Praise for the Second Edition:

'A well-balanced, thorough and lucidly written account...the best general history of the Liberal Party available.' – **Dr Stuart Ball**, *University of Leicester, UK*

Once teetering on the brink of oblivion, the British Liberal Party has again re-established itself as a major force in national and local politics. David Dutton's approachable study offers new insights into the waning, near death and ultimate recovery of the Liberal Party from 1900 to the present day. Discussions of politics, philosophy and performance are all skilfully interwoven as Dutton demonstrates how the party has become, once more, a formidable player on the political stage.

The second edition of this established text offers:

- an entirely new chapter on the coalition government
- a chronology of key events
- numerous suggestions for further reading

This lively survey of British Liberalism from the era of Campbell-Bannerman to that of Nick Clegg reviews existing literature while offering its own distinctive perspective on one of the most compelling of political dramas.

David Dutton is Emeritus Professor of Modern History at the University of Liverpool, UK

British Studies Series

General Editor JEREMY BLACK

Alan Booth **The British Economy in the Twentieth Century**
Glenn Burgess **British Political Thought, 1500–1660: The Politics of the Post-Reformation**
John Charmley **A History of Conservative Politics since 1830 (2nd edn)**
David Childs **Britain since 1939 (2nd edn)**
John Davis **A History of Britain, 1885–1939**
David Dutton **A History of the Liberal Party since 1900 (2nd edn)**
David Eastwood **Government and Community in the English Provinces, 1700–1870**
Philip Edwards **The Making of the Modern English State, 1460–1660**
W. H. Fraser **A History of British Trade Unionism, 1700–1998**
John Garrard **Democratisation in Britain: Elites, Civil Society and Reform since 1800**
Brian Hill **The Early Parties and Politics in Britain, 1688–1832**
Katrina Honeyman **Women, Gender and Industrialisation in England, 1700–1870**
Kevin Jefferys **Retreat from New Jerusalem: British Politics, 1951–1964**
Kevin Jefferys **Sport and Politics in Modern Britain: The Road to 2012**
T. A. Jenkins **The Liberal Ascendancy, 1830–1886**
David Loades **Power in Tudor England**
Ian Machin **The Rise of Democracy in Britain, 1830–1918**
Allan I. Macinnes **The British Revolution, 1629–1660**
Alexander Murdoch **British History, 1660–1832: National Identity and Local Culture**
Anthony Musson and W. M. Ormrod **The Evolution of English Justice: Law, Politics and Society in the Fourteenth Century**
Murray G. H. Pittock **Inventing and Resisting Britain: Cultural Identities in Britain and Ireland, 1685–1789**
Nick Smart **The National Government, 1931–40**
Howard Temperley **Britain and America since Independence**
Andrew Thorpe **A History of the British Labour Party (3rd edn)**
Michael J. Turner **Britain's International Role 1970–1991**

British Studies Series
Series Standing Order ISBN 978–0–333–71691–5 hardcover
Series Standing Order ISBN 978–0–333–69332–2 paperback
(*outside North America only*)

You can receive future titles in this series as they are published by placing a standing order. Please contact your bookseller or, in the case of difficulty, write to us at the address below with your name and address, the title of the series and one of the ISBNs quoted above.

Customer Services Department, Macmillan Distribution Ltd, Houndmills, Basingstoke, Hampshire, RG21 6XS, UK

A History of the Liberal Party since 1900

Second Edition

David Dutton

First edition 2004
Second edition 2013

Published by
PALGRAVE MACMILLAN

Palgrave Macmillan in the UK is an imprint of Macmillan Publishers Limited, registered in England, company number 785998, of Houndmills, Basingstoke, Hampshire RG21 6XS.

Palgrave Macmillan in the US is a division of St Martin's Press LLC, 175 Fifth Avenue, New York, NY 10010.

Palgrave Macmillan is the global academic imprint of the above companies and has companies and representatives throughout the world.

Palgrave® and Macmillan® are registered trademarks in the United States, the United Kingdom, Europe and other countries

ISBN 978–0–230–36188–1 hardback
ISBN 978–0–230–36189–8 paperback

This book is printed on paper suitable for recycling and made from fully managed and sustained forest sources. Logging, pulping and manufacturing processes are expected to conform to the environmental regulations of the country of origin.

A catalogue record for this book is available from the British Library.

A catalog record for this book is available from the Library of Congress.

10 9 8 7 6 5 4 3 2 1
22 21 20 19 18 17 16 15 14 13

Printed and bound in China

For Ralph and Judy White

Contents

Acknowledgements

Though this book makes use of a considerable amount of original archival material, it inevitably owes much to the work of other scholars. Some indication of my debt is given in the notes and the Guide to Further Reading. I also owe a debt of gratitude for the help I have received from the staff of the libraries and archives in which I have worked.

In addition, I should like to thank Jeremy Black for inviting me to write the book; Terka Acton and Sonya Barker at Palgrave Macmillan for their help and support; the late Lord Renton of Huntingdon for sharing with me his fascinating memories of the National Liberal Party; the Rt Hon. Lord Owen for discussing with me the troubled history of the Alliance; Philip Bell, Duncan Brack, Mark Egan and Ralph White for subjecting my first draft to critical but sympathetic inspection and thereby saving me from numerous blunders; and Alison Bagnall, Val Fry, Gaynor Johnson, Lucy Mills, Paula Mills, Pauline Oliver and Peggy Rider for invaluable help in producing a final typescript. None of the above, of course, bears any responsibility for remaining errors of commission or omission.

For permission to reproduce material in their possession or in which they hold the copyright I am pleased to thank the Rt Hon. Lord Ashdown, the Earl Baldwin of Bewdley, Mrs Joanna Clement-Davies, the Flintshire Record Office, the Lord Gainford, Sir William Gladstone, Mrs S. G. Graham, Captain J. Headlam and the Durham County Record Office, Sir Charles Hobhouse, the Liverpool Record Office, Miss Ishbel Lockhead, Mr Alexander Murray, the Orion Publishing Group, the Rt Hon. Lord Owen, the Rt Hon. Lord Rodgers of Quarry Bank, Mr Michael Rowntree, Mr John Simon, Mr Matthew Simon, Mr Mike Thomas, the Viscount Thurso, MP, the trustees of the Trevelyan Family Estate and the Rt Hon. Baroness Williams of Crosby. Permission is also gratefully acknowledged to reproduce material which first appeared in the following articles: 'On the Brink of Oblivion: The Post-War Crisis of British Liberalism', *Canadian Journal of History*, 27(3) (1992), pp. 425–50; '1932: A Neglected Date in the History of the Decline of the British Liberal Party', *Twentieth Century British History*, 14(1) (2003), pp. 43–60, by permission of Oxford University Press.

Every effort has been made to trace all copyright holders, but if any have been inadvertently overlooked the publishers will be pleased to make the necessary arrangement at the first opportunity.

DAVID DUTTON
Liverpool, 2004

The formation of the coalition government in May 2010 provides an obvious opportunity to bring the story up to date and I am grateful to Sonya Barker at Palgrave Macmillan for encouraging me to do so, and to Jenni Burnell and Keith Povey (with much help from Elaine Towns) for bringing the project to completion. Acknowledgement is made to Aitken Alexander Associates Ltd as holders of the copyright in the papers of Violet Bonham Carter.

DAVID DUTTON
Dumfries, 2012

Introduction

The Scope of this Book

The modern Liberal Party has already attracted a wealth of historical attention. Granted that the last purely Liberal government came to an end as long ago as 1915, that attraction might fairly be deemed excessive. In the twentieth century as a whole, the Liberals could claim nothing better than a poor third place in terms of electoral success, significantly behind their Conservative and Labour rivals. Yet the lack of Liberal success at the polls proved no barrier to continuing historical curiosity. Indeed, it was the party's decline rather than its brief exercise of power that acted as a magnet to academic investigation.

It cannot be denied that, for a period of at least 40 years or, according to some interpretations, considerably longer, the Liberal Party was in a process of remorseless and seemingly irreversible decay. This story had all the ingredients of a good whodunnit – a gruesome death, several plausible suspects, a compelling array of character parts and, in all probability, a generous sprinkling of red herrings. The subject attracted some of the best and most persuasive of modern British historians. Yet the debate was sometimes conducted with a predictability of argument and an absolutism of analysis that did not help historical understanding. 'Labour' historians preached the inevitability of their party's rise at Liberalism's expense, reluctant to believe that chance and fortune could play any part in the outcome of events. Their 'Liberal' counterparts sometimes appeared too keen to argue that Liberal decline need never have happened, turning a blind eye to long-term changes in politics and society that were unlikely to help their party's cause. After all, the decline of the British Liberal Party was no isolated happening, being matched by a contemporaneous experience in many other European countries, strong – perhaps compelling – evidence of the existence of

1

underlying forces at work. In the context of European democracy as a whole, the twentieth century saw continental Liberal parties failing to compete successfully with the rival traditions of Social and Christian Democracy. At the same time, both sides in the debate over Liberal decline tended to claim a monopoly of wisdom, unwilling to concede any strengths in their opponent's case. Yet, whatever the precise truth, it seems improbable that any monocausal explanation will suffice. The notion that Liberalism was already 'doomed' by 1914 is clearly incompatible with the suggestion that it was a perfectly healthy organism until it was ruined by the impact of total war. Yet it is entirely possible for a political party, as with any other organization, to contain elements of both strength and weakness at the same time, with the developing balance between the two at the mercy of the unfolding and unpredictable patterns of historical events.

Much of this debate's diversity is explained by a reluctance to define precisely whose decline is being analysed and explored. A political party is, after all, a multi-dimensional entity. If it is Liberalism as a political philosophy that is under scrutiny, then it is right to pay some attention to those Liberals whose intellectual outlooks found it difficult to encompass the requirements of a state whose government demanded an increasingly collectivist approach. Why, also, were some Liberal intellectuals able to transfer their commitment, apparently without too much difficulty, to the Labour or Conservative causes? Yet Liberalism was always a broad church and some Liberals clearly did adapt their thinking to changing circumstances. It is a striking feature of inter-war British history that the Liberal Party still managed to attract impressive and innovative intellectual support long after there was any realistic possibility of the return of a Liberal government. 'If the Liberals met their death during the war,' writes Michael Bentley, 'they did not do so at the hands of their thinkers.'[1] Indeed, it is arguably the triumph of the liberal state in recent times, albeit through the medium of Labour and Conservative governments, that justifies the disproportionate attention accorded by historians to the third party in the political system.

If it is the high politics of the Liberal Party – Liberalism at Westminster – that is being examined, then it seems reasonable to place more importance on the clashes of personality, the accidents of history, and the mistakes and miscalculations of a decision-making elite. But the decline of Liberalism in the country, a mass movement made up of activists and voters, may be something subtly different again. At the end of the day, the Liberal Party declined, in the sense of diminishing electoral success, because individual Liberal voters decided to change their party allegiance, or because the newly enfranchised among them failed to follow the voting patterns of their fathers and grandfathers. Though historians must generalize to make any sense of electoral politics, they should also be humble enough to recognize the individuality of the voter and the impossibility of determining precisely why electoral crosses of long ago were inscribed in one box on a ballot paper rather than another. In some ways, then, this is an appeal for liberal values – moderation, reasonableness and consideration for the other's point of view – to be applied to the study of the Liberal Party's decline. The explanation for what happened is undoubtedly complex; and it may also be more nuanced than has sometimes been allowed.

While the theme of 'decline' figures prominently in this book, it does not dominate the whole work. The passage of time enables the Liberal Party's downfall to be seen in a new perspective. Since the early 1960s, the party's fortunes have moved, however tentatively and sometimes uncertainly, in a positive direction. At the time of writing, it stands, in the guise of the Liberal Democrats, reinstated as a significant force in British politics and the junior partner in a coalition government formed in May 2010. The party's very survival, at a time when total extinction appeared to be its likely fate, and its subsequent substantial recovery pose historical problems as intriguing as that of its earlier decline. Furthermore, the perspective of the entire twentieth century draws attention to the way in which that century began and ended with evidence of the two left-of-centre parties working in co-operation with one another to the immense disadvantage of the Conservatives, and thereby opens up tantalizing excursions into the counterfactual realm of 'what might have been' if this co-operation had been maintained during the intervening years. These perspectives, in which the story of 'decline' is given an important but not all-encompassing place in the Liberal Party's history over the years since 1900, dictate the policy of this book to treat the whole period as evenly as possible, irrespective of the party's inherent strength at any particular moment.

Origins

'The only purpose of politics,' declared Lady Violet Bonham Carter, daughter of the Liberal Prime Minister, Herbert Henry Asquith, 'is the expression of one's deepest convictions – and their translation into facts.'[2] Naturally enough, those convictions will pre-date the establishment of a political party or movement designed to promote and enact them. Thus, in the British context, the philosophy of 'liberalism' has been traced back at least as far as the seventeenth century and the writings of John Locke (1632–1704). Locke claimed that individuals are born equal and free, that legitimate governments can only be created through a process of consent, and that, even when they have been created, the individual retains certain fundamental rights, such as freedom of conscience and belief. A 'liberal' political tradition may be discerned, independent of the embryonic political structure of Whigs and Tories that grew up in the late seventeenth and early eighteenth centuries, running through the English Civil War and the Glorious Revolution to a belief in the values underlying the American and French Revolutions in the later eighteenth century. It was associated with a defence of civil and religious liberties, a steadfast opposition to arbitrary government, the advocacy of a limited state, a belief in the rights of dissenting individuals and a faith in people's conscience as the most appropriate determinant of their actions. Taking a fundamentally optimistic view of the human condition, the Liberal approach was to preach moderation, reason and restraint, and to abhor extremism and bigotry. The struggle for liberty would enable human beings to live their lives to the full, maximizing the talents with which the Creator had endowed them.

The term 'Liberal' began to be used in the politics of post-Napoleonic Britain and was first officially adopted by a political party in the course of the 1847 General Election. Over the following decade, a recognizable Liberal Party began to coalesce around a number of groupings of which the Whigs, the Radicals and the Peelite free-trade Tories were the most important. History, in the quest for a precise beginning, has usually settled on a meeting in Willis's Rooms in 1859, when these groups agreed to serve in a government under Lord Palmerston, as the moment when the party formally came into being. By this time, Liberalism had taken on board the theories of economic liberalism propounded by Adam Smith, whose seminal work, *The Wealth of Nations,* had been published in 1776. Liberalism thus became synonymous with the doctrines of free trade and laissez-faire, and tended to attract support from the new industrial and commercial interests in opposition to the Tory landowners. Free trade, by facilitating economic relations between states, would help to foster harmonious diplomatic relations and build an international community from which war was excluded as an inherently unreasonable activity. Laissez-faire implied a more active role for the state than has sometimes been implied, not least because only the rule of law could prevent liberty degenerating into licence. Indeed, it was the function of the state to intervene to protect the free market, enforce competition and remove barriers. Looking back from the vantage point of the 1930s, the historian and Liberal intellectual, Ramsay Muir, insisted:

> It is often said that the Liberal party has stood for the policy of laissez-faire, or leaving things alone. This was never true; on the contrary the intervention of the modern State in industrial questions began with the first Liberal Government in 1832, and most of the functions which the State has assumed in this field have been due to Liberal legislation. There have always been a few Liberals who have been bitterly critical of any enlargement of the functions of the State. But there have always been others, more numerous, who were prepared for great enlargements.[3]

The Late Victorian Party

Under W. E. Gladstone, who led the party for most of the period between 1868 and 1894, Liberalism reached its zenith as a political movement. The party championed the causes of free trade, sound finance, religious toleration and a pacific foreign policy. Gladstone's first two governments (1868–74 and 1880–85) boasted substantial records of progressive reform. Yet even at this stage historians have discerned some worrying features, prompting some to suggest that, at the very time of its political pre-eminence, the party already contained the seeds of its later decay. More helpfully, it may be argued that the Liberal Party never displayed all the characteristics deemed necessary for success in the modern era. In particular, as Sir William Harcourt put it in 1891, 'like the Kingdom of Heaven, the Liberal party is a house of many mansions'.[4] Activists were attracted into Liberalism, not necessarily because they agreed with all its ideas, but in order to promote, and if possible to achieve, specific objectives such as temperance, franchise extension or church disestablishment. As a result, the party developed into 'a composite of [sometimes] mutually exclusive pressure groups',[5] prone to internal dissension and schism, and never attained genuine internal coherence. Thus 'the danger of division was always inherent in Liberal politics by the very nature of the party'.[6] In a revealing diary entry of May 1885, Gladstone recorded:

> Very fair cabinet today – only three resignations. Members of the cabinet who within the last month have, on one ground or other, appeared to consider resignation: Lord Chancellor, Lord Northbrook, Lord Hartington, Mr Chamberlain, Sir Charles Dilke, Mr Lefevre, Lord Spencer, Sir William Harcourt, Chancellor of the Exchequer. A majority.[7]

Regardless of the tendency of Liberal factions to go their own way, it was Gladstone's particular achievement to maintain an essential party unity by focusing Liberal attention on a succession of single great issues that needed to be tackled before further progress could be made on the often-disputed agenda of reform. Only when elevating the cause of Irish Home Rule to this status did his strategy unravel, prompting the split of 1886 with the defection of the Liberal Unionists. This development was not entirely negative, since the majority of defecting Whigs had been unlikely bedfellows of Liberal radicals and now found a more comfortable home in the ranks of Conservatism. But it was also Gladstone's achievement that a party born in the restricted electorate of the mid-nineteenth century had, by the 1880s, become in most parts of the country the principal party of the urban working class, enfranchised for the first time in substantial numbers following the passage of the Second Reform Act of 1867. Many trade unions appeared content to seek political representation through Liberal channels, leading from the 1870s to the emergence of a group of Lib–Lab working-class MPs, particularly in coal-mining constituencies.

By this time, the Liberals had taken on most of the characteristics of a modern political party. These included an important organizational structure operating beyond the confines of the Westminster village. The National Liberal Federation was founded in 1877 as a body independent of the parliamentary party, and represented the mass party in the country. From the outset it sought to influence party policy and, despite efforts, particularly after the split of 1886, to curb its pretensions in this direction, the potential for conflict with the party leadership remained. As late as July 1923 the *Liberal Magazine* described the NLF as an organization 'through which party opinion may be brought to bear on Members of Parliament'. The structure created in 1877 was to remain fundamentally unchanged until 1936, when the party's annual assembly agreed to replace the NLF with a new Liberal Party Organisation.

After the 1886 split the party remained in opposition for almost two decades, except for three years of unhappy minority government between 1892 and 1895. Gladstone's final retirement in 1894 removed the controlling influence of his masterful personality and allowed the party's inherent divisions to become ever more apparent. Liberal leaders turned their attention to personal rivalries and, in a mood of bitter recrimination, the party itself degenerated into a period of 'faddism', in which its members seemed concerned only to promote their own, often unrelated, single-issue causes. The danger existed that what had been until recently a successful party of government would become no more than an impotent party of protest. 'The overwhelming sense conveyed by Liberal history after 1895,' writes Michael Bentley, 'is one of shrinking horizons and a feeling of involution. What Liberals want to discuss is themselves: their leaders and their limitations, the poverty of their organization, the trouble caused by their own imperialists.'[8] Insiders predicted a further lengthy period on the opposition benches. 'The disease of the Party is deep-seated,' warned the chief whip. 'Time alone can eradicate it, and Time will take ten good years of its own self to do the job.'[9]

By the end of the decade the evolving crisis in South Africa had opened up new cleavages. After Gladstone's departure, Liberals such as Lord Rosebery demanded a reappraisal of the anti-imperialism with which the party was traditionally, though not always accurately, associated. Dubbing their opponents 'Little Englanders', the Liberal Imperialists insisted that the party must show that it, equally with the Conservatives, could champion and administer the great empire that Britain now headed. The outbreak of the Boer War in 1899 inevitably emphasized this latest line of division, with the party's radical wing blaming the Unionist government for engineering an unnecessary conflict. In the absence of any other viable candidate, Sir Henry Campbell-Bannerman was chosen as leader in the same year. While both sides welcomed the appointment of a man of the centre, the task of holding the warring factions together looked daunting. Indeed, the formation of the Liberal Imperial Council in 1900 and of Rosebery's Liberal League in 1902 seemed to presage a complete split. In all the circumstances, the party's performance in the 1900 'Khaki' General Election in reducing the Unionist government's parliamentary majority was a creditable and surprising one.

Also worrying, though, was the geographical pattern of the party's parliamentary representation. By the end of the nineteenth century, Liberalism looked increasingly like a party of the Celtic fringe, or at least of the non-metropolitan periphery. It remained well represented in Wales, Scotland and the North of England, where the nonconformist vote was strongest, but seemed incapable of winning a majority of English seats. In 1895, Liberals were successful in less than a quarter of English constituencies. This did not imply the imminent demise of the British Liberal Party, but it did perhaps suggest that Liberal government at Westminster was not necessarily the natural order of things.

For all that, as the new century opened the Liberal Party remained the only realistic alternative for those who rejected the notion of uninterrupted Conservative government. The Conservative–Liberal duopoly at Westminster was reflected in the political allegiance of the country's quality and mass-circulation newspapers. While Fleet Street was already a preponderantly Conservative realm, Liberalism was better represented in the country at large. Most regions and large cities could still boast a Liberal-supporting paper as well as a Conservative one. This situation would change dramatically in the decades to come. The decline of the Liberal Party was matched by a startling erosion of the Liberal-supporting press.

But the factor which, above all others, would determine the party's future prospects was its relationship with the working-class voter, especially in the context of a now irreversibly advancing democracy following a further extension of the franchise in 1884. It was, Herbert Samuel argued, 'the abiding problem of Liberal statesmanship to raise the enthusiasm of the working class without frightening the middle classes'.[10] By the 1890s there was clear evidence of the beginnings of an institutional separation between the Liberal Party and an increasingly organized Labour movement. The Social Democratic Federation had been founded in 1881 and William Morris's Socialist League in 1884, but neither developed into a mass movement. More importantly, the formation of the Independent Labour Party (ILP) in 1893 and the Labour Representation Committee (LRC) in 1900 bore witness to the limitations of Lib–Lab politics as previously practised and the Liberal Party's partial failure to contain the forces of Labour radicalism within the existing party structure. In places such as Manchester, ILP candidates started to make gains at the Liberals' expense in municipal elections. This is not to suggest that the working class was as a unified entity waiting to be represented by a new political party, but to the extent that an organizational separation between the Labour movement and the Liberal Party did take place, the potential for competition for the working-class vote was bound to increase.

Yet in most cases the working-class man was not pulled away from Liberalism by the attractions of a new creed. Ideology was much less important in the formation of a new political party than the desire of working-class men to secure representation in Parliament by members of their own class. Despite the existence of the Lib–Lab MPs, in most working-class constituencies the Liberal candidate was not a working-class man. The typical Liberal MP of this era was a middle-aged, middle-class businessman or lawyer with a public school or university education. Despite encouragement from the party leadership, most local Liberal Associations proved extremely reluctant to adopt working-class candidates, and it was this lack of response, rather than any conversion to 'socialism', however defined, that drove working-class men towards independent political action to further their sectional interests. By contrast, where Liberals were accommodating, the demand for separate Labour representation was reduced. The experience of some key figures of the early Labour movement is instructive. Keir Hardie, Arthur Henderson and Ramsay MacDonald all sought adoption as Liberal candidates before deciding that only a new political party could secure their goals. Turned down for the Liberal candidature at Dover, MacDonald was driven to 'the conclusion that there is no sympathy at headquarters with candidates who respond to Labour desires'. His 'greatest regret is that I am now driven to the conclusion of my friends of the ILP. I have stuck to the opinion that Liberalism was a sufficient gospel for the above politicians until but a few days ago.'[11] Yet, 'had MacDonald been able to say "I have a thousand pounds at my back and I am not in favour of the entire labour programme", the rascals would have gone for him. His enemies admit even now that he is far and away the best man. But he is tainted with Labour!!'[12] MacDonald joined the ILP in 1894 and stood as its candidate in Southampton the following year.

The Trades Union Congress of 1899 was dominated by complaints about the failure of the working class to secure their objectives through the vehicle of the Liberal Party, and provided the impetus behind the formation of the LRC the following year. The Taff Vale ruling of the House of Lords in 1902, which threw into question a trade union's basic right to strike, added greatly to the pressure for independent parliamentary representation, since only through a change in the statute law could this decision be reversed. That said, the LRC was not committed to a different programme from the Liberal Party. Indeed, it *had* no programme. Its task was limited to the election of MPs who would serve the interests of the working-class man. Historians have identified a considerable overlap between the aims and aspirations of the Liberal and Labour traditions at this time, seeing them as just two wings of the same 'progressive' movement. Furthermore, many LRC activists did not wish to see the LRC develop into a separate party. Their aspiration was for a pressure group, voting together on labour issues, but generally supporting the Liberal Party. On the other hand, there were those, particularly in the ILP, who *did* want an independent party ready to fight the Liberals as vigorously as it would the Conservatives. When the Liberal, Herbert Samuel, stood as the 'Liberal and Labour Candidate' at a by-election in Cleveland in 1902, a leading figure on the ILP's national administrative council, J. Bruce Glasier, was appalled:

> I cordially hope Samuel will be defeated. His insolence in using the title 'Labour' candidate proves the unscrupulous character of

the fellow. My idea is that we should issue a manifesto and get it into the press, reciting what was done by the Liberals to prevent a genuine Labour man being adopted and strongly repudiating alike the Imperialism and pseudo Labour pretensions of Samuel.[13]

So, as the new century opened, while the working-class vote had in no sense been lost by the Liberal Party, there were certainly those for whom this development was now a key objective.

The denigration of Samuel's efforts to bridge the gap between Liberalism and the Labour movement is striking, because Samuel was among the Liberal thinkers of this period engaged in what many historians have judged to be the most promising attempt to prepare the party to be a viable player in the electoral politics of the modern era. While in the 1890s Liberals at Westminster seemed determined to pull their party apart, an important rethinking of Liberal ideology was also taking place. An impressive group of academics and journalists, influenced by the Oxford philosopher, T. H. Green, had taken on the task of reinterpreting Liberalism for a new age. The starting point of the so-called 'New Liberals' was their belief that the central concept of 'liberty' had hitherto been defined too narrowly, being largely restricted to legal, political and religious issues. Now, not least because so many of the original objectives in these areas had been achieved – 'the old Liberalism had done its work'[14] – the quest for liberty should be extended to the social and economic sphere. The material condition of much of the population acted, in practice, as a restraint on the liberty of the individual. It was therefore the duty of the state – a state which the Liberals themselves had reformed and in which they could now place greater confidence – to create the conditions that would permit each individual to develop talents to the full. This implied the need for social reform carried out by a much more interventionist state than the Liberals had previously envisaged. Because of the cost involved, it also suggested a new attitude towards taxation and the use of the government's annual budget as an instrument of redistributive justice. As was argued in the first issue of the *Progressive Review*, published in October 1896, 'if Liberals still cleave to their honourable name they must be willing and desirous to assign a new meaning to liberty; it must no longer signify the absence of restraint, but the presence of opportunity'.[15]

Most of this reappraisal was carried out away from the coalface of party political conflict, but it had clear implications for the position of Liberalism *vis-à-vis* the evolving Labour movement. For Samuel, the purpose of the *Progressive Review* was to prevent a Lib–Lab split, which could only work to the Conservatives' advantage, and 'to forestall such a disruption of the progressive forces in British politics'.[16] For the journalist and academic, L. T. Hobhouse, 'the breach of principle' between Liberalism and Socialism was 'much smaller than might appear on the surface'.[17] Similarly, when in 1896, C. P. Scott of the *Manchester Guardian*, a leading organ of the new ideas, invited Hobhouse to join the newspaper, he stressed that

> the relations of Liberalism and Labour must govern the future of politics... The problem was to find the lines on which Liberals could be brought to see that the old tradition must be expanded to yield a fuller measure of social justice, a more real equality, an industrial as well as a political liberty.[18]

New Liberals moved easily towards the concept of an interdependent society, where individual citizens would contribute freely to the general good of the organic whole. This implied co-operation rather than confrontation between classes and was particularly important within a climate of mounting industrial militancy at the end of the century. It suggested that the Liberal Party should seek to bring the forces of capital and labour together, to settle industrial disputes harmoniously in the interests of society as a whole. Liberals therefore needed to counteract the arguments of those seeking to convince the working classes that their interests were fundamentally incompatible with those of the classes above them, whose unfailing inclination was to exploit workers for their own selfish financial advantage. Therefore, the more that members of the British working class developed a sense of their own distinct and corporate identity, the less purchase the ideas of the New Liberalism were likely to enjoy. But New Liberals themselves ran some risk that their own plans for social reform based on redistributive taxation would create social tensions and divisions rather than the unity and harmony they proclaimed. Thus while the New Liberalism offered tantalizing possibilities for the regeneration of the Liberal Party at the start of the twentieth century, it by no means represented a straight and uncomplicated path to political salvation. Furthermore, as the next chapter will consider, there was also the question of how far the work of writers and publicists would succeed in permeating the thinking and then determining the conduct of those who carried the Liberal standard in local and national politics.

1 Strange Death or Edwardian Summer, 1902–16?

Recovery 1902–05

The period between the end of the Boer War in 1902 and the General Election of January 1906 saw a transformation in the Liberal Party's fortunes. As a general rule it is governments that lose elections rather than oppositions that win them, but on this occasion the actions of the Unionists not only weakened their own party but also contributed directly to the strengthening of the Liberals by providing the latter with the factor they had patently lacked, at least since Gladstone's retirement – unity. The 1902 Education Act, with its marked bias towards Anglican schools, rode roughshod over the sensibilities of nonconformist opinion and greatly assisted the process of Liberal reunification. The Licensing Act of 1904, an apparent sop to the Unionists' supporters in the brewing trade, had very much the same effect. Organized Labour was alienated by the government's failure to introduce legislation to reverse the Taff Vale judgment of 1902 and by the scandal surrounding the exploitation of Chinese workers in the mines of the South African Rand. Even more important was Joseph Chamberlain's celebrated speech in Birmingham on 15 May 1903, in which the Colonial Secretary called for the ending of the prevailing system of free trade and the substitution of a regime of imperial preference. Chamberlain's initiative started a debate that was to dominate the last two and a half years of Balfour's government, thereby doing serious damage to the Unionist cause. Divided now between tariff reformers, free traders and Balfourite retaliationists, who would only impose tariffs in response to comparable action by foreign states, the government never again possessed the internal unity and cohesion necessary for an effective administration. Unionism was starkly revealed as an uneasy coalition of forces whose unity was overly dependent on the single issue of opposition to Irish Home Rule.

But Chamberlain's move also exercised a decisive influence over the Liberal Party, by calling into question the sacred creed of free trade, one of the few issues on which Liberals were fully united. Chamberlain was unequivocal about the advantages he believed the introduction of tariff reform would bring about: 'You have an opportunity,' he told his Unionist supporters. 'You will never have it again.'[1] But his words might just as well have been directed to the Liberal opposition. Campbell-Bannerman commented: 'This reckless – criminal – escapade of Joe's is the great event of our time. It is playing old Harry with all party relations... All the old war-horses about me... are snorting with excitement. We are in for a great time.'[2]

The changed political climate was soon apparent. Public opinion had begun to move strongly against the Unionists by 1904. Seven seats were lost in by-elections that year and a further seven in 1905. As early as October 1904, Henry Lucy noted 'a rare consensus of opinion' that the next General Election would result in a victory for the Liberal Party.[3] Seldom in British electoral history can a governing party have been more pessimistic about its prospects at a forthcoming poll. St John Brodrick, the Secretary of State for India, feared that 'we shall get hideously beaten', while Chamberlain himself privately predicted a combined Liberal–Irish majority of around 120 seats.[4] Finally, with his government visibly breaking up around him, Balfour resigned on 4 December 1905 and King Edward VII invited Campbell-Bannerman to form a minority Liberal administration. This task was successfully accomplished, in itself no small achievement, as the new Prime Minister had to overcome an attempt by three leading Liberal Imperialists to determine by themselves some of the key cabinet appointments. Asquith, Grey and Haldane had earlier concluded the so-called Relugas Compact, by which they determined not to serve under Campbell-Bannerman unless the latter agreed to go to the House of Lords, leaving Asquith as Leader of the Commons and Chancellor of the Exchequer. In addition, Grey was to be Foreign Secretary and Haldane Lord Chancellor. Campbell-Bannerman stood his ground and formed a cabinet on his own terms which left him in the Commons and firmly in control of the situation. It was an important moment, revealing that the new Prime Minister was made of sterner stuff than many of his colleagues believed. Then, on 16 December, Campbell-Bannerman announced the dissolution of Parliament for an election in January. Though Chamberlain's proposals had never become official Unionist policy, everyone recognized that the election would amount to a national referendum on the competing merits of tariff reform and free trade.

Given the seminal importance, particularly in terms of welfare legislation, of the Liberal government which would be endorsed by this General Election, it is necessary to determine the basis on which it was elected. The Liberal Party's campaign focused above all on the defence of free trade. Ninety-eight per cent of Liberal candidates included this issue in their election addresses. Liberals argued that, while Chamberlain's proposals might help a few specialist producers, they would in general damage the economy and in particular lead to an increase in the price of food. To this extent the party waged an essentially reactive campaign. Free trade was 'the great umbrella; fighting negatively, the Liberals got every disaffected element underneath it'.[5] Much of the Liberal campaign looked back to the nineteenth century, rather than forward into the twentieth, with Campbell-Bannerman standing for 'a policy covered by the oldest and best of political watchwords, "Peace, Retrenchment and Reform"'.[6] But it was also striking that more than two-thirds of Liberal candidates included social reform among their priorities. As the historian of the election notes, 'although the need to repeal or amend the Education and Licensing Acts of 1902 and 1904 came first in many Liberal minds, pledges made to other social reforms amounted to a recognisable and extensive commitment'.[7] Poor Law reform and pensions were particularly prominent. Quite how such reforms might be financed was, however, another matter. The fact that Campbell-Bannerman also promised a massive reduction in public expenditure did not suggest that the new government had thought through a clear programme, let alone costed it.

The 1906 General Election

The outcome of the election exceeded all Liberal expectations. The party's strength in the new House of Commons stood at 400 MPs, with the Unionists reduced to just 157. It was the biggest anti-Conservative majority for more than 80 years, and very few areas of the United Kingdom could now be described as Unionist strongholds. The Liberal tally included 224 gains and just eight losses, giving them a majority of 130 over all other parties combined. In practice, because the Labour contingent of 30 MPs and the 83 Irish Nationalists were hardly likely to vote with the Unionists, the government's effective majority over the opposition stood at an impregnable 356 seats. Surveying the picture in Lancashire, where the Liberals had done particularly well, the *Manchester Guardian* only slightly exaggerated what had happened:

> A candidate had only to be a Free-trader to get in, whether he was known or unknown, semi-Unionist or thorough Home Ruler, Protestant or Catholic, entertaining or dull. He had only to be a Protectionist to lose all chance of getting in, though he spoke with the tongues of men and of angels, though he was a good employer to many electors, or had led the House of Commons, or fought in the Crimea.[8]

Yet the dimensions of this Liberal triumph must be subjected to closer analysis. The sheer scale of the victory in terms of Commons seats, far beyond what the party had achieved in its Gladstonian heyday, has only added to the mystery of what now followed. Within two decades of this unprecedented triumph, Liberalism would be confined to the sidelines of British politics. But it is clear that the electoral system, which in future years would work consistently to the party's disadvantage, had exaggerated its performance in 1906. In terms of the popular vote, the gap between the two leading parties remained relatively narrow: 49.5 per cent for the Liberals against 43 per cent for the Unionists. On a simple system of proportional representation the Liberals would have secured 285 seats and the Unionists 236. Put another way, it took almost two and a half times as many votes to return a Unionist to Westminster as it did a Liberal. The margin of the Liberal victory reflected the fact that Liberal votes had been distributed to the party's greatest advantage, with a marked swing in those constituencies where Unionist seats could be captured. Against this background it becomes easier to see some merit in Alan Sykes' judgement that 'The 1906 success was not the continuation of Victorian supremacy but the aberration from the emerging pattern of Liberal weakness, caused primarily by the renewal of Conservative divisions and their adoption of deeply unpopular policies which reignited old Liberal passions for one last time.'[9]

Campbell-Bannerman's Government

For all that, the Liberal Party had, statistically at least, secured a
stunning triumph. Most of this book chronicles the party's (generally forlorn) attempts to secure political power. But in 1906 the
Liberal government held the reality of power in its hands. The
question now was the use to which that power would be put. It was
by any criterion an able administration. Campbell-Bannerman
could deploy the talents of three future Prime Ministers – Asquith,
Lloyd George and Churchill – as well as those of such accomplished political practitioners as Edward Grey, R. B. Haldane and
John Morley. By its end in 1915, the government could look back
on a distinguished legislative record, whose main components
would gain in lustre as the twentieth century progressed. But ultimate achievement should not be confused with original intent.
'With its connotations of social justice, state intervention and
alliance with Labour,' writes Peter Clarke, '[progressivism] aptly
describes the basis of Liberal policy after 1906.'[10] This is surely
a misreading of the evidence. The government arrived in office
without having worked out a clear or defined programme of legislation it wished to enact. Its members had been more successful
over the preceding three years in identifying what they opposed
than in delineating what it was they stood for. The government's
first burst of legislative energy thus gave a misleading impression.
The Trades Disputes Act of 1906 overturned the Taff Vale judgment and restored to trade unions the legal immunities in relation to strike action they had presumed they enjoyed prior to the
House of Lords' ruling. Significantly, the government in this case
dropped its own more cautious bill and accepted an alternative
drawn up by the parliamentary Labour Party. A new Workmen's
Compensation Act, a School Meals Act, based on a private member's bill introduced by a Labour MP, and Medical Inspections of
Children quickly followed.

This all gave a somewhat exaggerated view of the closeness
of the Liberal–Labour alliance and of the extent to which the
progressive spirit had permeated government thinking. In the
last days of the Unionist government, Lord Crewe had warned
Campbell-Bannerman that 'more than ever before the Liberal
party was... [on trial] as an engine for securing social reforms'.[11]
But the Prime Minister's attitude and that of most of his leading

ministers was more cautious. They recognized that measures to improve the condition of the working classes might well alienate the middle-class support that the Liberals could ill afford to lose. Campbell-Bannerman was therefore resolved to strike a balance, placing party unity before dynamic policies of reform. 'If we have two sops for Labour,' he told Asquith, 'we ought to have some other Bills of general interest to balance them.'[12] These 'other Bills', and in particular Education and Licensing measures to satisfy the traditional Liberal nonconformist vote, were at the forefront of the government's priorities. The other key measure of its first year in office, a bill designed to end the anomaly of 'plural voting', also seemed to hark back to an earlier, albeit unfinished, agenda of constitutional reform.

There was, then, a certain 'confusion of aims' in the government's strategy.[13] This was compounded by a seemingly intractable constitutional obstacle that had confronted earlier Liberal governments – the obstructive powers of the Unionist-dominated House of Lords. In the immediate wake of electoral defeat in January 1906, the Unionist leader, Arthur Balfour, conscious of his party's continuing strength in the upper chamber, had made the cavalier statement that his party 'should still control, whether in power or opposition, the destinies of this great Empire'. In practice, the Unionist leadership behaved somewhat more circumspectly than these words implied, weighing up the likely popular reaction to each individual piece of proposed legislation before deciding what to do. As a result, while the Liberals' Education and Plural Voting Bills were wrecked, the Trades Disputes Act was allowed to pass on to the statute book with little resistance. In June 1907, Campbell-Bannerman moved a resolution that the Lords' powers to reject or amend bills coming up from the Commons 'should be so restricted by law as to secure that within the limits of a single Parliament the final decision of the Commons shall prevail'. But granted that any legislative constitutional changes would themselves need to get through the upper house, it was by no means clear how this aspiration could be achieved.

The Liberals found little from which to draw comfort in 1907. The Irish Councils Bill, designed to devolve power to Irish local government, was badly mishandled and had to be withdrawn. With the ministry 'apparently drifting into a period of futile and aimless endeavour',[14] the economic climate now began to show a marked deterioration, with unemployment climbing alarmingly. For Chamberlainites, these developments seemed to presage the imminent collapse of the government's free-trade finances and gave an enormous boost to the cause of tariff reform within the Unionist ranks. Protective measures, it was argued, could safeguard British jobs. Election results suggested that the political tide was already moving against the government. As early as November 1906 the municipal elections witnessed heavy Unionist gains. Then, in 1907, the government lost three by-elections (one to Labour – 'the most deadly blow the Liberal party has ever received at our hands'[15] – one to the Unionists and one to an independent socialist candidate), followed by three more (all to Unionists) in the first three months of 1908. By that time it was clear that Campbell-Bannerman's premiership was nearing its end. His first year in office had been marred by his wife's illness and death; and during the second his own health began to collapse. In April 1908 he was obliged to resign and, too ill to leave 10 Downing Street, he died there before the month was over. During its brief lifetime his government had shown some creditable signs of reforming zeal, without suggesting any significant developments in the general scope of public policy. The one exception perhaps was Asquith's 1907 Budget, which asserted the important principle of differential rates of taxation in raising that on unearned income to one shilling in the pound.

Asquith Takes Over

The governmental reorganization that followed Campbell-Bannerman's resignation marked a distinct change in the balance of forces at the top of the Liberal Party. No one seriously questioned Asquith's claim to the succession. But the new Prime Minister himself was not the key to the change. 'His concept of progress was limited,' writes Cameron Hazlehurst. 'He gave intellectual assent to much of the new Liberalism; he gave it no passion or inspiration.'[16] Lord Riddell offered a comparable contemporary assessment. Asquith was 'really an old-fashioned Radical of the Manchester school, who [was] leading a heterogeneous band of followers'.[17] Of greater significance was the promotion of David Lloyd George to the Treasury from the Board of Trade to fill the vacancy created by Asquith's elevation and the appointment to

Lloyd George's old place of Winston Churchill, who joined the cabinet for the first time. These ministerial changes initiated the most constructive era in the history of the Liberal government and the period that provides the most telling evidence of the influence of New Liberal thinking within the party's upper reaches. Lloyd George, in particular, seemed to recognize that, if his party was to thrive in the era of mass politics, it needed to respond to the problems generated by an industrial society. 'L. G. is the only leading man who has the courage to attack the rich and powerful,' declared Lord Riddell. 'All other leading politicians deal with the stock political commodities, such as Home Rule, Disestablishment, Tariff Reform ... L. G. says what the mass of the people feel but cannot express.'[18] Over a period of four years the government introduced old-age pensions (long promised by both leading parties), established labour exchanges and trade boards, created a National Insurance scheme to cover sickness, invalidity and unemployment, and passed a Miners' Minimum Wages Act. Each measure combined caution in its specific immediate provisions with far greater long-term significance with regard to assumptions about the role of the state and its duties towards its citizens. But we should be hesitant to suggest that all this Liberal legislation necessarily led to a strengthening of the electoral relationship between the party and the working-class voter. Old-age pensions seem to have been well received. The rewards (5s. a week) were relatively small and the qualifying age (70) high, but the take-up was bigger than expected and by 1914 nearly a million people were receiving state pensions at a cost of more than £12 million per annum. Some other Liberal reforms were, however, less welcome, either because they smacked of paternalistic interventionism or because they came at a price. National Insurance benefits, unlike old-age pensions, were dependent on direct contributions and, even if the benefit was greater than the contribution – '9d. for 4d.' – for large numbers of working people on low incomes it nevertheless involved their first and unwelcome experience of taxation by central government.

Accompanying changes to the taxation system, particularly those embodied in the 1909 Budget, were equally, if not more, significant. This established the principle that the annual Finance Bill could be used to finance new areas of spending by the state, and that it was a proper function of government to redistribute wealth from the better-off to the poorer members of society.

After extensive cabinet debate, Lloyd George introduced what was his first Budget on 29 April 1909, Asquith having taken responsibility for that of 1908 despite his elevation to the premiership. It was, he declared, 'a war budget... for raising money to wage implacable war against poverty and squalidness'. The Chancellor sought to raise an additional £13.6 million in taxation. He proposed to increase income tax and to subject annual incomes of over £5,000 to a supertax. Additional death duties would raise £4.8 million and stamp duty £1.25 million. There would be additional duties of £1.8 million from spirits and £2 million from tobacco, together with a £2.25 million rise in the cost of liquor licences paid by publicans and brewers. The proposed land taxes represented a fundamental departure, even though the estimated revenue to be generated was modest. Lloyd George proposed a 20 per cent tax on the increments of land value, a halfpenny in the pound tax on the value of undeveloped land and a tax of 10 per cent on the value of leasehold reversions. Even so, this was more a case of Lloyd George attacking his traditional enemy, the landlord, than a significant move in redistributive taxation.

Accurately predicting many of the Chancellor's ideas, his junior minister, Charles Hobhouse, had foreseen that 'such proposals, if propounded to the country, ought to insure the rejection of the budget by the Lords [and] enforce a dissolution'.[19] Nevertheless, the general consensus of recent historiography is that Lloyd George, in introducing his Budget, had no devious plan to goad the Unionist peers into rejection and thus towards constitutional and electoral suicide.[20] The government's need for extra revenue was genuine enough, not least to finance pensions and to carry out its naval building programme to counter a perceived German threat. With an anticipated budget deficit of £16–17 million, the Chancellor had no alternative but to introduce some startling measures. But Lloyd George may well have foreseen that, by going so far as to undermine the revenue motive for tariffs, his Budget was likely to provoke Unionist tariff reformers into some strenuous form of resistance. If he could raise the necessary income by means of ordinary taxation, then one of the most powerful arguments in favour of tariff reform would be refuted decisively. Asquith himself had conceded that 'if it could not be proved that Social reform... can be financed on Free Trade lines, a return to Protection is a moral certainty'.[21] The Budget also confirmed the Liberals' long-standing argument that, by requiring a tax on the food of ordinary people, protection was an essentially unfair device that now compared unfavourably with Lloyd George's more 'democratic' proposals. Many tariff reformers rapidly concluded that attack was the best form of defence and, goaded by some inflammatory pronouncements by the Chancellor, began to argue for the outright rejection of the Finance Bill. Indeed, since the case for tariff reform, now dominant in the Unionist ranks, could only be given its chance if the Bill was stopped in its tracks, the party leaders moved inexorably towards rejection by the Lords as the summer of 1909 progressed. Finally, on 16 November, Lord Lansdowne, as leader of the Unionist peers, gave notice of the fateful amendment that would destroy the Finance Bill. Thus was the well-established principle – that financial measures fell outside the remit of the upper chamber – defied and a first-class constitutional crisis created. With the Budget rejected, the business of government became impossible and a General Election a constitutional necessity. And, despite the Liberals being forced to the polls much earlier than they might have planned in the context of seven-year parliaments, it was a contest that the government had some reason to welcome. Lloyd George's Budget had, it seemed, forced the Unionists into a morally untenable position as the defenders of a reactionary alliance between food-taxers and hereditary peers, opposed to the people of the country and their budget.

Constitutional Crisis

No party could draw total satisfaction from the election results of January 1910. The most striking feature was the complete erosion of the Liberals' independent Commons majority secured just four years before. Though the Unionists had failed to maintain their by-election momentum of 1907–09, losing seats taken in the three previous years, they did regain 116 seats lost in 1906, recovering their traditional status as the majority party in England. Overall, the Unionists now held 273 seats compared with the government's 275. In terms of percentages of the popular vote, the figures were 46.9 and 43.5, respectively. Unionist gains appear to have owed more to the renewed support of voters who had abstained in 1906 than to Liberal defections. Crucially, despite the narrow gap between the two main parties, the Liberals could expect to rely on 40 Labour and 82 Irish Nationalist members in the new House to safeguard their parliamentary majority and their government's continued existence. As will be seen, however, the support of the minority parties, especially the Irish, would come at a price.

There was a widespread feeling that the cry of 'Peers versus People' had saved the situation for the government. The fact that Unionists had gained seats, particularly in the South of England, owed more to a general recovery of support in their traditional strongholds after the exceptional results of 1906 than it did to any great appeal exercised by tariff reform or the party's stance in the constitutional crisis. But not all the novel features of 1906 had been reversed. A number of working-class constituencies, particularly in London and Lancashire, Unionist before 1906, did not return to the fold. This, taken with the effective containment of any significant further advance on the part of the Labour Party, suggested that the Liberals had been markedly successful in attracting the working-class vote. One Unionist candidate suggested that working-class constituencies in Lancashire, Yorkshire and Cheshire had been lost by his party because 'masses of the extremely poor have been attracted by the Lloyd Georgian programme of vague suggestions that something is to be given to them, which at present belongs to somebody else. They do not know what it is, but want to take their chance of getting it whatever it may be.'[22]

'The big thing,' wrote Beatrice Webb at the end of November 1910, 'that has happened in the last two years is that Lloyd George and Winston Churchill have practically taken the *limelight*, not merely from their own colleagues, but from the Labour Party.'[23] The practical effect was that, after January 1910, the electoral map was redrawn more clearly on class lines than ever before. Though the average swing to the Unionists across the country from 1906 was 4.3 per cent, this figure masked a wide range whose effect was to leave Britain broadly divided between a Liberal-dominated North of England, Scotland and Wales and a Unionist-controlled South. Mrs Webb noted 'the dividing of England into two distinct halves, each having its own large majority for its own cause: the South Country – the suburban, agricultural, residential England – going Tory and tariff reform, and the north Country and dense industrial populations (excluding Birmingham area) going radical socialist'.[24]

Though confirmed in office, the Liberal government had, to a large extent, lost control over the political agenda. The Irish

Nationalists, by contrast, were quick to appreciate the strength of their position. Parliamentary arithmetic now made possible – or, from an Irish point of view, inevitable – the introduction of a third Home Rule Bill, something the government had deliberately excluded when in possession of an independent Commons majority and therefore having no need of Irish support. But the prerequisite would be action to curtail the powers of the House of Lords; otherwise any Home Rule measure would be likely to suffer the fate of its predecessor of 1893. Not until April 1910, however, when the government made clear its intention to introduce a Parliament Bill, did the Irish help to get the Finance Bill through the Commons. Having lost the vote in the country, the Lords now withdrew their opposition and the Budget of 1909 belatedly became law. But a further impediment to Lords reform, not to mention Home Rule, lay in the King's insistence that the government should hold a second General Election before he would agree to create enough new Liberal peers to ensure that the upper chamber agreed to its own emasculation. It was in this situation that Edward VII died suddenly on 6 May and, in an attempt to effect a compromise that would spare his inexperienced successor George V a number of difficult decisions, four senior representatives of each of the two main parties met in a constitutional conference over the summer and early autumn.

Much mystery and speculation surrounded the course of these inter-party discussions, largely because, though negotiations proceeded over several weeks, no record was published either at the time or subsequently, and perhaps also because of the intrusion of Lloyd George's dramatic and unexpected proposal for a coalition government. But it would appear that, without compromising on fundamental principles, each side genuinely sought to reach a settlement. Soon after the conference resumed in October after the summer recess, negotiations reached an impasse. Basic agreement seemed to have been reached on the submission of deadlocked legislation to a joint sitting of the two Houses of Parliament, but the sticking point was whether, as the Unionists insisted, constitutional changes including Home Rule should be excluded from this provision and submitted instead to a referendum. At this point, however, consideration of such constitutional niceties was pushed temporarily to the periphery by Lloyd George's bold suggestion that the outstanding issues of the day could best be resolved by the formation of a coalition government. The Unionists showed some interest before drawing back. The Chancellor's motives for putting forward this proposal remain a matter of debate. He may have been considering how to ease the passage of the National Insurance legislation to which his fertile brain had now turned, but it also seems likely that he shared the irritation, frequently voiced over the preceding decade by radical politicians from all parties, at the sterility of the party political struggle. His attitude at other times in his long political career supports the view that, though he lived and died a Liberal, he was never as wedded to the notion of the party for its own sake as were most of his political contemporaries. Lloyd George had political goals and his party was never more than a vehicle helping to achieve them.

When the government compromised to the extent of suggesting that a General Election should intervene on the next occasion that a Home Rule bill was rejected by the Lords, but on this occasion alone, and that subsequent Home Rule measures should be treated like ordinary legislation, it was clear that the Liberals had gone as far as they could. But it was also clear that the Unionists would not accept a settlement on such terms. Not surprisingly, the conference was wound up at its 22nd session on 10 November. A further General Election was now inevitable, though the King insisted on waiting for the Lords to reject the Parliament Bill before granting a dissolution. Jesse Herbert, Treasurer of the Liberal Central Association, the body charged with maintaining communication throughout the party, suggested that the Liberal and Labour parties stood to gain about 30 seats in England and Wales, while the Unionists were clearly apprehensive about the country's verdict. Under pressure from moderates in his own ranks, Balfour was obliged to water down his party's commitment to tariff reform. On 29 November, only days before voting began, he announced at the Albert Hall that, if the Unionists were to win the election, no taxes would be imposed on food until the electorate had had the opportunity to express its views on this single issue in a referendum.

In the event, the electoral outcome was something of an anticlimax. The December poll saw only marginal overall changes from that of January. The Liberals and Unionists now both held 272 seats; and Labour's tally went up slightly to 42. In fact, more seats had changed hands than these figures suggested. The Liberals won 23 seats from the Unionists, but suffered 25 losses, including one to Labour. Even so, the transfer of votes was on a relatively small scale. The government would remain in power, still dependent on the support of Labour and the Irish Nationalists. In the short term it could now proceed with the Parliament Bill. Under its terms, the Lords would not in future be able to amend or reject a financial bill; any other legislation rejected by the Lords would become law automatically, provided that not less than two years had elapsed between its introduction and its third reading in the Commons; and the maximum life of a Parliament would be reduced from seven years to five. Asquith's trump card was the promise, secretly extracted from a reluctant monarch shortly before the December election, that the latter would, if needed, be ready to create the requisite number of peers to ensure the bill's passage. Even so, a substantial number of Unionists preferred to 'die in the last ditch' rather than surrender their powers voluntarily. In the event, enough Unionist peers went into the government lobby on the cru-cial vote on 10 August 1911 to cancel out the 'ditchers', while the majority of their number followed the lead of Lord Lansdowne and abstained.

Irish Home Rule

The curtailment of the powers of the House of Lords opened up the prospect of a further tranche of reforming legislation from the government, of a kind that might previously have had little chance of success. Yet it is hard not to conclude that, after the passage of the National Insurance Act later that year, the government lost some of its momentum. At the level of personnel, the departure of Churchill to the Admiralty in October 1911 was a significant loss from the forces of progressivism on the domestic front. As First Lord of the Admiralty, Churchill had different priorities. He had 'become quite a Tory,' noted Lloyd George in 1912. 'He has changed immensely.'[25] More generally, the change was in large part the inevitable consequence of a renewed fixation on the problems of Ireland. Between 1906 and 1910, Ireland had occupied a lowly position among the government's priorities. As previous Liberal governments had burnt their fingers badly on this issue, this was scarcely surprising. The limit of the government's ambitions had been to try to satisfy the Irish with minor reforms, while preparing the electorate for the possibility of Home Rule at some time in the future. In November 1905, Campbell-Bannerman had revealed his cautious step-by-step approach to the Irish Nationalist leadership. While he would not pledge his party to full Home Rule in the new Parliament, he did intend to enact 'some serious measure which would be consistent with and lead up to the other'.[26] In the event, the ill-fated Irish Councils Bill of 1907 represented the sum total of the government's endeavours. While there were still Liberals who regarded the quest for Home Rule as something of a crusade, the majority had come to agree with Joseph Chamberlain that it was 'death and damnation' for their party as a whole.

After 1910, however, Home Rule was the issue that dominated the government's thinking and latterly its parliamentary agenda, right up to the outbreak of the First World War. The two General Elections of 1910 recreated the parliamentary situation of 1886 and 1892 in the sense of leaving the Liberal government dependent for its continued survival on the support of the contingent of Irish Nationalist MPs, who were insistent on seeing their aspiration for Home Rule satisfied. The 1910 election results were, in the words of George Dangerfield, 'like historical graffiti, the naughty calligraphy of Fate itself'.[27] But the key difference in the post-1910 situation was that the passage of a third Home Rule Bill would not, thanks to the Parliament Act, fall victim to the immovable Unionist majority in the upper house. Indeed, the destruction of the Lords' veto added an element of precision and predictability to the bill's parliamentary progress. Contemporaries could now calculate, accurately enough, the cumbersome yet inevitable timetable by which Home Rule would wend its way on to the Statute Book. Even allowing for the full exercise of the Lords' remaining powers of delay, Ireland would become self-governing by the summer of 1914. In the intervening period, the government could expect to be fully occupied. Unionists would respond to the challenge of Home Rule with every bit of the passion and determination with which Liberals might defend free trade.

Home Rule thus became an obsession for government and opposition alike, with genuine conviction on both sides of the argument rather than the stylized rhetoric that so often accompanies political debate. Mounting tension in Ireland was characterized by the growth of armed volunteer forces on both sides of the argument, carrying with them at least the threat of civil war.

At the height of the crisis, one cabinet minister recorded: 'History if it concerns itself with us at all will write us down as either the most patient, wise, foreseeing Govt. this or any country ever had, or else as the inept, blind and cowardly crew that ever disgraced Downing Street. No middle judgement will be possible.'[28] Yet it is doubtful whether the Liberals, any more than their Unionist opponents, derived any significant electoral advantage, at least on the British mainland, from the stance they adopted. Rather, the Irish problem appears as an enormous distraction, a throwback to the constitutional struggles of the nineteenth century, even though its resolution would continue to elude successive British governments for the remainder of the twentieth century. Meanwhile, Asquith's government missed possible opportunities to advance its own cause. In November 1911, the Prime Minister announced that the government would bring in a Franchise and Registration Bill designed to grant full manhood suffrage and at the same time remove the anomaly of plural voting. Significantly, and despite the fact that the cabinet was deeply divided on the issue, the bill was drawn up so as to permit the introduction of an amendment to enfranchise women on the same basis as men. This duly happened. In January 1913, however, the Speaker ruled that the amendment would so transform the nature of the bill as to render it invalid. This ruling was of questionable merit, but there was no obvious way in which it could be challenged, and the government decided to drop the whole measure.

As the Home Rule Bill progressed, both sides became anxious to secure a compromise settlement, based probably on the exclusion of Protestant Ulster from the bill's provisions. Both sides, however, were wary of the potential reaction of extremists in their own ranks. For the Liberals, this meant ensuring that they could carry the Irish Nationalists with them. In the event, agreement on the details of a compromise – which counties might be excluded and for how long – proved elusive, and historians can only speculate as to what would have happened if the enactment of Home Rule had come up against the steely determination of Protestant Orangemen to resist government from Catholic Dublin. As it was, only the coming of the war in Europe in August 1914 forced the Irish issue on to the legislative back-burner. On 24 July, as a last-minute conference at Buckingham Palace to try to break the Irish deadlock collapsed, the Foreign Secretary informed his colleagues of the text of an ultimatum sent to Serbia by Austria-Hungary. As Churchill memorably recalled:

> [Edward Grey] had been reading or speaking for several minutes before I could disengage my mind from the tedious and bewildering debate which had just closed. We were all very tired, but gradually as the phrases and sentences followed one another, impressions of a wholly different character began to form in my mind ... The parishes of Fermanagh and Tyrone faded back into the mists and squalls of Ireland, and a strange light began immediately, but by perceptible gradations, to fall and glow upon the map of Europe.[29]

Nor was Ireland the government's only worry in the last years of peace. The campaign of the militant suffragettes provided a considerable distraction. Then the period after 1911 saw an unprecedented wave of industrial unrest, with strikes and lockouts hitting large parts of British industry. More than 40 million working days were lost in 1912 alone. Some of these strikes carried a syndicalist undertone, threatening the overthrow of capitalism and the setting up of a workers' republic, though economic factors were the more usual cause. By 1913, moves had been made to co-ordinate the activities of the railwaymen, miners and transport workers in a so-called Triple Alliance. The control of these unions over the country's transport gave them the capacity to call something approaching a general strike. In 1913, the cabinet itself was badly shaken by the Marconi Scandal, which threatened the careers of three government ministers – Lloyd George, Herbert Samuel and Rufus Isaacs – and the former chief whip, the Master of Elibank. Accused of what would today be called 'insider trading', the four men had probably been unwise and lacking in candour rather than genuinely corrupt. 'There was no corruption,' judged the new Tory leader, Bonar Law, 'but they acted imprudently and improperly.'[30] More generally, both the cabinet and the parliamentary party seem to have been more divided than in earlier years. Issues of defence policy were often the cause. Thirty-seven Liberal MPs voted to reduce military and naval expenditure in March 1911. The following July, 23 members opposed the supplementary naval estimates, and, in March 1913, 14 Liberals again defied their government over increased naval expenditure. Churchill's appointment as First Lord of the Admiralty only exacerbated the problem, as he now 'embraced the cause of naval might as eagerly as he had [once championed] retrenchment'.[31] In his new post, Churchill clearly intended to secure peace by preparing for war. Added to this was a growing personal opposition from many of his cabinet colleagues, who objected to his overbearing manner and tendency to intervene in each and every cabinet discussion, no matter how far removed from the First Lord's departmental concerns. Though Churchill's estimates for 1913–14 got through the cabinet without difficulty, trouble erupted when, at the end of 1913, he proposed an additional increase of £3 million. At one point, half a dozen cabinet ministers, including Lloyd George, seemed likely to resign unless Churchill backed down or he himself resigned. 'The Government may break up on the question of the Navy estimates,' judged Reginald McKenna in January 1914.[32] In the event, by the middle of February the crisis had passed with no resignations tendered. Churchill promised to effect substantial reductions in expenditure the following year. The resolution of disputes such as this was perhaps Asquith's greatest skill as Prime Minister. His readiness to skirt around awkward issues and post-pone difficult decisions, and his ability to charm, cajole and con-ciliate his colleagues all helped to hold an exceptionally talented but often potentially divergent cabinet together. In the context of war there would be a downside to this style. For the time being, however, it worked well.

The Land Campaign

The troubled history of the last years before the outbreak of the First World War, compounded by knowledge of the fate that awaited British Liberalism in the years to come, makes it all too easy to take a very gloomy view of the party's likely prospects. But several historians have drawn attention to clear signs that, regard-less of Ireland and other problems, the government, and in par-ticular Lloyd George, were beginning to embark on a second wave of radical reforms. Despite opposition from fellow Liberals, Lloyd George was determined to push ahead. As C. P. Scott recorded:

> There were of course people in the party who in their hearts hated all reforms and he constantly came across nominal Liberals whose one cry was 'Why not let it alone?' They did not realise that for

Liberalism stagnation was death. The worst kind of Tory was the nominal Liberal.[33]

The new focus of the Chancellor's attention was the land, and his proposals included establishing security of tenure for tenant farmers and creating Wage Boards to set minimum wages for agricultural workers. There were plans too for the towns, involving rating reform to facilitate improvements in urban housing. Like so much else, these schemes, launched in the autumn of 1913, fell victim to the changed priorities of the war years. But 'most of the signs that are available suggest that the land campaign had every chance of success when war intervened to transform the political landscape'.[34] More generally, the land campaign offers clear evidence that the government had not run out of steam in 1914, and indeed that it was succeeding in placing the opposition on the back foot as far as the forthcoming General Election was concerned. This was particularly the case with regard to English rural constituencies, two-thirds of which were in Unionist hands. The Unionists' response to Lloyd George's initiatives was slow and uninspiring. Their difficulty was that any counter-policy to alleviate the lot of the rural working class would run the risk of alienating their traditional support among the land-owning community. By June 1914, Sir Arthur Steel-Maitland, the Unionist Chairman, privately conceded that his party had completely lost the initiative on the land question, and that Unionist prospects for the coming autumn looked extremely unfavourable.[35]

The renaissance of Liberal radicalism was also evident in Lloyd George's 1914 Budget, the first £200 million Budget in British history. This provided for grants of more than £4 million to local authorities to subsidize the rates, to be paid for by a rise of 2d. in income tax (to 1s. 4d.), and increased supertax and death duties. This represented a significant extension of the principle of graduated taxation and a further step in wealth redistribution, and has been described as marking 'the climax of the fiscal strategy of the New Liberalism'.[36] But the Budget provoked strong opposition within the ranks of the parliamentary Liberal Party. A group of around 40 MPs organized themselves under the leadership of the wealthy Liverpool ship-owner and MP for Hexham, Richard Holt. Historians have disputed the importance of the so-called 'Holt Cave'. Some have suggested that the actions of Holt and his colleagues represented a significant body of opposition to the general progressive direction of government policy, including Lloyd George's land campaign. Contemporaries were struck by the wealth of the Cave's members, with *Punch* making fun of the Adullamite activities of 'Holt's Cave for Plutocrats'. These were the men with most to lose from the Chancellor's policies, which were directed even more markedly at the rich than had been the People's Budget of 1909. One former cabinet minister judged the group to be 'a clique of rich men determined to read a lesson to L. George by resisting a budget which taxes them'.[37] Holt led a deputation of between 40 and 50 MPs that met Asquith on 15 June. The Prime Minister's failure to satisfy the rebels resulted in a letter to *The Times* on 18 June, which even Asquith found 'a very able document'.[38] The Cave's efforts ended with the government withdrawing some of its proposals and agreeing to halve the projected increase in income tax. This, it has been argued, 'clearly defined the limits of [the Liberal] Party's tolerance for social and economic change'. Possibly, indeed, 'the budget debacle of 1914 marked the end of the New Liberalism'.[39]

This is an exaggeration. Recent research has stressed the fluid composition of the Holt Cave, whose numbers fluctuated during the brief weeks of its existence between 15 and 60 members. According to Ian Packer, it was 'by no means a straightforward expression of anti-progressive sentiments' but rather 'a disparate group of MPs whose membership and grievances varied enormously'.[40] Furthermore, Packer has shown that the government's concessions had more to do with procedural difficulties of its own creation than with pressure applied by Holt and his associates. So the Cave may have been less significant for the Liberal Party's long-term evolution than was once thought. That said, it is difficult to ignore Holt's own analysis. The Cave, he said, was 'a combined remonstrance by business men and some survivors of the Cobden–Bright school of thought against the ill-considered and socialistic tendencies of the Government finance'. The government had 'certainly travelled a long way from the old Liberal principle of "retrenchment" and I deeply regret it'.[41] Holt himself, and presumably at least some of those who acted with him, represented a continuing strand of non-interventionist, laissez-faire Liberalism that was out of sympathy with the New Liberalism and with much that the government had been doing since 1908. Even one of Lloyd George's cabinet colleagues had earlier found it difficult to accept a Chancellor of the Exchequer who urged expenditure rather than economy, and who seemed 'to have no idea that he is the guardian of the public purse'.[42]

Doomed to Oblivion?

By the outbreak of war, the Liberal Party had – albeit with some support from its allies – emerged victorious from three successive General Elections. The next contest would have to be held before the end of 1915, and not all Liberals looked forward to it confident of victory. But nor, for that matter did the Unionist opposition, some of whose leaders were privately anticipating a fourth successive defeat. Though the outcome of a General Election that was never held must necessarily remain uncertain, what can be said is that the Liberals were trying to create the most favourable conditions for their next appeal to the country by pushing through a bill to abolish plural voting. This anomaly, it was believed, had added as many as 30 seats to the Unionist tally in December 1910. The government's measure awaited its third and final reading in the Commons when the coming of war disrupted the whole pattern of its planned legislative programme. At the same time, Liberals believed that Lloyd George's land campaign would lead to gains rather than losses in English rural seats in the forthcoming contest. And even if a 1915 General Election had resulted in a Liberal defeat, this is the nature of the democratic process and such an outcome should not be equated with the party's total disintegration and the end of its claims to be a party of government.

In such a situation it might seem bizarre, absurd indeed, to suggest that the historic Liberal Party was in any sense 'doomed' to oblivion by the time that Gavrilo Princip fired his fateful shots in the Balkan town of Sarajevo. Hindsight, however, imposes a heavy burden. The short timescale of the party's decline in the decade after the First World War, and its replacement by Labour as the leading opponent of the Conservatives, has encouraged the belief that Liberalism must already have been fatally wounded before the coming of European war. Since the mid-1930s, when the young Oxford-educated historian, George Dangerfield, penned his celebrated *Strange Death of Liberal England*, historians have been engaged in 'the scholarly pursuit of listening to the heartbeat of the Edwardian Liberal Party in order to record its formal death'.[43] Dangerfield's analysis, expressed in compelling if somewhat melodramatic prose, contains two essential elements. Most famously, he suggested that Liberal England died 'strangely' in the period 1911–14, the victim of a pattern of violence made up of the intransigence of the House of Lords, the militancy of the trade unions, the excesses of the suffragettes and the fanaticism of the Protestants of Ulster. The coming of external war provided a fitting climax to this pattern of internal violence. In the face of this concerted onslaught, Liberalism – moderate, rational and tolerant – collapsed and died, an anachronistic relic of an age that had now passed.

No serious scholar would now subscribe to anything like this thesis. Fundamentally, no 'pattern' of violence ever existed, merely an 'accidental convergence of unrelated events',[44] the sorts of problems that it is the business of elected governments to confront and resolve. By 1914, some of these problems had indeed been resolved; and others, though serious, were fully capable of resolution. Furthermore, the supposed link between international and domestic violence is an illusion. But Dangerfield also made a more challenging suggestion. Writing from a perspective when not only was the decline of Liberalism an issue of contemporary politics, but also, regardless of the setback of 1931, the Labour Party appeared to be engaged in an inexorable rise from its foundation in 1900, he pointed to a causal link between the two phenomena. Indeed, for the Liberal Party, the writing was already on the wall in the hour of its greatest electoral triumph in 1906:

> The Liberal Party which came back to Westminster with an overwhelming majority was already doomed. It was like an army protected at all points except for one vital position on its flank. With the election of fifty-three Labour representatives, [a total which Dangerfield reaches by adding those Lib–Lab MPs who took the Liberal whip to the representatives of the newly formed Labour Party] the death of Liberalism was pronounced; it was no longer the Left.[45]

Expressed in more measured, but still forceful, terms, the relationship between the pre-war Liberal and Labour parties has become a central component of the historiographical debate over

Liberalism's decline. Put simply, argument has raged, and still rages, over whether the Liberals were in the process of being over-taken by Labour even before European war distorted the pattern of domestic political development, or whether they remained in 1914 the undisputed party of the British working class, with the pretensions of the Labour upstart held firmly in check.

The Labour Challenge and the Progressive Alliance

The idea that there was something 'inevitable' about the rise of Labour and its consequent destruction of the Liberal Party has exercised a strong appeal for Marxist and quasi-Marxist histo-rians in particular, and Labour historians in general. In their vision, a growing understanding that the interests of employer and employee, of capital and labour, were ultimately incompatible (something Victorian Liberalism had always denied), was bound to find expression in new political organizations based on the spe-cific interests of the working class. Thus the establishment of the Labour Representation Committee in 1900, and its rapid trans-formation after the 1906 General Election into the Labour Party, signalled the eventual destruction of the Liberals, even if that pro-cess was partially concealed before 1914 by the restricted nature of the Edwardian franchise.[46] The pattern of pre-war Liberal elec-toral success was therefore nothing more than a deceptive Indian summer, quickly revealed as such when the Representation of the People Act (1918) signalled a significant move towards full democ-racy. According to Henry Pelling, Liberalism's demise was not the consequence of wartime quarrels or the erosion of Liberal values: 'Rather it was the result of long-term social and economic changes which were simultaneously uniting Britain geographically and dividing her inhabitants in terms of class.'[47] The period before 1914 saw the growth of 'a sort of undogmatic "Labourism"' – a feeling that 'the Labour Party, and not the Liberal, was the party for working men to belong to'.[48] If this transformation did not immediately translate into electoral success for Labour, that did not matter. The Labour Party's greatest strength lay in its extra-parliamentary organization in the trade union movement, where the period 1906–14 saw a growth in the number of affiliated members from 900,000 to more than 1.5 million. More recently, Ross McKibbin has confirmed the rise of 'an acutely developed working-class consciousness', reflected above all in a flourishing trade union movement:

> The eclipse of the Liberal Party was not due to 'the war', or a wrong-headed pursuit of laissez-faire, or the split between Asquith and Lloyd George, or the conversion of the workers to socialism, but to a slow change in the way popular affiliations were decided. As political allegiance became more and more determined by class self-awareness, the Liberal Party found it could make no claim on the loyalties of any class.[49]

In such a scenario, the impact of war might have accelerated the pattern of change, but it did not initiate it. The triumph of Labour and the collapse of Liberalism were already well advanced by 1914.

These 'Labour' interpretations have inevitably been challenged by historians with a more sympathetic disposition towards the Liberal Party. Writing in the mid-1960s and early-1970s, respectively, Trevor Wilson and Peter Clarke[50] pointed to the fundamental strength of pre-war Liberalism. Whatever caused the party's eventual replacement by Labour, it was not to be found in the Edwardian era. Wilson, explicitly, and Clarke, largely implicitly, sought to divert attention to the 'accidents' of the war years as the source of Liberal decline. Clarke's analysis provided a particularly telling response to the 'inevitabilists'. Basing his study on the electoral politics of Lancashire, he did not deny that political allegiance by 1914 had come to be determined largely by the question of class. Rather, he confirmed that by 1910 the 'change to class politics was substantially complete', and clearly reflected in the electoral map of that year when the prosperous south returned, by and large, to the Conservative fold after the aberration of 1906. There were, therefore, no signs that such a transformation would be accompanied by the supersession of one party by another. Instead, it appeared that 'both Labour and Liberalism would be subsumed in progressivism'.[51] In other words, enough common ground existed between Edwardian Liberalism and the preponderant Social Democratic wing of the Labour Party to produce eventual fusion – if the First World War had not intervened. By adopting the ideas of the New Liberalism, as exemplified in the legislation enacted by Lloyd George and Churchill, and publicized through the circle surrounding C. P. Scott, editor of the *Manchester Guardian*, the Liberal Party had successfully adapted to the new era of class politics and, in so doing, had entrenched itself as the party of social reform and of the British working class. Nothing, according to Clarke, suggests that the party was in serious difficulties before the coming of war. Indeed, the evidence indicates that Liberal success would have continued, 'if not to the degree of 1906, at least at a level markedly above that of the Gladstonian party'.[52]

Such starkly different interpretations are not easily reconciled. Their incompatibility demands that the history of Liberal–Labour relations in the decade before the First World War be reviewed. As is well known, in September 1903 the Liberal and Labour parties had entered into a secret electoral pact signed in the names of Herbert Gladstone, the Liberal chief whip, and Ramsay MacDonald, Secretary of the Labour Representation Committee. From a Liberal point of view, the need for such a pact might seem unclear. But that is to see the question through the perspective of the party's electoral triumph of 1906. At the time of the pact's signature over two years before, the Liberal Party had been out of power for eight years, during much of which time it had not even appeared to be a viable alternative government. For the best part of two decades, with the exception of three unhappy years in office between 1892 and 1895, the party had been permanently confined to the opposition benches. In 1903, however, Gladstone and MacDonald identified a common purpose in defeating a Unionist government whose fortunes had begun to wane but which might still emerge victorious at the next General Election if the progressive vote was split by Labour and Liberal candidates competing against one another. The dangers to Liberalism of three-cornered contests had been highlighted by Labour's victory in July in a by-election in Barnard Castle, County Durham, at which the Liberal candidate had come bottom of the poll. The pact also offered Liberalism the chance to confirm its working-class appeal by aligning itself with an avowedly working-class organization, while at the same time offering the opportunity to limit the financial demands on hard-pressed party funds.

Yet, as some contemporaries recognized and as later historians have been quick to point out, the pact was not necessarily an unmixed blessing. Liberals faced a dilemma that had some parallels with the one confronting their successors nearly 80 years later at the formation of the Social Democratic Party. By admitting Labour's organizational independence, the pact created the possibility that the new party, now virtually guaranteed a significant bridgehead in the next Parliament, might become a Trojan horse threatening the Liberal Party's supremacy on the left wing of British politics. In short, Liberal benevolence might have the effect of 'nursing into life a serpent which will sting their Party into death'.[53] Jesse Herbert, Gladstone's secretary, who played a leading role in the negotiations leading to the pact, set out the potential hazards with commendable fairness:

> Are the principles and objects of the LRC such as to justify such a benevolent attitude? Will the success of the Liberal party at the polls be too dearly purchased at the price? Ought the Liberal party to prefer defeat rather than assist in any way to foster the growing power of the Labour Party?

On balance, however, he had no doubt about the compelling electoral advantages:

> The gain to the party through a working arrangement would be great, and can be measured best by a comparison of the results of 'no arrangement' with those of 'an arrangement'. Should [LRC supporters] be advised to vote against Liberal candidates, and (as they probably would) should they act as advised, the Liberal party would suffer defeat not only in those constituencies where LRC candidates fought, but also in almost every borough, and in many of the Divisions of Lancashire and Yorkshire. This would be the inevitable result of unfriendly action towards the LRC candidates. They would be defeated, but so also should we be defeated.[54]

Fundamental to the willingness of the Liberal leadership to enter the 1903 pact was the perception that Labour still represented a kindred spirit rather than an ideological challenge. Gladstone, who had long encouraged Liberal constituency parties to look favourably on the claims of working-class candidates, readily accepted MacDonald's assurance that 'the candidates of the LRC will be found to be in almost every instance earnest Liberals, who will support a Liberal Government'.[55] The chief whip could find 'no material point of difference' between the two parties in

terms of policy.[56] MacDonald himself predicted the evolution of
'a united democratic party appealing to the people on behalf of
a simple, comprehensive belief in social reconstruction'.[57] Such
hopes seemed to be confirmed by the sort of Labour men who
were successful at the 1906 General Election. Though many professed themselves to be 'socialists', they were in practice 'really no
more than advanced Liberals'.[58]

At all events, few could question the effective working of the
pact at that election. The results seemed to vindicate the strategy
of avoiding a division in the anti-Unionist vote, while at the same
time confirming Labour's continuing electoral dependence on
the Liberal Party. Gladstone thought the pact 'the chief factor'
in his party's unprecedented triumph.[59] Thirty-one of the LRC's
50 candidates stood without Liberal opposition. Of these, 24 were
successful. But only five LRC candidates prevailed in the face of
Liberal opponents. Strikingly, in Scotland, where the pact did not
apply, there were 10 three-cornered contests and the Liberals were
defeated in six seats which they might otherwise have won. Jesse
Herbert celebrated the Liberals' achievement:

> The sum of the matter is that in England and Wales Liberals and
> Labour-men held 367 seats out of 495, i.e. a majority of 239, and
> there are only 2 cases in which we have any ground for complaint
> against the Labour people, and one case in which they have just
> ground of complaint against us. Was there ever such a justification
> of a policy by results?[60]

It is thus possible to argue that a relatively small concession on
the part of the Liberal Party had enabled it to contain Labour's
challenge and ensure continuing Liberal leadership of the progressive left in British politics. For all that, the election for the first
time of a substantial body of Labour MPs could not be ignored.
Symbolically, the LRC now formally renamed itself the Labour
Party. The Unionist leader, Arthur Balfour, seemed to anticipate
Dangerfield when he drew dark parallels between Labour's gains
and recent revolutionary events in St. Petersburg. More cautiously,
it may be noted that the British electoral system makes it extremely
difficult for new parties to establish a parliamentary presence. For
Labour, this hurdle had now been overcome, courtesy of their
Liberal partners. But did the new party's band of MPs pose, as

Dangerfield suggested, a long-term, if not immediate, threat to the Liberal Party? David Powell has suggested that 'once the Labour party had come into existence, it rapidly acquired an identity and momentum of its own and was able to present itself as a credible alternative focus for working-class loyalties'.[61] Such an analysis is certainly logical. Whether this is what actually happened over the following eight years is more open to question.

The Parliament of 1906 saw no real change in the relationship between the two parties, at least at the level of national politics. Labour and socialist candidates secured spectacular by-election gains at Jarrow in the North-East and Colne Valley in West Yorkshire in 1907 and at Sheffield, Attercliffe in May 1909, but these were more representative of a predictable slump in the government's mid-term fortunes, against the background of a trade recession, than of any fundamental change in voting patterns. For the most part the pact of 1903 was maintained, though MacDonald had one eye open to the chances of extending Labour representation in order to conduct future negotiations from a position of greater strength. The most significant event of the period was the ballot conducted by the Miners' Federation of Great Britain in 1908, which resulted in a clear though not overwhelming majority in favour of affiliation to the Labour Party. As a result, the latter's nominal strength in the Commons rose to 45, though most of the mining MPs who now joined Labour continued to co-operate with the Liberals in their own constituencies, and three chose to stand again under their old Lib–Lab colours in the General Election of January 1910. Against this background, Labour's performance at that election – three gains and five losses producing a total of 40 MPs – was scarcely a stunning advance. Though the extent of the Unionist recovery left Labour (along with the Irish Nationalists) in a strong position, the dynamics of the Liberal–Labour relationship still seemed to be weighted heavily in the Liberals' favour. In essence, the Liberals had allowed the pact to continue on the basis of what had happened in 1906, but with no new concessions. J. A. Pease, the party's new chief whip, argued that Liberals should 'respect the seats which at the last General Election returned Labour Representation candidates and that the LRC organisation should respect other progressive candidates standing for seats held by other Labour representatives or Liberals in 1906'.[62] Labour and Liberal candidates opposed one another in 24 constituencies, none of which returned Labour MPs, and in 20 of which Labour came bottom of the poll. In December 1910, Labour's overall tally went up to 42 seats, but once again victory in triangular contests proved beyond them. Overall, the results of the two General Elections 'appeared to confirm what Liberals had emphasised for some years; that Labour's success in elections was directly related to the extent to which they were willing to co-operate'.[63] Labour seemed to be dependent on Liberal support to win seats; but there were seats which the Liberals could hold in the face of Labour opposition.

In the absence of evidence from a 1915 General Election, the by-election statistics for the years 1911–14 have been subjected to more than usually detailed scrutiny, without, it has to be said, any defini-tive conclusion being reached about what this information tells us of the health of the Liberal Party or the condition of Liberal–Labour relations at the start of the war. Certainly, the Liberal gov-ernment experienced a disappointing run of by-election losses. The beneficiaries, however, were not Labour but the Unionists, to whom the Liberals lost 15 seats, leaving the Unionists the largest party in the Commons by a clear margin. Some of these seats were lost in straight fights, but Labour intervened in 11 formerly safe Liberal constituencies, causing five seats to fall to the Unionists. 'As a result of three-cornered contests,' warned C. P. Scott in July 1912 through the pages of the *Manchester Guardian*, 'it is quite pos-sible that while Liberalism and Labour are snapping and snarling at each other the Conservative dog may run away with the bone.'[64] By 1914, this alarm had spread to the heart of the Liberal govern-ment. In a speech at Ladybank in Fife, Scotland, in April, Asquith pointed out that all but one of the Liberals' losses over the previous two years had been the result of a 'split in the forces of progress'. Indeed, when Unionist candidates took seats on a minority vote, Liberals were still inclined to stress that the combined Progressive vote showed that, while the government's candidate might have been defeated, its policies had not.

What deductions may safely be drawn from these figures? Many believe that the most important feature of the electoral history of the immediate pre-war period is the weakness of the Labour Party. Both Roy Douglas, writing of Labour's 'decline', and Peter Clarke have emphasized that Labour came third in 14 three-cor-nered contests in industrial constituencies between 1911 and 1914.

'With two or three possible exceptions,' writes Douglas, 'there was not a constituency in the land which Labour could be tolerably certain of holding if both the Liberals and the Unionists chose to field candidates; and there were not many where, in such circumstances, Labour could even expect a second place.'[65] Labour seemed unable to offer a distinctive alternative to Liberalism and could only muster the support of those trade unionists who felt obliged to back a candidate of their own class. In general, Liberals were still attracting the bulk of the working-class vote. 'The reason why the Labor [*sic*] Party has been able to make so little of a fight against Liberalism,' declared *The Nation*, 'has been that Liberalism has gone so far in the direction of the Labor [*sic*] Party.'[66] As a result, few leading Labour figures were anticipating a significant Labour breakthrough. Indeed, in 1913, Philip Snowden declared that 'the present Labour representation in parliament is there mainly by the goodwill of the Liberals, and it will disappear when that goodwill is turned into active resentment'.[67]

Yet this same evidence has been used to produce a very different interpretation. According to Ross McKibbin, though Labour was not yet winning by-elections, its vote was often impressive, especially in constituencies which it had not previously contested. Where Labour had already stood at the General Election, it often improved on its earlier performance. In Holmfirth, West Yorkshire, in June 1912, Labour took 28.2 per cent of the vote compared with 14.9 per cent in January 1910. What was happening amounted to a steady erosion of Liberal support, which was to have profound long-term implications. He accepts that Labour's challenge was not ideological, but points to a growing feeling that the Liberals had ceased to be the party of the working class, while 'in some perceived if indefinable way the Labour party was'.[68] But, for McKibbin, the level of Labour support was less significant than the fact that Labour was now far more ready to compete with the Liberals for the same vote. In short, he points to the breakdown of the Progressive Alliance and the damage this would do to the Liberals' position at the forthcoming General Election. Had that election taken place in 1915, McKibbin believes that Labour would have contested up to 170 seats. Sensing the danger, the *Liberal Magazine* called, in the summer of 1914, for 'a policy of accommodation between Liberal and Labour, which will reproduce in the constituencies the co-operation which obtains at Westminster'.

But such was the growing spirit of Labour independence in the country that, even if it had been proposed by the party leadership, the Labour movement as a whole would not have accepted a renewal of the sort of electoral arrangement that had protected the progressive vote in the last three national contests.

Regional studies have confirmed the complexity of the overall picture. Both the viability of the Progressive Alliance and the electoral fortunes of the Liberal Party itself varied considerably from region to region. Martin Petter notes a 'curious contrast' in Liberal–Labour relations 'between harmony in Parliament and friction in the constituencies', a conclusion endorsed by George Bernstein's examination of the situation in Norwich, Leicester and Leeds. In municipal politics, Labour candidates seemed more prepared than they were nationally to stand as 'socialists', thereby differentiating themselves from Liberalism and undermining the viability of a progressive alliance between the two parties. Liberals were 'unable to come to terms with a movement which insisted upon espousing an ideology so hostile to their own'.[69] Electoral contests between the two parties were frequent in the West Riding of Yorkshire and, according to Keith Laybourn and Jack Reynolds, revealed considerable Labour progress at the municipal level as early as 1906, and possibly irreversible Liberal decline before 1914. 'By any yardstick,' they conclude, 'Labour had made substantial political gains in West Yorkshire between 1906 and 1914. Whilst Liberalism remained the preponderant force at the parliamentary level, the roots of its parliamentary success were being rapidly eroded by Labour at the local level.'[70] In the North-East, Liberals seem to have made a considered decision as to whether to oppose LRC candidates on the basis of the latter's views, and whether they were compatible with Liberalism. But here the Liberal position was much stronger than in the West Riding. The period after 1906 witnessed a successful Liberal counter-attack in the North-East which held Labour firmly in check.[71] London was, predictably, *sui generis*. Paul Thompson sees the Liberal recovery that took place in the first decade of the new century as being based on a 'temporary revival of Nonconformist and trade union support and of old radical political issues', which could not disguise an otherwise 'disastrous decay' dating from the late nineteenth century. The Liberal Party lacked a firm basis of electoral support among London's working classes, even though the Labour challenge came relatively late on the scene.[72] Many of these local findings have been confirmed by Chris Cook's wide-ranging study of pre-war municipal elections. He draws a picture of serious Liberal decline in many areas, together with a failure to define a clear electoral strategy in relation to Labour. In some areas Liberals were already starting to join forces with the Conservatives in an anti-Labour front. But Cook stresses that the main beneficiaries of this Liberal retreat were the Conservatives and that, apart from a few heavily industrialized areas in the large cities, Labour's advance remained negligible or non-existent.[73]

Duncan Tanner provides one further twist to this historiographical plot. The strength of his argument derives from the wide-ranging nature of his research and his unwillingness to make unsustainable generalizations. Tanner discovered enormous regional variations in the strength of the Progressive Alliance and in Labour's capacity for independent action. Overall, Labour was 'comparatively strong where the Liberal party was weak [but] unable to seriously rival it in most Liberal areas'.[74] He shows that Labour–Liberal by-election contests in the years 1911–14 were no more numerous than in the corresponding period of the 1906 Parliament and suggests that these contests should be viewed less as evidence of the collapse of the Progressive Alliance than as skirmishes in an on-going tactical battle. 'Threatened campaigns were part of the process of public negotiation which characterised the Progressive Alliance' and suggestions that Labour would field around 150 candidates had also been current prior to the General Elections of 1910.[75] Tanner argues that, but for the war, there was every likelihood that the two parties would have brokered some new electoral arrangement. National Executive Committee lists prepared for a meeting in June 1914 indicate that in many parts of the country the electoral pact of 1903 was continuing to hold. Nationally, Labour had not so far developed the sort of political strength needed to sustain an expansionist strategy. As a result, a General Election in 1914 or 1915 would probably have witnessed a Labour campaign that was a 'little larger' than in 1910, and Labour–Liberal conflict 'a fraction more pronounced', but in general 'history was about to repeat itself'.[76] Tanner concludes that there is no real evidence that the Labour Party in 1914 was in any sense on the verge of replacing the Liberals as the leading party of the left.

A 'New Liberalism'?

The viability of the pre-war Liberal Party was not solely dependent on the strength of Labour's challenge. Its own intrinsic vitality must also be considered. After all, it was central to Peter Clarke's thesis that the Liberals had adapted successfully to the changing electoral conditions of the twentieth century in a way that undermined the very need for a specifically working-class party. But there was always a suspicion that Lancashire, the focus of Clarke's analysis, was untypical of the country as a whole, even though contemporaries certainly recognized its importance in determining the outcome of national contests. As a result, much detailed work has been done to assess the extent to which the doctrines of the 'New Liberalism' had genuinely gone beyond the realm of journalists and intellectuals to penetrate both the party at Westminster and the country at large.

The evidence suggests that the process was far from complete. Lloyd George, at least, seemed to recognize the importance for the party of policies that dealt with the 'condition of the people'. 'Liberalism,' he declared in October 1906, 'will never be ousted from its supremacy in the realm of political progress until it thoroughly deserves to be deposed for its neglect or betrayal of the principles it professes.'[77] As has been seen, however, the election of 1906 was largely a victory for traditional Liberal values, and the Campbell-Bannerman government was very much in the mould of typical Liberal cabinets of the nineteenth century, with only the Trades Disputes Act of 1906 fully reflecting the impact of Progressive politics. The advent of Asquith's administration provided a fresh impetus, and by 1914 the government had an impressive record of social legislation, involving state intervention on an unprecedented scale. Old-age pensions, insurance against sickness and unemployment, labour exchanges, school meals and the tentative introduction of progressive, redistributive taxation all indicated a willingness to intervene in the actions of the free market to the benefit of the working man and his family, which stood in marked contrast to the presumptions of the Gladstonian era. Nineteenth-century notions of the minimal state had finally been abandoned. But it would be unwise to suggest that the New Liberalism now completely dominated the party or the government. It is striking how much of the progressive legislation passed after 1908 was the work of just two cabinet ministers – Lloyd George and Churchill – assisted by a few like-minded junior ministers, most notably C. F. G. Masterman. 'I don't know exactly what I am,' confessed Masterman in 1912, 'but I am sure I am not a Liberal. They have no sympathy with the people.'[78] 'Rival Liberal strands,' argues Duncan Tanner, 'were still strongly represented' in the government. The diary of Charles Hobhouse represents an on-going critique, written from the perspective of traditional Liberalism, of what he considered to be the socialistic excesses of his cabinet colleagues, Lloyd George and Churchill. Traditional Liberal concerns – temperance, free trade and religion – remained firmly on the party's agenda. One estimate suggests that only about a tenth of the parliamentary party were 'advanced radicals' and perhaps a fifth strongly committed to interventionist policies.[79] Edwardian Liberalism, concludes Geoffrey Searle, was 'Janus-faced', looking back to the traditional doctrines of Cobden and Bright as much as it projected forward to the social democracy of the later decades of the twentieth century.[80] Michael Bentley notes in the papers of the leading party figures of this time an absence of evidence of progressive motivation. He is struck by the fact that

> A pragmatic imperialist with a revulsion from philosophy of all kinds [Asquith] held the premiership during just the period when progressivism is meant to have flowered; and that his closest collaborators…injected prominent offices of state with the Oldest of Liberalism and treated progressivism with a mixture of suspicion and contempt.[81]

Similarly, David Powell believes that those same leaders were hamstrung by their social background in fully understanding and thus responding appropriately to the needs of the working class, leaving them insufficiently committed to the sorts of changes demanded by the trade union movement.[82] George Bernstein develops the same point. Even when the impact of the New Liberalism was at its height, Liberals still recognized limits beyond which they would not go on issues of fundamental concern to the working class, such as the right to work, strike action and a national minimum wage. 'If the emergence of class politics meant that working people wanted a party whose first priority was the concerns of the poor and the working class then they would have to look elsewhere.'[83]

The motivation behind the government's social reform legislation was complex and varied. Genuine philanthropy was accompanied by a keen awareness of the benefits accruing to the country as a whole through the elimination of poverty and distress. Indeed, those Liberals who expressed sympathy for working-class aspirations often did so primarily in terms of the possible electoral advantages for themselves. With a measure to deal with unemployment, suggested J. A. Pease in 1908, 'we shall be able to resist Tory reaction and Socialism and drive a wedge between the practical and impractical Labour politicians'.[84] Though his words were no doubt coloured by dismay that the government had taken the country to war, C. P. Scott's comments in August 1914 are instructive: 'We have I think no longer a Liberal Government – had we really one before?' He felt able to contrast what existed with what he wanted – 'a real Liberal Government resting on Radicalism and Labour'.[85]

Regional studies have also done much to qualify the conclusions drawn from Clarke's analysis of Lancashire. Generalization remains dangerous, but overall the impression is that in most of the country the New Liberalism had not by 1914 transformed an older pattern of political debate. In areas such as the North-East, West Yorkshire, London and Wales, it was still the traditional Liberal issues of individualism, free trade, nonconformity, retrenchment and temperance that dominated the party's agenda. In an important study of the politics of Norwich, Leeds and Leicester, George Bernstein showed that such questions were far more important for provincial Liberals than was the new programme of social reform.[86] In West Yorkshire, Liberalism remained 'dominated by the factory master and Nonconformity' and, 'unbending in its support for self-help and charity', showed few signs of trying to capture the working-class vote by way of progressive social policies.[87] This survival of an older Liberalism did not necessarily indicate that the party was in electoral difficulties. Walter Runciman's victories in Dewsbury, West Yorkshire, 'sprang from the unexhausted seam of nineteenth-century Liberalism'.[88] Liberalism's hold in the North-East had hardly been affected by Labour's challenge before the outbreak of war, while Wales, where the pre-war Liberal ascendancy was complete, 'remained sunk in the politics of nostalgia and its Gladstonian past... The new liberalism barely existed.'[89] But the absence, or at least the relative weakness, of the New Liberalism in these areas does surely place a searching question mark over the party's long-term capacity to withstand the advance of an avowedly working-class political movement.

Conflicting theories and evidence, marked regional variations and a series of unanswerable 'what if' questions posed by the coming of European war do not lead easily towards confident conclusions. But the attempt must at least be made. Because, if Labour in 1914 was indeed on the verge of replacing the Liberals as the main non-Conservative force in British politics, then the debate on the decline of the Liberal Party might effectively stop at this point. If, on the other hand, Liberalism remained a viable, indeed a vibrant, political force at the outbreak of war, then attention must shift to what happened during the war itself and possibly also to the post-war era. The most optimistic case sees the Liberal Party fully grounded in working-class support on the basis of an interventionist ideology of social reform, capable of absorbing the non-socialist wing of the Labour Party and of developing in the years ahead into something like the Democratic Party in the United States. At the opposite end of the scale, Liberalism had already surrendered the advantage to Labour in a new era of class-based politics and was only maintaining a tenuous hold on power by virtue of a series of passing advantages – the restricted franchise, Labour's financial difficulties and a crumbling electoral alliance.

Neither of these absolutist interpretations seems tenable. Labour was not on the verge of triumph in 1914, but nor was the Liberal Party without its problems. The Liberals still attracted the allegiance of large swaths of working-class support; they had not surrendered control of industrial Britain. The party was certainly weaker in 1914 than in 1906. But whether this 'decline' was merely the natural fate of a party that had been in government for eight years and whose level of support was reverting to what it had tended to enjoy in the late nineteenth century, after the aberration of 1906, or whether it was part of underlying trends that boded ill for Liberalism in the long term is almost impossible to determine. Much of the electoral support the party had lost since 1906 had transferred to the Unionists rather than to Labour. Profound social and economic changes were taking place, but no clear *national* pattern is discernible and no general statement seems applicable to the country as a whole. Such changes would have continued whether or not the war had intervened, though the timescale of change in the absence of a war, and the scope this would have afforded for Liberal adaptation, is entirely problematic. The argument that Liberalism had been saved by its intellectual vitality, by 'the medicinal powers' of the New Liberalism that had sufficient purchase on the working-class vote to counteract the growth of socialism, is unconvincing.[90] The new ideas seem to have exercised less influence on the party at Westminster and in the country at large than was once claimed. Significantly, Liberals won three successive General Elections primarily on issues determined by their Unionist opponents – free trade and the House of Lords. There is also evidence to suggest that issues such as wage rates and job security loomed larger among working-class priorities than did the sorts of social reform introduced by the Liberal government, however significant these might have been in the long-term history of welfare provision. This was by no means fatal for the Liberal Party. The ideas of an older Liberalism could still deliver electoral success, as the experience of Wales and elsewhere showed, but in the longer term the party surely needed to recognize that issues of class were coming to replace religious rivalries as the key determinant of voting behaviour.

All this suggests that the future of the Progressive Alliance was of fundamental importance. As noted earlier, in the three General Elections of 1906 and 1910, the Unionists' share of the vote ranged from 43.6 per cent to 46.9 per cent, but Labour and the Liberals managed their relationship so as to keep the Unionists out of power. In 1922, the Conservatives were to secure a comfortable Commons majority on the basis of just 38.2 per cent. Almost certainly, then, the outcome of the 1915 General Election would have been decided by the development of relations between the Liberal and Labour parties, rather than by the performance of the Unionists. The larger the number of Liberal–Labour contests, the greater the probability of a Unionist victory. Some sort of renewed electoral deal might have been stitched together in time for the coming General Election, but it is well to remember that there had always been a strand of Labour thought, particularly within the ILP, that was inherently suspicious of pacts with the Liberals and anxious to raise the banner of socialism 'out of the slough of [Liberal] individualism'.[91] The potential clearly existed for Labour, assisted from 1911 by the introduction of payment for MPs, to become a stronger element within the British political system.

And, even assuming some new arrangement had been reached for 1915, the question remains over how long it would have been content to exist as the junior partner of the Liberal Party. Once freed from the dominant Liberal agenda of constitutional reform, Irish Home Rule and the disestablishment of the Welsh Church, Labour would have the chance to outbid the Liberals on specific working-class issues.

In the longer term it is reasonable to question the viability of a party whose candidates and organization remained overwhelmingly middle-class, presenting itself as a party, or even *the* party, of the working class. With hindsight, the Liberals' failure to adopt more working-class men as parliamentary candidates emerges as a fundamental error. Many working men had been driven to Labour not in the quest for socialism but simply to secure representation of their own class interests. The intense industrial unrest of the years immediately preceding the First World War indicated some measure of working-class disenchantment with the Liberal government, a sign perhaps that belief in the identity of interest between the forces of labour and those of capital was losing its appeal. The loss of the institutional support of the trade unions, whatever the voting behaviour of individual trade unionists, was a further matter of concern. Chris Wrigley has pointed to the significance of the Trade Union Act of 1913, which partially reversed the Osborne Judgment of 1909 and allowed unions to hold ballots to authorize the setting up of political funds. By the beginning of 1914, trade unions with a membership of more than 1.2 million had voted in this sense. 'These votes,' writes Wrigley, 'ensured Labour's post-First World War electoral finances, and in themselves reflect an element of the explanation for the rise of the Labour party and the decline of the Liberal party in the early twentieth century.'[92] As this account moves to a consideration of the impact of the war years, its cautious judgement must be that Liberalism in 1914 was a varied, but generally robust, political force – but one beset by more than its fair share of problems.

The Impact of War

'Liberalism tore its heart out between 1914 and 1918 in a private agony about true and false Liberals, right and wrong Liberalism.'[93] At one level it is difficult to dispute Michael Bentley's verdict.

The party, which entered the First World War in August 1914 under the leadership of Herbert Asquith with more than eight continuous and largely distinguished years in government to its credit, left the conflict badly divided, about to be humiliated in the Coupon Election of December 1918, held just weeks after the armistice came into force, and destined never again to form a government in its own right. That election saw the independent party, the governing party of 1914, still headed by Asquith, reduced to a rump of fewer than 30 MPs. Few would fail to include the impact of war in any list of the factors that contributed to the party's demise. Indeed, the more evidence that has been accumulated to show that the party was in no imminent danger of collapse in 1914, the more significance must be attached to the war as the key explanation of what occurred subsequently. Even so, the precise effect of four years of unprecedentedly intense conflict, the first total war in British experience, remains a matter of considerable controversy. Geoffrey Searle has identified three broad explanations of what happened. Some historians have focused on the accidents of history whereby key individuals – Lloyd George, Asquith and their followers, although the precise division of responsibility has been a further matter of vigorous debate – contributed by their mistakes and misjudgements to their party's decline. Others attach the greatest importance to the processes of social change, begun or perhaps only accelerated by the war, which created a system of class-based politics in which Liberalism, having coped perfectly well before 1914, found itself outflanked by an advancing Labour Party. Finally, and most seductively, there are those who stress the inability of Liberalism as a political creed to cope with the demands of modern warfare.[94] 'It was their principles,' asserts Kenneth Morgan, 'which the very fact of total war with the unbridled collectivism and the "jingo" passions which it unleashed, appeared to undermine.'[95] In the memorable image of Trevor Wilson, the war was like a 'rampant omnibus' which, out of control, mounted the pavement and ran over an unsuspecting pedestrian. That pedestrian, the British Liberal Party, may have had its pre-war problems but it was perfectly capable of survival – until confronted by the unequal odds of the First World War.[96]

Each of these ideas might have some validity, but none on its own provides a complete explanation for the transformation which, whenever it began, had clearly overtaken British politics by the end of 1918. It is easy to suggest that the very coming of European war represented a contradiction of basic Liberal principles of internationalism and the primacy of reason over force. When Percy Illingworth, the party's chief whip, learnt of the outbreak of hostilities, he was heard to mutter, 'liberalism is dead'.[97] Yet the first point to note is not the damage that the coming of war did to the Liberal Party but the fact that both party and government escaped from this potentially traumatic event largely unscathed. Indeed, at this stage at least, the war seemed likely to inflict more damage on the Labour movement than on the Liberal Party. ILP Socialists, including Ramsay MacDonald himself, opposed the war from the outset, whereas the majority of the parliamentary party followed the lead of the patriotic and non-ideological working man in backing the government. Despite the long-term ascendancy of Sir Edward Grey on matters of foreign policy, there had always been more potential within the Asquith cabinet for a major split in this area than on any other issue. For much of the crisis of August 1914, moreover, Asquith could not rely on a majority of his cabinet colleagues to endorse a declaration of support for France. This is not to argue that a large and committed anti-war group of fixed resolve ever existed inside the cabinet. Rather, there were as many as 10 or 12 waverers, who felt varying degrees of disquiet at the prospect of intervention. But these men lacked genuine agreement among themselves and they produced no leader. Lloyd George, whose past history perhaps cast him as the likely leader of a radical protest, was among the first to be won over to the Asquith–Grey camp. As the crisis developed, moreover, it became clear that Britain would intervene. The only remaining question was the political complexion of the government that did so. Asquith handled the situation with consummate skill, making sure that the waverers understood that any substantial number of resignations would lead to a coalition government, a development which, as one of them argued, 'would assuredly be the grave of Liberalism'.[98] As a result, only the veteran Morley, by now a quaint survivor of Gladstonian days, and the working-class man, John Burns, withdrew from the cabinet, the pair creating scarcely a ripple in the government's equanimity.

This situation was matched inside the House of Commons, where the vast majority of the parliamentary Liberal Party had little difficulty in accepting Britain's declaration of war on 4 August.

The crucial factor for most Liberal MPs was the German violation of Belgian neutrality, which enabled the government to present British participation as a moral issue rather than a question of *realpolitik*. Before the Belgian issue arose, it was another matter. As Richard Holt wrote on 2 August, 'it is impossible to believe that a Liberal government can be guilty of the crime of dragging us into this conflict in which we are in no way interested'.[99] Yet a week later his mood had changed dramatically: 'I had thought we might and should have kept out of the war but when Germany decided on an unprovoked attack upon Belgium, whose neutrality Germany equally with ourselves had guaranteed, it seemed impossible for us to stand by.'[100] Many Liberal politicians, who had been ready as late as 3 August to join peace rallies, were reconciled to, if not enthusiastic about, the fact of war only a day later. By insisting, prior to the violation of Belgian neutrality, that Britain was not bound to any particular course of action, Asquith could carry the vast majority of the parliamentary party with him. The public justification of Britain's involvement might not have matched the actual motivation of the key figures inside Asquith's cabinet, but it all amounted to a remarkably successful example of the government's skills of policy presentation.

At the same time, a significant minority of Liberals did refuse to endorse the government's line. C. P. Trevelyan, who resigned from his post as Parliamentary Secretary to the Board of Education, soon found himself co-ordinating the activities of around two dozen Liberals who wanted to work with Labour opponents of the war. The numbers involved were less significant than the coming together of radicals from differing political traditions and the scope this created for a transference of political allegiance. Trevelyan invited Ramsay MacDonald to a dinner of Liberal dissidents 'for the purpose of considering joint action and the creation of a new Parliamentary Party which will take action immediately, more particularly after the war has spent itself a little and which may be a permanent combination. They ask me to lead it both in the House and the country.' As MacDonald later noted, 'clearly wartime conditions raised prospects of political realignment'.[101] Another dissident Liberal recorded the outcome of the dinner:

> MacDonald, E. D. Morel, Angell, Ponsonby, Trevelyan – we talked until late last night about the organisation that will be required in

future to advocate a safe foreign policy and the way in which this will probably effect [*sic*] parties in the future. It's early days to speak yet but it looks to me as if this war will probably result in the creation of a new party composed of men from both the Radical and Labour parties.[102]

Outright opposition to the war was difficult in the prevailing atmosphere of patriotic enthusiasm that greeted the outbreak of hostilities, but many doubters found it easier, now that war was a reality, to focus their concerns on the means by which it was conducted. They argued that Britain must fight on the basis of 'liberal' principles and avoid at all costs adopting the tactics of 'Prussianism', against which, after all, the war was being waged. This sort of thinking was behind the formation of the Union of Democratic Control (UDC) which held its first meeting in September. Here, radical Liberals encountered and exchanged ideas with like-minded men from other parties. The meeting was attended by a number of prominent Liberals including Morel, Ponsonby, Trevelyan, F. S. Cocks and C. Roden Buxton, but also by well-known figures from the ILP. The UDC developed gradually into an important conduit, easing the passage of many Liberals into Labour's ranks. Such movements did not reflect ideological conversion but rather the closeness of existing views compounded by a shared hatred of secret diplomacy and wartime jingoism, and a mounting suspicion that the Liberal leadership could no longer be trusted to uphold Liberal values. Their new party, deserting Liberals hoped, would prove to be more 'liberal' than the one they had left. It was the beginning of a process by which 'the Labour Party via the ILP was able to sap the intellectual strength of the Liberal Party'.[103] By the early 1920s, Trevelyan, Ponsonby and Morel were all Labour MPs under MacDonald's leadership. Trevelyan, who served as President of the Board of Education in the first two Labour governments, reflected, shortly before his appointment to a Labour cabinet, on the formative importance of the war years to the political journey travelled by men such as himself: 'Nothing could shake our feeling which grew during the war years that there is no one except you [MacDonald] who is big enough to give Europe the necessary lead.'[104]

The waging of the war undoubtedly contributed to the erosion of Liberal principles and values. As one Liberal MP warned, 'it would be a tragedy worse than war if, in order to win the War, England ceased to be the beacon of freedom and liberty which she has been in the past'.[105] Some Liberals clearly feared the slippery slope. 'Do you imagine,' warned Trevelyan, 'that, if you start with this [seizure of UDC pamphlets] you are going to be able to stop? The outcome before long must be that you will have to begin imprisoning men for their opinions.'[106] But compromise was inevitable. The Defence of the Realm Act, 'which wipes out Magna Carta, the Bill of Rights, etc, in a few lines',[107] curtailed traditional liberties; the restrictions placed on the freedom of the press and the internment of enemy aliens flew in the face of conventional Liberal presumptions; the National Registration Bill of July 1915 was widely interpreted as preparing the way for full-scale conscription; and McKenna's Budget of October 1915, which imposed heavy duties on a wide range of luxury goods, represented a renunciation of the sacred Liberal creed of free trade. The clear temptation is to interpret the later split between Asquith, Lloyd George and their respective followers as just the visible manifestation of a more fundamental divide based on a parting of the Liberal ways along ideological lines. But to suggest that Liberalism, as a laissez-faire philosophy, proved to be intellectually defenceless in the face of the necessary wartime encroachments of a collectivist state would be to impose an all too simple, if convenient, explanatory straitjacket on a complex set of events. In the first place it does scant justice to the way in which Liberalism had already abandoned much of its nineteenth-century outlook long before war broke out. It fails, in short, to allow for the impact of the New Liberalism on the party's outlook and ideas. Indeed, it has been suggested that, by 1914, the Liberal Party was more committed to the notion of state intervention than were the Conservatives.[108] Second, it is striking that most of these measures were enacted successfully by a Liberal government, or at least by Liberal ministers within a Liberal-dominated coalition, prior to the crisis of December 1916, and without apparently doing any irreparable damage to the coherence of the party at Westminster. Indeed, a group of Liberal MPs from across the party spectrum in the so-called Liberal War Committee were among the most ardent advocates of compulsory service. Some even went out of their way to insist that this was entirely compatible with their Liberalism. Furthermore, once the focus is shifted from the parliamentary arena to Liberalism as a national movement, it appears that such measures were accepted with little difficulty.[109] The Liberal Party, in fact, proved to be a more flexible and pragmatic body than has often been allowed, or than is indicated in the surviving documentation of articulate but not necessarily typical individuals. Third, the divisions of December 1916 did not, at a personal level, accurately reflect the attitudes struck before that date. Committed Asquithians, supported by the impeccably 'liberal' *Westminster Gazette*, proved as ready as Lloyd George's followers to swallow apparently illiberal measures. Ministers cannot be slotted neatly into opposing camps labelled 'laissez-faire' and 'control'. Rather, opinions varied depending on the particular issue at stake. McKenna, Runciman and Haldane backed the idea of government intervention to ensure the country's self-sufficiency in the production of aniline dye – whose importance extended beyond the colouring of cloth to the manufacture of high explosives and poison gas – and did so against the combined opposition of Asquith and Lloyd George.

Coalition and Conscription

For many Liberals, however, the issues of the formation of a coalition and the introduction of conscription were of a different order. The two were linked in the sense that it was widely recognized that the presence of Conservatives inside the government made the abandonment of the voluntary principle markedly more likely. Historians have long picked over every available piece of evidence without reaching a definitive conclusion about the pressures that persuaded Asquith to take the opposition parties into his administration in May 1915. As one has written, 'unless the papers not so far available to researchers happen to contain an unusually convincing letter in the hand of one of the three men responsible for the decision, this question seems well placed to defy solution indefinitely'.[110] For long the debate alternated between the contending theories of a dispute at the Admiralty between the First Lord and the First Sea Lord over the conduct of the Dardanelles operations and an impending crisis over the supply of munitions to the Western Front as the primary factor forcing Asquith into the embrace of his Conservative opponents. More recently, it has been suggested that Asquith, unwilling to face the uncertain prospect of a wartime General Election, was a

more proactive architect of the First Coalition than these explanations would allow, an analysis that fits more comfortably with the
continuing Liberal domination of the coalition cabinet and, in
particular, of the great offices of state. Though Conservative pressure did oblige the Prime Minister to drop Haldane from the government and remove Churchill from the Admiralty, the paucity
of Conservative representation in the reorganized government
remains striking, with the Tory leader, Bonar Law, securing no
more than the Colonial Office. In the present context, however,
the motivation behind Asquith's actions is less important than
their consequences, though uncertainty about that motivation did
contribute greatly to the feeling of unease that now pervaded the
parliamentary Liberal Party.

The end of what proved to be the last purely Liberal government in the country's history provoked intense opposition among
the rank and file. Asquith announced the formation of a coalition without warning or preparation, and 'told that all the "cream"
of our party...were in open revolt...wouldn't stand it at any price
and were passing hot resolutions against it', had to act decisively to
fend off a party revolt.[111] On this occasion at least, Richard Holt
expressed the feelings of a broad spectrum of Liberal opinion:

> Why this has happened is not clear to anyone. There has been
> a campaign in Lord Northcliffe's press, but that could not have
> produced the result, and a quarrel between Winston Churchill
> and Lord Fisher at the Admiralty. Liberal opinion is dissatis-
> fied and many Liberal members...are vexed and suspicious. The
> PM attended an impromptu meeting of Liberal members on
> Wednesday 19th [May] and alleged foreign affairs of an unreveal-
> able character as his reason in a speech impressive but not ulti-
> mately convincing.[112]

Those who had felt misgivings about the actions of their own
government had fewer qualms about giving voice to their concerns now that a 'mongrel coalition' was in power. But what did
the new government portend? 'Nothing will persuade me,' wrote
Charles Hobhouse, 'that this is not the end of the Liberal party as
we have known it.' Those Liberals who prostituted themselves by
sharing power with Conservatives would become 'responsible for
measures you disapprove, but cannot in the supposed "national"

interest reject'.[113] C. P. Trevelyan concurred: 'This is the end of
the Liberal Party. Now all Liberalism will be abandoned and we
shall live under conscription and martial law.'[114] As the bonds
linking the party leadership to its nominal followers became
strained, groups of dissidents began to organize themselves. Sir
Charles Nicholson, MP for Doncaster, was the head of a small
group known originally as the 'seven wise men'. 'We are meeting
regularly,' recorded Holt in June 1915, 'and discussing the situation with a view to giving the Government a Liberal pull whenever
possible.'[115] One of their first concerns was the growing campaign
for conscription.

Conscription was, wrote H. W. Massingham, an 'all-dominat-
ing anxiety', whose introduction would mean the end of national
unity, leaving the Liberal Party 'not merely suspended but broken
for ever'.[116] For many Liberals, even among those ready to make
compromises in the interests of military victory, conscription represented a step too far that would violate the most sacred principle
of individual liberty – a man's right to decide for himself whether
he would fight and quite possibly die for his country. Asquith himself was far from enthusiastic. In August he recorded the warnings
of his own chief whip:

> Gulland... tells me that he gets letters from Liberal chairmen etc.,
> all over the country denouncing Lloyd George as a lost soul, and
> some of them predicting that conscription would bring us to the
> verge, or over the verge of revolution. I have had several interviews
> with colleagues – Harcourt, Simon etc. – all strong in the same
> sense.[117]

By the end of the year this issue was threatening to cause a serious rupture inside the cabinet as well as the parliamentary party.
McKenna, Runciman and Simon all indicated that they would
have to consider their positions if the government went ahead.
Asquith responded by appealing to his colleagues not to deliver 'a
shattering blow to the Government and I believe to the National
Cause'.[118] Worse was to follow, however, when Edward Grey, the
Foreign Secretary, indicated that, should McKenna and Runciman
resign, he would feel obliged to follow them. Though Grey was
no longer the force he had been until the outbreak of war, his
departure might still have had fatal consequences for Asquith's

continued premiership. For perhaps the last time, the Prime Minister displayed the skills of man-management that had kept his talented but sometimes wilful cabinet together for the previous seven and a half years. While he worked on Grey, Maurice Hankey, Secretary to the War Committee, sought the possible basis of a compromise. In the event, only Simon, the Home Secretary, resigned, immovable on the basic proposition that it was wrong to compel a man to be a soldier against his will. In the Commons, 35 Liberals voted against the government in a division on the conscription of single men on 6 January 1916. But unease went much deeper than this figure suggests. Many more abstained, while others were cajoled into supporting the government in the knowledge that defeat would lead to its fall and a probable Conservative victory in the subsequent General Election. A few months later, 41 Liberals recorded their votes against the conscription of married men. 'With this wanton breach with historic Liberalism,' recorded *The Nation*, 'that great movement practically comes to an end, and a new alignment of parties must gradually take place, with new leaders to conduct it.'[119] The fact that Lloyd George appeared to have helped force Asquith's hand on this issue, and that personal relations between the two men were never quite restored afterwards to their former cordiality, made these words prophetic. 'None of the Radicals in the Cabinet is working with [Lloyd George]', recorded Lord Riddell as early as November 1915. 'He finds his supporters amongst the Conservatives.'[120]

The Fall of Asquith and the Rise of Lloyd George

Over the months that followed, Asquith failed to mould the coalition government into an effective instrument for waging war. In the allocation of ministerial portfolios he tried to strike a balance between those who still sought to protect Liberal values and those who called for more far-reaching intervention on the part of the state. It was not an easy position to maintain. 'During 1916,' writes Peter Clarke, 'the Liberal dilemma became sharper. Liberal methods could only be vindicated by military victory; yet victory seemed unattainable without abandoning Liberal methods. It sometimes seemed as though Asquith's Liberal credentials were only being confirmed by his apparent readiness to lose the war.'[121] Asquith himself satisfied neither side in the debate.

To the interventionists, his approach was too lackadaisical and his commitment to victory at whatever cost open to doubt. A group of about 40 Liberal MPs in the Liberal War Committee did not conceal their dissatisfaction with Asquith's leadership. They called for further measures of national mobilization and for action against shirkers and unpatriotic dissidents. To the guardians of true Liberalism, Asquith's record was already tarnished by what he had done, or allowed to be done, since the outbreak of war. Almost certainly his own powers were beginning to wane. As early as November 1915 one of his backbenchers described him as 'a tired, almost broken man': 'I have my doubts whether he is really strong enough in nerve and will power to go through.'[122] The balance between the virtues and faults of Asquith's peacetime leadership did not change significantly. But in a wartime context the latter became increasingly apparent. Ministers commented on his indecisive and excessively indulgent chairmanship of the cabinet. Stories abounded of his ability to find the time to play bridge while affairs of state were left in abeyance. Asquith was badly shaken when his youthful confidante, Venetia Stanley, announced her engagement to one of his own ministers, Edwin Montagu, in May 1915. The death in action of his eldest son, Raymond, in September 1916 left him deeply depressed. That autumn he became increasingly withdrawn and difficult to approach, absenting himself from several meetings of the cabinet. 'It is difficult to avoid the conclusion,' judges Cameron Hazlehurst, 'that the strain of the war premiership, augmented by ill health and private grief, had rendered him unfit to continue at the head of the nation's affairs.'[123]

Above all, however, Asquith's fate was tied to the British war effort and dissatisfaction with his leadership was primarily a function of the country's inability to secure the often-promised victory. The year 1916 saw British pride badly shaken at Jutland and British manpower drained on the Somme, and still there was no prospect in sight of an end to the war. Against the background of the coalition, new political alignments began to take shape around the issues of the day, particularly the question of grand strategy. These alignments were not constant and there was much regrouping in the face of a changing political agenda. Nothing predetermined the eventual split between Asquith and Lloyd George, and indeed the two men came together again over the issue of a possible Irish settlement in the spring of 1916. Gradually, however, the debate at the heart of the administration began to crystallize around Asquith's failure to streamline the machinery of government to provide an effective decision-making body that could respond quickly to the developing war situation. In particular, after he succeeded Lord Kitchener as War Minister in July, Lloyd George emerged as the leader of those determined to secure fundamental reforms. By this time he was of the view that the Liberal Party had, 'so far as the war was concerned, become the Conservative Party. Any criticism of the War Office or the Admiralty...was regarded by the Liberals in Parliament as an indirect attack on the Prime Minister and they had become a positive hindrance to any reform.'[124] Furthermore, with Bonar Law's position as leader of the Unionist Party by no means secure, the two men came to see the possibilities of a mutually advantageous partnership. Strikingly, Margot Asquith reacted to Lloyd George's appointment to the War Office with deep foreboding for her husband's future: 'We are out,' she insisted, 'it can only be a question of time now when we shall have to leave Downing Street.'[125]

The outcome of the final crisis of December 1916 was determined as much by chance and miscalculation as by intrigue and ambition. The issue at stake was the creation of a small war cabinet and, more particularly, the membership of it. Lloyd George later declared that he 'neither sought nor desired the Premiership'.[126] The first proposition is probably wholly true; the second partially so. What Lloyd George was determined to secure was executive control over the war effort. If this could be done while Asquith remained as Prime Minister, so be it. In the event, however, Asquith was persuaded that such an arrangement would have involved an unacceptable affront to his own standing and self-respect. In this situation, the first wartime coalition came to an end. More important, Asquith and Lloyd George, for more than eight years the indispensable axis of the British government, went their separate ways. As a former Liberal chief whip put it, 'theirs has been the most formidable political combination that this country has ever known. Look what has been achieved within the last ten years.'[127] The new government still had a Liberal at its head but, as Charles Hobhouse noted, 'if [Asquith] yields to George, taking Grey with him, the last remnant of liberalism and moderation vanishes from the Government'.[128] As Lloyd George formed a new coalition, in its heavy dependence on Conservative support different in kind from that of his predecessor, the question now was whether the Liberal Party itself had been dealt a mortal blow.

2 The Liberal Civil War, 1916–35

Beyond the Point of No Return?

So much has been written of the Lloyd George–Asquith split of December 1916, identifying it as a seminal moment in the Liberal Party's fortunes, that it is tempting to assume that the formation of the second wartime coalition marked a point of fundamental and irreversible division, after which little could be done to halt the processes of political decline. Arguably, however, it was less the fact of the split than its duration that did the party the most damage. What is beyond dispute is that between 1916 and 1923 – and, even in 1923, reunion and reconciliation were at best only partially secured – the Liberal Party moved from being the leading party of government into the position of the third force in British politics. In the same seven-year period, the Labour Party moved from the periphery of the political spectrum, first to the status of official opposition and then to the verge of forming its first, albeit minority, government. As the third party, the Liberals would have to operate within an electoral system that fails to convert a minority party's share of the popular vote into a commensurate share of seats in the House of Commons. This fact in turn has the further long-term effect of discouraging the electorate from backing such a party, out of a desire to use their votes in support of a realistic contender for government. Once a party is consigned to the 'third party trap', therefore, it becomes increasingly difficult to escape from it, because of the self-perpetuating nature of its predicament. But was the Liberal Party's descent into this status inevitable? There are, of course, strong arguments that it was destroyed by long-term structural changes in British society and politics. But a study of the decade and a half following the events of December 1916, during which period the Liberals remained a significant political force, lends weight to the view that

the party was as much the victim of avoidable events as of ineluc-
table forces.

For some Liberals the war had certainly created a crisis of ideals
and values, with which they struggled to cope. For such men, the
Lloyd George–Asquith split afforded the opportunity to reassert
true Liberalism, rescuing it from the contaminating constraints
of association with an alien political philosophy. Richard Holt
epitomized this point of view: 'L. G. has behaved scandalously,' he
declared, 'and the section of the Liberals he takes with him are certainly not men conspicuous for their character.'[1] But to recognize
such individuals is not the same as suggesting that the 1916 split
symbolized a fundamental ideological division in Liberal ranks
between those capable of adapting to the demands of total war
and those doomed to perish as they sought to uphold an outdated
political philosophy that had no place in the increasingly collectivist twentieth century. A. J. P. Taylor once speculated that the split
reflected 'a division long a-growing' along class lines. But detailed
analysis has failed to reveal any clear differentiation along generational, occupational, ideological or class lines. Nor were pre-war
divisions accurately reflected in the new alignments.[2] In broad
terms, it is possible to suggest that the right wing of the party now
looked to Lloyd George while the left turned to Asquith, but the
critical consideration was an assessment of the abilities of the two
Liberal leaders to manage and win the war. Such a judgement cut
across all other patterns of division, placing Liberals of every hue
in each camp. But what really confused the picture was the stance
of the two leading protagonists. According to their pre-war pedigrees, it was by any analysis Asquith, the old Liberal Imperialist,
who should have headed the right and been a more natural ally
of the Conservatives, leaving the radical Lloyd George to champion the voice of pure Liberalism. The false position in which both
men, especially Asquith, now found themselves did much to determine relations between the two factions for the remainder of the
war and beyond.

Though he no longer headed the government, Asquith retained
most of the apparatus of power in the Liberal Party within his own
hands. Party headquarters, funds and officials remained under
his control, and he enjoyed the support of the National Liberal
Federation. The party's chief whip, John Gulland, also committed himself to Asquith. Most of the Liberals who agreed to join

the Lloyd George government were figures of the second rank. The appointment of Churchill was for the time being blocked by Conservative opposition. Even the number of rank-and-file MPs ready to back the new Prime Minister appears to have been exaggerated by the over-enthusiastic Dr Addison, who was now promoted to the post of Minister of Munitions. Many of those whom Lloyd George was encouraged to regard as fully committed supporters actually voted against him in key parliamentary divisions in the second half of the war. In practice, nothing that could be described as a Coalition Liberal Party existed before the autumn of 1918. Lloyd George relied heavily on Conservative support to supplement a shifting band of Liberal backers, the consistent core of which comprised no more than 50 MPs. But if Asquith held most of Liberalism's trump cards, his was not an easy hand to play. Barry McGill has defined his predicament as 'how to use his political prestige and his power as a party leader to support the war effort, without identifying himself and his followers with the government'.[3] This was never going to be an easy task, but it would be difficult to suggest that Asquith carried it out successfully. In particular, he proved an immense disappointment to those Liberals who, *faute de mieux*, had rallied to his standard in December 1916. Many of these had been uncertain from the outset about British participation in the war, and critical of many of the actions of the wartime government of which he had been the head. One practical result of Asquith's stance was that a precarious party unity was maintained. Liberal whips continued to canvass the whole of the parliamentary party. Each side recoiled from any step that would formalize existing cracks into a permanent division. On several occasions between the spring of 1917 and the end of the war, Lloyd George put out feelers to see whether Asquith could be persuaded to rejoin the government. But the latter remained aloof, revealing that, while the breach in the Liberal ranks had yet to be institutionalized, much ill-feeling would have to be overcome before unity could be restored. 'Under no conditions,' Asquith insisted in May 1917, 'wd. I serve in a Govt. of wh. LlG was the head. I had learned by long and close association to mistrust him profoundly. I knew him to be incapable of loyalty or lasting gratitude.'[4] Asquith, in fact, nurtured a sense of grievance about the way he had been treated in December 1916, which he never lost and which was shared by many of his closest associates.

Liberal politics would continue to be scarred by such bitterness until his death and beyond.

But the policy of offering general support to the government from outside its ranks also had the practical effect of condemning the party's Asquithian wing to political impotence at a time when it urgently needed revitalization. 'My old party, the Liberals, are not fertile at present,' noted the former Lord Chancellor, Lord Haldane, in November 1917. 'The feeling is that their work is over for the present.'[5] In particular, Asquith proved incapable of reclaiming for Liberalism the leadership of the radical left in British politics, leaving this position to be appropriated by Labour. Not surprisingly, after 1916 'Labour became a more serious positive political force, the Liberals a less serious opposition'.[6] Equally predictably, the tendency for radical Liberals to transfer to the Labour Party, which had begun earlier in the war, continued apace. R. L. Outhwaite, R. C. Lambert, H. B. Lees-Smith and Joseph King were among Asquithian MPs who, by the end of the war or soon afterwards, had cut themselves adrift and joined the Labour ranks. This steady draining away of the radical content of the Liberal Party – one estimate suggests that between 1917 and 1919 as many as 2,000 Liberal activists joined the ILP alone – would have important consequences for the character of the post-war party and its ability to compete in the new political environment that emerged after 1918.

In so far as a coherent Liberal opposition to the Lloyd George government emerged between December 1916 and the November 1918 armistice, it did so despite rather than because of Asquith. Listing those who were prepared to negotiate with the German government, Lloyd George's whip, Frederick Guest, included in the summer of 1918 'the Asquithians (except Mr Asquith)'.[7] Assiduous attendance in Parliament and purposeful leadership of his followers would, according to Holt, have enabled Asquith to recapture the initiative and put a rapid end to 'the L. G. villainy'.[8] But Asquith would not play the part that Asquithians had hoped he would. None the less, a group of Liberals gradually developed the habit of opposing the government. In March 1917, 46 Liberals voted against the Cotton Duties Bill, while 59 supported it. An analysis of 11 key wartime divisions shows that 24 Liberal MPs went into the opposition lobbies on at least seven occasions.[9] By the end of the year, another unlikely alignment came into being as radical Liberals responded enthusiastically to the suggestion of Lord

Lansdowne, the former Unionist Foreign Secretary, that the war should be brought to a compromise conclusion before civilization itself was destroyed in the futile attempt to achieve outright victory. What was different about the celebrated Maurice Debate of 9 May 1918, which resulted from the publication of a letter from the recently removed Director of Military Operations charging that Lloyd George had misled Parliament about the strength of British forces on the Western Front, was that this was the only occasion when Asquith and the Asquithian whips gave their backing to a division against the government. With Conservative support, Lloyd George survived easily, but it was striking that as many as 98 Liberals backed Asquith and only 72 supported Lloyd George. Yet it is doubtful whether Asquith derived much benefit from his change of approach. Having demoralized his followers for so long, he now forfeited his claim to patriotic self-restraint. At the same time, he mishandled the parliamentary occasion by choosing to focus on the technical question of setting up a select committee rather than calling Lloyd George to account. *The Times*, drawing attention to the 'debut of an organized Opposition', believed that the first step had been taken 'towards what may become a permanent cleavage'. Moves were made to turn the Coalition Liberals into a separate party organization, and negotiations began for an electoral pact with the Conservatives.

The Coupon Election

That election was planned initially as a wartime contest but, because of the sudden collapse of German resistance from the late summer onwards, took place just a month after the armistice. Lloyd George had no fixed view of the political basis upon which the election should be fought. He expected Labour to remain within the coalition and had not excluded the possibility of a Liberal reunion. Gradually, however, the logic of his close partnership with the Conservatives and their numerical dominance within his government became compelling. Lord Derby, Britain's ambassador in Paris, recorded a revealing conversation with the Prime Minister in early November:

> Lloyd George then said that the Liberal Party had been trying to get him very hard to go back to them. They told him that they quite

understood if he went back he would be the Prime Minister and
they would get rid of Asquith, but he told them 'No', that that would
not be playing the game by our [Conservative] Party.[10]

Even so, Lloyd George sought almost to the end to bring Asquith
back into the fold. In early October, Lord Murray of Elibank, acting as intermediary between the two men, was authorized to offer
Asquith a deal that included his appointment to the Woolsack in
a reconstructed government. Asquith's refusal seemed to Murray
to be of more than passing importance: 'Unless I am very much
mistaken, in these two conversations I have been present at the
obsequies of the Liberal Party as I know it.'[11]

As many contemporaries recognized, the 1918 General Election
was of far greater significance than the split of two years before in
determining the Liberal Party's fortunes. According to Asquith,
writing in 1926, 'the disintegration of the Liberal Party began
with the Coupon Election...It then received a blow from which it
has never since recovered.'[12] Herbert Gladstone concurred: 'The
result of 1918 broke the party, not only in the ... Commons but in
the country. Local associations perished or maintained a nominal existence.'[13] As late as 1928, Lord Crewe was still describing
ongoing party squabbles as 'perhaps the inevitable result of the
infamous 1918 Election'.[14] But such judgements did not reflect a
clear ideological or even policy division between the two Liberal
factions contesting the election. The campaigns of coalition and
independent Liberals revealed no great differences. In his first
major campaign speech, Asquith concentrated his attack on the
Conservative element in the government, while defining himself
as a Liberal 'without prefix and suffix, without label and hallmark
of any sort and description'. Lloyd George assured a delegation
of Manchester Liberals that he remained a Liberal, that he would
never call on anyone to sacrifice Liberal principles and that, while
continuing the coalition was the condition for successful reconstruction, his government would put forward 'a great Liberal
programme'.[15] Indeed, most Liberals could applaud the recogniz-
ably Liberal content of the coalition manifesto. While limited measures of protection were proposed to safeguard key industries from
foreign dumping, the essentials of free trade were maintained.
In addition, Lloyd George promised Irish Home Rule (with safe-
guards for Ulster) and church disestablishment for Wales.

The problem lay not in policy but in Lloyd George's ready acceptance of the bargain struck by Guest with the Conservatives, that only 150 Liberal candidates would receive the letter of endorsement, or 'coupon', signed by Bonar Law and himself. In the circumstances of 1918, amid the euphoria surrounding the recent military victory, this imprimatur represented a virtual passport to Westminster for its fortunate recipients. Until the coupon was issued to his Conservative opponent, recalled Percy Harris, the sitting MP for Harborough, 'all had been going well, but now my friends melted away like snow in the night'.[16] But the paucity of favoured Liberals obliged Lloyd George to endorse large numbers of Conservatives against representatives of his own party. By this act he created lines of division that were altogether more rigid than any drawn up in 1916, while putting himself permanently beyond the political pale as far as most Asquithians were concerned. In Yorkshire, for example, where the party's parliamentary representation had been largely Asquithian, it was Lloyd George's supporters who were now elected. Yet rank-and-file Liberals retained their earlier loyalties, thereby undermining the party's unity within the local constituencies.[17]

Finding themselves in opposition to 'couponed' candidates, Asquithian Liberals had little with which to tempt the voter. Asquith's own election address reiterated the classic doctrines of Gladstonian individualism, but seemed to have abandoned the social priorities of the New Liberalism with which his pre-war government had been so closely associated. It was all very disappointing for the dwindling band of Liberal radicals, keen to take up again the progressive themes that the war had inevitably sidelined. Campaigning in Manchester, E. D. Simon began by welcoming the challenge of producing a party programme to 'put against the excellent programme prepared by [Sidney] Webb for Labour'. He had made a clear decision that 'the Liberal Party is the right place for me notwithstanding the attractiveness of the Labour programme'. By polling day, however, he was bemoaning 'the utter lack on the part of the Liberal Party, and the [Manchester] candidates in particular, of any knowledge of or interest in industrial problems and the great question of equality between the two nations of England'.[18] Matters became no easier for uncouponed Liberals as the campaign progressed and government spokesmen responded to the increasingly shrill demands in the popular press for the draconian treatment of the defeated German enemy. Simon was horrified by the way Lloyd George, 'following the irresponsible levity and the lust for blood of the yellow press', had 'reduced the election to the lowest level of demagoguery'.[19]

Overall, it is hard to resist the conclusion that the Liberal Party of 1918 was no longer, as it had been at the outbreak of war, the major party of the British working class. Its own problems and divisions were compounded by the way the war had helped to develop a unified class-consciousness, where earlier distinctions between skilled and unskilled workers were less sharp, and which translated into a belief that the Labour Party represented the natural vehicle for working-class aspirations. As only 258 Asquithian candidates, compared with 358 Labour ones, stood for more than 700 seats, many erstwhile Liberal voters looking to oppose the government had to choose between voting Labour and abstention.[20] With the pre-war progressive alliance consigned to history, existing patterns of party allegiance may well have been broken. But any analysis of electoral behaviour in 1918 must encompass the impact of the Representation of the People Act, or Fourth Reform Act, passed earlier in the year, as a result of which the electorate was almost three times as large (21.4 million) as it had been at the previous contest in December 1910 (7.7 million). Allowing for deaths in the intervening period and for those too young to vote in 1910, only about a quarter of the electorate of 1918 had previously entered a polling booth. Much interest and considerable controversy has attached to the way in which these newly enfranchised voters exercised their political voice.

The Franchise Factor

An important article published in the mid-1970s seemed for a time to have discovered the elusive explanatory factor in the replacement of the Liberals by Labour as the main force of the progressive left.[21] Historians had become increasingly aware that the Second and Third Reform Acts of 1867 and 1884 had fallen some way short of creating universal manhood suffrage. The franchise was significantly limited by difficult residence qualifications, which meant that only about 60 per cent of adult males were on the electoral register at any one time. Though only about 12 per cent were formally excluded, the remainder changed residence too regularly or merely failed to register. Thus, it was now argued, a restricted pre-war franchise that left about half the working class without the vote had inevitably limited Labour's ability to tap into its natural constituency of support. When full male suffrage was achieved in 1918, the effect was entirely predictable. A working-class electorate turned to Labour, as it would probably have done before 1914 had the opportunity been open to it. Thus a genuinely democratic pre-war franchise would have enabled Labour to challenge the Conservative–Liberal duopoly far more effectively than it did and, while 'we cannot say how many votes the introduction of universal franchise was worth to Labour...we can say that it was a critical element in the emergence of the party as a major political force'.[22] Moreover, the post-war electorate, swamped by less sophisticated voters from the lower social classes, was one to which the Liberals, with their demanding political ideas, found it increasingly difficult to appeal. In this analysis, the war's significance in determining the changing fortunes of the parties of the left was clearly diminished. What happened after 1918 would probably have happened before 1914 had the advent of full democracy not been delayed.

This seductive theory has been attacked at many levels and is now largely discredited. In the first place, it tends to overlook the fact that the greatest single addition to the electorate in 1918 came from the newly enfranchised female vote rather than additions to the ranks of the male franchise. Then, as Duncan Tanner has shown, not all the voteless men of the pre-1918 era were working-class, and therefore natural, but frustrated, Labour supporters. The existing bias of the constitution favoured householders over lodgers, irrespective of class or income. Many middle-class men had been prevented from voting either because their work made them too mobile or because of the complexities of the voting qualifications relating to lodgers in the pre-1918 period. Tanner concludes that the difference between the pre-war electorate and its much larger post-war equivalent was not substantial in class terms and insufficient to explain a significant change in the electoral performance of the Liberal and Labour parties, a line of argument that tends to reinstate the war's importance in transforming voting behaviour.[23] Three-quarters of the newly enfranchised male voters were not permitted to vote in municipal elections, yet the Labour Party flourished in such contests after 1918. By contrast, in areas such as the East End of London, which had a particularly low parliamentary franchise before the war, the post-war Liberal performance remained relatively strong. Furthermore, advocates of the 'franchise factor' have assumed too readily that what did happen after 1918 would necessarily have happened before 1914, had a more democratic electorate existed at that time. By under-estimating the size of the pre-war working-class vote, they tend to ignore the success of Edwardian Liberalism in presenting itself as the natural and legitimate party of the British working class. The real question to be asked is why the Liberals were unable to main-tain that image in the post-war era.

Recent research suggests that the bias of the pre-war franchise was more apparent in terms of age than of class. Thus it may be that the Liberal Party's mounting problems in the decade after 1918 had less to do with a transfer of allegiance to Labour on the part of existing working-class voters than with the Liberals' fail-ure to attract a sufficient proportion of successive cohorts of new working-class voters as they qualified, by age, to vote. The gener-ation that came of age in the second and third decades of the century underwent 'increasingly similar educational experiences, increasingly similar leisure pursuits, and increasingly similar work-ing conditions', which inclined them towards a 'more inclusive and less hierarchical identification of their class and its particular needs' – in other words, a growing propensity to vote Labour.[24] As a result, existing Liberal voters died off and were not, despite the usual tendency of children to copy their parents' voting pat-terns, replaced in sufficient numbers from the next generation. Such an interpretation is consistent with the Labour Party's steady progress, largely at the Liberals' expense, throughout the 1920s, whereas the 'franchise factor' explanation in its crudest form would be more compatible with a 'big bang' of Labour advance as soon as the franchise was widened in 1918. As it was, Labour improved its share of the poll at *every* election between December 1910 and May 1929, a fact easily lost sight of because the vagaries of the electoral system produced a Labour government in January 1924 but consigned the party to opposition again the following October.

One thing the Representation of the People Act (1918) did not do was to change the country's basic voting system. A Liberal tradition in support of Proportional Representation as a natural component of a fully democratic franchise could be dated back to J. S. Mill, and the cause attracted the support of a number of radical Liberal MPs of the Edwardian era. But the party as a whole remained unenthusiastic on the issue, not least because it benefited from the existing 'first-past-the-post' system in its electoral strongholds of Scotland, Wales and the North of England. None the less, in 1912 Asquith had toyed with the idea of a PR experiment based on 150 constituencies across the country. Significantly, the Speaker's Conference of 1918 proposed the introduction of the 'single transferable vote' system of PR in boroughs with three or more MPs, a change that might have improved the Liberal Party's subsequent fortunes dramatically. But agreement could not be reached by the two Houses of Parliament, the cabinet was hesitant, and the reform was never introduced. In the crucial Commons votes on the issue, Liberals divided fairly evenly, but the majority of Lloyd George's supporters were hostile to the suggested change.

Two Liberal Parties

Whatever the forces at work, nothing could conceal the enormity, at least in statistical terms, of the catastrophe inflicted on British Liberalism by the 1918 General Election; 133 Liberal Coalitionists were returned, though these were easily outnumbered by 335 Conservatives. But only 28 Asquithians – and the term has to be used loosely, as these were men who were opposed to or not supported by Lloyd George rather than followers of the party leader – took their seats in the new Parliament. At the same time, Labour's representation increased to 63, with a further 10 MPs elected as Labour supporters of the government. Though the results were delayed to count the service votes, many Liberals sensed their fate before it was announced. 'It seems pretty clear that the poll yesterday was disastrous,' recorded Richard Holt. 'I saw some politicians and found the same impression everywhere – complete defeat of the Liberal party.'[25] E. D. Simon 'drove round the Committee Rooms and Polling Stations of Manchester' and had 'no doubt that we are badly beaten'.[26] All the Liberal ex-ministers who had gone into qualified opposition in December 1916 now went down to defeat. Asquith himself was ousted in East Fife, which he had represented for 32 years. In Frome, Somerset, the Liberal candidate and, apart from a short break, its sitting member since 1892, now lost his deposit. According to *The Times*, only three non-coalition Liberals with any front-bench experience survived the slaughter: George Lambert, F. D. Acland and William Wedgwood Benn. When a journalist asked John Simon, defeated at Walthamstow, to comment on this rout, he responded bravely: 'We have been snowed under, but snow melts.' Thirty years later, he added a telling postscript. 'But while snow melts, it may in the meantime crush the life out of that which it has buried.'[27]

That said, the party's plight, at this stage at least, can easily be overdrawn. The salient feature of the Coupon Election was the overwhelming personal triumph of Lloyd George. 'There has never been an election like this one in its one-man nature,' wrote Edwin Montagu in a comment that combined flattery of his political master with objective observation. 'Somebody said to me the other day that the only speeches in the papers were your speeches, that the only thing the country listened to was what you said.'[28] So great indeed was the personal endorsement registered by the electorate that it seems reasonable to suppose that Lloyd George would have been victorious in 1918 whatever the political organization he had headed, including a united Liberal Party. Even in defeat, such a party would have had much greater prospects of recovery, while Lloyd George would have been well placed to inherit its formal leadership whenever Asquith chose to stand down.

The reality in 1918, however, was that the Liberal Party was divided, that it would stay divided, and that its divisions would become deeper during the remaining years of the coalition government. Between the elections of 1910 and 1918, independent Liberalism had gone from governing to third-party status without alighting at an intermediate position. Now, with Asquith, whatever his failings, out of Parliament, the party scarcely cut an impressive figure. From an admittedly limited pool of parliamentary talent, the somewhat dull figure of Sir Donald Maclean was chosen as sessional chairman pending Asquith's assumed return to the Commons. Meanwhile, the party seemed shrouded in gloom, completely overpowered by the magnitude of the disaster that had befallen it. Preoccupation with the divisions in its own ranks impeded any remaining hope of building on pre-1914 foundations to develop policies to respond to the mass working-class electorate.

Ramsay Muir later recalled the condition of the party in the immediate post-war period:

> What was left of the Liberal party was a merely negative and queru-
> lous faction, mumbling the shibboleths of the xix cent. and not
> even capable of understanding the change of orientation implicit
> in the pre-war legislation and demanded by the postwar situation.
> Liberalism stood for nothing but complaints of LG, and therefore
> it sank to futility...It had to be given a 'constructive programme',
> not as a bait to catch the electorate, but as a means of keeping its
> soul alive.[29]

Defeat at East Fife gave Asquith, now in his sixty-seventh year,
the opportunity to retire gracefully from the scene. Instead, he
clung on for eight more years to the reins of leadership, motivated
as much as anything by a determination to deny Lloyd George
any chance of the succession. He appears to have believed that
a revival was just around the corner and that he was destined to
lead the party back to the promised land of Liberal government.
These years formed a sad postscript to a distinguished career and,
as even his most sympathetic biographer concedes, did nothing
to enhance his historical reputation.[30] Indeed, it is impossible to
escape the conclusion that the post-war Asquith was but a shadow
of his former self, using, as Edward Grey put it, 'the machine of a
great political brain to rearrange old ideas'.[31] Asquith did return
to Parliament following a by-election in Paisley in 1920, but the
position scarcely improved afterwards. He had little to offer in
terms of energetic new ideas and seemed curiously incapable of
taking an effective stand against the government, despite – or perhaps because of – his intense hatred of its leader. The Asquithian
court resembled 'an extra-parliamentary conclave of the elder
venerated, meeting in spacious drawing-rooms to await the second
coming'.[32]

Asquith's uninspiring leadership and his inability to exercise
any great impact on national politics had a debilitating effect on
his party. 'The leadership is an immense drawback in the eyes
of many people,' complained Henry Gladstone, 'because it leads
them to the conclusion that there is no alternative Govt. to LG's.'[33]
Yet the establishment of an active leadership was a fundamental
prerequisite for the party's rehabilitation: 'The party is not in a

position to run itself.'[34] Such thinking gave rise to a half-hearted attempt to bring Edward Grey, despite his failing eyesight, back into the centre of Liberal politics, either to lend some backbone to Asquith or ultimately to replace him. If the latter option could be arranged, thought the Liberally minded Conservative, Lord Robert Cecil, 'the Liberal Party has a great future before it'.[35] Some believed that a political realignment, including the re-creation of something like the pre-war progressive alliance, offered the best chance of salvation. 'A Grey Cecil Asquith Government is the best hope,' argued Herbert Gladstone. 'They would get much support from Thomas, Clynes and the moderate Labour men.'[36] In what was for many an act of self-delusion, Liberals continued to believe that the two parties of the left represented complementary wings of the same movement. Yet most of those for whom this was true had already made the transition to Labour or were contemplating doing so. Radical Liberals could make this transition without undergoing any dramatic conversion. They moved to Labour not because they were changing their own views but because Labour now had a stronger claim to traditional Liberal values and aspirations than did the Liberal Party itself. E. D. Simon pondered the possibilities of a parliamentary career:

> the question of Liberal and Labour parties seems likely to become acute. A modified radical party would suit me best, or a new combination of radical Labour if only that could be brought about... But about four fifths of the people whose political views I admire are in the Labour Party! Of course if I do go for Parliament it would be rather nice to stand for Withington; and if I made up my mind and worked for it I could probably be Liberal (or for that matter Labour!) candidate next time.

But few Asquithian stalwarts would have accepted Simon's contention that 'economic equality (at least of opportunity) is probably the acid test as to whether the Liberal party still represents a Liberal spirit'.[37]

What is most striking about the post-war Liberal Party is the picture of a backward-looking movement that had cut itself adrift from the New Liberalism of earlier years. The party failed to develop relevant social and economic policies to confront the problems of industrial Britain. Outdated nineteenth-century slogans were unlikely to entrench the party in a solid base of working-class support, yet this is precisely what most leading Liberals proceeded to offer. 'The party leaders,' recalled Simon, 'still lived in the old idea of laissez-faire; their only industrial policy was free trade.'[38] The unrelated John Simon offered confirmation. His major preoccupations remained free trade and 'economy', a crusade to reduce wasteful government expenditure. Traditional laissez-faire would, he believed, open the way for social progress, industrial prosperity, security of employment and a high standard of living. In similar mode, Maclean had 'nothing heroic to offer. I believe we will only get things adjusted naturally by...simple commonsense and homely wisdom...the only way to get back to national health is by way of economy.'[39] Henry Gladstone sought refuge in the familiar platitudes of his father's generation: 'Peace, Retrenchment and Reform, the fine old watchwords are again the necessity of the moment.'[40] 'All too plainly,' concludes Michael Bentley, 'liberalism was out of date.'[41] The traditional issues that had dominated Liberalism's nineteenth-century agenda – political and religious emancipation, disestablishment, the Lords veto, licensing reform, home rule – had now either been resolved or else were incapable of exciting the enthusiasm of earlier years. In their place, the party failed to develop a new agenda of social and economic reform, despite the promising start made in the two decades before the First World War.

So, while many Liberals in the early 1920s still looked wistfully to a partnership with Labour, these same men often also voiced an unqualified opposition to Labour's commitment to state regulation and public expenditure. 'The weak point in the situation apart from Libs and Labour opposing each other,' suggested Henry Gladstone, 'is the extravagant policy of Labour. They don't seem to mind how much money is spent on Home Depts.' If only Labour would postpone the nationalization of minerals, including mining royalties, he would 'not be so much afraid'.[42] Yet even a more imaginative Liberal approach than this would have been unlikely to prompt a favourable Labour response. While welcoming individual defections, Labour now opposed realignment with the Liberals on strategic rather than specific policy grounds. Its leaders, particularly Ramsay MacDonald, saw that it was in Labour's long-term interest to maintain the lead it had established over the independent Liberals in 1918 and to drive them into a permanent third-party position, thus leaving Labour as the only viable alternative to Conservative government. 'By the 1920s,' concludes Peter Clarke, 'the ideological convergence of Liberals and social democrats was matched by a tactical divergence...much to the frustration of those of a progressive outlook.'[43]

Whatever may be said of the Liberal Party, Liberalism was not wholly moribund in this period. During the winter of 1918–19, a group of Manchester businessmen began meeting on a regular basis at the home of E. D. Simon, a local manufacturer and expert on housing, to discuss industrial questions. Initially, the reaction of the party leadership was discouraging, but in June 1920 Simon recorded: 'we sent a resolution to the Leamington meeting of the NLF demanding an industrial policy. To our surprise, instead of hostility, we were received with open arms, given seats on the platform, and our resolution accepted by the official gang.'[44]

At a meeting at Simon's Herefordshire farm in the spring of 1921, attended by Ramsay Muir, Professor of History at the University of Manchester, and Edward Scott, son of the proprietor of the *Manchester Guardian*, the notion of the Liberal Summer School was devised. The idea was to provide a forum where a range of social and economic issues could be discussed, from a Liberal point of view but separate from any formal party structure. The Summer School, which met for the first time in Grasmere in September 1921, would bring together the Manchester group and a number of Cambridge intellectuals including J. M. Keynes, Walter Layton and Hubert Henderson. 'I am really hopeful', recorded Simon, 'that it will be the beginning of a genuine awakening of thought and study in Liberal circles.'[45] Over the decade, the movement sought to build on the foundations of the New Liberalism of the pre-war era in the direction of greater state intervention without going down the path of doctrinaire socialism. It was hoped that it would have the sort of impact upon the Liberal Party that the Fabian Society had exercised over the Labour movement.[46]

The influence of the Summer Schools was most marked in the second half of the decade, once Lloyd George had assumed the party leadership. For the time being, however, the immediate problem was the reunion of the party's severed wings. In the early days of the post-war coalition, the lines of Liberal divisions were far from clear. There was some movement between the two groups, generally in the direction of the Independent Liberals, or 'Wee

Frees' as they came to be called, while, in the House of Lords, Liberals continued to behave very much as a single party under the leadership of Lord Crewe. The selection of George Lambert, who had not received the coupon, as parliamentary chairman of the coalition Liberal group, suggested a conciliatory attitude towards the Asquithians. A joint committee to promote unity met on several occasions early in 1919 before negotiations broke down in March. Most Liberals could find something to applaud in the government's programme. At least until the economies effected by the 'Geddes Axe' from August 1921, Liberal influence was fully apparent in the coalition's policies of social reform and reconstruction. Despite the passage of the Safeguarding of Industries Act in 1920, Britain remained in essence a free-trade country. Individual measures could still prompt the reassertion of an essential Liberal unity. Seventeen Coalition Liberals supported a motion moved by the Asquithian, Wedgwood Benn, to delete moves towards Imperial Preference from Austen Chamberlain's budget of April 1919, while many more abstained. Only the government's repressive policies in Ireland, perhaps, and in particular the excesses of the notorious 'Black and Tans', suggested that Lloyd George had lost touch with his Liberal roots. In a letter to *The Times* in April 1921, John Simon condemned the government's Irish tactics as 'politically disastrous and morally wrong ... exposing us to the scorn of the world'.

But what really stood in the way of reunion was the intransigent opposition of the Asquithian leadership, in no mood to forgive Lloyd George for what he had done. 'I would not trust him,' confessed Henry Gladstone. 'I am not sure I would not prefer to vote for a Tory rather than a man who would support Lloyd George and his Coalition for another five years.'[47] Matters came to a head at the meeting of the National Liberal Federation General Committee at Leamington in May 1920. Here the Coalition Liberal delegation, led by the Attorney General, Sir Gordon Hewart, walked out in protest against the patent hostility of the Wee Frees. Over the following months, area federations and constituency parties found themselves having to choose between the two factions. Only in Wales did the Lloyd Georgeites retain the upper hand. In many local associations, the result of bitter in-fighting between the two groups was an almost complete collapse of both organization and activity. Even then, most Coalitionists continued to hanker after reunion, but Lloyd George remained aware of the danger of alienating his Conservative partners, on whose parliamentary backing his premiership ultimately depended. Concerned, as throughout his career, with policies rather than parties, he saw little future for Liberalism in the post-war era, and seemed more interested in the possibilities of a wide-ranging political realignment. 'The so-called Liberal party,' he told Lord Riddell in 1919, 'consists mostly of plutocrats who have no sympathy whatever with the aspirations of the mass of the people.'[48] 'Liberal labels,' he warned his ministers, 'lead nowhere: we must be prepared to burn them.'[49] But Lloyd George failed to carry his Liberal supporters with him in the quest for a new centre party, and by the spring of 1920 had few options left other than to convert the Coalition Liberals into a permanent organization. Guest set himself the aim of creating a local Coalition Liberal Party in every parliamentary constituency, but the task proved much more difficult than he had expected.

With division ever more firmly entrenched, it was scarcely surprising that Liberalism failed to benefit from the government's mounting unpopularity. Three early by-election victories in March and April 1919, at which substantial government majorities were overturned, proved deceptive. During the Parliament as a whole, Independent Liberals came third in 15 out of 24 three-cornered contests. Only two further by-election gains were recorded before the 1922 General Election, both in rural seats with a strong Liberal tradition. In industrial, working-class constituencies it was Labour, with 13 gains over the course of the Parliament, that profited from the government's misfortunes. Particularly worrying was the evidence of what could happen if the party remained divided. When, at the end of 1919, a vacancy arose in the Spen Valley division of Yorkshire following the death of the sitting Coalition Liberal member, the local Liberal association, anxious now to run an Independent Liberal, selected the former Home Secretary, Sir John Simon. Up to this point, Lloyd George had happily supported Coalition Conservatives against Asquithians, but had stopped short of engineering a direct contest between competing Liberals. At Spen Valley he took a different line, putting forward a Coalition Liberal candidate. As the Liberal vote would clearly be split, it is evident that the Prime Minister's desire to exclude Simon was more important than the election of a government supporter: 'I don't care who wins if that blighter is last.'[50] The outcome of the by-election was entirely predictable. The Coalition candidate siphoned off enough Liberal votes from Simon to deliver the seat to Labour. The Spen Valley result would later be seen as a signal moment in Labour's transition to the status of a party of government.

The fall of Lloyd George's government in October 1922, following the decision of rank-and-file Conservative MPs to reject the advice of their leader, Austen Chamberlain, to fight the next election still bound to the coalition, offered an obvious opportunity to repair the breach in the ranks of the Liberal Party. But the decision of the new Prime Minister, Andrew Bonar Law, to call an immediate General Election offered no time for such a development to take place, even had the will existed on the part of the two principals, Asquith and Lloyd George. As a result, and with the Conservatives also divided between the adherents of the new government and those, led by Chamberlain, who hankered after a renewed coalition, the 1922 General Election represented 'a state of confusion unknown in any former election. The old party lines [were] gone.'[51] Some Liberal candidates stood as unequivocal adherents of one or other Liberal leader, others tried to paper over the party's divisions, and some campaigned specifically for reunion. As Lloyd George recalled:

> the Liberals spent a great part of their strength in fighting each other. It was the hardest job I ever had and I hope never to have such another...You never knew from what quarter the attack would come and the conditions varied from constituency to constituency. The people who were helping each other in one constituency would be fighting in the next.[52]

The Asquithians, in particular, seemed ill-prepared. A few weeks before the election, Maclean found Asquith 'devoted to bridge and small talk, doing no real work and leaving the party leaderless'.[53] With only 328 candidates for a Parliament of over 600 seats, the Independent Liberals could not realistically expect to control the outcome of the election without the co-operation of Lloyd George and his followers.

But this was an important contest. The unique circumstances of 1918 and the very existence of a coalition had not provided the easiest background against which to assess the standing of the parties in the newly unfolding post-war political environment. Despite the new lines of division, the election of 1922 represented a return to something like the normal pattern of domestic politics. Perhaps the most striking feature was the extent to which, with the Liberals still focusing on an essentially pre-war agenda, Labour had now taken over as the party of the industrial working class. Campaigning for her father in Paisley, Asquith's daughter, Violet Bonham Carter, sensed the change of mood resulting from high levels of unemployment: 'In places where there was no distress or unemployment – Huddersfield for instance – one felt quite different straightaway. There Liberalism had the democratic wind – or a gust of it – and there was no bitterness in the fight.'[54] But Liberals were also in danger of being outflanked on the right. Bonar Law's Conservatives had taken over the fight for retrenchment and decontrol, on which many Asquithians had campaigned since the end of the war.

In the event, neither Liberal faction had much cause for satisfaction. The Independent Liberals gained 43 seats, with a final total of 54, a considerable improvement over their 1918 performance. But 14 seats were lost, 9 of them to Labour, and their showing in mining seats, where they had done well before 1914, was especially disappointing. Their best results came in straight fights with the Conservatives in those traditionally Liberal rural constituencies lost in the peculiar circumstances of 1918. The performance of the Lloyd Georgeites was, if anything, even worse. They won just 62 seats, against 133 in 1918, going down badly in industrial areas. But the Liberal performance must also be seen in the overall party political context. Contests among themselves may have cost the Liberals up to fourteen seats, mainly to the advantage of Labour. Had these seats stayed in Liberal hands, the combined Liberal total might have been enough to deprive Labour of the psychologically important status of 'official opposition' to which it now rightfully laid claim. Also striking was the fact that, taken together, Labour and the Liberals, partners in the old Progressive Alliance, captured 58.6 per cent of the popular vote. The Conservatives, with just 38.2 per cent, won 483 Westminster seats and a Commons majority of 75. In the Liberal landslide of 1906, the Progressive parties had won 54.9 per cent of the vote against the Unionists' 43.6. However it was analysed, the 1922 result offered Liberals little solace. 'People have either gone back to Conservatism or have swung right over to Labour,' suggested John Simon. He sensed a 'very grave danger' that Liberalism could be 'crushed out between the upper and nether millstone', but took comfort in the belief that there was a great deal of sympathy for the party in the country that had not been expressed at the polls.[55] C. P. Scott of the *Manchester Guardian* was altogether more brutal; the result, he believed, was even worse than in 1918, 'because there was less excuse for it'.[56]

In fact, the 1922 General Election showed how difficult it would be for the Liberals to re-emerge as serious contenders for power in the new three-party system which, for the time being, had been superimposed on a political structure best suited to just two competitors. The combination of the first-past-the-post electoral system and a preponderance of three-cornered contests in the elections of the 1920s produced a succession of unrepresentative results in which marginal shifts in votes could lead to significant changes in parliamentary representation. Sometimes this worked to the advantage of the Conservatives; and sometimes Labour benefited. But Liberalism almost invariably lost out. By 1922, the disadvantages of third-party status were already becoming apparent. In rough terms the combined party had secured nearly 30 per cent of the popular vote but less than 20 per cent of the seats in the new Parliament. The Conservative election campaign had been focused on the Labour challenge, deliberately to polarize the debate and at the same time to squeeze out the Liberal Party as a largely irrelevant factor. If Liberalism was to have any chance of recovery, it needed to define its specific position in the changed political spectrum with far greater clarity than it had achieved so far.

Baldwin Forces Reunion

A further prerequisite of a Liberal revival was a reunion of the party's warring factions, if for no other reason than that the party needed access to Lloyd George's political fund, derived largely from the sale of honours during his premiership, to sustain its electoral viability. The auguries, however, were not good. 'While my opinion is all for reunion,' wrote Lord Cowdray, 'I consider, if reunion involved in any way our acceptance of Lloyd George, that we cannot afford to pay such a price.'[57] An early approach from Lloyd George was coolly rebuffed. The question of leadership was obviously a potential stumbling block, especially as the Asquithians moved quickly to block the Welshman's claims to the succession. Asquith and John Simon decided that Simon should become deputy leader, and the latter agreed to give up all his legal work, which might interfere with his new parliamentary duties. With Asquith now 70 years of age, Simon clearly anticipated that he rather than the ageing leader would be the driving force in the party's parliamentary activities. But merger with the former coalitionists would throw Simon's eventual claim to the succession into question. 'The whole problem of Liberal reunion,' reported the *Evening Standard,* 'will soon resolve itself into the single question of Liberal leadership. Asquith, Lloyd George or Simon.' A short session of the new Parliament began on 20 November and ended less than a month later. George Lambert attempted to summon a joint meeting of MPs from both groups, but neither leadership responded positively. 'Because ... I have tried to avoid the peril of Liberal disunion,' he complained to Herbert Gladstone, 'the rival Popes of Liberalism have placed me on the index of the politically damned.'[58]

Lloyd George, however, became increasingly convinced of the need for reunion and, in the spring of 1923, made a series of speeches urging this cause as the precondition of Liberal revival. 'If we do not reunite,' he insisted, 'Liberalism is done as a national driving force.'[59] A motion in favour of reunion was signed by 73 Liberal MPs in March, but the annual meeting of the National Liberal Federation at Buxton ignored insistent demands from the constituencies. Nevertheless, two by-elections, in Anglesey and Ludlow, Shropshire, saw Coalition Liberals and Asquithians coming together spontaneously; efforts towards reunion began in other constituencies; and by September more than 50 local Liberal and National (Lloyd Georgeite) Liberal associations had merged. But what no one could have anticipated was that Stanley Baldwin, the new Conservative Prime Minister, would succeed, where Lloyd George and other Liberals had failed, in giving the final push towards bringing the two factions together. Baldwin had taken over from the ailing Bonar Law in May, with the parliamentary majority secured by the latter the previous November still intact. In a speech in Plymouth on 25 October, however, he declared his wish to secure a fresh mandate to introduce tariffs. He was impeded in doing this by a pledge given by Law not to impose them without the nation's express approval.

The effect on Liberalism was dramatic. At this time there was still no single issue as likely to cement the disparate strands of Liberalism into a single whole as the defence of free trade. This issue had the potential to give the Liberals a tactical advantage over Labour, perhaps the only question that could still do so. Once Lloyd George had returned from a visit to the Unites States, a combined committee of Liberals, including Asquith, Simon, Lloyd George and Sir Alfred Mond, managed to hammer out a joint election manifesto and it was agreed that Liberals would fight as a united party across the country. It was also announced that candidates would take to the field in sufficient numbers to make the party a practical alternative to the Conservative government. For this to happen, of course, Lloyd George's financial support was imperative. Asquith had no alternative but to bite the bullet, but he evidently felt uncomfortable when he and Lloyd George appeared together on the same platform in Paisley: 'I have rarely felt less exhilaration than when we got to the platform amid wild plaudits and a flash-light film was taken, "featuring" me and Ll.G separated only by the chairman.'[60]

The Liberals' campaign rested overwhelmingly on a negative defence of free trade. Lloyd George was almost alone in making a few more radical and constructive statements. While this approach enabled the party to pick up the votes of free-trade Conservatives and retain its traditional support in rural areas, it also helped to take the party's eye off its real enemy, Labour, which on the question of tariffs found itself in the same camp. The Liberals thus adopted an essentially backward-looking stance, which did little to put down new roots for the electoral contests of the future. 'Every speech delivered in the course of this electoral campaign,' declared the *Western Mail*, 'lends emphasis to the fact that Liberalism is living in the dead past.' Yet, in purely statistical terms, the results represented a distinct revival in Liberal fortunes. With 30 per cent of the popular vote, 158 MPs were elected. But not all features of the election outcome gave cause for satisfaction. The Liberal revival, concentrated in rural and middle-class areas, was largely at the expense of the Conservatives. The party found itself winning seats that had returned Conservatives even in 1906, scarcely evidence that it was retaining an image of left-of-centre progressivism. More than 60 seats were won in straight fights and might be vulnerable in the event of future Labour intervention. Most disturbing was the party's failure to make significant inroads into the Labour vote. Indeed, the flag of Liberalism was still retreating in industrial Britain as the party suffered a net loss of 10 seats to Labour.

Holding the Balance

The most significant feature of the election result was the failure of any one party to secure an absolute majority. Though the Conservatives, with 258 seats, remained the largest single party, the combined Labour and Liberal contingents represented a clear majority for free trade after an election fought specifically on the question of tariffs. Holding the balance of parliamentary power, a contingency to which the leadership appears to have given little prior consideration, Liberalism now faced a tactical dilemma – the creation of its own relative success at the polls. The party's long-term future might well depend on the correct decisions being taken. The unenviable choice lay between sustaining a Conservative government that had just been defeated on a central plank of its programme, and installing a minority Labour administration in its place. This fundamental issue found the party leadership badly divided. Their indecision reflected a failure since 1918 to get to grips with the 'impact of Labour' and its implications for Liberalism's survival as a potential party of government. Should Labour be regarded as an ally, a rival or a mortal foe? It also stood as testimony to the continuing mutual distrust of the Lloyd George and Asquith factions, despite the shotgun reconciliation that had recently taken place.

The option of keeping the Conservatives in power was soon ruled out. As E. D. Simon, elected for the Withington division of Manchester, explained:

> if we now support the Conservatives, Labour will represent it as a capitalist combination to keep them out of power and will undoubtedly gain hundreds of thousands of votes by it. The one way of ensuring a Socialist Government in full power in the course of the next few years would be for us to come to an agreement to keep the Conservatives in power now.[61]

Thereafter, agreement was harder to secure. When Liberal leaders met soon after the election to settle their immediate policy,

Asquith urged that the party should vote with Labour to turn
Baldwin out when the new Parliament met and then, assuming
Labour succeeded in forming a government, the Liberals should
combine with the Conservatives to oust that as well. After that,
with no one ready to force yet another election, the King would
have to invite Asquith to form a government. Such a sequence of
events would at least succeed in maintaining the Liberal Party's
distinctive identity in the eyes of the electorate. Lloyd George,
however, was unconvinced, and the meeting adjourned without a
final decision being reached. By the time it reconvened, Asquith
had modified his stance and was no longer prepared to go beyond
voting out the existing Baldwin government. The Liberal attitude
towards any subsequent Labour administration would be non-
committal. Though Asquith's new approach smacked of the fatal
'wait and see' style that had discredited his wartime premiership,
Lloyd George, who clearly envisaged sustaining a Labour government in office, accepted it as a step in the right direction. This,
in essence, is what happened when Parliament reassembled in
January 1924.

But the dangers from a Liberal perspective were obvious. The
Liberals were voting Labour into office without really considering
what they would do subsequently, and without trying to extract
any policy commitments, such as electoral reform, of benefit to
themselves. An appropriate line might have been a fixed-term
arrangement on the basis of an agreed legislative programme.
The parliamentary arithmetic, was, moreover, against them. As
there were more Conservative MPs than Labour, it would not be
enough for the Liberal Party to abstain if Labour was going to survive for any length of time. The Liberals did not have the option
of merely acquiescing with the Labour government; they had to
support it positively. When Asquith told the parliamentary party
that a Labour government could hardly be tried out under safer
conditions, he was probably fully justified. But his further remarks
were totally unfounded: 'It is we, if we understand our business,
who really control the situation.'[62]

Those Liberals who still spoke the language of the Progressive
Alliance saw enormous possibilities opening up. As Labour
unfolded its legislative programme, E. D. Simon enthused about
the 'immense field of constructive work in which we could fruit-
fully co-operate...Foreign Affairs, Unemployment, Education

and Housing are the most important'.[63] In the government's early months he remained optimistic:

> Up to now the Labour Government has shown a real desire to avoid impracticable and Socialistic legislation, and to concentrate on practical social reforms on Liberal lines as for instance the removal of the unemployment gap, the extension of the Trade Facilities Act, and more generous administrative provision for the needs of education and public health. In other words they are acting almost exactly on the lines of a Liberal government. By far the best chance for the continuation of such legislation is for the Liberals to maintain Labour in power.[64]

But by the end of Labour's first brief term in office, Simon's mood had completely changed. 'The session as a whole,' he confessed, 'was a tragedy.' The two parties could, he believed, have stayed together 'for years', enacting a far-reaching programme of radical legislation. What had gone wrong? Simon enumerated his points of explanation:

1. A considerable section of Liberals didn't want radical legislation.
2. A section of Labour – Wheatley and Co. didn't want radical legislation. MacDonald joined them and Sidney Webb in having as their first object to kill the Liberal Party – as the only means of an ultimate Labour majority.
3. Liberal leadership was lazy and aloof. Not only did they not consult one another, but they made no real attempt to consult Labour.
4. The vacuity and self righteousness of R[amsay] M[acDonald] and his unfortunate habit of telling lies in the House made co-operation very difficult. No Labour leader ever thanked a Liberal for support or help, though for 6 months the Liberals as a whole gave them really good support.[65]

Both in his focus on Labour's attitude and his disappointment at the Liberals' own performance, Simon got to the heart of the matter. Labour would not play the part that the Liberals had mapped out for them. The Labour leadership was clear in its view that the destruction of the Liberal Party was a necessary precondition of their own party's further advance. In taking office, MacDonald saw it as his primary task to establish Labour's credentials as a respectable and moderate party of government rather than to embark on some far-reaching radical agenda in conjunction with the Liberals. 'The only kind of cooperation which is possible,' insisted MacDonald, 'is the cooperation of men and women who come over and join us.'[66] Indeed, in the broader context of the electoral history of the 1920s as a whole, it is evident that Labour was determined to pursue this strategy, thus abandoning the possibility of a short-term Liberal–Labour preponderance, even at the cost of allowing the Conservatives a near stranglehold on government. Even those such as Lloyd George, who were keen to sustain Labour in office, became disillusioned by the response given to the Liberal hand of friendship. 'Liberals are to be the oxen,' he complained in April 1924, 'to drag the Labour wain over the rough roads of Parliament for two to three years, goaded along, and at the end of the journey, when there is no further use for them, they are to be slaughtered. That is the Labour idea of cooperation.'[67] But many Liberals voiced their indignation in a way that suggested ignorance of the game Labour was playing. Vivian Phillipps, the chief whip, found MacDonald's behaviour particularly disappointing: 'Not only does he appear not to seek our goodwill and cooperation, but on several occasions it has seemed as if he went out of his way to make it as difficult as possible for us to back him.'[68] In this situation, the Liberals were unlikely to derive much benefit from having put Labour into office. Those who had voted Liberal to resist the dangers of socialism realized either that the Conservatives represented a more effective bulwark or else that Labour was not as dangerous as they had supposed and might even serve as the vehicle for those radical aspirations that had previously attracted them to Liberalism.

Irrespective of Labour's long-term strategy, the parliamentary Liberal Party remained deeply divided in its attitude towards the government. Even on the initial vote, bringing down the Baldwin government and opening the way to a Labour administration, 10 Liberals voted in the Conservative lobby. Thereafter, the shallowness of the reconciliation effected by Baldwin's pronouncement on tariffs was soon revealed. Lloyd George's point-blank refusal to amalgamate his Political Fund with the diminished financial resources of the Asquithian party was indicative of an ongoing absence of confidence and goodwill. The party could still not present a united front on major policy issues. Percy Harris, MP for Bethnal Green, South West, recalled 'a distinct cleavage of thought' apparent at every party meeting: 'The old Coalitionists were always looking for excuses to vote with the Tories, while the Independent Liberals were pressing for radical reforms and were only too glad to support legislation of a kind they had been advocating for years.'[69] On questions such as Labour's decision to discontinue development of the Singapore naval base, and the Eviction Bill in April, the whips could exert little discipline. E. D. Simon, perturbed at the party's 'utter failure of leadership', and holding Asquith particularly responsible, vividly described how Liberal policy was determined in the latter case:

> There were about a dozen present and we were unanimously and strongly of the opinion that [the government's bill] was grossly unfair to the particular landlord whose tenant happened to be unemployed, and utterly indefensible ... Mr. Asquith said nothing, but after fifteen minutes discussion ... the matter was practically settled, the only question being who was to speak and how the case should be put. At that moment in came Lloyd George. He had not looked at the bill: it was explained to him, and he immediately said 'This will never do. There are millions of tenants who may be unemployed and if we oppose this they will say we are against them and goodbye to their votes.' ... He went on like this for ten minutes ... but I assumed that he would be tactfully suppressed by Mr Asquith. To my absolute horror, all Asquith said was 'Very well, in view of what you say, perhaps you will put the case for us in debate'. And immediately broke up the meeting, without giving any opportunity for further discussion![70]

In similar vein, Wedgwood Benn recorded the frustration that ultimately propelled him into Labour's ranks:

> Policy at the present moment is very difficult. Mr A of course works in the background with Conferences with the Mausoleum. LLG will appear from time to time to force the Party into stunts. Party meetings are difficult to hold, but without them, trouble will ensue. Brilliant nagging at the Government is all very well but seems to me to lead nowhere.[71]

It was not surprising that there was talk of holding a regular 'Gladstone dinner' at the National Liberal Club, 'something to collect all Liberals, none of whom feel too enthusiastic about their leaders at the present moment'.[72]

Liberals were in fact now facing the problem inherent in their third-party status of defining their position in relation to two larger parties. Caught inevitably somewhere in the middle of the Labour–Conservative electoral contest, they struggled throughout the decade to determine whether their basic inclination was to lean to the left or the right. Their inability to give a single, coherent answer to this question would lead ultimately to a further, catastrophic, breach in the party's ranks. Yet just as Labour would no longer play the role of pliant partner, so too the attitude of many Conservatives had also undergone a fundamental change, with the Liberals' decision to allow Labour to form a government often proving the turning point. Since 1918, Austen Chamberlain had consistently sought a partnership with Liberalism as the only reliable means of preventing the advent of socialist government. But he was appalled by Asquith's decision to let Labour take office. The change in his attitude was evident in the no-confidence debate on 21 January which finally brought down Baldwin's government:

> [Asquith] has taken his choice and he has by that choice constituted his own immortality. He will go down to history as the last Prime Minister of a Liberal Administration. He has sung the swan song of the Liberal Party. When next the country is called upon for a decision, if it wants a Socialist Government it will vote for a Socialist; if it does not want a Socialist Government it will vote for a Unionist. It will not vote again for those who denatured its mandate and betrayed its trust.[73]

A week later, Chamberlain wrote to his colleague, Samuel Hoare, explaining that the Conservatives' task was now 'to smash the Liberal party'. Two-thirds of it, he claimed, was already Labour in all but name and the task of Conservatism was to draw over and eventually absorb the other third – rather as the Liberal Unionists had been absorbed into the Unionist Party.[74] Leopold Amery was of the same mind. As he explained to Baldwin, the real division in politics now lay between constructive Conservatism and Labour Socialism. It was in the interests of both to clear the ground of the Liberal Party, which stood for nothing except 'an organized hypocrisy'. The two leading parties could each hope to pick up the larger share of the Liberal carcass, but the 'great thing is to get the beast killed and on that we can be agreed'.[75] While, then, there are good reasons for dwelling on the damage that Liberalism did to itself in the decade and a half after the Lloyd George–Asquith split of 1916, it is also plausible to argue, as did many contemporary Liberals, that the party was the victim of a two-pronged pincer assault launched by its political opponents.

Liberalism was 'rescued' from its dilemmas when the Labour government decided to turn a Liberal proposal to set up a Select Committee into its handling of the so-called Campbell Case (designed in fact to offer the government a means of escape from a crisis created by its own ineptitude) into a vote of confidence. There was no need for the government to take the Liberal amendment, as opposed to the original Conservative motion of censure, as an issue of confidence. John Simon declared that to do so would be like a man who had been asked to produce a document from his drawer preferring to burn down his own house. But the Liberals could not stop the Conservatives supporting their amendment, and Labour probably preferred facing defeat on this matter rather than on a proposed trade treaty with Soviet Russia, where Liberals and Tories were also expected to vote together. The government fell by 364 votes to 198. But the act of 'rescue' was only nominal. While the end of the Labour government did free Liberals from the intolerable burden of sustaining an opposing party that offered nothing in return, it also made another General Election inevitable. The party could scarcely afford this in purely financial terms, and its outcome would reveal the extent of the Liberal collapse that had been predictable since the party's decision to install Labour in power. On the day Labour fell, Wedgwood Benn wrote in his diary of the 'suicide of the Liberal party'.[76]

In late April, Herbert Gladstone had advised Asquith of the imperative need to secure enough financial support to guarantee a sufficient number of candidates at the next election. In practice this meant courting Lloyd George, and difficult negotiations went on throughout the year. Lloyd George, however, was disinclined to relinquish control over what was his chief negotiating counter in the party's internal power struggle, at least not without the guarantee of a degree of control over Liberal policy and strategy, which the Asquithians were reluctant to concede. Sir Robert Hudson found one 40-minute session with Lloyd George so 'poisonous' that he 'took to [his] bed with a temperature the next afternoon'.[77] In the event, Lloyd George agreed to contribute just £50,000 for the campaign of October 1924, about a quarter of the sum needed to meet the party's anticipated costs. As a result, the Liberals could field no more than 340 candidates, effectively disqualifying themselves at the outset as serious contenders for power. 'We could not make candidates without straw,' recalled Herbert Gladstone, 'and straw was denied us.'[78] At one point the figure looked likely to be even lower. As the chief whip put it: 'This was the death-blow. We had assumed that reunion meant reunion of resources...We had striven at every stage to meet Ll. G's views in the long-drawn-out negotiations and we now found ourselves left without the means to put more than 300 candidates in the field.'[79] But financial worries merely compounded the problems of a party which, at constituency level, was both divided and demoralized. Even Lloyd George conceded that the Liberals went into action looking like a 'disorganized rabble'.[80] In the emotionally charged atmosphere of the campaign, with the Conservatives playing on the red scare of the Zinoviev Letter, Liberals found it difficult to project a distinctive identity. The party's manifesto was an uninspiring document, highly critical of Labour's performance in government but offering little as an alternative, especially in terms of economic policy. Calls for temperance and free trade were beginning to look curiously dated. Post-war electoral history suggested that the party's best hope lay in an appeal to the largely non-unionized working class of the countryside, but there is no evidence that the leadership tried to point the party in that direction.

After an uninspiring campaign in which even Lloyd George seemed unable to raise much enthusiasm for his party's prospects, the Liberals confronted a predictable disaster. The Conservative party secured a landslide victory with more than 400 seats in the new House. Though Labour lost nearly 40 seats, its percentage of the vote actually increased. It could look back on its first experience of government with some satisfaction. Its day would come again. But for the Liberals the result was, in Sidney Webb's words, 'the funeral of a great party'.[81] With just 42 MPs returned, three-quarters of the parliamentary party had gone down to defeat, including Asquith at Paisley. The progress made in 1923 at the expense of the Conservatives in rural and middle-class constituencies was emphatically reversed. Throughout the land only seven Liberals prevailed in three-cornered contests. As many as 31 candidates defending Liberal seats finished third behind Labour and the Conservatives. Though eight gains were recorded against Labour, compared with sixteen losses, seven of these were in constituencies where no Conservative took the field. The fall in the Liberal vote from 4.3 million in 1923 to 2.9 million was less dramatic, especially in view of the reduced number of Liberal candidates. But the result emphasized the extent to which the third-party trap was now beginning to bite. Liberals were still polling respectably enough, but an average 30.9 per cent of the vote per opposed candidate was insufficient to win many seats in the existing electoral system. At least the party's manifesto appeal for 'a real correspondence between Parliamentary representation and electoral strength' was well timed.

The 1924 results need to be set in a somewhat broader chronological context. Three General Elections had taken place in just two years and, despite some passing signs of encouragement for Liberals, the overall effect had been to confirm the two-party pattern that was to dominate British politics for the next half century, with the Conservatives and Labour the only serious contenders for power. The Liberals had been relegated firmly to third place in a system that operates to the advantage of just two players. The political objectives of both Labour and the Conservatives involved squeezing out the Liberal Party from the electoral frontline and this had largely been achieved. Labour had mounted a successful challenge to the Liberals in industrial Britain; and the Conservatives were well advanced in a similar campaign in suburban and rural areas. For the foreseeable future, Liberal prospects looked bleak, not least because the party no longer enjoyed an easily identifiable constituency in the electorate. This placed it at a grave disadvantage in the increasingly class-based politics of the time, as becomes clear when the electoral history of the decade is considered as a whole. 'The Liberals in the 1920s,' writes Geoffrey Searle, 'were quite successful in winning seats... their problem was rather one of holding on to their gains.'[82] With few constituencies that could now be regarded as safely, or even characteristically, Liberal, the party lacked the solid base from which to launch a successful revival.

Nor did the picture look significantly better at the level of municipal politics. The period since 1918 had witnessed an intensive Labour challenge in local elections, which the Liberals had been unable to resist. Indeed, the latter suffered a net loss of seats every year during the 1920s except for 1922. This Liberal decline was matched by a steady fall in the number of their municipal candidatures, even at times when the national party showed signs of renewal, so that by 1929 less than one in eight of those standing in provincial borough elections was a Liberal. In many towns, a Liberal presence was only maintained as a result of anti-socialist municipal alliances with the Conservatives. But while such pacts might delay the final extinction of Liberal representation, they ran the parallel danger of the progressive loss of a distinct Liberal identity, which encouraged the transfer of allegiances to one or other of the two main parties.[83]

Lloyd George Takes Control

As the dispirited band of MPs gathered at Westminster after the 1924 General Election, Liberalism seemed in danger of total disintegration. A gathering of Liberal leaders organized by Lord Beauchamp was 'knee-deep in condolences and tears'.[84] The shallowness of the reconciliation effected in defence of free trade was only too apparent. Unlike the 1923 election, that of 1924 had swung the party's internal balance of power in Lloyd George's favour. Over half of the surviving parliamentary party were former coalitionists. But hatred of Lloyd George himself had not abated. 'I could very well stand LG's defeat,' confessed Henry Gladstone, 'for Asquith's disappearance from the House must otherwise promote him to a position which he is not worthy to hold. I fancy distrust of LG has a good deal to do with the Liberal smash.'[85] Walter Runciman judged that personal difficulties were more acute than ever and could never be resolved as long as Lloyd George 'insists on pushing himself as leader or deputy leader'.[86] In fact no one sought to deprive Asquith of the nominal party leadership. At the same time, it was unlikely that he would ever again secure a seat in the Commons and, indeed, early in the new year he accepted a peerage, going to the Lords as the Earl of Oxford and Asquith. In his absence, attention shifted to the position of sessional chairman. John Simon urged that the post should remain vacant, with Godfrey Collins, the new chief whip, taking the chair at party meetings. This idea was put forward when Liberal MPs met on 2 December to decide the matter. It was rejected by 26 votes to 9, after which an amendment was carried to appoint Lloyd George. After the latter took the chair, Simon swallowed his pride and appealed for unity and comradeship. Though Asquith would retain the formal leadership until October 1926, the era of Lloyd George's ascendancy had begun. None the less, on the day after the party meeting, 11 Liberal MPs, with Runciman as their chairman, formed a 'Radical Group', pledged to working with the rest of the parliamentary party but effectively disowning Lloyd George's authority. The designation of the Gladstonian businessman, Runciman, as 'radical', especially in contrast to Lloyd George, epitomized the kaleidoscopic confusion that had come to characterize Liberal politics. Personality rather than doctrine, and specifically a hatred of Lloyd George, seemed to be the new group's primary motivation. Its members secured their own room in the Commons and began to issue their own whip. Liberalism's internecine conflict showed no sign of coming to an end.

With a comfortable parliamentary majority, Baldwin's Conservative party was likely to be in office for four or five years. Labour was established equally firmly as the alternative government. It was now apparent that the Liberals had been the least successful participants in the post-war political contest. Their image remained largely negative. They were against excessive state power, against militant trade unionism, against waste, socialism and jingoistic imperialism, but in favour, it seemed, of very little apart from prudent economy and free trade. Their position in the political spectrum was somewhere inside the comfortable middle ground, between the supposed extremes of their Labour and Conservative rivals, within which space their leaders mouthed reassuring platitudes which failed to inspire. 'Look neither to the right nor to the left,' Asquith told his audience in October 1926 at the time of his final retirement, 'but keep straight on.' In this situation, many Liberals, activists and voters alike, would inevitably be pulled towards the positive qualities of the other two parties, each of which, without being as extreme as Liberal spokesmen claimed, could better achieve Liberal aspirations, whether these were to oppose socialism or to promote radical change. Indeed, some seemed curiously satisfied with the idea that Liberalism's remaining function was to infuse Liberal values into the other two parties. E. D. Simon drew a distinction between the survival of the party and that of its philosophy, while Maynard Keynes suggested that possibly the party could best serve the state 'by supplying Conservative Governments with Cabinets and Labour Governments with ideas'.[87] Meanwhile, those Liberals who had sought to inject a new vigour into the party and interest it in a social and industrial agenda tailored to the 1920s had received scant support from the party leadership – the Asquithian 'mausoleum' as Wedgwood Benn styled it. The leadership, aware that its past was more glorious than its present (and in all probability than its future), was all too inclined to live in that past 'and regard it as the whole duty of a Liberal to cheer lustily when Gladstone, or Free Trade, or Home Rule are mentioned'.[88] Appropriately, it was Gladstone's son, Herbert, a still influential figure in the party's inner councils throughout the decade, who best articulated this deeply engrained strain of reaction. In 1927, by which time Lloyd George was trying to do something about the situation, Gladstone wrote:

> The programme, I confess, does not attract me. Land comes from the stockpot in a new dress but carries no inspiration. Coal and Power is not a political question at all. In my view, apart from Free Trade and the League of Nations, there are two questions which in sheer Liberalism stand out first and foremost, drastic retrenchment founded on policy and licensing not founded on fanaticism.[89]

By the middle of the decade those genuine radicals who had not already deserted the Liberal ranks faced a clear dilemma. As E. D. Simon explained soon after the 1924 election:

> The big decision I have to make as regards my individual political work is whether I should
>
> 1. do all in my power to help to revive the Liberal Party at the next election ...
> 2. do the same kind of thing, but half-heartedly, giving only limited time to it.
> 3. withdraw from national politics altogether for the present.
> 4. join the Labour party.
>
> My political aim is to give the best chance to every child, and to remove the excessive inequalities of today. That is practically the aim

of Labour. At Dundee I agreed with my extreme Labour audiences as regards political aims far more than with my Liberal chairman. All the enthusiasm and driving force is in the Labour Party, except for a few fanatics on land, or temperance or Free Trade.[90]

To his credit, Lloyd George now began to address this problem. Finally abandoning his earlier flirtation with the Conservatives, he set about taking Liberalism to the left, not towards doctrinaire socialism, but adopting a clearly radical agenda that would win public support and offer hope of returning himself to power. He now realized that Asquithian Liberalism would lead (as arguably it did in 1931) to Conservatism. Negative anti-socialism was the proper stance of a Conservative. But Liberals needed not so much to oppose the socialists as to compete with them on an alternative platform. The country was gripped not by political extremism but by the moderation of the centre-left and centre-right against which Liberalism could offer a radical alternative. Lloyd George was not, he stressed, a socialist, but a Liberal who believed that the elimination of private enterprise and individual incentive would be disastrous for the country's well-being. At the same time, it was not enough for the Liberals to take satisfaction from belonging to a party of noble principles and a glorious record. Much work and sacrifice was needed before the party could apply those principles to the needs of the day and thereby make that record even more glorious.[91] The ultimate aim, according to Frances Stevenson, was a new political alignment: 'D[avid]'s idea is to go definitely towards the *Left*, and gradually to co-ordinate and consolidate all the progressive forces in the country, against the Conservative and reactionary forces. Thus he will eventually get all sane Labour as well as Liberalism behind him.'[92] But the task would not be easy, not least because most of Lloyd George's existing supporters, a legacy of the Coalition, were men of the right, while Asquith 'who is really a Whig is accepted as a better Liberal than he'.[93]

Lloyd George's first initiative was to take up once again the land question with which his fertile brain had been engaged in 1914 before international developments compelled a reordering of everyone's priorities, including his own. The report of the Land Inquiry Committee was published as *Land and the Nation* in October 1925, and soon became known as the Green Book. Radicals were excited and enthused but the proposal to end private ownership of agricultural land by making farmers into 'cultivating tenants', supervised by county committees, aroused considerable opposition. But beyond specific policy difficulties lay the fact that Lloyd George was still not in position to direct the Liberal Party. Asquith held on to the shadow and in some ways the substance of power from his base in the Lords, for no other reason it seemed than to deny Lloyd George his inheritance. More and more Liberals recognized that it was time for the old man to go, but, as Lady Kennet noted, 'few cared to be rude to Mr. Asquith. Oh dear!', she continued, 'how I wish he could have died when he should in 1916. What a great name my beautiful friend would then have left.'[94] Lloyd George now regarded his nominal chief as a 'silly old man drunk with hidden conceit', but seemed prepared to bide his time.[95] Time, after all, was on his side, at least in terms of the party's internal politics, and so was money, which remained the younger man's whip hand. 'There was nothing for it,' conceded Herbert Gladstone, 'but to maintain amicable relations or keep on endeavouring to bring [Lloyd George] over to our views.'[96] In practice, neither strategy proved possible. Relations between the two factions continued to deteriorate throughout 1925 before reaching breaking point in May of the following year.

The event that brought matters to a head was the General Strike. The Liberal shadow cabinet declared that society was obliged to secure victory over the strikers, but from the outset Lloyd George blamed the government for the crisis and called for a negotiated settlement. In a significant if controversial intervention on 6 May, John Simon, with the authority he derived as one of the country's leading barristers, declared the strike illegal. Every trade union leader was guilty of incitement to breach of contract and liable therefore to damages 'to the uttermost farthing of his personal possessions'. When the shadow cabinet met again on 10 May, Lloyd George pointedly absented himself, instead writing to the chief whip to express his unwillingness to be associated with any declaration against the strike that failed also to condemn the government's handling of the situation. Lord Oxford's initial response was one of no more than mild displeasure, but his colleagues saw in this latest divergence the chance of a final break with Lloyd George. As had often been the case since 1916, the leader's followers were more Asquithian than Asquith himself. An increasingly acrimonious exchange of correspondence ensued, most of it published in the press, which seemed to indicate a readiness on both sides to push matters to an open rupture. The climax came when twelve members of the shadow cabinet sent Oxford a public letter of support, amounting to an indictment of Lloyd George's actions since the reunion of 1923, and in particular denouncing his manipulation of his private political fund. His actions during the General Strike had to be 'regarded in the light of this general position'. The letter concluded:

> We have done our best in the highest interests of the cause of Liberalism to work with Mr Lloyd George in the consultations of the party and we regret to say that we cannot any longer continue to work with a colleague who, in our judgement, is not worthy of the trust.[97]

But the Asquithians had miscalculated. The party at large was sick of the perpetual infighting and regarded this latest attack on Lloyd George as little more than victimization. The latter, moreover, still commanded majority support inside the parliamentary party. The annual meeting of the National Liberal Federation at Weston-super-Mare, Somerset, on 17 June offered Oxford a last chance to regain control over the situation. Less than a week before the meeting, however, he suffered a serious stroke that removed him from the political stage. With Oxford out of action, most Liberals saw that they needed Lloyd George. The mood was for reconciliation. To be leaderless was one thing; to be penniless quite another. John Simon's private secretary summed up the situation:

> Undoubtedly the preponderating desire of the delegates [at Weston] was that the recent published correspondence should not split the Party. While reaffirming its confidence in Lord Oxford as Leader, the Conference was equally emphatic that Lloyd George must be associated with the Party. How that was to be achieved I am afraid the delegates did not trouble to think about. All they were concerned with was that the Party should not be torn asunder.[98]

In October, Oxford finally resigned the leadership. Though he had attached his colours firmly to Oxford's mast ever since 1916, Richard Holt now passed a harsh but valid judgement. He was 'in some ways a great figure, yet he succeeded to the leadership when the party was in overwhelming strength and he left it a ruin, sunk lower than any great party ever sank. It is impossible to acquit him of the major responsibility for this event.'[99] While some hoped that Simon would emerge as the champion of an Asquithian succession, most realized that, for the party to have any future at all, it had to capitulate to Lloyd George, or at least to readmit him fully to the Liberal fold. In the words of the *Manchester Guardian*: 'Many people in the party, not specifically associated with one side or the other are hoping that in the entirely different situation caused by Lord Oxford's resignation the leading signatories [to the letter to Oxford of 31 May] may find it possible to make a gesture of reconciliation.'[100] Asquith's daughter put the matter more bluntly. The choice was whether 'to starve or be bought'.[101] In November the Million Fund Administration Committee, set up after the last General Election, narrowly agreed to accept Lloyd George's terms for a massive grant from his political fund. It was, thought Holt, an 'iniquitous transaction', but for all that it was inescapable.[102] Without Lloyd George, the party faced imminent bankruptcy. Having captured the party organization, he began to remove entrenched Asquithians from its bureaucracy. The Liberal Party was now effectively his. The only question was whether the takeover had come too late, both for himself and for the party.

Many regretted what had happened. '*If* Grey were younger and had his eye-sight,' bemoaned Violet Bonham Carter, 'if Simon were even 3/4 of a man and had an ounce of courage and a few strong ounces of blood and a heart that beat. But these are all fairy-tale dreams.'[103] In fact, while Simon drifted away from domestic politics, accepting the chairmanship of the Indian Statutory Commission, Grey took the lead in organizing the dissidents into the so-called Liberal Council. Runciman became the new group's chairman and effectively its parliamentary leader. Almost a party within the party, the Liberal Council claimed to represent a pure and uncorrupted form of Liberalism. It hoped to field candidates in opposition to Lloyd Georgeites at the next election. For the Asquithian old guard, the winning of power for the Liberal Party was evidently less important than thwarting Lloyd George's hopes in the same direction. So the Liberal civil war continued. The respected former cabinet minister, Herbert Samuel, was made chairman of the Liberal Party organization in 1927 in an attempt to effect a bridge between the contending factions, but the appointment was only a partial success. Runciman's wife, Hilda, refused to let Lloyd George speak on her behalf in a by-election at St Ives, Cornwall, in March 1928, while a year earlier Runciman had declared that what was needed was a Gladstonian policy, which 'the average non-political citizen...does not feel he can get...from the Liberal party'.[104]

Intellectual Revival

But most Liberals were content to see what Lloyd George could do, and it seems clear that the Welshman's ascendancy provided the party with a sense of purpose that had been lacking for many years. Building on the foundations laid down earlier in the decade by the Liberal Summer School movement, and bringing that body to the forefront of the party's activity, Lloyd George proceeded to endow Liberalism with a distinctive set of policies, relevant to the times, such as had largely been lacking since before the war. It represented a belated correction of the anomalous situation that had existed since 1916 when, *faute de mieux*, Asquith had become the nominal leader of the progressive Liberals. For a brief interlude the party displayed at its heart an intellectual liveliness that belied its gravely weakened political standing. In a post-Keynesian age, the policies projected in these years appear somewhat less compelling than was once the case, yet it is hard to deny that out of Liberalism's intellectual renaissance emerged those ideas that revolutionized British society in the post-Second World War era. The Liberal Industrial Inquiry, set up in 1925, brought together an impressive array of politicians and economists, including E. D. Simon, Walter Layton, Maynard Keynes, Herbert Samuel, Ramsay Muir and Lloyd George himself. Their report was published in February 1928 as *Britain's Industrial Future* – the 'Yellow Book'. It argued that, in modern conditions, the traditional antipathy between individualism and socialism had become unreal, and put forward far-reaching proposals for government planning of and intervention in the economy. Then a committee headed by Lloyd George, his former secretary Lord Lothian and the sociologist Seebohm Rowntree set about drawing up plans for national development schemes. The report, *We Can Conquer Unemployment*, published in March 1929, envisaged a vast public works programme, with an emphasis on road-building and housing, and this formed the basis of the party's manifesto for the General Election later that year. Looking back at the end of the decade, E. D. Simon reflected on the achievements of the Summer School movement:

> A great success – I knew exactly what I wanted. I learnt from Webb and Tawney the necessity of an industrial policy – the Liberal leaders ignored it. Through the Summer School we both [Simon and Ramsay Muir] worked out the policy and in just under 10 years effectively imposed it on the party. Biggest achievement the Yellow Book...I think it is a model of what political parties ought to do in an ideal democracy!

With more prescience than he could have known, Simon added 'whether it is of any use to the Liberal party politically is another and less important matter'.[105]

For a time, however, Lloyd George's imagination and energy seemed able to inject new life into Liberalism, both as a political force and as an intellectual movement. In March 1927, the party captured Southwark North, in London, from Labour. Further by-election gains followed at Bosworth, Leicestershire (May 1927), Lancaster (February 1928), St Ives (March 1928), Eddisbury, Cheshire (March 1929) and Holland-with-Boston, Lincolnshire (March 1929). After such a run of successes, few contemporaries could have guessed that Holland-with-Boston would be the Liberals' last by-election gain for almost 30 years. But perceptive observers did sense the limits to this latest Liberal revival. The party's victories were confined almost entirely to agricultural constituencies. After Southwark, all the gains were from the Conservatives and, over the Parliament as a whole, it was Labour that made most progress at the expense of an increasingly unpopular Conservative government, with no fewer than 12 gains overall. Lloyd George himself was worried that Labour would still not co-operate with the Liberals, even if the consequence of a continuing split in the progressive vote was to be further Conservative victories. 'If Tavistock [in Devon] goes the same way [as Cheltenham, Gloucestershire],' he wrote in September 1928, 'then it means that Labour in their blind jealousy of Liberalism are more intent on doing us in than in putting the Conservatives out.'[106]

The leader's mood at the beginning of 1929 was far from sanguine. 'I am fighting with an army paralysed by divided generalship,' he confided to his secretary and mistress. 'It is cankered with jealousy and suspicion.'[107] None the less, when Baldwin called a General Election for 30 May, many Liberals believed that their party once again had a realistic prospect of seizing power. Donald Maclean declared that it was well within the bounds of possibility that Liberals would be forming the next government, while some activists even spoke of repeating the performance of 1906. Almost all seemed ready to put past differences aside to make the most of the opportunity offered. 'Of course you and I can never trust the man,' admitted Henry Gladstone to his brother, 'but there he is the only possible leader for the time being.' A few months later he was ready to admit that 'new life' had been put into the party by Lloyd George's campaign, and that 'no Liberal of any colour will have a chance of getting into Parliament without making unemployment a first plank in the policy of the Liberal party'.[108] Richard Holt, making a sixth and final attempt to return to the Commons in North Cumberland, found a 'strong feeling that Ll G. has touched the popular imagination and that we ought not to throw cold water on his schemes'.[109] Even John Simon managed to pose as a loyal acolyte of Lloyd George. Back in September 1928, between two visits to India, he had warned that the party should not go into the next election 'like a cheap-jack in the fair' offering a 'patent remedy' to cure unemployment. Coming shortly after the publication of the Yellow Book, his words had understandably been interpreted as a stricture on his own party's proposals. Now, however, he explained, although without total conviction, that he had been referring only to protection and socialism as spurious cures for the problem of unemployment, and he expressed his unqualified support for 'the remarkable man who now leads the Liberal party'.[110] Runciman also modified his campaign to maintain an appearance of unity, though his ultimate aim remained to get enough like-minded Liberals elected to be able to snatch control of the party from Lloyd George after the election.

That election was the most competitive of the decade and as such provides the best guide to the underlying strength of the three main parties. More than three-quarters of all constituencies witnessed three-cornered fights and the Liberals themselves put 513 candidates into the field. For the Liberal Party, the most important feature of the results was confirmation of its third party status. Its representation went up to 59 MPs, compared with 40 in

1924. But these figures concealed more complex trends. Instead of building on their 1924 baseline, the Liberals contrived to lose 19 of the seats won that year while gaining 35 new ones. The party made a net gain of 28 seats from the Conservatives but suffered a net loss of 15 seats to Labour. Thus, in the contest that really mattered, Liberalism was still losing ground. Indeed, the most depressing feature was the continuing erosion of the party's position in the industrial areas of London, Lancashire, Yorkshire and the North-East. Labour, which now emerged as the largest single party in the new Parliament, had confirmed its status as the natural party of the British working class. Despite stressing the issue of unemployment, the Liberals had done worst in the largest cities. Arguably, they would have been better advised to focus their campaign on the needs of rural voters, that section of the electorate where the Liberal appeal remained strongest, than on the urban unemployed, most of whom were already firmly in the Labour camp.

In terms of votes the picture was somewhat more encouraging. More than five million electors (because of a further extension of the franchise in 1928, a higher figure than Liberals had ever secured before), 23.4 per cent of the total, had supported the party. But these figures only underlined Liberalism's dilemma. Its support was now spread too thinly to be effective within the existing electoral system. There were very few solidly Liberal constituencies, let alone areas, and only 15 candidates had secured an absolute majority of votes cast. The party's compelling need for electoral reform was starkly revealed. On average, there was one Liberal MP for every 91,000 votes; one Conservative for every 34,000; and one Labour member for every 28,000. 'You can imagine,' John Simon told the Indian viceroy, 'that our Liberals feel rather sore about this.'[111]

Labour Returns to Power

Once again, then, the Liberal Party had to decide how to respond to a minority Labour government. At least it had the advantage compared with 1924 that, with Labour now the largest single party, the government could survive a Liberal abstention and beat off Conservative opposition in the Commons with its own votes. In the wake of the election Liberals suffered what had now become the ritual of further defections. W. A. Jowitt, elected in the party's colours, found his way into the Labour government as Attorney-General, while Freddie Guest, having lost his seat in Bristol, defected to the Tories. For the time being, however, most Liberals seemed agreed on the need for united action to safeguard their party's existence. At the first party meeting after the election, John Simon 'smote his breast and declared that except on matters which could only be fitly decided in the sacred court of conscience – or words to that effect – no matter of opinion would induce him to do other than follow the crack of the whip'.[112] Seeming to have learnt from the experience of 1924, Lloyd George voiced his determination to secure reform of the electoral system, 'a speedy redress of this glaring wrong'. But E. D. Simon found the general tone of his leader's speech 'threatening', instead of 'looking forward to legislation on the fruitful field which is common to both parties'.[113]

Gradually, however, two distinct points of view emerged, or rather two extremes between which the by no means numerous members of the parliamentary Liberal Party placed themselves at assorted points. E. D. Simon, looking benignly on early evidence of Labour's plans for social reform, believed that 'in the national interest... it is quite clearly up to us to keep them in power and do all we can to help them to carry out an effective progressive policy'.[114] At the same time, he recognized that, from a party point of view, the position was more complex. If Liberals enabled Labour to complete a two-year programme of constructive reform, the government would get the credit. If, on the other hand, the Liberals turned out Labour prematurely, the country would resent it and punish the Liberals accordingly. But another group of Liberals, not interested as was Simon in 'economic equality', viewed Labour's proposals without enthusiasm. The parliamentary progress of the government's Coal Bill, published in December 1929, revealed the extent of Liberal divisions. On its second reading, the official Liberal stance was to oppose the bill, but two Liberals went into the government lobby while a further six abstained. At the committee stage, four Liberal MPs voted against a Liberal amendment and eight abstained. Any hope of consistency was doomed by marked changes in Lloyd George's own position. After a year of Labour government, Simon sensed three distinct phases in the leader's outlook: 'We have... had three periods during the year; a first one of peace, followed by one of war; then again a peaceful period. Now, judging by the last meeting, Mr Lloyd George intends another period of war.'[115]

By the second half of 1930, John Simon had emerged as the leading critic of Lloyd George's strategy. In the face of rapidly mounting unemployment the Labour government seemed to have few ideas and even fewer solutions. It was striking that when Oswald Mosley, one of the few ministers with a strategy to tackle the problem, resigned from the government, Simon wrote to express his 'great admiration'.[116] Then, in late October 1930, just before the opening of the new parliamentary session, Simon wrote to Lloyd George, giving advance notice of his current feelings on relations with the Labour government. He argued that, after 17 months in power, Labour had proved a complete failure in almost all departments. As a result, Liberals were deriving no benefit from the present situation, but were exposing themselves to the reproach that they were trying to save their own skins by avoiding another election. Simon announced that, should the government attempt to reverse the Baldwin government's trade union legislation, he would not be able to support them and on a vote of confidence would go into the Conservative lobby: 'We are in danger of carrying offers of assistance to the point of subservience and I do not believe that this is the way in which Liberalism is likely to become a more effective force in national and Imperial affairs.'[117]

At the heart of this dispute lay an issue that had become central for all Liberals in the era of three-party politics, but which had not needed a response when the Liberal Party itself had been one of the two contenders for power. Where exactly did it stand in relation to Labour and the Conservatives? 'The fundamental question for the Liberal Party,' wrote E. D. Simon,

> which has never been properly discussed at a party meeting, is whether, broadly, in the present circumstances, we prefer a Labour Government, with ourselves holding the balance, or whether, on the other hand, we should prefer to force a General Election, which would almost inevitably result in a Conservative Government with a large majority over both the other parties combined.[118]

Liberalism's inability to answer this question with a single voice signalled the outbreak of yet another, potentially fatal, phase of its self-destructive civil war. While John Simon now wished to bring the government down at the earliest opportunity, Lloyd George moved towards the idea of a formal pact with Labour. The stances taken by the two men involved a curious piece of symmetry. Lloyd George, who had worked in coalition with the Conservatives until 1922, now seemed ready to co-operate with Labour. Simon, who began the decade expressing sympathy with the objectives if not the means of the Labour Party, was about to open negotiations with the Conservatives which would eventually propel him into high office in the Conservative-dominated National Government. These personal political odysseys serve to emphasize the impossibility of subjecting the kaleidoscopic pattern of post-war Liberal politics to neat patterns of ideological division and interpretation. The very diversity of Liberal thinking, once seen to be one of the party's strengths, was now contributing to its undoing. Nothing revealed this more clearly than the issue of free trade, the ark of the Cobdenite covenant that had remained for so long an article of faith for all who professed to be true believers in the gospel of Liberalism. Rather like Home Rule after 1886, free trade had become the indispensable cement holding together the party's disparate strands. Over the course of the 1920s, however, as the British economy faced new and apparently intractable problems, particularly the ever-mounting levels of unemployment, even this most sacred of doctrines came under review. The First World War had fractured the once unassailable principles of internationalism and rationalism upon which it was based. As Keynes told the Summer School in 1925, 'we have to invent new wisdom for a new age'.[119]

Keynes and E. D. Simon were in fact among the first Liberal intellectuals to challenge the doctrine of free trade. Keynes became committed to the idea of tariffs during the course of 1930, while Simon found himself asking whether traditional free trade, appropriate when Britain was the undisputed workshop of the world, was still relevant in the changed circumstances of the twentieth century. At the Summer School of 1930 he called for a free and open enquiry into the whole subject, and suggested the advisability of a 10 per cent tax on all imports apart from raw materials. By the following March, John Simon also stressed that he was 'not going to shut out of [his] mind the consideration of fiscal measures which may be found to be necessary, even though they involve steps which in times of prosperity and abounding trade

Liberals would never contemplate'.[120] For many it was simply the case that, while theoretically desirable, free trade made no sense in a world where other nations imposed tariffs.

The extent of the party's disarray became apparent when Parliament reassembled in the autumn of 1930. When the Conservatives put down a motion on the King's speech, the official Liberal line was to abstain, but five Liberals, including John Simon and the chief whip, Sir Robert Hutchison (who promptly resigned), voted with the Tories, while four others went into the government lobby. Hutchison 'created a record by issuing a whip ... and then voting against it himself'.[121] Yet, at the meeting called to choose the chief whip's successor, only 30 Liberal MPs bothered to attend. Leading party members assembled on 20 November to hear Lloyd George propose a formal pact with Labour for two years. Simon spoke forcefully against this plan. The Labour government was already discredited and nothing would be gained by putting Liberal assets into a bankrupt concern. Indeed, at a subsequent General Election, Liberal candidates could scarcely criticize a party they had helped to sustain in power. The meeting broke up, having established little except the extent of the party's divisions. At a further meeting a week later, Lloyd George suggested a pact for a shorter period than two years in return for the introduction of the Alternative Vote, which, some Liberal strategists believed – probably erroneously – would double Liberal representation in the Commons. Simon, backed by Lord Reading, the Liberal leader in the Lords, opposed the whole notion of a bargain with the government. An arrangement for one year would turn into a bargain for two, since after twelve months it would be said that more time was needed to secure concessions from the government. Confusion again prevailed:

> Something was said at the end by Lloyd George about the difference between an agreement and an understanding and the conference ended ... without any clear information either as to what Lloyd George ... intended to say to the Cabinet Ministers, or as to what account might hereafter be given of the result of their further conversation.[122]

In the first months of 1931 the Liberal Party visibly collapsed as a unified political force. The parliamentary party degenerated into little more than a disorganized rabble. 'I am all for the party being independent and having a mind of its own,' conceded Archibald Sinclair, the new chief whip, 'but if individual members claim the same right, it is impossible for us to work effectively in the House of Commons.'[123] While Simon negotiated with the Conservatives about the possibility of their support at the next General Election for himself and those Liberal MPs prepared to follow him, Lloyd George moved closer to Labour, assuring George Lansbury that 'the great majority of our party are in accord with yours in the general line of advance for the next ten years'.[124] By the summer he seems to have been in talks with the government about a formal coalition that would have seen him become Leader of the House and Foreign Secretary or Chancellor. In the meantime, Simon, accompanied by Hutchison and Ernest Brown, formally resigned the Liberal whip on 26 June. The occasion was the Liberals' confused parliamentary response to the government's land tax proposals, a cause to which Lloyd George had first attached himself before the First World War. The specific issue scarcely merited Simon's withering indictment that the parliamentary party had reached a 'lower depth of humiliation than any into which it had yet been led'.[125] But in truth Simon's actual departure only symbolized a breach that had been growing ever since Labour took office.

National Government and Liberal Nationals

'The effect on the party is serious,' judged one Lloyd George supporter. This was a considerable understatement. Beatrice Webb was nearer the truth when she predicted the dissolution of the historic Liberal Party.[126] Had events been allowed to run their course, it seems probable that the Conservatives and the Simonite Liberals would have tried to eject the government once the House reassembled after the summer recess. As it was, such plans were overtaken by the dramatic internal collapse of the Labour cabinet. With the pound under severe pressure and the government unable to agree on a package of economy measures, the cabinet tendered its resignation on 23 August. On the following day, however, MacDonald re-emerged with the King's commission to form an all-party administration, charged with tackling the country's growing economic crisis. Lloyd George had been taken seriously ill in late July and it was his deputy, Herbert Samuel, who handled negotiations on behalf of the Liberals. In an atmosphere in which the King urged the party leaders to put the national interest first, Samuel had little alternative but to agree to Liberal participation. He and Reading now took office as Home and Foreign Secretary, respectively, in a new ten-man cabinet, while Donald Maclean, as President of the Board of Education, Sinclair as Scottish Secretary, and Crewe as Secretary for War, also took senior posts. The decision was warmly endorsed by the party as a whole; even Lloyd George gave guarded support from his sickbed. The new government pushed though a package of economies, but failed to 'save' the pound, which was forced off the Gold Standard on 21 September.

Though Simon had not received office in the National Government he was ready to offer his wholehearted support. On 23 September, 29 Liberals joined Simon, Runciman and Leslie Hore-Belisha in a memorial to the Prime Minister, supporting any measures the cabinet thought necessary to deal with the deficit in the balance of trade. As free-trade Liberals fully understood, this was meant to imply tariffs. Simon now accepted the invitation of more than two dozen Liberal MPs to lead the so-called Liberal National group, and on 5 October they formed a separate organization for the specific purpose of contesting the next election in alliance with the Conservatives and with MacDonald's tiny band of National Labour supporters. The holding of that election was bitterly opposed by the still ailing Lloyd George, and somewhat less strenuously by Samuel and Reading. Their reasons were clear enough. On the one hand the Conservatives were now looking to the electorate to provide a mandate to introduce tariffs. At the same time Liberals had good reason to fear the consequences of an election from a purely party point of view. Lloyd George's financial support had ended in June 1930, with immediate consequences for the party's grass-roots organization. As a result, Liberals had contested only a small percentage of the by-elections held during the lifetime of the Labour government, passing up several opportunities where Liberals had performed respectably in 1929. In those contests where Liberals did take part, they performed disastrously.

But, against Liberal opposition, a General Election was called for 27 October, with the government seeking a 'doctor's mandate' to continue its economic policies. Internal cabinet difficulties were papered over with the suggestion that each party should put forward its own programme under a blanket of anodyne words supplied by the Prime Minister. But Lloyd George denounced the election as 'an incredible act of reckless and criminal folly', while the growing separation of the Samuelite and Simonite factions was underlined by the differing situations their candidates faced in the constituencies.[127] While Conservatives opposed Samuelite Liberals in 81 seats, only four constituencies witnessed a clash between Conservatives and Liberal Nationals. Thus, while the Samuelites fielded 112 candidates, itself a somewhat pathetic total, their individual chances of victory were generally lower than those of the 41 Simonites. Liberal morale was low; the enthusiasm of 1929 had passed. The Samuelites offered little beyond an appeal for sacrifice at a time of national emergency, and an increasingly hollow faith in free trade. Maclean, wary of any perception of an alliance with the Conservatives, had little to contribute:

> the only thing left to us was to make it clear to the country that we had not supported the decision to have the election and that we had been prepared to continue the necessary effort to stabilize financial credit, and that we were facing the issue as free traders. That, at any rate, would be a clear, understandable position what-ever the result...We should maintain the existence of the party and avoid any responsibility for what was coming, namely another coupon Election.[128]

The outcome of the election was a major setback, only partially concealed by the peculiar circumstances in which it was held. The Conservatives returned no fewer than 473 MPs; Labour was reduced to just 52, the first real setback in its apparently inexorable rise over the previous 30 years. On the surface, the Liberals had done better; there were 33 Samuelites, 35 Liberal Nationals and 4 followers of Lloyd George. But the Liberal 'advance' compared with 1929 reflected only the electorate's temporary alienation from a Labour Party that the National Government had successfully presented as running away from its responsibilities in the face of a national emergency. Only 10 Liberals had been successful in the face of Conservative opposition. Thirteen seats won in 1929 were now lost, all to Conservatives, while 26 new gains were made, all at Labour's expense. Overall, the Liberal vote had fallen by more than three million, largely because of the reduction in the number of candidates. But it was striking that, in 51 constituencies fought by all three parties in both 1929 and 1931, the Liberal share of the poll dropped by 7.5 per cent, suggesting a measurable move to the Conservatives. Despite the latter's overwhelming strength in the new Commons, MacDonald was keen to emphasize the continuing 'national' character of his government. Though Reading and Crewe now retired, John Simon was rewarded for his loyalty by appointment to the Foreign Office, while Runciman became President of the Board of Trade. But was this, as Lloyd George had predicted, 'the death warrant of the Liberal Party as a separate Party'? 'You may have Ministers who are nominally Liberal in the so-called National Government,' he warned, 'but they will only be a miserable row of plucked boobies.'[129]

There has been widespread agreement among historians that the 1931 General Election marked the end of the road for the historic party of Gladstone and Asquith, at least in terms of its aspirations to be a party of government, and that there now began Liberalism's 'long diminuendo'.[130] Optimists, of course, were ready in 1931 to twist statistics to their own satisfaction. If the various Liberal factions were added together, a combined total of 72 MPs was reached. This enabled Walter Rea, soon to become the Samuelites' chief whip, to argue that Liberals were once more the second largest party in the Commons, with 20 seats more than Labour. Such a claim was disingenuous. Whatever had happened to its Commons strength, Labour's vote had held up quite well in 1931 – 30.6 per cent of the total compared with 37.1 per cent in 1929 – and was in any case nearly three times as large as the combined total of the assorted Liberal groupings. That said, it is at least arguable that the body of the Liberal Party was not yet a corpse and that the possibility of a partial recovery still existed, not least because of the huge setback the electoral system had administered to Labour. That party had suffered a considerable blow, not least in terms of its credibility as a party of government, because of the circumstances in which MacDonald's administration had collapsed. The apparently irreversible advance of the previous decade, achieved largely at Liberal expense, for the time being at least, had been arrested.

The key factor in the Liberal performance in 1931 was that, largely because of individual constituency arrangements reached by the various components of the National Government, the number of Liberal candidates fell from 513 in 1929 to just 160 in 1931. Thus, if many Liberal MPs now owed their presence in the Commons to the forbearance of the Conservatives, it was also true that many Conservative votes and probably some Conservative MPs were equally the consequence of the absence of Liberal candidates. Indeed, the 1931 election was held in such peculiar circumstances that it was unlikely to offer a reliable barometer of underlying Liberal support. It seems unrealistic to think that the potential reservoir of Liberalism in the country had dried up as dramatically or as quickly as the 1931 results suggested. After all, a little over two years earlier, almost a quarter of the electorate had registered support for Lloyd George's party. Furthermore, even in the Parliament of 1931, a united Liberal Party, outside the National Government, might have re-emerged as a significant challenger to the dominant Conservatives, especially in the context of Labour's disarray. Lloyd George certainly sensed an opportunity: 'If the Liberal Federation were to raise the standard,' he insisted, 'and bring out a resounding policy [at the annual meeting of the National Liberal Federation] at Clacton, millions of those who formerly looked to the Labour Party with hope, would rally to that standard.'[131] Early by-elections testified to the Liberals' opportunities. Labour's financial embarrassment was the main reason why no Labour candidate entered the field in as many as five by-elections in 1932. Meanwhile, there were some signs of a Liberal resurgence. In the absence of a Labour candidate, the Liberals performed respectably at Henley, Oxfordshire, on 25 February, cutting the Conservative majority by almost 50 per cent. At Dulwich, South London, in early June they moved up to second place from their third position at the General Election. Then, on 22 July and against most expectations, the Liberals held on to North Cornwall, despite the decision of the Conservatives, still their nominal partners inside the National Government, to field a candidate against them. Again, the Liberal performance was boosted by the absence of a Labour opponent. Sinclair enthused that this was the first time since the General Election that a government supporter had managed to increase his majority.

Yet, if the Liberals were going to stage a comeback, perhaps not to power but at least to the status of a significant parliamentary force, their basic requirement was unity. The formation of the National Government in August had partially concealed the reality of a divided party. That government was one that both the Samuelites and Simonites supported; both factions were now represented inside the cabinet. As long as the two groups remained within the same government, or both moved into opposition, there was always the possibility that they would eventually reunite. Certainly, the rank and file of both groups did not seem to believe that there had yet been an irrevocable parting of the ways. In the autumn of 1931 it did not seem inconsistent to be a member of the Liberal National group and also to belong to the Liberal Party itself. One Liberal National MP recorded attending a Liberal Party meeting on 2 October, before moving on to a gathering of the Simonite group.[132] But the following months would reveal that key figures in the Liberal National ranks, particularly Simon himself, stood very self-consciously in the way of reunion. The Liberal civil war, which had begun 15 years before, was ready to inflict one final and almost fatal body blow.

Once the election was over, Samuel moved rapidly to mend broken Liberal fences, only to meet with an unequivocal rebuff from both Lloyd George and Simon. The former, who had, of course, objected to holding an election, now insisted that he was not prepared to hold office again inside the parliamentary party, preferring to plough a lonely political furrow at the head of his tiny family grouping of MPs. Quite soon, his inclination was no longer 'in the direction of regaining the Liberal Party with its cranks and hypocrites at the top who all hate me and have always done so'.[133] Simon offered feeble excuses to avoid attending a meeting of Liberal leaders, and then gathered the courage to suggest that such a meeting should be postponed for the time being. The Samuelites issued a Liberal whip to all those MPs whose candidatures had been endorsed by local Liberal associations, but Simon's supporters chose instead to accept the government whip. Simon seemed more concerned about his relationship with the Prime Minister than that with his erstwhile Liberal colleagues, arguing at a dinner of his followers that 'the great thing was to assure Ramsay that he had a solid block behind him, irrespective of the Tories'.[134]

But at least both groups insisted that they remained 'Liberals'. If major divisions over policy could be avoided, the two factions might gradually coalesce, despite Simon's unhelpful attitude. Ironically, therefore, it was the issue of free trade, the issue that had brought Asquithians and Lloyd Georgeites to a qualified rec-onciliation in 1923 and remained for many Liberals the acid test of any potential adherent's credentials, which now ensured that there would be no coming together of Liberalism's disparate strands. If some Liberals continued to regard free trade as part of the par-ty's holy grail – 'I will vote regularly and persistently against this deadly tariff danger,' insisted Maclean[135] – for others it had lost its supreme significance in a rapidly changing world. Many now saw tariffs as a temporary tactical expedient, to be negotiated away when international circumstances changed. As Clement Davies later explained, the imposition of measures of protection by for-eign countries meant that 'we had to take some counter-measure in order to bring these other countries to a sense of reality'.[136] Early in 1932, the government's Import Duties Bill nearly provoked a major cabinet crisis. Superficial unity was maintained when min-isters agreed to follow Lord Hailsham's novel suggestion that, on this one issue, the traditional doctrine of collective cabinet respon-sibility should be suspended, thus allowing members the luxury of agreeing to differ. The agreement to differ did not prompt any sig-nificant movement inside the Liberal Party. But it did contribute to a growing mood of bewildered confusion about what Liberals were doing within the National Government. Divisions became public when, on 24 February, an amendment was moved in the Commons to exclude food from the list of commodities that would be subject to duties. The Samuelites voted as a group in support of this amendment but the Simonites were divided – 10 following their Liberal colleagues, but nine backing the government. This might have been the occasion for compromise but such thoughts appear not to have entered Simon's mind, convinced as he now was of the need for protectionist measures. In the current state of the national economy, it was 'no good prescribing a long sea voy-age as a cure for persistent haemorrhage; you must try to stop the bleeding'.[137] Simon's vision of the future appeared not to encom-pass Liberal reunion:

> I have a feeling that, after the experience through which we have passed, both in peace and in war, it may very well be that there will emerge an outlook on current political questions which will not be confined to any one of the old political parties and in which we shall be able really to influence one another.[138]

A further important step towards the formalization of divisions within Liberal ranks was taken in July 1932, with the setting up of the Liberal National Council. Designed as a rallying point for those Liberals wanting to give wholehearted support to the National Government, it was also part of a concerted effort by the Liberal National leadership to present their group rather than the Samuelites as the true standard-bearers of Liberalism in the country.

Matters came to a head later in 1932, when the government succeeded in negotiating the Ottawa Agreements to establish a scheme of Imperial Preference. For most Free Trade Liberals this was the last straw. But the Prime Minister was keen to keep the Samuelites inside the government in order to maintain the pretence of an all-party administration and thus to justify his own position at its head. 'If you go,' he pleaded with Samuel, 'I am no longer the head of a combination ... I should be regarded as a limpet in office.'[139] As MacDonald had only managed to bring a small number of Labour MPs into the National Government, the Liberals enjoyed an importance beyond their numerical strength. Their presence helped to conceal the essentially conservative nature of the programme upon which the cabinet had embarked. Simon, however, urged that the presence of the Liberal Nationals alone would suffice to sustain the government's 'national' credentials, while the Liberal National President of the Board of Trade, Walter Runciman, pressed for the immediate filling by Liberal Nationals of any governmental vacancies caused by the resignation of free traders in response to Ottawa: 'This is partly for the look of the thing – preserving the broad base – and partly to keep alive loyalty to the government in circles which had Liberal antecedents.'[140] Senior Liberal Nationals were fully aware of the enormous importance of what might now happen: 'Assuming we continue our support of the Government,' wrote the group's chief whip, Geoffrey Shakespeare, 'our lines of communication with the Liberal party will be cut for ever. Ottawa will be our Rubicon. There can be no re-crossing.'[141] Such a price was only worth paying if the Liberal Nationals could secure assurances from the Conservatives regarding the content of the government's future programme, the allocation of government posts vacated by Samuelites and the withdrawal of Conservative opposition at constituency level at the next election.

By the early autumn, Simon had succeeded in striking as good a bargain as he could have hoped for from the Conservatives. He met Baldwin on 27 September and followed up his interview with a letter the following day. His chief concern was with 'the prospective electoral position' of his Liberal National group 'who represent a large body of Liberal opinion'. Once Samuel and his followers left the government, 'the position of these friends of mine in the constituencies will be much more difficult and they will very soon be exposed to every sort of attack and pressure from the organisations who approve Samuel's démarche'. [142] Simon argued that the Commons division on the second reading of the bill implementing the Ottawa Agreements should be seen as the acid test. He hoped that those Liberal Nationals who then supported the government could be assured that they would not face Conservative opposition at the next General Election. In the circumstances there was more than a trace of hypocrisy in Simon's scribbled note of pained regret passed to Samuel at the cabinet meeting of 28 September, at which the latter and his colleagues finally announced their resignations. A private letter to Lady Hilton Young came closer to expressing Simon's true feelings: 'Samuel has chosen an amazing moment to go, for the whole world is now rocking and in the middle of an earthquake it will not be much good to howl "Ottawa".'[143]

While Baldwin pondered Simon's proposals, the Liberal Nationals had good reason to be pleased with the governmental reshuffle necessitated by the Samuelites' resignations. The appointment of Godfrey Collins to the vacant Scottish Office meant that there were now three Liberal Nationals in the cabinet. At the same time, several others, including Leslie Hore-Belisha and Leslie Burgin, were promoted within the government's junior ranks. It was said that rank-and-file Conservatives were dismayed by the allocation of posts that had given the Liberal Nationals an influence within the administration out of proportion to their numerical strength. Baldwin then sent Simon a 'letter of reassurance' about the position of sitting Liberal National MPs and gave public expression to his message in a speech at Blackpool on 7 October. His statement that those who backed the Ottawa Bill 'right through' should not suffer was, he informed Simon, received enthusiastically. Though Baldwin had to remind him that local Conservative constituency parties were not under the direct control of Conservative Central Office, Simon was 'entitled to assume that support will be forthcoming for those Liberal Members of Parliament who are prepared to give consistent support to the Government'.[144] The position of the Liberal Nationals was thus secured. But how long they would be able to maintain any genuine independence of the Conservatives was another issue. One suggested that Ottawa might lead to a new alignment of political parties: 'It may mean the creation of a Centre or National Party to face the country when next the opinion of the electors is sought.'[145] Just as likely, however, the Liberal Nationals would soon be subsumed within the ranks of the Tory party.

Into the Wilderness

By contrast, the position of Samuel's independent Liberals was becoming anomalous in the extreme. Though they had left the administration, they continued to occupy government benches in the Commons. Samuel was concerned that, in crossing the floor, he might suffer the loss of further MPs. For another year, therefore, the Liberals stayed on the government's side of the House amid mounting protest from the party's rank and file, an eloquent commentary on their ill-defined identity. 'The longer we remain in our present position,' warned Sinclair,

> the more inglorious, embarrassing and insignificant it becomes. Our speeches of criticism of the government and manifestos of Liberal policy will make no impression so long as it lasts; and while it is true that it would be disastrous to go into opposition at a time and manner that commanded no public interest or support, I doubt if we can remain where we are for long without witnessing the complete disintegration of the party.[146]

By the autumn of 1933, even Samuel recognized that this state of affairs could continue no longer: 'the party would fade away'.[147] But when the move did take place, the party suffered further damage. As Samuel had feared, several MPs remained on the government's side of the House and eventually joined the Liberal Nationals.

The events of 1931–33 were of crucial long-term importance for the Liberal Party. It may be argued that, by his withdrawal from the National Government on a point of principle and his eventual resumption of opposition status, Samuel ensured that the party would survive as an independent entity in British politics. But the circumstances in which these events occurred meant that the party was now a less effective force than ever before. British politics would be re-established on a two-party basis and, despite its performance in the 1931 General Election, the path was clear for the Labour Party to re-emerge as the only viable alternative to the Conservatives. Despite Lloyd George rejoining the Liberal Party in November 1935, the Samuelite–Simonite split of 1932 proved to be permanent. For some time the Samuelites behaved as if this latest breach could be healed. In late November 1932, Henry Morris-Jones found them making 'desperate efforts to win over Simonites'.[148] A year later, Samuel was still proclaiming that his aim was to gather together all Liberals. In 1934, the *Liberal Magazine* suggested that the Liberal Nationals were bound in the course of time to reunite with the Liberal Party. But the Liberal National leadership had made its choice, and that choice precluded reunion. The years ahead would witness several attempts to restore Liberal unity but to no avail, though many individuals did continue to cross over from one group to the other. Drawing ever closer to their Tory allies, the Liberal Nationals (restyled the National Liberals in 1948) maintained a theoretically independent identity into the 1960s before finally fusing with the Conservative Party.

The continued existence of the Liberal Nationals prevented Liberalism from maximizing its potential vote at a time when the mainstream party continued to decline remorselessly. Liberal Nationals were in place and tended to remain so in constituencies where a significant Liberal tradition persisted. One option was for the Liberals to try to reassert their claim to that tradition. But, after burning their fingers in a by-election in East Fife in Scotland in February 1933, they drew back from challenging Liberal Nationals in their constituencies. As a result, only in Oldham, Lancashire, and Denbigh, North Wales, did the two factions confront one another in the 1935 General Election. Some confusion thus persisted through the 1930s and into the post-war era as to who really represented true Liberalism. In 1937, a former Liberal Party treasurer used the argument of reclaiming sole ownership of the Liberal name to justify his suggested strategy of destroying the Liberal National Party.[149] More important, the close association of the Liberal Nationals and the Conservatives enabled the latter to broaden their appeal to the electorate to attract the residue of the Liberal vote, especially in constituencies where no Liberal candidate came forward. Philip Snowden, Labour's former Chancellor, who left the National Government at the same time as Samuel, summed up the situation as early as January 1933: 'the Simonite Tories keep up the pretence of being Liberals in order to secure the support of innocent Liberals for the Tory Party'.[150] This strategy was employed deliberately by Baldwin in the 1930s and by an array of post-war Conservative leaders, including Churchill. It contributed to the telling argument that there was no longer any need for a Liberal party *per se*; the Conservatives had been liberalized from within. The Tories thus managed to keep a firm grip on the spectrum of political opinion that was vital to the Liberals if they were ever to revive, even as a third force in British politics.

This situation left the independent Liberals, even after they crossed over to the opposition benches, with a crisis of identity. Two years of struggling to come to terms with a minority Labour government had been followed by a similar period of disarray over the issue of participation in the National Government. Even now, however, the Samuelites had difficulty in differentiating themselves from the government. The National Government had taken over the traditional Liberal rallying cries of retrenchment and sound finance, but without appearing unduly reactionary or illiberal. 'So long as Baldwin presses so far to the middle and is at war with his Diehards,' commented Sir William Sutherland, Lloyd George's former Press Secretary, 'it is not clear where Samuel is going to crash in with a separate identity and policy.'[151] A reluctance persisted to oppose a government set up to deal with a national emergency:

> Therefore in the opposition which it will be the duty of the Liberal Parliamentary Party to offer in the House of Commons ... there will be no resort to those traditional tactics of Parliamentary warfare which are aimed at the indiscriminate obstruction of Government business and are animated by a desire to thwart, embarrass and trip up the Government by every legitimate Parliamentary resource.[152]

One Liberal activist complained that, while the man in the street knew roughly what a Socialist state and a Conservative one would mean, 'he has precious little notion of the Liberal state'.[153]

An attempt to hammer out a coherent set of Liberal policies began under Lord Lothian's auspices in the autumn of 1932 and continued throughout the following year. But agreement on issues other than free trade proved elusive. Even on this question, the commitment of some Liberals was weakening, not least because improvements in the balance of payments suggested that the introduction of tariffs was having a beneficial effect. One leading Samuelite admitted that 'the possibility of a world system of complete free trade has gone and probably will never return'.[154] At this time, Liberals needed the fertility of a mind such as Lloyd George's, but it was not available to them. Samuel was an able parliamentarian but he lacked the qualities of inspirational leadership of which his party was in desperate need. Lloyd George's interventionist philosophy was gradually abandoned. According to one Liberal newspaper, many in the party were 'not in love with the proposals which emanate from some of their leaders for borrowing and spending huge sums of money'.[155] Sinclair's biographer has captured well the increasingly conservative image projected by the party in the early 1930s: 'When it came to policy the party would henceforth follow the path of caution, returning like wounded animals to the safe lairs of the past, espousing free trade, justice and equality, none of which was directly relevant to Britain's immediate problems. The Yellow Book gathered dust on Liberal shelves.'[156] The radicalism that had characterized the Summer School movement of the early 1920s and the Lloyd George revival later in the decade retreated once more to the periphery of the Liberal Party. It was still there. Ramsay Muir, for example, published *The Liberal Way* in 1934. He suggested, *inter alia*, that the Bank of England 'ought to be freed from any suspicion that its powers might be used for party ends' – an idea not acted on until the late 1990s.[157] But Muir's was no longer the public face of British Liberalism.

It is difficult to escape the conclusion that many leading Liberals were losing faith in themselves, with inevitable and disastrous consequences for the party in the country. Muir, a man who had done much to keep alive the flame of independent Liberalism, now took 'a most gloomy, almost a despairing view of our prospects. We are beaten in advance by the public idea that we are done for, and this affects our own people.'[158] Sinclair warned of a 'real danger' that the party would 'cease to be regarded as an effective fighting force'. A shortage of both money and personnel in the constituencies made it hard to 'maintain...activities at a level of intensity over a prolonged period'.[159] The decline of Liberalism as a force in local government continued apace. Apart from 1931, the party suffered a net loss of council seats each year as the decade progressed. The process of decay was particularly marked in the industrial towns of the North and Midlands. A few scattered gains at Conservative expense in middle-class seaside resorts afforded scant compensation. Symbolically, even in Manchester, with its long radical tradition, Liberals effectively gave up their independence when, in 1931, they joined the Conservatives in an anti-Labour pact.[160] By 1933, with Labour showing signs of moving back to the political centre ground, Lothian concluded that the Liberal Party's position was 'almost hopeless'.[161]

The loss of Lloyd George had inevitable financial implications. By 1931, revenue from the Liberal Central Association's subscription list had fallen to about £500 per annum. Party headquarters was in effect being maintained by Lloyd George, who had earlier promised a sum of £30,000 for the next General Election. When, however, that election was held in circumstances of which he disapproved, Lloyd George withdrew his offer and the election was fought by means of a hastily raised fund of just £17,000. From the Whips Office, Harcourt Johnstone, who expended much of his private wealth trying to keep Liberalism afloat, bemoaned the 'worry and strain of trying to carry on the organisation of a political party without knowing for two months in advance whether the inevitable liabilities can be met or not'. He doubted whether he had 'ever in these 10 miserable, discouraging years...been so sorely tempted to chuck the whole thing and be a free man again'.[162] In brief, the Liberal Party could no longer pose as a credible party of national government. Its resources were insufficient and its local base too attenuated to play the role it had just about sustained throughout the 1920s. The logical option might have been to focus on a clearly targeted narrow front in those areas of the country, such as the South-West, where Liberalism remained a viable political force. An alternative would have been to seek an alliance with Labour in the face of the Conservatives' overwhelming strength in the Commons. But most of the party's leading figures 'still regarded politics purely in terms of major international and domestic issues, which meant that they were unable to adopt an alternative role based on low politics'.[163] As a result, the party tried hard to convince itself that revival was at hand, and that a Liberal government remained a realistic proposition rather than a self-deluding pipe-dream.

Liberals thus had no real reason to face the 1935 General Election with anything other than apprehension. There was little sign of a clear and viable political identity emerging. On some social issues, the party seemed indistinguishable from Labour. On other matters, however, differentiation from the National Government was not easy. By May 1935, the Liberals were ready to support the government's policy of increased expenditure on defence. By-election performances since going into opposition had been distinctly poorer than before this move. At Cambridge in February 1934, the Liberal share of the vote fell from 25 per cent in 1929 to just 7 per cent. A week later at Lowestoft, Suffolk, the corresponding fall was from 31 per cent to 10 per cent. Largely for financial reasons, the party failed to contest seven of the twelve by-elections held between April and December of that year. The fiction was maintained that the party would contest the General Election on a broad front, thus offering voters the realizable prospect of a Liberal government. To declare otherwise would be to invite 'a scream of rage from all the Party Organizations and an immediate collapse of the Associations which had been told that it was not intended that they should contest the election'; 'We must try to keep up the bluff until the last moment,' declared Harcourt Johnstone, 'or decide here and now to disband the Liberal Party as an organized political entity.'[164] Attempts to restore Lloyd George to the party's inner councils broke down over the Welshman's efforts to radicalize the Liberals' programme for the forthcoming contest. After this he showed a growing readiness to endorse selected Labour candidates and, early in 1935, launched his New Deal campaign aimed at bringing together all those of progressive views who were critical of the National Government's performance.

In the event, Baldwin, Prime Minister since June, called the election for 14 November. As late as June, fewer than 100 Liberal candidates were in place. Last-minute funding for those willing to subscribe to Lloyd George's Council of Action helped to bring the total up to 161. But the resulting narrow-front campaign was not one for which the party had carefully planned. It represented no more than the tactics of necessity and, in any case, many constituencies were fought where the Liberals entertained no hope of success. The brief Liberal manifesto contained no surprises and aroused little interest. Several national newspapers ignored its publication. Its stirring title, *A Call to Arms*, seemed curiously ill-chosen. Even the *News Chronicle*, the only mass-circulation national newspaper to offer its support, noted that the Liberals would 'be lucky to hold what they have'.[165] It was somewhat strange that two of the three Liberal radio broadcasts were delivered by Lloyd George, whose connection with the party was now tenuous, and Lord Snowden who, despite a close association with Samuel since 1932, was still best remembered as Labour's Chancellor of the Exchequer. Samuel's own broadcast on 6 November conceded that the government had made some progress since 1932, but argued that issues such as the Means Test, high unemployment and the Ottawa Agreements remained to be tackled. Where no Liberal was standing, he urged support for candidates who had satisfied the scrutiny of Lloyd George's Council of Action questionnaire. But that still left about 300 seats where Liberal voters were offered no guidance. Perhaps it was not needed. Much of the National Government campaign, not least its apparently firm commitment to the Covenant of the League of Nations, was geared towards that band of centre opinion that Conservative Central Office believed held the key to its return to office. In his broadcast on behalf of the government, Simon stressed that Liberalism was distinct from the Liberal Party and assured Liberal voters that they could place their trust confidently in Baldwin.

After what most observers judged to be a feeble campaign, Liberals should have been prepared for a result of unmitigated disaster. With only 6.4 per cent of the total vote, the party saw just 21 MPs returned to the new Parliament. Apart from Archibald Sinclair, the party's entire front bench, including Samuel, narrowly ousted by the Conservatives in Darwen, Lancashire, went down to defeat. Meanwhile, despite a net gain of 94 seats for Labour, the National Government remained firmly entrenched, with an over-all majority in excess of 250 seats. It was rewarded for seeing the country through the worst phases of the international depression, its reputation reinforced by the expectation of even better times to come. Perhaps as many as 150 of the Conservatives elected in 1931 had owed their success to their 'National' credentials. The fact that many of them held on to their seats in 1935, by which time the Liberal Party was once more in opposition, was indicative of Baldwin's success in convincing the electorate that his version of Liberal Toryism had now captured the vital centre ground of British politics. The government had retained the support of a substantial proportion of the country's 'Liberal' vote. As a result, and for the first time in the twentieth century, the Liberal Party itself appeared entirely irrelevant to the country's political fortunes. Its small band of MPs could exert no influence in the face of the parliamentary arithmetic of the day. Whether the victim of suicide or murder, the body itself seemed indubitably dead.

3 So Few and So Futile, 1935–55

A Spiral of Decline

In the 20 years after the General Election of 1935, the Liberal Party showed few if any signs of genuine revival. All the statistics and indices of decline, already established, continued to move in an unfavourable direction. The debilitating haemorrhage of Liberal votes seemed to have no end. Both in Parliament and local government the reduction of Liberal representation continued apace. The parliamentary party of 21, bequeathed by Herbert Samuel to his successor, went down progressively at succeeding General Elections, reaching an all-time low of just five MPs following the loss of the Carmarthen by-election in February 1957. Ironically, the victor in this contest was Lloyd George's daughter, Megan, newly welcomed, like so many radical Liberals before her, into the ranks of the Labour Party. Five months earlier, a Gallup poll had put the party's national support at a derisory 1 per cent of the electorate. Municipal elections continued to witness a fall in the overall number of Liberal candidates, and in the percentage of those who were successful at the polls. The proportion of council seats won dropped from 14 per cent in 1931 to just 7.2 per cent in 1938.[1] The existing tendency of Liberal councillors to form local pacts with their more numerous Conservative counterparts intensified. Bristol was among the important cities where Liberals in the 1930s submerged their identity within an anti-Socialist alliance. This trend may have saved individual Liberals from exclusion from their councils, but it did nothing to preserve a separate and recognizable Liberal identity, and it stored up problems for any future attempt to redefine independent Liberalism. In many ways, the logical conclusion to this spiral of decline was the complete elimination of the Liberal Party, at least as a national political force. Many saw its survival as no more than 'the obstinate refusal of a

128

dying party to accept [its] fate'.[2] Yet survive it did, even though this survival owed less to rational calculation than to the unshakeable conviction of a small band of dedicated followers that better days would eventually return.

Archibald Sinclair, chosen to lead the parliamentary rump following the electoral debacle of 1935, faced a disheartening future. Demoralized by the loss of key colleagues and with benefactors and supporters continuing to leave an apparently sinking ship, he personally doubted whether the Liberals could possibly sustain their credentials as a nationwide organization for much longer.[3] With the periodic subventions from Lloyd George's political fund now consigned to history, finance remained the party's most obvious headache. Despite hopes that their base of financial support could be broadened, the Liberals continued to rely on the generosity of a small number of wealthy benefactors. But the available cash was seldom adequate. Over the next decade, the party's annual income never reached £15,000 and sometimes struggled to attain half that figure, a slim foundation for a supposedly national party.

The state of the party's organization was the easiest cat to kick. The Meston Committee was set up with a broad remit to propose changes. Its major recommendation led in 1936 to the replacement of the National Liberal Federation by the Liberal Party Organisation, with the aim of creating a single policy-making body, though in practice authority over policy remained divided. None the less, some improvements did result and the party was certainly in better heart in the late 1930s than during Samuel's leadership. More fundamental issues witnessed less progress. Perhaps the most basic were the party's identity and place within the political spectrum, and its resulting best strategy for the future.

It was not obvious by the mid-1930s what made independent Liberalism distinctive. Sinclair would mouth platitudes about a non-socialist alternative to the Conservative-dominated National Government, but convincing voters of the viability of this image was another matter. Lothian had identified the problem as early as 1933:

> From a party point of view Liberalism is in an almost hopeless position, so long as Baldwin is leader of the Conservative Party and Arthur Henderson the leading figure in the Labour Party. [The point was equally valid once Attlee became Labour leader in 1935.]

> Both are democrats, liberally minded, supporters of disarmament
> and the League of Nations, and constitutionalists. Both, too, are
> moderate tariffists, even friendly, in theory, to free trade.[4]

For all its subsequent bad press, the National Government was in no
sense an administration of the far right. Its leading Conservative
members, such as Baldwin, Neville Chamberlain and Samuel
Hoare, had well-established moderate, even liberal, pedigrees,
while right-wingers, including Churchill, were kept firmly on the
political sidelines. In part, this was a matter of conviction. But
Conservative strategists also believed that, by shifting the party's
centre of gravity leftwards, Conservatism could appeal to a broader
electorate, including the supposedly still large 'Liberal vote', than
would otherwise be the case. The National Government's electoral
supremacy throughout the decade lends a measure of credibility to this analysis. As Lothian reflected in the wake of the 1935
General Election, while a distinctive Liberal attitude to public
affairs appeared to persist, the voters seemed to identify it with
Baldwin.[5]

Not least of the Conservative leader's advantages in developing this strategy was his ongoing partnership with the Liberal
Nationals. As the Conservative leader once commented of his block
of 'Liberal' supporters, 'they are my body guard'.[6] The continuing existence of the Liberal Nationals sowed seeds of confusion
in the minds of some electors about who in fact now represented
the authentic voice of British Liberalism. In policy terms, by the
middle of the decade little seemed to divide the two Liberal factions other than their attitudes to the existing administration. But,
spared Tory opposition at the recent General Election, the Liberal
Nationals had become the numerically stronger parliamentary
body.

The Liberals' quest to establish a distinctive identity was not
helped by their own continuingly equivocal attitude towards the
Liberal Nationals. After the experience of the East Fife by-election
in February 1933, the mainstream party was extremely reluctant to
confront Liberal Nationals in their own constituencies, or even to
set up rival local Liberal Associations. As a result, only two isolated
contests took place between the competing groups at the 1935
General Election. Liberal Nationals were thus allowed to hold the
field in many constituencies where there was a significant Liberal

tradition. As Sinclair wrote as late as 1937: 'We at Headquarters cannot – at any rate yet – countenance attacks upon seats held by Liberal National members of Parliament. They have not yet done it to us openly, and we should have to consider very carefully before we took the initiative against them.'[7] The position did change somewhat after the St Ives by-election that June, when Isaac Foot came close to defeating the Liberal National candidate. Even so, a tendency remained to look upon the Liberal Nationals as errant sheep who would one day return to the fold, and it was striking that the Liberal Year Books continued to list Liberal National organizations among those of the Liberal Party itself until the end of the decade.

The period before the outbreak of war saw few new developments in party policy. In 1939, J. L. Hammond commended Lord Crewe for his consistency to 'Mr Gladstone's principles' without apparently seeing that Crewe's ongoing commitment to the Liberalism of the nineteenth century was part of the party's problems.[8] Ironically, while the radical ideas worked out in *Britain's Industrial Future* and *We Can Conquer Unemployment* began to find their way into the thinking of such bodies as Political and Economic Planning and the Next Five Years Group, becoming by the mid-1940s part of a new orthodox consensus, their importance within Liberal circles declined. With Baldwin's Conservatism espousing the more traditional Liberal virtues of fiscal prudence and retrenchment, Liberals had little beyond the increasingly weather-worn slogan of 'free trade' to call their own. But free trade had lost much of its electoral appeal in the face of mounting unemployment and a stagnant economy. It also hindered attempts to carve out an electorally attractive agricultural policy for those rural areas where a residual inclination towards Liberalism was probably strongest. No single Liberal ideology prevailed at this time; the party embraced both planners and free marketeers. On balance, however, 'the Liberal Party was consistently libertarian rather than collectivist. It placed the greatest stress upon the basic importance of the individual, saw the government's role as sustaining his rights [and] was aware of the dangers of the concentration of economic and political power.'[9]

It was foreign policy that offered Liberals the clearest opportunity to strike out on their own and to differentiate themselves from the Conservative-dominated National Government. The turning point was the Hoare–Laval crisis of December 1935. Coming only months after a General Election in which all parties had competed with one another to convince the electorate of their commitment to the principles of the League of Nations, this attempt to buy off Mussolini's aggression at the territorial expense of the African kingdom of Abyssinia suggested a lack of good faith on the government's part. Donald Johnson, who had contested Bury, Lancashire, for the Liberals at the election, recalled that while 'the Hoare–Laval Plan did not save Abyssinia or even a portion of it, it did ... save the Liberal Party for a further lease of life'.[10] A plausible case has been made for a viable Liberal alternative to the government's appeasement of the European dictators. Until 1938 this involved 'making it clear that the League was capable of, and willing to, remedy grievances through formal procedures which would lead to economic disarmament'.[11] By 1938, recognizing that the League was all but dead, Liberals moved towards a stance of ensuring that all concessions had behind them the threat of force from a powerful alignment of states ready to act if Germany or Italy broke their agreements. The Liberals' position was similar to Labour's but free of the latter's reluctance to accept the need for rearmament.

Sinclair himself deserves credit for his honourable stance during a decade that ruined the reputations of so many of his political contemporaries. He retained, for perhaps too long, an idealistic faith that the League could still play an effective role in international affairs. In 1938, however, he urged a strong stand over Czechoslovakia, and after Munich condemned the government's successive retreats in the face of aggressive dictatorships. But the divisions that had plagued Liberalism when it was a much larger parliamentary force had not gone away now that it was reduced to a rump. In the key Commons debate on the Munich settlement in early October 1938, 14 Liberals voted against the government, but four voted in support and two did not vote at all. Over the introduction of conscription early in 1939, Liberal divisions were even more apparent, with six MPs voting in favour and seven against. A Liberal alternative to the government's policy may have been articulated by Sinclair, but it was not espoused by his predecessor, Herbert Samuel, whose support for Munich prompted Neville Chamberlain to offer him a cabinet seat. Arguably, of course, 'appeasement' was the authentic and tragically mistaken view of liberalism (if not of Liberalism) in the inter-war years – the unshakeable belief in man's rationality and a refusal to contemplate his complete corruption by the forces of evil.

At all events it seems unlikely that the party's approach to international affairs did much to enhance its electoral prospects. Sinclair recovered his optimism, buoyed up by a mini-revival in the party's electoral fortunes in 1937 when, in addition to near misses at St Ives and North Dorset, Donald Johnson polled respectably at Bewdley, Worcestershire, vacated when Baldwin moved to the House of Lords. Confident that Liberal revival lay on a tantalizingly close horizon, Sinclair was at first cautious about alternative strategies of electoral pacts and co-operation urged upon him by other senior Liberals. Lothian, for example, contemplated the need for Liberals to join either the Conservative or the Labour Party and to 'liberalise from within'.[12] Others called for Liberal participation in a Popular Front to oppose the National Government at home and fascism abroad, and the last years of peace saw several examples of electoral co-operation. Liberal MPs such as Wilfrid Roberts and Richard Acland regularly appeared on Labour platforms, and even Sinclair showed interest, while remaining reluctant to compromise the party's independence. Whether such co-operation would have been repeated at the next General Election remains unclear. In the event, the promising performances of 1937 proved to be no more than a typical mid-term reaction against the incumbent government. In 1938, the party contested just two of 18 by-elections. T. L. Horabin held on to North Cornwall in July 1939, but there seems little reason to question his opinion that there was no prospect of any substantial Liberal gains in the General Election widely anticipated for the autumn of that year.[13] In the view of the admittedly not impartial Hugh Dalton, the party had become 'a living corpse'.[14]

Over the 1935 Parliament as a whole, the parliamentary party cut a poor image, regardless of some impressive personal performances by Sinclair. One MP recalled that, while Liberal MPs met on a weekly basis to decide their voting intentions, in the event each tended to vote as he or she wished.[15] Too much work fell on the shoulders of a small, if willing, band. As Percy Harris, the party's chief whip, remembered ruefully:

'Speaking on behalf of my honourable friends', I would say, to the jeers of the honourable members opposite, looking to the left of me, only to find I was alone on the bench. It was a great experience: I learnt every move in the game and I hope it was worth while, though I sometimes doubt it. Certainly Liberals outside knew little of the work I was putting in to save their heritage for them.[16]

Second World War

The coming of European war in September 1939 disrupted the normal patterns of political development in Britain, not least because it postponed for the duration of hostilities the, by then, imminent General Election. Prime Minister Neville Chamberlain invited the Liberals, along with Labour, to join his government, but both parties declined. With no position in the War Cabinet on offer, the Liberals decided that they would be obliged to accept joint responsibility for government policy without sharing control over its creation. In May 1940, however, Churchill formed a genuinely all-party coalition in which Sinclair became Secretary of State for Air, while Harcourt Johnstone and Dingle Foot took junior positions at the Board of Trade and the Ministry of Economic Warfare, respectively. For the first time, therefore, since the Samuelites' resignation in 1932, Liberals returned to the seats of power. Though not a member of the War Cabinet, Sinclair took part in the crucial discussions of late May 1940 over whether to open peace talks. Yet it is doubtful if the party derived any long-term advantage from its occupation of office, with Sinclair incurring criticism for failing to exert influence over the general tone of the government. If anything, the circumstances of wartime exacerbated the internal divisions that had plagued it for at least a generation. Sinclair's understandable absorption with the Air Ministry deprived the party of a sense of leadership and direction, while encouraging the suspicion that he might ultimately follow the example of so many Liberals before him and defect to the political enemy. 'I feel sure,' noted Violet Bonham Carter in June 1944, 'that Archie's one desire is to remain with W[inston] and continue to work in much the present set-up.'[17] Sinclair had served as second-in-command to Churchill with the 6th Royal Scots Fusiliers in the First World War and there were those who believed that he continued, metaphorically at least, to stand to attention when in the Prime Minister's presence. Those Liberals for whom no government office was found grouped themselves, almost as a party within the party, under Percy Harris. Even here, divisions persisted over the extent to which the government could legitimately direct and manage the wartime state, divisions that were bound to become acute once attention turned to the problems of reconstruction and the sort of society that the Liberals wanted to see emerge when peace returned.

As in the First World War, the politicians of the three main parties responded to the grave external threat from Hitler's Germany by declaring a moratorium on domestic politics with the suspension of by-election contests, allowing the incumbent party to nominate an unopposed successor in the event of a vacancy. Before long, however, this self-denying ordinance began to create frustration among the Liberal rank and file. When attempts to move a resolution against the Party Truce were thwarted at the 1941 Assembly, the Liberal Action Group, later renamed Radical Action, was formed that November. The founders included Lancelot Spicer, Honor Balfour, Everett Jones and Donald Johnson, and they were later joined by more prominent Liberals, including Clement Davies, Megan Lloyd George and Tom Horabin. Over the following three years, several known Liberals stood at by-elections as 'independents' and often achieved respectable polls, benefiting, like the short-lived Common Wealth Party, from the national wartime swing against the Conservatives. Johnson came close to victory at Chippenham, Wiltshire, in August 1943, while Miss Balfour all but regained Darwen, Lancashire, Samuel's old seat, that December. The following February, Mrs Corbett Ashby secured 44 per cent of the vote at Bury St Edmunds, Suffolk.

These performances encouraged many Liberal activists to believe that their party was on the brink of a great resurgence, held back only by the constraints of the wartime truce and the delay in holding a general election. Such thinking received apparent endorsement from the increasingly 'liberal' ethos that came to permeate the war years. John Maynard Keynes and William Beveridge, two men whose ideas seemed set to dominate the postwar world, were, after all, both Liberals, and the latter entered Parliament as a beneficiary of the by-election truce as member for Berwick-upon-Tweed in the North-East in October 1944. Beveridge himself 'believe[d] genuinely in the Liberal Revival of which [he] spoke'.[18] But he probably overestimated the party's readiness to move towards the sort of state-regulated economy he espoused. It was striking that when two veteran Liberal peers discussed their party's approach to the parliamentary debate on the Beveridge Plan, Lord Crewe merely informed Lord Samuel that 'he might say something very briefly in general support of the proposals though not making any direct attack on the Government' – scarcely a ringing endorsement of the most significant blueprint for social progress since before the First World War.[19] Nine Liberal MPs, including T. L. Horabin, went into the opposition lobby in protest at the government's lukewarm reception of the Beveridge Report. The party proved incapable of taking any real advantage of Beveridge's sudden and spectacular prominence. Two revealing Mass Observation reports summed up its problems. That of March 1942 noted: 'Over and over again we come back to the widespread feeling, among pro-Liberals, anti-Liberals and apathetics, that the Liberals are essentially *something of the past* rather than *of the future*'. Three years later, Mass Observation found a basic feeling of goodwill towards the Liberals but also a sense that a vote for the party would be a wasted one.[20] Thus, while the mood of the times 'may technically have been more liberal than socialist... this was a technicality which the party could not exploit'.[21] The fruits of wartime hopes and aspirations for a better world were preparing to fall into the lap of Clement Attlee, not that of Sinclair or any other Liberal.

As in 1931, the existence of a coalition brought Liberals and Liberal Nationals into the same administration, and renewed talk of reunion was almost inevitable. On this occasion the initiative came from Ernest Brown, who took over the leadership of the Liberal National group in December 1940. From the outset, however, there was a suggestion that Brown's approach was largely tactical – 'to put ourselves right with our Liberal supporters in the country who might accuse us of maintaining divisions against Liberals' – and even that it had been 'decreed' by Churchill, who saw the fusion of the sundered wings of Liberalism as the first stage in the development of a broad anti-socialist alliance to confront the Labour Party in the post-war era.[22] At all events, Sinclair was willing to explore the possibility of reunion, not least because it seemed, in the face of Radical Action's advance, to offer the chance to strengthen Liberalism's right wing.

Talks began in the summer of 1943. But Sinclair was careful to stress his primary concern to ensure the survival of the Liberal

Party as an independent political force. In practice, this meant that the Liberal Nationals would have to sever their Conservative associations for the negotiations to have any chance of success. As Sinclair told his fellow Liberals: 'I want to see the Liberal Party strong, united and reinforced by all men and women who subscribe to its principles, will support its policy and will resolutely maintain its identity and independence. On that basis I shall be very glad to talk things over with Mr Brown.'[23] When, therefore, at the end of October 1943, Brown made explicit his opinion that a National Government should continue even after the end of the war, any possibility of formal Liberal reunion was effectively at an end, even though desultory talks continued into the following year. Dingle Foot, dismissing the Liberal Nationals as 'Vichy Liberals', reassured Megan Lloyd George that 'nothing remotely resembling a basis of agreement ever looked like emerging'.[24] But Clement Davies, only recently returned to the Liberal fold, offered a more interesting interpretation of the 1943 negotiations:

> One set of people, namely so-called leaders, desire amalgamation so that they would join with Winston Churchill in forming a Centre Party; the others, like myself, feel that for a considerable time men have borne wrong labels. And that there are, in both branches, Radical elements which should join together with the object of carrying out a true Liberal or Radical policy which would certainly be opposed by Winston Churchill and the Tory Party.[25]

A feeling that the political tide was running their way caused many Liberals to rejoice at the breakdown of these negotiations. But their optimism was misplaced. Though the Liberals were the first of the three main parties to set up a reconstruction committee as early as the autumn of 1940, this was not generally indicative of their preparation for the return of normal party politics. The party's organization atrophied during the war years at all levels. As Percy Harris later recalled:

> Up to 1944 it was almost impossible to persuade Liberals to take any active interest in party politics or even to consider adopting candidates. It was not until early 1945 there was any real awakening of activity among the Liberals in the constituencies, and the same applied to possible candidates.[26]

Violet Bonham Carter, going through a list of English seats and candidates, was 'depressed by the tracts of Liberal wasteland'.[27] The chief whip pressed the need for a major publicity campaign in 1944, but Sinclair, constrained by his loyalty to Churchill's government, refused his consent. In October 1944, the parliamentary party accepted a resolution to 'put forward, without any commitments to any other parties, the largest possible number of candidates in complete independence, presenting the party's independent programme'.[28] Sinclair had wanted the wartime coalition to continue until the Japanese were defeated, a task which, it was widely believed, would require an additional 18 months or two years of attritional fighting. In February 1945, however, the party conference voted to leave the coalition as soon as the European war was over, a decision that scarcely gave the Liberals time to recover from their wartime inertia or to arrive at a coherent picture of what the party now represented. A last-minute upsurge of enthusiasm could not make up for several years of organizational neglect.

The General Election of 1945

In the circumstances, it was perhaps not surprising that Liberalism gave out different and sometimes confusing messages during the 1945 election campaign. The election addresses of Liberal candidates showed a greater diversity and inconsistency than those revealed by their political opponents. That said, the party's manifesto was probably the most left-wing on which it campaigned in the whole of the twentieth century. While stressing a belief in private enterprise and the value of individual effort, it said that Liberals would demand nationalization 'without hesitation' where this was the most economical option: 'Where there is no further expansion or useful competition in an industry or where an industry or group of industries has become a private monopoly, Liberals say it should become a public utility.' In addition, there were calls for extensive state control over the use of land, and a statement that Liberals would not be satisfied until a separate dwelling had been provided for each family at a reasonable rent. The tone of the manifesto owed much to the Liberals' expectation of a Conservative victory, and their need to differentiate themselves from that party rather than from Labour.

Against this, Sinclair, certain that the relevance of traditional Liberalism had not diminished, tended to conduct the party's campaign much as he might have done in the 1930s. But the themes that had given the party strength and vitality in earlier decades no longer had the same appeal in post-war Britain. After the sacrifices of the struggle against Hitler, the electorate wanted something more tangible than a high-minded reassertion of abstract values: 'its ideals of freedom and tolerance; its assertion of the principle that every human being, and not merely the specially privileged, is a personality with a right to a reasonable share in the moral, intellectual and material progress of the world'.[29]

The Liberal campaign never captured the popular imagination, not least because the other two parties, recognizing that the real contest lay between themselves, paid it scant attention. In his celebrated 'Gestapo' broadcast, Churchill contented himself with the assertion, which would become a Conservative commonplace over the next decade, that 'there is scarcely a Liberal sentiment which animated the great Liberal leaders of the past which we do not inherit and defend'.[30] Even after listening to a speech by Beveridge in Edinburgh, an observer concluded that 'the old fire of Liberalism ... was now almost extinct'.[31] Beveridge and his ideas naturally figured prominently in the Liberals' campaign, but without redounding significantly to the party's advantage. Despite his Liberal credentials, Beveridge's ideas were not a Liberal monopoly. With varying degrees of emphasis, most of his plans had found their way into the electoral programmes of the Labour and Conservative parties, and the growing 'liberal' consensus in the country did not necessarily presage Liberal success at the polls.

The party's other basic difficulty was to convince the electorate that it was a serious aspirant for power. In the end, despite more ambitious predictions, only 306 candidates were nominated, a figure insufficient to constitute a Commons majority even had every one been elected. Of this number, as many as 87 per cent were fighting an election for the first time. Some were so inexperienced as to do the party little credit on the hustings. In any event, Gallup polls since 1943 had seen Liberal support stuck at around 10 per cent, rising to a peak of just 15 per cent in June 1945. Though such statistics enjoyed less credibility than has since become the norm, the best that the party could realistically hope to achieve was to hold the balance of power in a hung Parliament.

In such a situation, potential Liberal voters would wish to know where the party's support might go. But when asked this question, Sinclair replied that 'it would be unwise and impractical to try to decide now what form of government should be constructed in a parliamentary situation which none of us can accurately foresee'.[32] The party's manifesto clearly implied a leaning towards Labour; but the ever-present Liberal emphasis on 'freedom' ultimately suggested a stronger affinity with the Conservatives.

In all the circumstances, the electoral outcome was entirely predictable. The party secured just 2.2 million votes, about 9 per cent of those cast. Liberal support per opposed candidate fell from 23.9 per cent in 1935 to 18.6 per cent a decade later. In parliamentary terms the position was far worse. Liberalism's pre-dissolution strength of 18 MPs was reduced to 12. As had become the norm at pre-war elections, there were a number of high-profile casualties. Sinclair lost by 62 votes in Caithness, Scotland, while Percy Harris and William Beveridge were also defeated. This left Gwilym Lloyd-George, Minister of Fuel and Power since 1942 but whose commitment to Liberalism was now a matter of speculation, as the only surviving MP who had ever held government office. Liberalism now seemed to be a party of the Celtic fringe, emphasizing its remoteness from the seats of power. Six of the surviving MPs sat for rural Wales. Four MPs were returned in the absence of Conservative opponents and four without Labour opposition. Only perhaps the outposts of Cardiganshire and Montgomeryshire now looked securely in Liberal hands.[33] Nor was the party strategically well-placed to stage an effective comeback at the next election. Only 8.8 per cent of Liberal candidates secured second place, while 84.9 per cent came third.[34]

Officially the party put a brave face on what had happened: 'Though this figure [of 2.25 million votes] fell considerably short of what was expected, it demonstrates quite clearly that there exists a substantial body of voters who are not prepared to compromise their Liberal principles and whose views are not adequately represented by either of the larger parties.'[35] Even in private correspondence Samuel reacted with a blind optimism that might have been a necessary ingredient in the party's survival but that flew in the face of all logical calculations: 'The result of the election here was a reversal of all our hopes for the Liberal Party. But a change might come as suddenly in the opposite direction, and we regard it as our duty to maintain the Party in being for any future eventuality that might arise.'[36] In fact, it was difficult to conceal the enormity of the catastrophe that had occurred. Six months later, the November municipal elections provided a sad but apparently inevitable reaffirmation of this verdict. The party lost 111 of the 245 council seats it attempted to defend, and now controlled not one of the 80 county boroughs. Only in a handful of textile towns in Lancashire and Yorkshire did it remain the strongest party. There seemed no way of stopping, let alone reversing, the downward and inexorable spiral of decline.

The reaction of the *Manchester Guardian* symbolized the party's problems. This once steadfast bastion of Liberal support commented that, while the adoption of proportional representation might offer the party a viable future, 'under the present system its hopes must be slender'. Under the editorship of A. P. Wadsworth, the newspaper had moved towards increasing support for Labour as the only realistic vehicle of radical progress, and the 1945 General Election effectively ended the formal links between the *Guardian* and the Liberal Party.

Survival under Clement Davies

Once the dust of electoral battle had settled, the parliamentary party's first task was to choose a new leader. From a rather bizarre process in which the MPs – many of whom did not know one another well – discussed the qualities and credentials of each other in turn, Clement Davies, MP for Montgomeryshire since 1929, emerged as the parliamentary party's choice. Even so, he was not formally appointed to the wider position of party leader, not least because of an expectation that Sinclair might soon return to the Commons. The latter's victorious Conservative opponent in Caithness had earlier pledged to stand down in Sinclair's favour, but in the event never did so.

The somewhat erratic course of Davies's political career up to that point is important in trying to make sense of the direction in which he might now try to steer the party. Davies had joined the Liberal National ranks in 1931, but insisted, as did most Liberal Nationals, on his continuing personal commitment to Liberalism: 'I stood as a Liberal. I was nominated by the Liberals as a Liberal. I remain a Liberal,' he told his electors in 1935. But he left the

Simonite faction in 1939 and organized an all-party 'ginger group' opposing the continuation of Chamberlain's premiership in the winter of the phoney war before playing a crucial, if little appreciated, role in bringing down the government in May 1940. Unrewarded by the new Prime Minister, he became for a time an independent critic of Churchill before rejoining the mainstream Liberal Party in 1942 and becoming prominent inside Radical Action. In June 1945, he offered a clear statement of his position within the political spectrum: 'I stand on the side of the progressive. If two parties such as Labour and Conservative were equally balanced then I would vote Labour. Members of the Labour Party and myself can walk side by side for a long way. There are many things on which we agree.'[37] His own election address advocated the nationalization of coal, transport, electricity and even the land. This clear leftward inclination was evident when Davies made his first Commons speech as parliamentary leader. He gave the new Attlee government a warm welcome, wishing it well and rejoicing at the end of the Tory regime with its 'reaction and chaos'. A more traditional Liberal such as Sinclair, still optimistic that his own political career had been interrupted rather than ended, was worried that Davies might even try to outflank Labour from the left, instead of concentrating on such time-honoured Liberal virtues as individualism, freedom and free trade.

Broadly speaking, Clement Davies's Liberal Party continued in this vein for the first two years of Labour government. Davies looked forward to promised Labour initiatives in health and social insurance as the implementation of Liberal policies going back to the great reforming government of 1905–15. 'It would be ignoble to hinder that work,' he insisted in July 1946, 'merely because it happens to be in the hands of other people to promote.'[38] Yet any overall assessment of Davies's 11-year leadership of the party must conclude that the period as a whole witnessed Liberalism moving distinctly to the right. This about-turn is not easily explained. Davies's own thinking clearly underwent a transformation. Before the end of 1947, by which time the Labour administration had experienced its first major crisis, he had become critical of the government's centralizing and illiberal tendencies: 'Everything is being organised from the centre,' he complained, 'and the centre is a small oligarchy. Freedom is threatened by conscription for the Army in peacetime and now by the direction of labour in industry. Hitler and Mussolini began their appeal to the people as Socialists.'[39] But regardless of any change in Davies's own thinking, it would have been an almost impossible task to lead Liberalism, or at least the rump that survived as a parliamentary force, in the direction upon which he had apparently embarked in 1945. No matter how far the party's strength in the Commons diminished, it never succeeded in speaking with a single voice. Indeed, the divisions of earlier years, which could sometimes be passed off as the dissent of the party's periphery, seemed to indicate a more fundamental cleavage now that the number of Liberal MPs only just exceeded single figures. The same party that encompassed the radical Megan Lloyd George, who retained the attitude with which Davies had begun in 1945 of broad sympathy for Labour, also contained a laissez-faire purist such as Rhys Hopkin Morris, MP for Carmarthenshire, who remained immovably hostile to all signs of government direction – 'subsidies, restrictions, planning, everything in fact that the Labour Government stood for'.[40] In broad terms, the party was divided between those who wanted a basic anti-Tory orientation and those whose primary concern was resistance to the spread of socialism. But this crude division masked a kaleidoscope of views extending across the full spectrum of historic Liberalism. As Davies put it in 1950, 'there is no Party but a number of individuals who, because of their adherence to the Party, come together only to express completely divergent views'.[41]

Increasingly, Davies despaired of giving *any* sort of lead to the parliamentary party. His priority, like that of Harold Wilson in the Labour movement 20 years later, was progressively reduced to trying to hold it together. He complained in 1950:

> My own position is one of almost supine weakness, for if I give full expression to a definite course of action that at once leads to trouble and a definite split. It is that split that I am so anxious to avoid. We have suffered so much in the past from these quarrels ... Any further division now would, I fear, just give the final death blow.[42]

Perhaps more than any of his predecessors, Davies had to take into account the attitude of the party outside Parliament. Reduced by electoral vagaries to a largely rural and Celtic rump, the parliamentary party had never been 'less representative of the Party as a whole. Its ten members,' argued Violet Bonham Carter in 1949, 'are constantly at variance with one another, with the Liberal Party Organisation and with their colleagues in the House of Lords.'[43] Figures such as Lady Violet, who never succeeded in getting elected to the Commons, enjoyed at least as much influence as the majority of her parliamentary colleagues. In any case, by 1948, those colleagues had begun to go their separate ways. The debate over the government's plans to nationalize the iron and steel industry saw the first significant divisions within the parliamentary party. 'I was elected to the House as a Liberal,' noted W. J. Gruffudd, member for the University of Wales, 'which means, as things are at present, that I can be eclectic in my politics.'[44] At the 1948 party assembly, radical Liberals looked on askance as the right called for a drastic reduction in government expenditure and, in an early anticipation of Thatcherite Conservatism, argued that council tenants should be given the right to buy their homes.

While most commentators have adopted a broadly sympathetic attitude towards Davies's leadership, pointing in particular to his successful resistance of a deadly Tory embrace in 1951, it is difficult to avoid the conclusion that the party was left to drift with little sense of purpose or direction while he remained at the helm. He claimed to define a distinct niche for the Liberal Party of the late 1940s: 'Do not run away with the idea that Liberalism provides the middle way between the other two,' he insisted in 1949. 'Still less that it is a compromise between them. Liberalism is a distinct creed – a distinct philosophy; distinct from Socialism, from Communism and from Conservatism.'[45] But it is doubtful whether many of his followers fully understood what the creed was, or even whether a consensus existed about it. Instead, Liberals 'have teetered between the other two parties like a drunken referee who despite his size is constantly trying to separate the heavyweights and fell each of them with a blow which is neither a left nor a right'.[46] Jo Grimond, first elected to Parliament in 1950, recalled that loyalty, gratitude and admiration bound him to Davies, 'but I was never quite sure on what branch he could finally settle'.[47] More significantly, the ordinary Liberal voter was often left confused, especially in constituencies where no Liberal candidate was standing.

Yet it is open to question whether any alternative leader would have been more successful than Davies in carving out a distinctive

Liberal identity in the decade after the end of the war. The debate over the existence or otherwise of a post-war political consensus lies outside the scope of this study. But it seems incontrovertible that the gap between Britain's two major parties did narrow substantially after 1945. On the one hand, the Conservatives reacted to the shock of electoral defeat by committing themselves to a moderate programme of pragmatic policies firmly grounded within the political parameters established by Attlee's government. On the other, that same government had by 1947 abandoned most of its pretensions to genuine socialism, preferring instead the techniques of Keynesian demand management to finance the emerging Welfare State. Ironically, therefore, while Labour and the Conservatives competed with one another in terms of their espousal of the ideas of two outstanding Liberals – Keynes and Beveridge – little scope was left in which a separate Liberal Party could flourish. In an 'era of centrist politics, there was no room for a centre party'.[48]

Ironically, too, while little seemed to divide the two political giants, at least in terms of their immediate party programmes, the two sides' partisans were ready to stick with their chosen course with unquestioning loyalty and zeal, apparently believing that an unbridgeable divide separated them from their political opponents. Labour was remarkably successful in holding on to its electoral support through the vicissitudes of government. Even in defeat in 1951 the party managed to poll 48.8 per cent of the popular vote. In that election, as much as 96.8 per cent of the total vote was shared between Labour and the Conservatives; in 1955 the comparable figure was 96.1 per cent. Class-based voting was now at its height and few electors seemed uncertain as to where their allegiance lay. Not surprisingly, surviving pockets of Liberalism were to be found in those relatively remote areas – rural Wales, the Highlands and Islands of Scotland, and South-West England – where the politics of class had found it most difficult to penetrate and where a stubborn individualism persisted. In what most viewed, however inaccurately, as a clear choice between the political heavyweights, many erstwhile Liberals determined either that Labour had become the modern vehicle of their progressive instincts or else that the liberalized Conservative Party of Butler, Eden and Macmillan was their best chance of resisting the encroachments of the 'socialist' state. Donald Johnson was among the latter group. Concluding that 'the main political objective of any liberal-minded person in the present day world must inevitably be the defeat of socialism', he joined the Conservative Party in 1947.[49]

Nor did Liberalism's problems disappear when the Conservatives returned to power in October 1951. Despite dire Labour predictions about the consequences of a Tory victory, Churchill's government made few radical deviations from the path already charted by its Labour predecessor. The term 'Butskellism' may miss some of the nuances of subtle difference between the economic management strategies pursued by the two administrations, but it remains a revealing contemporary observation on a broad pattern of continuity. Liberalism was not well placed to break out from, or even to challenge, this prevailing consensus. Davies was not a particularly original thinker in terms of policy initiatives, though he encouraged the idea of co-ownership in industry and he did commit his party to support British participation in the early moves towards greater European integration. Davies praised the Schuman Plan of 1950 for a Coal and Steel Community as the greatest step towards peace in the annals of European history. In part, this enthusiasm could be traced back to Gladstonian idealism about the concert of Europe; and in part, it suggested that Liberals were readier than their political rivals to come to terms with Britain's diminished status in the era of the superpowers. To their credit, moreover, postwar Liberals confronted the political dimension of the European movement head-on, in a way that their Labour and Conservative opponents did not. But Europe was not at the forefront of the political agenda until at least the 1960s. In this situation, only the themes of free trade and proportional representation really served to set Liberalism apart, and the former now looked increasingly anachronistic, sitting uneasily alongside prevailing assumptions about a planned and tightly controlled economy, while causing embarrassment over protection and farm subsidies for a party now largely confined to agricultural constituencies.

Resisting the Tory Embrace

In this situation, the danger clearly existed that Liberalism might be swallowed up by one of the other two parties. In the event, it was relations with the Conservatives that dominated the party's strategic thinking throughout the post-war decade. Even in the 1945 campaign, Churchill had reminded Liberal voters of his own Liberal past, urging them to support the Conservatives as the only viable means of thwarting socialism. The Liberals tried to use their election broadcasts to fend off Churchill's unwanted advances, while the *Manchester Guardian* poured scorn on the idea that Conservatism now embraced the central tenets of Liberal belief.[50] As the Conservatives of the late 1940s adopted an increasingly progressive stance, however, the *Guardian*'s conclusion looked open to challenge. Furthermore, such was Labour's margin of victory in 1945 that many Conservatives concluded that their chances of reversing the result next time would be negligible unless the majority of the more than two million Liberal voters could be induced to join the Conservative camp.

In September 1945, a letter appeared in *The Spectator* from Quintin Hogg, MP for Oxford and a leading light in the Tory Reform Group, a body that pressed the Conservative leadership to adopt a positive attitude towards the Beveridge-inspired social reforms that Labour was now enacting. Claiming to speak for 30 or 40 Tory MPs whose views 'showed no striking difference from the Liberals', Hogg suggested that 'if only the Liberals would come and help...we could, together, capture the Conservative Party'.[51] By early 1946, informal discussions were taking place within a small committee of Conservatives and Liberals chaired by the future Chancellor of the Exchequer, Peter Thorneycroft. It was decided to draw up a joint policy statement entitled *Design for Freedom*. Progress was such that, by November, a rather alarmed Liberal Party headquarters was obliged to issue a statement denying rumours of a Liberal–Conservative pact.[52] By the following January a draft document was ready, and only when Davies spoke out against it at Colwyn Bay, North Wales, in February 1947 did this particular initiative collapse. Liberal headquarters now called on Liberals to dissociate themselves from the *Design for Freedom* movement and reaffirmed the party's independence.[53]

In the meantime, a somewhat different approach had been adopted by Harold Macmillan, who had lost his Stockton-on-Tees seat in the North-East of England to Labour at the General Election. From personal experience, Macmillan understood how important Liberal votes might be for the future salvation of the Conservative Party. Returning to Parliament in the Bromley, Kent, by-election of November 1945, he noted that, while the Labour vote had remained 'uncomfortably high', support for the Liberal candidate had slumped disastrously, falling by more than half from the General Election figure.[54] Macmillan even toyed with the idea of dropping the name 'Conservative', since it failed to reflect the sorts of moderate and progressive ideas he was keen to advocate and which alone could woo further Liberal voters. He aired these themes at Conservative rallies in the summer of 1946 and elaborated his views in an article in the *Daily Telegraph* that October under the heading 'Anti-Socialist Parties' Task: The Case for Alliance or Fusion'. This article, intended to coincide with the opening of the Conservative Party Conference, urged Liberals and Conservatives to come together to promote a policy 'not of passive anti-Socialism, but of an active and dynamic character'.[55] But the mood of the Conference was not with Macmillan and, for the time being, his ideas were allowed to lapse.

If a merger with the Conservatives threatened to result in the extinction of British Liberalism as an independent political force, reunion with the Liberal Nationals offered a more constructive and less suffocating prospect. In particular, it would make it harder for the Conservatives to lay claim to be the true inheritors of Liberal traditions because of their close association with the Liberal Nationals. In the summer of 1946, the Liberals and Liberal Nationals of London quietly came together and there was some optimism that this merger would be repeated elsewhere. But the leadership of neither wing showed total commitment to the further healing of old wounds. Davies, still espousing the left-wing views that had characterized his recent election campaign, was wary that reunion might undermine his hope of turning the Liberals into a radical, but non-socialist, third force in British politics. By contrast, the Liberal National leadership, aware that its parliamentary strength – down to 13 seats after the 1945 election – was largely a function of Conservative acquiescence at constituency level, was keen not to break its relationship with the Tories completely. Nevertheless, tentative discussions took place between Ernest Brown and the Liberal peer, the Duke of Montrose, in the course of 1946. It became clear that it was the independence of any fused party rather than detailed policy issues that posed the most significant stumbling-block to agreement. Faced with Liberal National insistence on a definite arrangement for Liberal representation in a future Conservative government, the negotiations stalled by the end of the year.[56] In the wake of the failure of this final effort at Liberal reunion, the Liberal National and Conservative parties rapidly formalized their association. Under the Woolton–Teviot accords of May 1947, the two parties were effectively fused at constituency level. It was agreed that, in constituencies where each party had an existing organization, a combined association would be formed under a mutually agreed title. In constituencies where only one of the parties had an organization, that body would consider enlarging its membership to include all who supported joint action against socialism. As a result, in the 1950 General Election, 53 candidates stood under such assorted labels as National Liberal and Conservative; Conservative and National Liberal; Conservative and Liberal; and Liberal and Conservative.

Davies's fears for Liberal independence were well founded. The success of the Woolton–Teviot agreement encouraged renewed Conservative efforts to swallow the bigger fish of the Liberal Party itself. In April 1947, Woolton, as Conservative chairman, proclaimed that the great need was for those who understood the threat of socialism to unite. In practice, this meant supporting the Conservatives as the only party capable of forming a non-socialist government. Macmillan also re-entered the fray, taking his message to a rally at the Gladstonian shrine of Hawarden Castle in North Wales. Here he asked: 'What divides – at this moment – the Liberal and Conservative parties? What separates them? Nothing – except the memories of the past... Each condemns with equal vigour the grave mishandling by the present socialist Government of our internal and external economy.'[57] As a consequence of the Woolton–Teviot agreement, 1947 saw the setting up, in constituencies such as Dunstable, Bedfordshire, Bideford, Devon and North Angus in Scotland, of so-called 'Liberal and Conservative Associations'. These derived from meetings at which actual Liberals were either greatly outnumbered or actively excluded. Liberal headquarters felt obliged to issue a 'Declaration of Independence' and warned that Conservative Central Office was pursuing a deliberate and carefully conceived campaign to destroy the Liberal Party's constituency organizations. Valiantly, the call went out to 'all Liberals throughout the country to stand firm against Conservative overtures and to concentrate their energies upon preparing for the coming fight'.[58]

Unfortunately, many on the Liberal Party's right wing were increasingly ready to respond positively to Conservative advances. Optimism about Liberal prospects, widespread in 1946, had soon begun to evaporate. As so often in the past, the party had put its faith in structural reorganization as the panacea for future recovery. After the electoral disaster of 1945 many remained convinced that a revivified party organization was the means of converting the millions of potential Liberal voters – the 'Liberals-but' who had been uncovered in public opinion surveys – into actual crosses on ballot papers. An eight-member Committee on Reconstruction was set up in the autumn of 1945 to produce a prescription for revival. Its report, *Coats off for the Future!*, was presented to the spring assembly in 1946 amid scenes of renewed energy, enthusiasm and confidence. But the situation on the ground was less encouraging. By-elections still indicated a falling Liberal percentage of the popular vote. In the second half of 1947, Liberal candidates contested five seats, but lost their deposits in four of them. Discussions with the chief whip, Frank Byers, convinced Lady Violet Bonham Carter of the possibility of the party being wiped out completely as a parliamentary force at the next General Election. She and Byers calculated that, even if every Liberal candidate took 15 per cent of the Labour vote and 10 per cent from the Tories, the net result would be a gain of only six seats nationally. More probably, there would be substantial losses among the party's 10 remaining MPs if they faced three-cornered contests. The alternative, Lady Violet concluded, 'would be a deal over seats with the Tories with PR as a condition and an agreed programme. I shldn't like it and it might split the Party in half and give the Left Wing to Labour. I see all the rocks and shoals very clearly but I *fear* complete Parliamentary extinction.' [59]

In a rare letter to Megan Lloyd George, Lady Violet spelt out her anxiety. She confessed that she no longer believed that the Liberals could stage an effective comeback, certainly not by 1950. Only electoral reform would ensure the ultimate survival of any third party.[60] It was difficult to say more than this to Megan Lloyd George, but a month earlier Harold Nicolson had gained a clearer picture of Lady Violet's thinking:

She abuses the Government for abandoning all moral principle. Until now she had believed that the Liberal Party were closer to the Socialists than to any other party. Now she doubts it...No, she feels closer to the left-wing Tories today. All of which suggests that the Liberal Party are about to create a common anti-communist front.[61]

In fact, Asquith's daughter had already begun to sound out her friend and her father's one-time colleague, Winston Churchill. The latter's response was vague but not entirely discouraging:

> stressed the need for Lib. Independence – no alliances etc. – but 'Lay off a little against us. We might help each other – make some arrangement which would be mutually convenient etc.' I said that only *an issue* cld determine such an alignment – not a cold-blooded arrangement. *I* cldn't deliver the goods. Could *he do so*? Cld he for instance 'deliver' Electoral Reform?[62]

Liberal disunity became increasingly apparent during 1948. The year began with rumours that Megan Lloyd George was about to join Labour, but in February she told the Cambridge University Liberal Club that the Liberal Party was moving not to the right but to the left. This claim reflected little more than her own wishful thinking. At the beginning of the following year, Davies made a vain attempt to impose unity on the party by appointing Lady Megan as deputy leader. Despite her new status, however, she made few efforts to moderate her views, calling on the party to adopt a truly radical programme and adding, rather provocatively, 'of course, that means shedding our Right Wing'. The *Western Morning News* responded: 'There have been hurried consultations between some of the other leaders of the party, who interpret this statement as a declaration of war against, perhaps, a substantial majority of its members... Lady Megan's attitude, far from bringing unity, might split the party.'[63] Along with such colleagues as Dingle Foot, she continued to urge the party to align itself unambiguously on the left, and frequently found herself at odds with the majority of her colleagues on policy issues. Discussions on the state of the economy highlighted the differences of approach. The left was fearful of being seen to accept too much of the Conservative critique of government policy. As Foot put it:

> It looks to me as if the Tories... are girding themselves up for an attack on the social services... and a rise in unemployment figures.

> To my mind it would be fatal for us to lend ourselves, even by
> inference, to this campaign... Even if we have to preach a form of
> austerity... we should do it as *defenders* of the social services and full
> employment and not as an alternative gang of destroyers.[64]

In the meantime, Davies's efforts to boost his party's self-
confidence were rebuffed by his colleagues. His claim, reported
in *The Economist*, that the party had doubled its membership
appeared to be based on nothing more concrete than the findings of a Gallup Poll about the numbers of those who said they
would vote Liberal, and on the large and enthusiastic audiences
attending Liberal rallies. Yet, warned Violet Bonham Carter, such
evidence could scarcely justify the conclusions Davies had drawn,
and his assertions would prove embarrassing if challenged.[65] As
the 1945 Parliament drew towards its close, such internal dissen-
sions scarcely augured well for the party's electoral prospects.

By contrast, the Conservative Party went into the 1950 General
Election in an optimistic mood. The ageing Labour government
appeared to have run out of steam, while the Liberals seemed to
pose few threats. The Tories again strove to present themselves as
the true heirs of the great Liberal tradition, even if this meant sow-
ing confusion in the minds of the electorate. Liberals could only
respond by insisting that the differences between Liberalism and
Conservatism were fundamental, and that the intimacy between
Conservatives and National Liberals was an entirely different
matter.[66] As the election approached, Lord Moynihan, chairman
of the Liberal Party Organisation, tried to clear up any confusion, suggesting to Woolton that Conservative and Conservative-
supporting candidates should be prepared to fight the contest as
Conservatives and that 'the name "Liberal" should not be used by
them in order to confuse the issue'. Woolton replied, with some justification, that the National Liberals had as much right as anyone
else to use the word 'Liberal' in their title.[67] At this point the party
leaders entered the dispute. At his adoption meeting in Woodford
in Essex, Churchill spoke scathingly of 'the very small and select
group of Liberal leaders who conceived themselves the sole heirs
of the principles and traditions of Liberalism and believed themselves to have the exclusive copyright of the word "Liberal"'.[68] Two
days later, Churchill and Lord Rosebery, President of the National
Liberal Council, issued a joint statement containing a rather

half-hearted call to 'Liberal–Conservative' candidates to use the prefix 'National' whenever a candidate from the mainstream Liberal Party was also standing. Clement Davies felt bound to protest and there was even talk of the Liberals taking legal action. But Davies was wide open to Churchill's rejoinder that he himself had been happy enough to carry the label 'Liberal National' for the best part of a decade.[69]

From the Liberal point of view, this wrangling over nomenclature was an unwanted distraction, but it showed how unsuccessful they had been since 1945 in staking out a viable political identity of their own. And internal party disputes remained just beneath the surface. Against Davies's wishes, the party's annual assembly went ahead immediately prior to the election. The leader's private comments are instructive: 'My one prayer now is that there will not be much discussion, debate or disputing. Now is the time when we should agree upon the spirit, and not debate the finer points. We must have unity and also show that we are a Party of action, and not a debating society.'[70] As at all General Elections during their years in the political wilderness, the Liberals faced a difficult decision as to whether to fight on a broad or a narrow front. The argument was finely balanced. Those who favoured the former line saw it as the best means of giving national credibility to the small number of candidates who had a realistic chance of success, by encouraging potential Liberal voters to believe that the party remained a national political force. Those who supported the narrow front wished to concentrate the party's limited resources and avoid a large number of humiliating results in individual constituencies. In the event, 475 candidates were nominated, 169 more than in 1945. Even this decision did not command unanimous support. Two Liberal peers, Lord Reading and Lord Rennell, who for some time had been showing signs of dissatisfaction with party policy, argued that the party was in danger of spreading its resources too thinly. 'Of course what they really mean,' complained Davies, 'is that there should be some kind of pact with the Tories.'[71] Only tactful handling by the party's veteran leader in the upper house, Lord Samuel, prevented another damaging row.

At a national level, no formal pact was made between Liberals and Conservatives, despite the claims of many observers that, without it, the anti-socialist vote would be split. Churchill wrote to Davies shortly before the dissolution, suggesting an arrangement between their parties: 'There is a real measure of agreement,' he claimed, 'between modern Tory democracy and the mass of Liberals who see in Socialism all that their most famous thinkers and leaders have fought against in the past.'[72] In Huddersfield, West Yorkshire, a local arrangement was arrived at whereby the Conservatives agreed not to contest the town's west division, while the Liberals stood down in the east. In Dundee the local parties seemed near to agreement, but were thwarted when Liberal headquarters in London put up their own candidate independently of the Dundee Liberal Association. Elsewhere, Liberal headquarters tried to turn the Tory argument on its head, suggesting that in constituencies such as Bethnal Green in East London it was the Conservative who should stand down, since only the Liberal could possibly defeat Labour. The Conservatives refused further concessions, though in three other constituencies – Carmarthen in Wales, and Greenock and the Western Isles in Scotland – no Conservative stood and local support was given to the Liberal candidate.

For the most part, the Conservatives were left with the telling argument, 'robustly declared in hoardings, speeches, and election addresses', that a vote for the Liberal Party was a vote wasted.[73] The claim carried credibility. Opinion polls and general perception suggested that the gap between the two leading parties was narrow, while few believed that the Liberals by themselves could achieve very much. This theme was taken up in the press with the *Daily Telegraph* emphasizing the futility of running so many candidates, while the *Sunday Times* stressed the need for a common stand against socialism and criticized the vanity of Liberals for refusing to recognize reality. Churchill conducted a skilful campaign, blaming the Liberals for their refusal to co-operate, while emphasizing his own liberalism and the lack of substantial differences between the two parties by offering Violet Bonham Carter one of the broadcasts allocated to the Conservatives.

The Liberal manifesto, *No Easy Way*, failed to make much of an impression. Many of its proposals appeared to be insufficiently distinctive, while no single theme or concept ran through the whole document. It tried to strike a balance between Liberalism's warring factions by putting forward a right-leaning approach in economic policy and a leftward incline in the social sphere. The Conservatives drew attention to a considerable measure of overlap with their own statement, *This Is the Road*; but the Labour Party tended to ignore it.

By comparison with the major parties, the Liberals' national campaign of 1950 looked amateurish. Five years of supposed preparation since the previous election had borne little fruit. Shortage of money limited the number of paid agents and workers, while on the hustings the party suffered from a lack of big names. Recognizing that their individual success was by no means assured, figures such as Davies, Sinclair, Byers and Megan Lloyd George concentrated their electioneering in their own constituencies. As the campaign progressed, the Liberals' argument that they were now fielding enough candidates to secure a Commons majority began to appear a sham. Many of those standing were adopted very late in the day, lacked credibility as aspiring politicians, and were not even well-versed in the policies of their party. As one veteran Liberal commented: 'I felt in listening to a good number of speeches that our candidates made a poor impression, rather as if they thought it was fun to stand if their expenses were paid, but they had very little to say except rather out-of-date appeals to party feeling.'[74]

The historian of the 1950 election has commented on the Liberal performance that 'to win 9 seats with 475 candidates, and to lose 319 deposits...was a defeat on a scale which it would be hard to parallel'.[75] Jeremy Thorpe, then at Oxford, likened the result to a replay of the charge of the Light Brigade.[76] Frank Byers narrowly lost his seat in North Dorset; Sinclair failed to regain Caithness; only Jo Grimond's success in Orkney and Shetland offered a crumb of comfort. Violet Bonham Carter captured the mood of despair as the results came in: 'Two of our dear supporters slunk in with a N[ews] C[hronicle] looking shattered. One hardly dared look at them. It was like meeting after a death.'[77] It is true that the party's total vote increased to 2.6 million, but as the Liberals were fielding 50 per cent more candidates than in 1945, this was scarcely a noteworthy achievement, especially as the overall turnout was up by nearly four million. As few as 3.8 per cent of Liberal candidates even managed to finish second; 93.2 per cent were in third place. The Liberal vote was evenly distributed by class, age and sex, and, while this might imply that Liberalism still had a universal appeal, it also suggested that there was no likelihood of a future electoral breakthrough under a first-past-the-post voting system.

As in 1945, party headquarters responded to disaster with defiance: 'The Liberal Party carries on. Let there be no doubt about that.' But much of the press was highly critical. *The Times* highlighted the 'national disservice' that Liberal intervention had occasioned, and suggested that in future the party could best serve the interests of Liberalism by allowing its supporters to judge for themselves which of the two larger parties could do more to put the Liberal spirit into practice. The *Daily Mail* agreed. The Liberal effort had 'chiefly served a wrecking purpose', but now 'the game [was] up'. Even the still generally sympathetic *Manchester Guardian* wondered whether the Liberals' thinly scattered vote could really form the future basis of a national political party. Davies, while maintaining a brave public face, privately admitted that the party now faced a more difficult situation than at any time since the Parliament of 1929. He took refuge in the iniquities of the electoral system and was soon writing to Attlee to press the case for electoral reform. But it was perhaps Harold Nicolson, a Liberal at heart though the Liberals were the one party he never formally supported, who expressed the most common sentiment. 'I am sorry, of course, for the Liberals,' he admitted, 'but they asked for it.'[78]

From a Conservative point of view, the problem was clear enough. During the campaign, the veteran Tory MP, Cuthbert Headlam, had expressed his 'great fear' that 'the infernal Liberals are going to queer our pitch all over the country'. He found the division in the anti-socialist ranks 'really amazing' and failed to understand why people who appreciated the menace of socialism insisted on fighting one another simply 'because in the past their parents and grandparents fought each other as Tories v. Whigs or as Conservatives v. Liberals'.[79] Arguably, Headlam's fears had been proved correct. It was widely assumed that the Conservative and Labour parties had polled at something like their full strength. The outcome was a Labour Commons majority of five over all other parties combined. Yet between them the Tories and Liberals had captured about 1.85 million more votes than the victorious Labour government. The conclusion was not difficult to draw. The problem was how best to get those who had voted Liberal on this occasion to vote Conservative at the next – and probably not long delayed – election. In March, Churchill proposed the setting up of a shadow cabinet committee to 'go into all the questions open between Conservatives and Liberals and to see what can be done to secure greater unity among the forces opposed to Socialism'.[80] Attlee made fun of the Conservatives' courtship of the Liberal Party. Were the intentions of the Leader of the Opposition honourable or not?

> He has been a very ardent lover of this elderly spinster, the Liberal Party. The elder sister – the National Liberals – was married long ago; she is now deceased. This now is the younger sister, but she is getting on. I can never make out whether [Churchill] is going to play Petruchio or Romeo. He has given her a slap in the face, then offers her a bunch of flowers.[81]

Attlee's sarcastic tone may well have been designed to strengthen Liberal resolve to resist the Conservative embrace, since by-elections afforded some evidence that former Liberal voters were more likely to go to the Tories than to Labour. Undeterred by Attlee's wit, Churchill continued on his chosen course. To the backbench 1922 Committee he declared on 16 May that Conservatives had to obtain Liberal support both as individuals and, if possible, as a party, not by any political deal but by proclaiming the fundamental principles on which those who voted against socialism were agreed. On 29 April, Woolton insisted that he did not know 'of any practical issue on which Liberals and Conservatives are not agreed', a claim that prompted Davies to reiterate that there was no intention of compromising the independence of the Liberal Party.[82] The Conservative chairman's statement followed the formal defection of Lords Reading and Rennell to the Conservative camp, a move that seemed, in Lord Salisbury's words, 'to underline the broad measure of agreement which exists between those who believe in the free way of life, to whatever party they have hitherto belonged'.[83] When Lords Willingdon and Cowdray also left the Liberal Party in early May, it seemed that the process of defection might escalate out of control.

Davies suggested that what was needed was a short statement of Liberal principles, defining what was distinctive about Liberalism and the belief in which was fundamental to being a Liberal. Yet it was striking, and perhaps indicative of the difficulties the party faced at the time, that the leader should make this suggestion without stating what that distinctive Liberal creed actually was.

His predecessor, on the other hand, was thinking in more practical terms. According to Sinclair, the electorate had lost faith in the capacity of Liberal candidates to win seats and were now tending to vote against the candidate they liked least, rather than for the candidate they liked best. He judged, therefore, that all other considerations must be subordinated to the attainment of electoral reform. It was the duty of those with responsibility for the party's future 'not to indulge in the luxury of expressing heroic sentiments', but to ensure that the party survived. The way forward was an arrangement with the Conservatives along the lines of the Huddersfield pact, limited to the next General Election and based on a concrete Conservative pledge to introduce a measure of electoral reform in the next Parliament if they were returned to power.[84] Violet Bonham Carter's thinking moved along similar lines. The party leadership, she believed, had been irresponsible. Their attempts to convince the public that the Liberal Party could form a government had been either fraudulent or so out of touch with reality 'as to disqualify those who made them from any claim to political *sense*'.[85]

The possibility of the Conservatives espousing a system of proportional representation was less remote in 1950 than it has since become. Harold Macmillan, more than ever convinced of the need for an alliance with the Liberals, saw 'a great deal to be said, in principle, for an experiment in Proportional Representation, limited to the big cities. It could do no harm and might do good.'[86] Even Churchill was favourably disposed and, according to Nigel Fisher, made a moving but unsuccessful appeal to the 1922 Committee to be allowed to pursue an agreement along these lines.[87] 'On Electoral Reform,' R. A. Butler confirmed, 'the battle is only too seriously engaged.'[88] During the summer, Churchill entrusted to Butler, in conditions of great secrecy, the task of negotiating with the Liberals in the person of Lady Violet. Butler's position on the liberal wing of Conservatism had been assured by his part in remodelling party policy in the late 1940s. The aim was a pact for the next election, and in June Butler drew up a document entitled 'Overlap Prospectus of Principles'. The two negotiators were agreed that there should be no joint endorsement of a common programme but merely a statement of the general principles on which both parties were agreed. Though Lady Violet regarded it as the key issue, Butler urged her not to press electoral reform for the time being lest it damage the whole negotiating process. In any case, Conservative Central Office seemed less enthusiastic about the whole enterprise, and Woolton delayed making a firm approach to Davies on seats. In the event, the talks ground to a halt by the end of the summer, partly because of the outbreak of the Korean War and partly because of the differing priorities of the two sides.[89]

Whether Davies went along wholeheartedly with these negotiations, whether indeed he accepted Sinclair's arguments for an electoral arrangement, is unclear. In stating the Liberal position to Churchill and Woolton, Davies was at pains to emphasize not only that the Liberals must remain an independent party, but also that there could be no national agreement on the allocation of constituencies whereby one party would undertake to withdraw its candidate in favour of the candidate of the other party. Such an agreement, he insisted, would never be accepted by the Liberal rank and file.[90] Despite this hesitation, the Liberals were evidently moving closer to the Conservatives than at any time since the end of the war. Yet it was not a direction in which a substantial minority of the divided parliamentary party wished to travel. By the autumn of 1950, three MPs – Lady Megan Lloyd George, Emrys Roberts and Edgar Granville – supported by figures such as Dingle Foot and Philip Hopkins, had begun to organize a rearguard action against Davies's drift to the right. At a series of party meetings the left protested against the possibility of an electoral arrangement with the Conservatives. Davies claimed that the dissidents were 'concerned about themselves only and think that their best chance lies in help from Socialists'.[91] In reality, his position was a difficult one, especially as he had issued a statement in the May issue of *Liberal News* to the effect that 'the Liberal leaders have no knowledge of Conservative intentions or of Conservative proposals and no negotiations are taking place'.

This renewed division made the parliamentary party something of a laughing stock. Its nine members – nicknamed by Labour the 'Nimble Nine' – might have been expected to exercise an influence out of proportion to their numerical strength in a Commons that was finely balanced between the two leading parties. Instead, as in 1924 and 1929–31, proximity to power had a counter-productive effect. Despite protesting his own powerlessness and even considering resignation, Davies was partly responsible for this confusion,

failing to provide the strong lead the situation demanded. A car-
toon in the *Sunday Graphic*, captioned 'Spring Double', pictured
him riding two horses, one named 'Labour' and the other 'Tory'. In
practice, the Liberal Party was reluctant to help the Conservatives
bring down Attlee's government. It was in no position, especially
financially, to fight another early election. Davies even sought an
agreement with Churchill to limit the number of parliamentary
divisions. Yet the regularity of these was part of the Conservative
strategy to bring the government to its knees.[92]

By the autumn of 1950, a mood of widespread depression seemed
to have gripped the party's senior figures. Davies tried hard to
rally the Liberal Assembly at Scarborough in Yorkshire, but his
claim that the party was united and free of jealousies and envy was
a hollow one. At the same gathering, Megan Lloyd George avoided
accusing the leadership of dealing with the Conservative enemy –
this might have necessitated revealing her own discussions with
Labour's Herbert Morrison about how to stop the Tories regaining
power – but still complained about the party's slippage towards
the right. Privately, Violet Bonham Carter warned Davies of the
possibility of electoral extinction. By-election results gave weight
to her fears. The Conservatives were enjoying a series of promising results, partly, contemporaries noted, because of a collapse in
the Liberal vote. Granted that the Liberals were unlikely to be in
a position to fight many seats at the next General Election, a pact
with the Conservatives made even more compelling sense from
Lady Violet's point of view.

After a meeting of Liberal leaders in October, at which majority opinion clearly favoured seeking regional arrangements on the
Huddersfield model, Lady Violet tried once more to stir Davies
into action. It was no longer possible to dodge the central issue –
'whether on balance we desire the return of a Socialist or a
Conservative Government next time'. Survival itself was the problem. If the party was reduced to only four or five MPs, as seemed
entirely possible, then 'we can no longer pretend to be a National
Party with rooms in the House of Commons, a Chief Whip, a Party
Broadcast etc'. A decisive declaration of intent might well split the
party, 'but better even a split with survival than a united death'.
Lady Violet felt that the party was drifting without purpose, that
an election might find it unprepared and that the time had come
to renew contact with Woolton.[93] Davies replied that he personally

was prepared to help bring down the Labour government, but that such a proposal would immediately prompt a party split. With another election likely within a matter of months, the Liberal Party again seemed on the verge of disintegration.

In the event, the election was delayed until October 1951. At the opening of the campaign, it was reported that the Liberals had 174 candidates provisionally adopted. Soon, however, many withdrew, while some constituency associations found that they lacked sufficient funds to support a contest. With the number of confirmed candidates dropping alarmingly, the party announced on 26 September that it had decided to fight on a narrow front. Just 109 candidates were put into the field. But this was less a matter of considered tactics than of necessity. The party 'appears, in fact, to have fought on as wide a front as was practicable'.[94] Nor were Liberal efforts even concentrated in the most promising locations. Seats such as Rochdale in Lancashire, Torrington in Devon, Caernarvon in north Wales and Salisbury in Wiltshire, where the party had performed respectably in 1950, were now left uncontested. By contrast, a number of hopeless battles were fought once again, including 29 where deposits had been lost at the previous election. Davies's claim that the Liberals had deliberately planned to contest selected seats does not stand up to scrutiny. At best, therefore, Liberals could only hope to hold the balance of power in a hung Parliament. The cry of 'wasted vote' was likely to be more potent than ever, unless the Liberals gave a clear indication of how they would employ their parliamentary strength. To quote a Conservative election leaflet, 'the Independent Liberal Party has no hope of power and to support a party without hope is itself a hopeless action'. Davies, however, refused to give any advance commitment of support to either of the two major parties, though it was widely noted that his broadcast on 28 September attacked only the Labour Party and contained little that would have caused exception for a Conservative. In practice, many former Liberal candidates in areas where no Liberal was standing showed their preference by throwing their weight behind other candidates, in most cases Conservatives. Among the minority of constituencies was Bristol North-East. Here, the secretary of the local Liberal association came out in favour of Labour shortly before polling day. In response, several Liberals, accused by the secretary of being National Liberals, wrote to urge support for the Conservatives.

Party organization was even weaker than in 1950. The number of full-time agents, which had stood at 140 in October 1949, was down to 44. In only a few seats could Liberals mount a full-scale campaign. Elsewhere, issuing an election address and holding a few poorly attended meetings was all that was attempted. The party faced 'an impossible task in trying with very limited resources to make the electorate aware of [its] continued existence and of the justification for it'.[95] Some Liberals seemed ready to forsake the traditional goal of electoral success for the more ethereal ambition of permeating the political thought of the other parties. The seeds of Liberalism, declared Jo Grimond during the course of the campaign, 'blow far and wide. We welcome it when they take root in the Conservative or Labour parties, but we must tend and water the plant from which they come.'[96] The Liberal Manifesto, *The Nation's Task*, stressed the importance of securing strong Liberal representation in the new Parliament in order to check the extremism of the other parties. But it gave no clear picture of Liberal policies. Apart from a commitment to Scottish and Welsh parliaments and a vague call for European unity, the manifesto contained little that was distinctively Liberal. Lord Teviot of the National Liberals seized the opportunity to argue that, as there was no fundamental difference in policy between Liberals and Conservatives, Liberals in constituencies with no Liberal candidate should be urged to vote Tory,[97] an invitation that Davies continued to resist.

Some limited efforts were made to extend the 'Huddersfield formula'. A comparable pact was reached in Bolton in Lancashire, where Conservatives did not oppose the Liberal candidate in Bolton West, while the Liberals stood down in Bolton East. In three seats in rural Wales, Liberals were not opposed by Tories, and in Dundee the Conservatives did not stand. Most strikingly, Violet Bonham Carter was not opposed in Colne Valley in Yorkshire, and Churchill made a point of speaking on her behalf. His theme was entirely predictable: 'I find comfort in the broad harmony of thought which prevails between the modern Tory democracy and the doctrines of the famous Liberal leaders of the past.'[98] For Labour, Attlee tried to counter this argument by suggesting that Liberals who accepted Conservative support ceased to be Liberals. One Conservative leaflet, which appealed to the memory of David Lloyd George, urging Liberals to make their votes effective and preserve Liberalism by voting Conservative, stirred up controversy.

His daughter Megan, insisting on her lifelong radicalism, pointed out that she had been faithful to the traditions of her father by supporting every measure the Labour government had brought before Parliament that had the effect of improving the lot of working people. In general, the Conservatives were more restrained in their quest for Liberal votes than in 1950, recognizing perhaps that too overt a courtship might be counter-productive.

Lowest Ebb

Probably no Liberal seriously expected anything but another electoral disaster. The party's vote slumped to under three-quarters of a million – less than 2.6 per cent of the total; its Commons representation fell from nine to six, while 66 candidates forfeited their deposits. Only a few pockets of genuine strength now remained, concentrated in Wales, Scotland and the West Country. Elsewhere, the Liberal vote was distributed fairly evenly, though it was strongest in agricultural areas. The modest figure of 20 per cent support was secured in just three urban seats. Only Jo Grimond was returned in the face of Conservative opposition, and it was a reasonable proposition that the party would have retained three seats at most if Conservatives had stood against all its candidates. *The Times* commented that the 'party, which for thirty years has fought to survive with almost incredible tenacity, has received a fresh blow'.[99] The *Manchester Guardian*, which had recommended a full term for Churchill as the country's best option, offered an even gloomier message:

> It is hard to see in this depressing picture much ground for building up a country-wide political party on the old model. Unless there is some change in the Conservative Party or some break-up in the Labour Party, the Liberal Party can look forward only to further attrition and further losses to the two major parties.[100]

Liberal votes certainly seem to have been decisive, but only in the sense of helping the Conservatives to secure a narrow, but still comfortable, majority of 17 over all other parties. The statistics suggest that few Liberals, deprived of a Liberal candidate in 1951, felt unable to register a vote, and that the majority of them transferred their support to the Tories. In constituencies where Liberals stood in 1950 but not in 1951, the swing to the Conservatives was greater than in the country as a whole. Something like 60 or 70 per cent of those who had supported Liberal candidates in 1950 seem to have transferred their allegiance to the Conservatives when a Liberal vote was no longer an option. This may have accounted for more than half the seats that the Conservatives won from Labour.[101] Harold Macmillan's contemporary assessment was that Liberal votes had been decisive in securing Conservative successes north of the River Trent, areas 'which have suffered under the Socialist tyranny'.[102]

If the election result were not bad enough, one further pitfall awaited the depleted party – albeit one dressed in an appealing disguise. Churchill's parliamentary majority was adequate enough and he had no real need to seek Liberal support. But the election had seen the defeat of those left-wing Liberals – Granville, Roberts and Megan Lloyd George – whose presence in the party's ranks was the most serious impediment to closer relations with the Tories. Perhaps Churchill was also keen to re-create the sort of 'National' rather than party authority, which he had enjoyed during the war, or he may simply have seen a golden opportunity to extinguish the party of which he had once been a member. At all events, Churchill decided to offer Clement Davies a cabinet post as Minister of Education.[103] Davies, who had never held government office, was keen to accept, but felt obliged to consult senior colleagues, including Lord Samuel, before giving his decision. On 28 October, party headquarters announced that Davies was unable to accept Churchill's offer, but that, in view of the government's narrow Commons majority, Liberals would be willing to give support for measures 'clearly conceived in the interest of the country as a whole'.[104] The decision was a crucial one, as even those such as Violet Bonham Carter, who urged Davies to accept, came to realize. So low were Liberal fortunes at this time that, had Davies accepted, the remaining party could easily have disintegrated. His refusal was probably the greatest act of service rendered to his party during 11 years as leader.

Defiance in adversity had become a Liberal trademark, but after 1951 it seemed particularly hollow: 'Our beachhead is not enlarged,' the party conceded, 'but it remains.' 'We refuse to be stamped out,' Davies told the Liberal Assembly the following year. 'In spite of all temptations we still prefer our own doctrine and we are determined to maintain our independence.'[105] Privately, he took comfort from the strength of Liberalism among the under-graduate population. He was, he insisted, less downhearted than in 1945 or 1950: 'I cannot give a reason for this. It is just a state of mind and may be quite illogical.'[106] At least the danger of assimila-tion within Conservatism had largely passed. Having achieved a majority government on the basis of their own efforts, the electoral imperative of the late 1940s appeared less acute in Conservative minds. In any case, it seemed logical to assume that the steady attritional erosion of the Liberal vote would continue, and that the party would eventually fade away without the need for further pacts or negotiations at a national level – and in particular without the concession of proportional representation. Thus the Liberal Party's very weakness in the early 1950s may well have proved its salvation. It had become too small to worry about.

But the party's problems were far from over. 'I truly believe, and, of course, I sincerely hope,' wrote Davies in the wake of the election, 'we have now reached the nadir and that from now on we shall begin to climb steadily the hill of prosperity.'[107] In fact, the situation continued to deteriorate. Liberals did badly in by-elections, contesting only eight of the 45 held during the 1951–55 Parliament and saving their deposit just once. Only a respectable second place in December 1954 on 36 per cent of the vote on a low turnout at Inverness, not even contested in 1951, provided a crumb of comfort. The position in local elections was no better. In 1950, only 2.2 per cent of borough councillors were Liberals; and by 1955 the figure stood at just 1.5 per cent. After 1953, Liberals were the largest party in just two borough councils, Huddersfield in Yorkshire and Mossley, near Manchester. The last geographi-cal strongholds of Liberal support seemed to be vanishing, with Labour steadily mopping up the nonconformist vote in rural Wales as the decade progressed. By 1955, the number of affiliated local associations fell below 300. As individual membership declined, the party's financial worries increased and its fragile dependence on the generosity of a few wealthy benefactors became ever more apparent.

In the Commons, the parliamentary rump under the age-ing Clement Davies presented an unimpressive picture. Most of the Liberals who enjoyed national recognition stood among the defeated. Violet Bonham Carter saw no future chance of securing election, except perhaps as a Conservative. Megan Lloyd George, concluding that she was 'too left for the modern Liberal taste',[108] announced in 1952 that she would not fight her old Anglesey constituency again and declined re-election as a party vice-president. Egged on by Philip Noel-Baker, her clandestine lover on the Labour front bench, she now stood aloof from such efforts as were made to sustain the radical tradition in Liberal politics and prepared the ground for her eventual move to the Labour ranks. Frank Byers had failed to regain his seat and now reconciled himself to an important but non-parliamentary role in the party's affairs. Donald Wade and Arthur Holt, the respective beneficiaries of the local pacts in Huddersfield and Bolton, were welcome additions to Liberalism's depleted ranks in the Commons, but they remained vulnerable to any future change of heart on the part of the Conservative Party.

The position in the House of Lords was little better. Sinclair had given up hope of returning to the Commons and, enthused 'by the prospect of leaving his cold hermitage in Caithness for the rhetorical delights of Westminster', was created a viscount in the 1952 New Year Honours List.[109] But plans that he should become party leader in the upper house were thwarted by his own ill health. Sinclair did not take his seat until 1954, and did not make his maiden speech until 1956. As a result, Samuel stayed on as leader in the Lords until 1955, when he was 85 years of age. A survey carried out at around this time revealed that, despite a nominal contingent of 46 Liberal peers, only 16 were deemed to be 'valuable attenders'. The average age of the party's 'first-line' in the upper chamber was 77.[110] The depths of the party's roots in history had been a major factor in keeping it going when so many other elements pointed towards extinction. Samuel's ministerial career went back to 1905 and his retirement cut a last tie binding Liberals to an earlier, happier age. Violet Bonham Carter admitted that it was 'hard for those who remember the great men of our Party to continue to serve its shadow among the lesser ones'.[111]

Inside Parliament, the Liberal Party proceeded to give general support to Churchill's government. Many took comfort in the belief that the Conservatives now embodied most of what was best in Liberal thinking: 'I am really inclined to think that it is the Tory party that is extinct, not the Liberal,' insisted Gilbert Murray. 'They have had to accept a more than half Liberal leader, and on the main lines of policy people like Winston and Eden scarcely differ from us.'[112] Four years later, this lifelong Liberal expressed satisfaction at a further Conservative General Election victory: 'Nearly all the educated people I meet are Liberal, but vote Conservative' – a course he himself had taken.[113] Such complacent thinking did not go unchallenged. The Radical Reform Group was set up in 1953 with the clear intention of challenging the preponderant free trade lobby. The Group argued for government intervention in the economy to regulate trade, maintain full employment and provide social security. The 1953 and 1954 Party assemblies witnessed heated debates between individualists, who continued to preach the time-honoured Liberal virtues of free trade, personal liberty and minimum government intervention, and radicals who traced their political pedigrees back via the interventionist policies of Beveridge and Keynes to the New Liberalism of the turn of the century. But to most observers such disputes seemed largely irrelevant. The public found little in Liberalism to give it a distinctive appeal. As one despairing Liberal candidate put it, 'our words cut no ice, for the single reason that we have nothing new, original or constructive to say. If we had something to say on these lines, the probability is that we should be branded as non-Liberals.'[114] In short, Liberals had become, as Churchill was reported as saying, 'so few and so futile'.

Against this background, the 1955 General Election offered little cause for optimism. From a Liberal point of view, it looked very much a re-run of 1951. Liberals fielded 110 candidates, just one more than at the previous election. The choice of seats seemed marginally more appropriate than four years earlier, and their campaigns were run somewhat more efficiently. Even so, a number of forlorn candidates were sent out to face inevitable slaughter and, compared with the better-resourced Labour and Conservative parties, the Liberals still looked amateurish. Bristol North was a constituency the party decided to fight as early as July 1954. Not until the following April, however, was a prospective candidate in place. But the local party, unable to afford the £12 a week salary required, still fought the election without a full-time agent. Even finding enough envelopes appeared to pose problems. The candidate himself 'was not able to give all his time to the campaign, and was handicapped in the early stages because he had no one to drive him round the constituency. He was not completely mobile until a supporter, able to drive a car, came back from holiday.'[115]

The Liberal manifesto accepted that the country had moved into somewhat calmer waters than had been the case four years earlier, but insisted that the party still stood as security against two class-based parties seeking to use their power in the interests of 'their particular clients'. It criticized both Labour and the Conservatives for the timidity of their approaches to European integration, warned about the dangers of inflation, stressed the need to scrutinize government expenditure, and reiterated earlier calls for Scottish and Welsh devolution and electoral reform. Its most distinctive features, suggested the *Manchester Guardian*, were 'an appeal to the middle-class vote and an attack, in the name of liberty, on the tendency of trade unions to limit the freedom of individuals within the unions'. It was no surprise when, a month before polling day, Megan Lloyd George announced her conversion to Labour, concluding that the Liberal Party had lost all touch with the radical tradition that had once inspired it. Talks with Conservative officials to see if the Huddersfield and Bolton arrangements could be extended soon collapsed in the face of unrealistic Liberal demands. While the party did not give any formal advice to Liberal supporters in constituencies where no Liberal candidate was standing, it was striking that the Tory lists included 13 candidates who had previously stood as Liberals, seven of whom were elected. Churchill, standing as a humble backbencher, restated his familiar refrain that a broad harmony now existed between the aims of the modern Conservative Party and those of the great Liberal leaders of earlier times.

Given all the circumstances, the electoral outcome was a cause for relief. Only perhaps in Inverness did the Liberals have any real chance of adding to their meagre parliamentary tally. In the event, no seats were gained, but none was lost either. For the first time since 1929 the party's position had not deteriorated compared with the previous General Election. Liberal statisticians derived a crumb of comfort from a marginal increase in the average Liberal poll from 14.7 per cent to 15.1 per cent. Most significantly, now that the post-war electorate had had an opportunity to taste a full term of both Labour and Conservative governments, the Liberal Party had begun to benefit from what would become one of its greatest assets, the protest vote. An examination of the constituency of Bristol North suggested that more than half the Liberal vote derived from dissatisfaction with the major parties rather than a genuine conversion to Liberalism.[116] For all that, whatever advance had occurred, it scarcely merited the ecstatic reaction of party headquarters: 'It is not just a "moral" victory,' insisted *Liberal News*, 'it is concrete progress on which we can begin at once to build for the full triumph at the next election.'[117]

The Bases of Survival

After more than 20 years of steady decline, the Liberal Party was still in business, just about a national force in British politics. This is a phenomenon worthy in itself of a word of explanation. John Stevenson has wisely written that 'the party's structure as a loose grouping of largely middle-class individuals, tied together by sentiment, friendship and voluntary commitment, was one well-adapted to survival and to resisting take-over'.[118] Within this context, tribute must be paid to key figures – parliamentarians, senior party officials and dedicated constituency workers – who managed to convince at least themselves that the Liberal cause was not lost, and that the flame must not be extinguished. During the 1950s, many local activists, anticipating the community politics of later years, saw the importance of contesting local elections as a preparation for fielding a Liberal candidate at a future General Election.[119] Even where a Liberal constituency association had ceased to exist, or had perhaps been taken over by the Liberal Nationals, small and often isolated branch associations kept the party's flag flying.[120] For nearly 20 years the Liberals of the tiny town of Langholm were the only organized body in Dumfriesshire, south-west Scotland, even though that constituency had regularly returned a Liberal MP in the decade after the First World War. Such organizations at least provided a foundation that could be built upon and developed in future years. Looking back from the more promising days of the early 1970s, Leonard Behrens recalled that one of the encouragements he had received when touring the country during two years (1955–6) as Acting President and then President of the Liberal Party Organisation was to find 'in every town and even in little villages groups of determined Liberals who, without any expectation of success, continued to keep the Party alive in preparation for the great days which are to come'.[121] The support of the press could often be important in convincing a locality that Liberalism remained a credible political force in that area. The *News Chronicle* was now the only broadly Liberal-supporting national title – though even its endorsement was not consistent and, in any case, it closed in 1960 – but there remained in the 1950s around 20 local newspapers which backed the party, helping to sustain Liberalism in such disparate locations as Carlisle in the North-West, Huddersfield in Yorkshire, Rochdale in Lancashire, Greenock in Scotland and Aberystwyth in Wales. In addition, it is clear that Liberalism survived on the strength of its own tradition, of voting Liberal from one generation to the next, all the party's remaining constituencies being ones of long-term Liberal strength. In only a handful of constituencies, however, were 'natural' Liberal voters – nonconformists, small-scale farmers and small businessmen – sufficiently numerous to make a Liberal victory likely. Such pockets of support continued, oblivious almost of what was happening to the party elsewhere in the country. Furthermore, no serious challenger to the Liberal Party had emerged for the third place in British politics, and there remained a sizeable number of voters who were wary of the duopolistic stranglehold of Labour and the Conservatives. These were fragile bases for survival, but offered just enough of a foundation to hand over a viable party into the more promising era that now followed.

4 Two Steps Forward and One Back, 1955–79

Grimond Takes Charge

At the beginning of 1956 both Clement Davies and Leonard Behrens, the party's acting president, published optimistic New Year messages, claiming that Liberalism was on the march again. Though such optimism prompted a measure of ridicule in the press and among political opponents, there was nothing surprising in these Liberal pronouncements. At least since the 1920s, the party's unrealistic and sometimes illogical pretensions had been an important factor in keeping it alive. Objectively, however, and despite the bottoming-out of the process of Liberal decline revealed in the recent General Election, there was little hard evidence to sustain such high hopes apart from an encouraging by-election result at Torquay, Devon, in December 1955, where the Liberal candidate took 23.8 per cent of the vote. Even when, the following February, with the Conservatives' post-election honeymoon rapidly receding in the face of a worsening economic climate, the Liberals secured 36.4 per cent at Hereford and 21.4 per cent at Gainsborough, Lincolnshire, any triumphal flag-waving was surely premature. Yet, with the hindsight of half a century, it is now clear that Davies and Behrens had at least an element of truth on their side. The Liberal tide had turned, and though there would be much ebbing as well as flowing in the years ahead, the process of revival had indeed begun.

Not surprisingly, not all Liberals had yet detected this turn-around in their fortunes. Frank Byers, for example, had begun to work out a plan for the next General Election that would have reduced the Liberals to the status of little more than a guerrilla force rather than a conventional political party. 'Operation Blackmail' involved putting up candidates in vulnerable Conservative seats with the aim of contesting, or not contesting, them as party

171

strategy determined: 'This wld. be the only way to make terms for ourselves with the Conservatives for the next Election.' Violet Bonham Carter was sympathetic to this idea, recognizing that, in the future, Liberals were only likely to win contests in straight fights, and that the Conservatives would only concede these if the Liberal Party was prepared to 'exploit real nuisance value' where the Tories themselves were in danger of defeat.[1] In practice, the threat that the Liberal Party might be swallowed up by the Conservatives, very real at the beginning of the decade, had largely passed, not least because the Conservatives had proved to themselves that they could defeat their Labour opponents comfortably while an independent Liberal Party continued to exist. But, at the same time, this experience also suggested that there was little scope to build on the example of Huddersfield-style co-operation. Two successive General Election victories weakened the case for anti-socialist pacts. Nor did it seem likely that Liberalism would fall victim to the Labour Party's embrace, largely because the evidence suggested that the presence of a Liberal candidate did more harm to the Conservatives than to Labour. Indeed, when Labour won a by-election in Gloucester in October 1957, this was widely attributed to the effects of a Liberal intervention. But while the risks of an overt takeover by one or other of the larger parties might have receded, Liberals in the mid-1950s still faced the likely, and equally damaging, prospect of the remorseless, attritional erosion of their support, both among the politically active and from within their now fragile electoral base. In July 1956, a significant group of defectors, including Dingle Foot and Wilfrid Roberts, went over to Labour, claiming that there was 'a great deal of common ground between Radicals and the Labour Party and that the differences between them now largely belong to the past'.[2]

One hoped-for possibility was that the electorate might grow tired of a second-term Conservative government and, in particular if economic problems continued to mount, turn to the Liberals rather than travelling the full distance to support the Labour Party. But in 1955 there seemed little prospect of such a development. Drawing on his long experience, Hugh Dalton described that year's General Election as the 'most tedious, apathetic, uninteresting' in which he had participated, the product of the electorate's inability to find grave fault with the way the country was being run.[3] In Anthony Eden, moreover, the Conservatives now had a new and comparatively young leader, a man with a long-standing 'liberal' pedigree with which to appeal to a broad spectrum of British opinion. That the Liberals would advance upon their recent marginal progress was, therefore, by no means inevitable. That they did so was the product of two important catalysts, the first within their own control, and the second entirely beyond it.

At the end of 1955, Clement Attlee retired after two decades of leading the Labour Party. His replacement was 49-year-old Hugh Gaitskell. This left Clement Davies, until recently the youngest of the three party leaders, now by some years the most elderly, and his recent record was not impressive. Illness had largely kept him out of the 1955 election campaign and he was in any case waging a personal battle against the ravages of drink. In private at least, many prominent Liberals, including Major-General Grey, the Party Treasurer, and Philip Fothergill, Party Vice-President, had concluded that it was time for a change. That change effectively took place at the 1956 Party assembly in Folkestone, even though in strict constitutional terms the decision did not lie within its remit. The youthful chief whip, Jo Grimond, found himself acclaimed as 'the white hope' of the future, even before Davies formally announced that he was stepping down. The later vote by the parliamentary party was little more than a formality. In practice, Grimond was the only viable candidate. Among the small band of Liberal MPs, only he combined an unequivocal and full-time commitment to the Liberal cause with a reasonably secure electoral position in his constituency. The outgoing leader was warmly received, though it is clear that 'gratitude for past service and relief at his decision to step down were mixed in about equal proportions'.[4] It was a wise move. As *The Economist* commented, 'pensioning off an old servant is a sad business, but when the Liberals have paid their tributes to Clement Davies, they are bound to feel relieved that their leadership, like that of the two main parties, has now moved into the next generation'.[5]

The Impact of Suez

Grimond's assumption of the leadership coincided with the early stages of a crisis for the government that would transform for years to come the relationship between the Liberal and Conservative parties. Opinions on the Eden government's conduct of the Suez adventure have differed violently, both at the time and in subsequent historiography. However, for the Liberal Party this was a watershed, all the more poignant because of the Prime Minister's well deserved reputation until this time for commitment to the principles of liberal internationalism. Violet Bonham Carter confessed that she had 'almost persuaded [herself] during the 51–56 Government [that] Toryism was shading into Liberalism'. Now, she insisted to a Conservative Suez sceptic, 'I feel there is reversion to type'.[6] Even so, the initial Liberal response to the crisis was far more equivocal than it later appeared. As Lady Violet recorded after a 'terrible' Liberal Party committee meeting:

> Jo ... says Nasser's action is the parallel of Hitler's when he invaded the Rhineland and that unless we bring about his fall the whole Middle East will go his way – nationalize their oil, threaten to cut us off etc. I think this is true. Yet I hardly feel that we can 'go it alone' and align world opinion against us.[7]

In the Lords, both Samuel and Sinclair supported Eden, and when Labour first divided the Commons on 30 October, three Liberal MPs, Davies, Roderic Bowen and Arthur Holt – who, after all, comprised 50 per cent of the parliamentary party – voted with the government. In the country too, many Liberal supporters found it difficult to criticize the government with the nation effectively at war.[8] As rumours spread, however, of British collusion with France and Israel prior to the latter's attack on Egypt, it became easier for Grimond to distance his party from the Conservative administration. For at least a generation, the Conservatives' image as the natural repository for the best traditions of British Liberalism had been destroyed. Many former Liberals returned to the party fold. Others looked to it for the first time. Rather like the Hoare–Laval Pact of 20 years earlier, Suez opened up new opportunities for redefining the Liberal Party in a way that clearly distinguished it from its political opponents.

Establishing a Liberal Identity

The replacement of a 72–year-old leader in poor health by a vigorous 43-year-old offered obvious advantages, especially when the new leader had Grimond's freshness, imagination, ability to communicate and striking good looks, which gave an impression of openness and reliability. The new man's personality would be a key factor in the Liberal Party's subsequent revival, but on its own it was not enough. The party was unlikely to make much progress until it succeeded in establishing a clear and identifiable image in the British political spectrum. The most common image of Liberalism at this time was that it was a compromise party that combined the better traits of its larger opponents. Many voters could only identify it in terms of what it was not, rather than on the basis of what it was. As late as 1959, a Gallup poll found that 59 per cent of the population had no knowledge of Liberal policies, a figure that included almost half of those who said they were going to vote Liberal. For too long the party had tried to define itself in terms of its two rivals, as a sort of moderating influence between the extremes of socialism and conservatism. This stance had many disadvantages. For those who accepted this caricature of British politics in the 1950s, Liberals offered themselves as a classless party to an electorate divided by class. For the more perceptive, who recognized that no vast chasm divided the Conservative Party of Harold Macmillan from that of Labour under Hugh Gaitskell, it left the Liberals with little political ground to call their own. As the Conservative, Angus Maude, pointed out:

> If anyone ... imagines that the Liberals are providing an essential moderating influence between a lot of revolutionary Socialists and a crowd of reactionary die-hard Tories, he should banish the idea at once. Both the big parties are chock full of people making sensible, moderate speeches to such an extent that the atmosphere often becomes positively stifling.[9]

On balance, by the time Grimond became leader, the party had become a largely right-leaning body, an anti-socialist rather than an anti-Conservative force in British politics. Its continuing commitment to free trade and low taxation did little to hone its progressive credentials at a time when Labour and the Conservatives were competing with each other in their claims to run the managed economy. Despite numerous defections to Labour, a strand of left-wing radicalism did persist, and the Radical Reform Group formally realigned itself with the party early in 1956. A contributor to an important volume on Liberal thought, published in 1957, insisted that 'by any strict use of language Liberals are the true Left, the real progressives', but objectively it was difficult to sustain such a contention.[10] Yet the fact that such diverse ideas could be embraced within one relatively small political grouping was still widely seen as a virtue. Writing in the month of Grimond's accession, the party president explained:

> We are a Party of individualists, with minds of our own. We do not take directions from our leaders: we combine to hammer out our policies. That is one of the reasons why it is not easy to be a Liberal, and why it is common for Liberals to disagree.[11]

To the wider public, however, Liberal diversity merely created confusion and was not conducive to building up the party's electoral appeal.

Grimond was a man of ideas. His literary output in terms of books, pamphlets and articles was considerable. In time, he came to dominate his party's thinking in a way that no leader had done since Lloyd George. Almost half of the party's manifesto for the 1959 General Election was his personal statement. His first period as leader, however, was not one in which he stamped his distinctive ideological imprint on the party. For the time being, traditional Liberal preoccupations with high taxation and government waste continued. In what was almost an anticipation of the Conservatism of Keith Joseph and Margaret Thatcher, Grimond warned that an overweening state would create a dependency culture. The population risked being lulled into the belief that it was right to transfer responsibility from individual enterprise to state activity at the cost of ever higher taxes. In similar vein, he singled out inflation as the most serious economic problem facing the country, and advocated monetarist solutions to curb it.[12] At the same time, Grimond's Liberal Party did adopt a distinctive position on two important policy issues. At the 1956 Folkestone assembly, the party passed a resolution calling for Britain's active participation in the setting up of a Common Market. This was just over a year after the powers of Western Europe had gathered at Messina, Sicily, to plan the next stages of European integration, a process from which the British Conservative government had quickly withdrawn. Grimond seemed at first to have misgivings. An article published in *Liberal News* in February 1957, apparently with his approval, suggested that Britain should join a free-trade area, but not a customs union. This stance was consistent with the party's ongoing commitment to free trade. By the end of 1958, however, by which time the European Economic Community (EEC) had become a reality, Grimond was ready to abandon his doubts about that body's common external tariff, won round by individuals such as his mother-in-law, Violet Bonham Carter, to the view that the Community provided the best approach to further European co-operation. The other policy development related to defence. In March 1957, the parliamentary party, at Grimond's prompting, stated that it was time for Britain to abandon the manufacture of its own nuclear deterrent and concentrate instead on nuclear research, to enable the country to continue to make a contribution to the protective shield provided by the United States. Coming in the wake of the Suez episode, this initiative helped to confirm the party's separation from the Conservatives.

Grimond's leadership saw early evidence of progress in two areas that would be vital to the party's recovery as a national political force – an improved performance in by-elections and a revival of its almost dormant base in local politics. Between Torquay, Devon, in December 1955 and Galloway, in south-west Scotland, in April 1959 there were 53 by-elections. Of these, the Liberals contested just 19. But, significantly, only one deposit was lost and in seven contests the party came either first or second. The Liberals began to understand the importance of a good by-election result, not only in the hope of increasing representation at Westminster, but also in raising the morale of party workers and focusing national attention in a way that was impossible in a General Election campaign. The curtain-raiser came at Rochdale, Lancashire, in February 1958 when the well-known media personality, Ludovic Kennedy, forced the Conservatives into third place, a sufficiently bad result to prompt an offer of resignation from the Tory chairman, Lord Hailsham. Then, the following month, Mark Bonham Carter, Violet's son and Asquith's grandson, snatched the Devon constituency of Torrington from the Conservatives. It was the first Liberal by-election gain for almost 30 years and prompted hyperbolic, if understandable, elation. Lady Violet recalled 'the strange sense of being a member of an army of liberation entering occupied territory which for years had been ruled by quislings and collaborators and that their day was over once and for all'.[13] Victory was particularly sweet since the defeated Tory had sought to tap into the historic traditions of West Country Liberalism by adopting the hybrid designation of 'National Liberal and Conservative'. In the wake of this triumph, Grimond began to expound the themes that would be so important for his repositioning of the party over the following years. The Liberals' task would be to 'carve out a niche for ourselves Left of Centre ... in the sense that we stand for personal freedom against authority ... in the sense that we believe there is still too much poverty, too many slums and too much cruelty ... in the sense that we want and mean to have a wide dispersal of property and power'.[14]

With little prompting from Grimond himself, the party also began to appreciate the importance of securing successes in local government, largely neglected by the Liberals for a generation, as a first foundation for the creation of a broader party base. In organizational terms it was obviously easier to compete with the major parties on a ward basis than across an entire constituency. The process of recovery had begun before Grimond took over the leadership, with modest gains registered in both 1955 and 1956. The improvement continued, and in 1958 the Liberals had their best results since before the war, with 54 gains notched up in the boroughs and 59 in the urban and rural district councils. In another anticipation of its later tactics, the party showed signs of varying its image and appeal to suit the demands of the locality being contested. In Exeter, the Liberal assault was mounted against the Tories; but, by contrast, Bradford Liberals still tended to work in partnership with the Conservatives to breach a Labour stronghold.[15]

It was tempting for party loyalists to be carried away by what were only modest advances from a very low baseline. Most new Liberal votes were coming from disgruntled Conservatives, registering a probably temporary displeasure at the apparent inability of Macmillan's succession of Chancellors to manage the managed economy. Even the victory at Torrington only cancelled out the loss of Carmarthen to Labour in February 1957, following the death of Sir Rhys Hopkin Morris. The parliamentary party's strength remained stuck at six, and jokes were still made at the Liberals' expense about party conferences being held in telephone boxes. Though the small band of Liberal MPs became markedly more critical of the Conservative government than it had been under

Davies, it failed to make a real impact in this period. More significantly, the extra-parliamentary party, though enthused by
Grimond's energy and commitment, was not necessarily moving
in step with its leader. The 1958 Torquay assembly was something
of a shambles, dominated, *The Economist* suggested, by a combination of 'vacuous youth' and 'blithering old age'.[16] The passage
of a resolution reaffirming the party's commitment to unilateral
free trade was hard to reconcile with Grimond's wish to locate
Liberalism at the heart of the modern political agenda. Some of
the surviving Liberal outposts that might have been expected to
provide a launch pad for future growth seemed curiously resistant to Grimond's message: 'Welsh Liberals increasingly appeared
a relatively conservative party, thus driving radical thinkers disillusioned with Labour into the arms of Plaid Cymru.'[17] Most disappointingly, it proved difficult, if not impossible, to sustain the
momentum of advance.

As the General Election approached, the majority of floating
voters drifted towards their natural points of allegiance. None the
less, the Liberals went into the contest with some grounds for optimism. Organizational revival was reflected in the party's readiness
to contest 216 seats, almost double the total of the last two elections.
The party's finances were on a more stable footing than they had
been for some time – by the end of 1957 the annual accounts had
been balanced at more than £24,000. Yet this was still a small sum
compared to the money available to the major parties, and there
remained relatively few constituencies where the Liberals could
conduct a comprehensive canvass or even spend the full amount
of money legally permitted. It was eloquent commentary on the
progress still needed that about three-quarters of the Liberals who
went to the polls in party cars reported that they had done so in
non-Liberal vehicles. Overall, the Liberals were still seen as 'the
largest of the minor parties, a federation of independently operating candidates rather than ... a broad national movement'.[18] The
manifesto *People Count* reiterated many well-worn themes, in particular that 'a Liberal vote is a protest against the British political
system being divided up between two powerful Party machines,
one largely financed by the employers and the other by the Trade
Unions'. It called for more money for education and roads, and
an increase in the old-age pension. But overall, the document
offered few specific policy promises, stressing instead the need for

a substantial Liberal presence in the new Parliament to 'save us from Tory or Labour reactionaries'. Such an aspiration hinted at the objective, which seemed at one point realizable, of holding the balance in the new Commons. Yet neither in the manifesto nor the campaign itself did Grimond clarify how Liberals would behave in such a situation.

Realignment and Revival

In the event, the result was both a considerable encouragement and a great disappointment. Granted that the doubling of the number of seats contested meant that the Liberals were fighting some less-promising constituencies, the average Liberal vote still rose from 15.1 per cent to 16.9 per cent. At the same time, the number of lost deposits fell to 55. In 16 more seats compared with 1955, Liberal candidates forced themselves into second place. The overall Liberal vote went up to 1.6 million, some 5.9 per cent of the total. But, on the debit side, the party still returned just six MPs. To Grimond's dismay, Bonham Carter failed to hold on to Torrington, but this loss was balanced by the victory of the youthful Jeremy Thorpe in the neighbouring constituency of North Devon. But by far the most promising feature of the result from Grimond's point of view was the effect it had on the Conservative–Labour contest, even though this was far from leaving the Liberals holding the balance of power. The government had now extended its majority to 100 seats. For the third successive election, Labour was on the losing side, defying the expectations of contemporary psephologists that the natural swing of the electoral pendulum would return it to power. Before long, commentators suggested that the Labour Party was in a state of terminal decline, increasingly deprived of its perennial power base among the manual working class, as an ever-expanding proportion of the electorate, benefiting from the unprecedented affluence of 1950s Britain, took on the characteristics of a middle-class lifestyle, including a propensity to vote Conservative. Grimond was quick to see the possibilities that such a situation might afford to the Liberal Party.

Grimond's aim was to secure a realignment of British politics that would create a more relevant division between the parties than existed by the late 1950s. The real divide, he believed, lay between progressives and conservatives and, while the Liberals might constitute the nucleus of a new progressive grouping, recruits would also have to be found inside Labour's non-socialist wing, and even among moderate Tories. Such a body could unite in support of individual freedom and responsibility, and a commitment to work towards equality of opportunity and international co-operation. The present party system had the practical effect of entrenching the forces of conservatism, whether of the right or the left, in power. Believing that the pattern of class voting was likely to decline, Grimond was the first Liberal leader since Lloyd George to see his party's salvation lying not purely in its own efforts but as part of a restructuring of Britain's political left. As soon as the election was over, he spelt out his vision:

> I would like to see the radical side of politics – the Liberals and most of the Labour Party – make a new appeal to people to take a more active part in all sorts of real political issues … There must be a bridge between socialism and the Liberal policy of co-ownership in industry through a type of syndicalism coupled with a non-conformist outlook such as was propounded on many issues by George Orwell.[19]

An article by Grimond in *The Times* three years later adds greater clarity: 'The divisions in politics fall in the wrong place. The natural breakdown should be into a Conservative Party – a small group of convinced Socialists in the full sense – and a broadly based progressive Party. It is the foundations of the last named that the Liberal Party seeks to provide.'[20]

In practice, the goal of realignment depended on a major split occurring within Labour's ranks. During the first three years of the new Parliament this looked to be a realistic proposition. Members of the Labour Party reacted in varying ways to their third successive electoral defeat, but as far as Hugh Gaitskell, the party leader, was concerned, the voters' message was clear: Labour had to modernize or perish. Influenced by the example of the German Social Democratic Party (SPD), he proposed that the party should drop the famous Clause Four of its constitution, which committed it to the principle of the public ownership of British industry. Though Clause Four was of largely symbolic importance, Gaitskell saw that if Labour remained stuck with its almost exclusively working-class image, it might never be elected again in a rapidly changing and increasingly affluent society. It was the beginning of a Labour civil war, in which the party leader took on his own left wing at successive party conferences, losing the battle over Clause Four but emerging victorious in the struggle to resist a commitment to unilateral nuclear disarmament. At one point it looked possible that the party's non-socialist right wing might break away in the manner anticipated in Grimond's vision of realignment. The Campaign for Democratic Socialism, set up immediately after Labour's 1960 Scarborough conference, where the left carried a resolution in favour of unilateralism but at which Gaitskell pledged to 'fight and fight and fight again' to save the party he loved, contained many similarities, even down to some of the personnel involved, with the breakaway of the Social Democratic Party two decades later. Quite possibly, moreover, Grimond could have worked amicably enough with many of the Gaitskellites, had Labour's left emerged triumphant from the party's internecine feuds. William Rodgers, the Campaign for Democratic Socialism's full-time organizer, later recalled being matched with Mark Bonham Carter in a *Sunday Times* discussion of the common ground between the Labour and Liberal parties: 'Although it was nearly thirty years before we found ourselves in the same party as Liberal Democrats, Mark and I reached a surprising measure of agreement.'[21]

Yet these optimistic signs probably served to conceal what was really happening on the electoral ground. The continuing progress of the Liberal Party among the voters was more the product of the Conservative government's unpopularity than it was of Labour's divisions. Macmillan's political touch rapidly deserted him after 1960. The image of 'Supermac' was replaced by that of an ageing, out-of-touch and increasingly accident-prone Prime Minister. The introduction of Selwyn Lloyd's pay pause in 1961 was probably more important in sustaining the momentum of Liberal electoral advance than were the chasms within the Labour Party displayed publicly at its Scarborough conference the previous year. Labour's unappealing image merely encouraged disillusioned Conservatives to stop at the halfway house of Liberalism rather than to travel the full distance and transfer their support to Labour.

The party was in any case ill-equipped to compete with Labour and the Conservatives on anything like equal terms. Liberal organization remained rudimentary compared with that of its opponents. The party went into the 1964 General Election with just

60 full-time agents; and its annual income stood at around £70,000. Party headquarters lacked the funds to provide a library service and even had to do without a typing pool. Too much depended on Grimond himself: 'You have taken all the strings into your own hands', declared the party's candidate at the Ebbw Vale by-election of 1960, 'and the whole success or failure of Liberalism now rests on your shoulders alone.'[22] That same candidate had recently resigned as Party Treasurer, complaining that the party organization must become a democratic body responsible to the party as a whole 'and not remain, as it is today, the preserve of a small private coterie'.[23] Grimond was restricted in Parliament by the talent available to him. In practice, he could rely on the services of just four MPs, including himself, and 'the amount of work required of Donald [Wade], Arthur [Holt] and Jeremy [Thorpe] [was] preposterous'.[24] Violet Bonham Carter described the parliamentary party's parlous position in July 1961:

> Wade is ill, Jeremy is ill, Clem [Davies] is a chronic absentee and useless when present. [Grimond] wrote imploring Bowen to be with him for the Berlin debate on Monday and to *speak* – and Bowen replied that he had 'a function'. He does damn all in the House. As Jo says – why go into it? [25]

For the moment, none of this seemed to matter. The evidence of a Liberal revival was there for all to see. By the end of 1959, party membership had risen to an estimated 150,000. By the winter of 1961–62 it had gone up to 250,000 and peaked at around 350,000 in 1963. The 1960 assembly at Eastbourne was the best attended since the war and enthusiastically endorsed the leadership's policy of seeking membership of the Common Market – this at a time when informed opinion at least was becoming aware of unflattering comparisons between Britain's recent economic performance and that of her continental neighbours. The decision to contest a by-election in Bolton East that November effectively ended an era of Conservative–Liberal electoral co-operation, and represented an important confirmation of Grimond's insistence that Liberalism was a party of the radical left, even though it left at least two of the party's small band of MPs dangerously exposed to a future Conservative challenge. His vision of Liberalism necessitated some adjustment to his policy stance. A continuation of the proto-Thatcherite programme of rolling back the frontiers of the state and allowing free rein to the workings of the market economy no longer made much sense, especially as the late 1950s and early 1960s witnessed the progressive departure of 'economic liberals' from the party's ranks. Instead, Grimond began to emphasize the need to modernize the British economy and shake it out of the lethargy into which it had increasingly fallen. The change was apparent when he addressed the Young Liberals in December 1961. In place of the traditional shibboleths of free trade and individual liberty, he stressed the importance of economic growth and regional development, calling for a wages policy and a national plan to guide the country's development in a new technological era. Grimond himself was an obvious asset. His youth and tendency to iconoclasm chimed well with the increasingly anti-establishment and anti-deference mood of the new decade – notwithstanding his own quintessentially establishment background.

The party made about 50 scattered gains in the local borough elections of 1960. The following year, almost 200 new seats were captured, leaving the Liberals as the largest group on such councils as Huddersfield, Yorkshire and Darwen, Lancashire, and in control of Bacup and Saddleworth in Lancashire, and Fletton in Cambridgeshire. But 1962, with the Conservative government embroiled in a succession of sex and security scandals, was the party's *annus mirabilis*. As many as 567 gains were recorded in the May council elections – nearly 400 of them from the Conservatives – while in March the party secured what remains to the present day its most celebrated single by-election victory. On 13 March, the Liberal candidate in Blackpool North did better than expected, cutting the Conservative majority from nearly 16,000 to just 973. The following day it was the turn of the voters of the Kent constituency of Orpington to go to the polls. Orpington was, it seemed, a rock-solid Conservative stronghold. The Tories had enjoyed a majority of 14,760 in the 1959 General Election. Now the Liberal candidate, Eric Lubbock, took the seat with a majority of 7,855. Even allowing for changes in the electoral register, about 10,000 former Conservative voters had moved over to the Liberal Party. 'We have been swept off our feet,' noted Harold Macmillan in the privacy of his diary, 'by a *Liberal* revival.'[26] A few months later, the Prime Minister dismissed seven members of his cabinet in a desperate attempt to breathe new life into the Conservative government. Briefly, anything seemed possible. A National Opinion Poll published on 28 March suggested that, on the question 'How would you vote in a general election held tomorrow?', the Liberals were in the lead with 30 per cent of the poll, with Labour having 29.9 per cent and the Conservatives 29.2 per cent. 'Orpington Man' was conceived as the symbol of the upwardly aspiring, professional, suburban commuter to whom Grimond's classless Liberal Party was uniquely well placed to appeal. The reality was somewhat more complex. The Liberals' gain was less dramatic than at first appeared, being the product of a carefully tended local base developed over the previous few years. By 1961, the party had raised its representation on the local 33-member Urban District Council to 12 seats. In addition, 'Orpington was no archetypal prosperous middle-aged established suburb, but an area of growth, conflict and change' in which the Conservatives had failed to respond to the interests and needs of newly arrived voters.[27]

As after Torrington, however, the Liberal tide soon began to ebb. Despite the party contesting all but one of the 17 by-elections held during 1962, there were no further gains. By October, the proportion of those intending to vote Liberal had fallen to 20 per cent. Three promising seats in West Derbyshire, Chippenham in Wiltshire and Colne Valley in Yorkshire all produced respectable second places but no new MPs. By 1963, the Liberal by-election vote was averaging 17 per cent compared to 28 per cent the previous year. The 1963 local elections witnessed a net gain of around 250 seats, a satisfying outcome by most criteria, yet a disappointment when set against the earlier trend.

What had gone wrong? As the next General Election approached, the Labour Party was again looking like a viable alternative government. This was largely Gaitskell's personal achievement, and his sudden death in January 1963 was in many ways a tragedy. But his successor, Harold Wilson, succeeded in binding the party together in a way that Gaitskell, with his obvious leanings towards the social democratic right, would always have found difficult. At the same time, the Conservatives responded belatedly to the Liberal challenge. In June 1962, Iain Macleod, the Party Chairman, was given the task of snuffing out the Liberal revival before it got out of hand. Many subsequent government policy initiatives, such as the abolition of Schedule A tax, were designed to win back the disgruntled middle-class voters who had flirted with the Liberals.

The Liberals' brief moment of policy distinctiveness also passed. Wilson quickly stole Grimond's clothes as he projected himself successfully as the youthful innovator of British politics who understood and could cope with the white heat of the techno-logical revolution. It was now the Labour leader who epitomized the widespread desire for a classless and modernized future. Even the last years of the Conservative ascendancy saw policy initiatives that stole the Liberals' thunder. In August 1961, the Macmillan government applied for British membership of the European Community (EC). The Tories were also converted to the virtues of indicative planning. With the setting up of the National Economic Development Council (NEDC) and the National Incomes Commission (NIC), and the introduction of a formal incomes pol-icy, Conservatism moved nearer than ever before to embracing the idea of the corporate state. In February 1963, the NEDC approved the ambitious target of a 4 per cent growth rate for the British economy. With the post-war consensus between Conservatives and Labour reaching its peak, despite the two parties' continu-ing capacity to vilify one another with apparently unrestrained fervour, little space remained into which to squeeze a third serious contender for power.

Liberal policy had in any case only played a small part in its electoral revival. As one activist recalled, 'there was not much knowledge of – still less enthusiasm for – any particular Liberal policies, either new or old'.[28] A poll in September 1961 revealed that under a third of declared Liberal supporters knew that their party favoured joining the Common Market. Two years later, a poll by NOP indicated the fragility of Liberal commitment. On a range of policy issues, from education to foreign affairs, Liberal voters consistently preferred the programmes of either the Conservative or the Labour Partys to the plans put forward by the Liberals themselves. This was not entirely surprising. The thousands of former Conservatives at Orpington had not suddenly been con-verted to a left-of-centre radicalism. Theirs was primarily a protest vote, subject to all the potential transience that implied. Grimond had been more successful in creating a vision of Liberal salvation than in working out how it would be achieved. He seems to have understood the paradox of the Liberal revival, while becoming intoxicated for a time by the sweet smell of passing electoral success:

> We cannot concentrate on certain issues and co-ordinate our work on them effectively until we find what issues Liberals really care about. This is the crux of the matter. I must confess failure here. For years Timothy Joyce supplied us with an admirable Public Opinion Poll which showed that many Liberals don't want to be Radical, they are comfortable, not very political, middle of the road people. I fear this may be true. If it is, it makes nonsense of nine-tenths of what the group at the top of the party are trying to say or do.[29]

Grimond's Strategy Unravels

These contradictions became more apparent in the General Election of 1964. Given Grimond's insistence that Liberalism was now a radical party of the left, it was inevitable that the thrust of the party's manifesto and campaign should be directed against the incumbent Conservative government. The manifesto, *Think for Yourself, Vote Liberal* was full of policy initiatives, drawing on the work of the party's new Research Department under Harry Cowie. Logically, however, the prospects of a realignment of parties would be strongest if the Conservatives secured their fourth successive victory. Only then would there be much likelihood of the Labour Party breaking up. By a ratio of about four to one, the Liberals' 365 candidates were fighting Conservative rather than Labour-held seats. It was here in middle-class suburbia that the party had been most successful in building up its organizational base. Thus, with Liberals largely picking up the votes of former Tories, their aim of forming the nucleus of a new opposition to Conservatism could only materialize if the Labour vote declined independently of anything the Liberals did. In practice, this did not happen. Labour's share of the poll increased marginally from 1959, when it had been heavily defeated. By contrast, the Conservative share fell by 6 per cent.

In many ways, the Liberal performance in 1964 gave cause for statistical satisfaction. At 11.2 per cent, the Liberal poll share had almost doubled since 1959. Even though 149 more constituencies were contested, the average Liberal vote went up from 16.9 per cent to 18.4 per cent, and only 53 deposits were lost. In 54 seats, the party came second and nine members were returned to Westminster, the first increase in Liberal representation at a General Election since 1929. All the victories had been secured in three-cornered fights. The most marked success was in terms of votes cast, more than 3.1 million, again the highest total since 1929. Yet, at another and more profound level, 1964 represented a considerable defeat, not least for Grimond himself. Labour's narrow overall victory by just five seats showed that the party had not become unelectable. In consequence, it set back any prospect of a realignment of the British political left.

The outcome of the 1964 election deprived the Liberal Party of the clear sense of political purpose that Grimond had developed over the previous Parliament. As one member of the party executive put it:

> Our trouble is simply that we need a strategy and don't have one. The party's principles aren't precise enough to tell us what to do without one, and without a strategy you're bound to get muddle. Why don't we have one? Because we were deprived of our traditional strategy by Labour's winning last autumn, and because the party hasn't been able to agree on a substitute. Most Liberals really have no very clear idea of where the party should go from here.[30]

The Conservatives were the obvious alternative for those who wanted Labour back in opposition, while the new government seemed determined to carry on without making obvious concessions to the Liberals. For a time, following the death of the Speaker and a by-election defeat at Leyton, in east London, it looked as if Labour would lose its parliamentary majority, necessitating some sort of arrangement with the Liberals. But Wilson cancelled out the numerical impact of the appointment of a Labour Speaker by tempting a Liberal, Roderic Bowen, to accept the Deputy Chairmanship of Ways and Means. Then, by avoiding such contentious legislation as the re-nationalization of steel, which would have prompted defections from his own right wing, Wilson managed to soldier on.

Adopting a stance of constructive opposition, the parliamentary Liberal Party determined to treat each government measure on its merits. By the end of May 1965, by which time they had been reinforced by the youthful David Steel's victory in a by-election in Roxburgh, Selkirk and Peebles, in Scotland, the Liberals had voted 40 times in the government lobby, opposed Labour on 85 occasions and abstained three times. Some of Labour's early initiatives, such as the creation of a Department of Economic Affairs under George Brown, separate from the Treasury, were in line with declared Liberal policy.[31] In general, however, Grimond found the new government insufficiently radical. On the other hand, he had no wish to force an early General Election, which might see the return of a Conservative administration.

Grimond's heart remained in the project of realignment, and in early June 1965 he put out a first feeler in an article in the *Sun*. 'If you are living on a small majority,' he suggested, 'it is common sense either to approach the Liberals...with proposals for active co-operation, or at least to concentrate your proposals within a range where their support is likely.'[32] Grimond spelt out his views in more detail in an interview published in the *Guardian* on 24 June under the somewhat exaggerated headline 'Coalition offer to Labour by Mr Grimond'. A few right-wing Labour MPs, including Woodrow Wyatt, evinced interest in Grimond's initiative, but in general its impact was more apparent among the parliamentary Liberal Party than within Labour's ranks. As before, Grimond had to work with those individuals whom the randomness of electoral fortune had returned to the Commons rather than with soul-mates of his own choosing, and two recent parliamentary recruits, Emlyn Hooson, who succeeded Clement Davies in Montgomeryshire on the latter's death in 1962, and Peter Bessell, newly elected in Bodmin, Cornwall, were among Grimond's sternest critics. By early August there were press reports of a right-wing revolt against the leadership.

Grimond found it difficult to follow his opponents' logic: 'There is only one course open to the Liberal Party,' insisted Hooson. 'That is to soldier on in complete independence of any arrangement with Conservatives or Labour and press for policies in which we believe.'[33] In abstract terms, there may have been something admirable in this sort of commitment to party political virginity. For a practical movement, however, interested in translating its ideals into concrete action and reality, it made little sense. The transition from a parliamentary party of ten to a governing majority in the Commons was likely to take the Liberal Party, unaided, decades to achieve. Moreover, for a party committed to electoral reform for more than a generation, it was almost a contradiction in terms to insist on maintaining the purity of Liberal doctrine, uncontaminated by association with any other party. Inter-party co-operation was likely to be both a prerequisite and a consequence of the introduction of proportional representation. As Grimond later explained: 'If electoral reform led to the results for which Liberals hoped and which statistics foretold, that is the fifty to seventy MPs to which our vote entitled us, then if government was to be carried on, coalitions of some sort would often be essential.'[34] Recognizing, however, that any formal approach to the Labour government would produce a serious split in the Liberal ranks, Grimond had to proceed with care. Through the good offices of the *Guardian*'s editor, Alastair Hetherington, Grimond held a private meeting with Wilson in early August. Though the Prime Minister was friendly and suggested that the government's planned legislative programme would be acceptable to the Liberal Party, he evinced no interest in a formal agreement. At the 1965 Liberal assembly, Grimond spoke bravely of Liberal teeth being in the real meat of power, but his words lacked substance. By the winter of 1965–66, the concept of realignment was to all intents and purposes dead. This situation left Grimond depressed and there were rumours at the beginning of the new year of his imminent resignation. In the event, with Labour's stock rising and every likelihood that Wilson would seize his chance and seek a renewed electoral mandate, Grimond determined to lead his party into the next election. But his creative contribution to Liberalism was effectively at an end.

Like its predecessor, the 1966 General Election was something of a curate's egg from the Liberal point of view. The party attempted to focus its resources on carefully targeted seats and, within a reduced total of 311 candidates, 87 constituencies contested in 1964 now had no Liberal standard-bearer. That said, in 33 seats the Liberals put up a candidate where none had stood two years before. Overall, the Liberal vote was bound to decline and it did so by almost 800,000, a fall of about 2.7 per cent in its share of the national vote. More disappointingly, the Liberal poll share fell in 278 of the constituencies also fought in 1964, rising in only 29. On the credit side, the vagaries of third-party politics worked for once to the Liberals' advantage, and their parliamentary representation rose to 12 MPs. The victories of Michael Winstanley in Cheadle, Cheshire, and Richard Wainwright in Colne Valley, Yorkshire, suggested that Liberalism was at least breaking out of its Celtic redoubt. Even so, ten of the party's MPs survived on majorities of under 2,500, while in only eight constituencies was a beaten Liberal within 5,000 votes of victory.

But the most striking feature of the results, and the one that provided a symbolic conclusion to Grimond's period as party leader, was the size of Labour's majority, which now stood at just under 100 seats. Grimond still spoke of the creation of a radical new coalition, uniting initially around the issue of British membership of the European Community but, as Hooson recognized, the election had 'definitely given Lib–Labory the axe once and for all'.[35] As the last remaining prospect of Labour's disintegration apparently receded, it was not long before Harold Wilson began to proclaim that his had become the natural governing party of British politics. The position of the Liberals, by contrast, seemed altogether less secure. Grimond's decade at its head had served to reveal a yawning gap between the Liberal voter and the vision with which the leader had enthused at least some of the party hierarchy. 'That we do better when a Tory government is in office,' Grimond later admitted, 'indicates that to some extent we are a haven for loosely attached Tories, disappointed in their government.'[36] Though written shortly after the events described, the verdict of the Nuffield historians merits repetition:

> Labour's comfortable victory in 1966 meant that the Liberals, although both their voting strength and their parliamentary representation had increased since Mr. Grimond became leader, had made no real strategic advance. In the weeks after polling day in 1966 it was no clearer than it had been ten years before how the Liberals were going either to form a new radical coalition with elements from both the Conservative and Labour parties, or to supplant Labour as the chief opposition to the Conservatives... to the extent that an opportunity existed [between 1964 and 1966], the Liberals failed to seize it.[37]

In January 1967, Grimond resigned as Liberal leader. He was still only 53 years old and it is difficult to escape the conclusion that, after just over a decade in the post, he felt that he had achieved all he could. Though his electoral strategy had disintegrated in the face of Labour's victories in 1964 and 1966, his legacy remained important and would be revived at a later date. Grimond had forced his party at least to consider its relations with other parties – not, as in the immediate post-war era, as a means of political survival, but in terms of bringing Liberals closer to government. In this sense he 'paved the way for inter-party co-operation that ultimately led to the formation of the Liberal Democrats in 1988'.[38] Two months after Grimond's resignation, Lord Rea, Liberal leader in the Lords, also stood down, in his case on grounds of ill-health. Rea's career had paralleled Grimond's, having taken over from Lord Samuel in 1955. His replacement was Frank Byers, ennobled in 1964. The latter's appointment offered some prospect that Liberal peers would be organized into a professional force for the first time for several decades. When Violet Bonham Carter had been belatedly elevated to the upper house in 1964, she had asked Rea how regularly the contingent of Liberal peers met, only to be told that they never did. By December 1968, *The Times* diary columnist offered a cautious tribute to what Byers had managed to achieve: 'Starved of new creations by the Conservatives, the Liberal Lords were an ill-organized band before Byers arrived. By common consent he does a good job leading what is still an awkward crew.'[39] Meanwhile, no obvious successor to Grimond stood out in the Commons, but in a vote among the 12 MPs, Jeremy Thorpe secured the support of half the parliamentary party, after which his two rivals, Emlyn Hooson and Eric Lubbock, withdrew. Though some senior figures doubted whether Thorpe possessed the necessary attributes of intellect and judgement, the general consensus was that the party had made the best choice from the available talent.

The Trials and Tribulations of Jeremy Thorpe

Thorpe's career is now so coloured by the way in which it ultimately collapsed, and by the charges and allegations from which his reputation has never fully recovered, that it remains difficult to assess his nine years at the helm with appropriate objectivity. Most of the writing about him ranges from the realm of 'investigative journalism' to that of the merely sensational and salacious. His own volume of reminiscences offers few insights. With hindsight, his leadership, sandwiched as it was between the clearer, more creative visions of Jo Grimond and David Steel, emerges as a period in which, regardless of some considerable electoral successes, the party drifted without a sense of conviction or underlying purpose. Instead, new Liberal revivals fed off Thorpe's very real but somewhat superficial qualities – his 'enormous flair, charisma, showmanship and boundless energy'.[40] He was effective as a communicator, an organizer and a fund-raiser. Interviewed by the *Observer* in 1973 he claimed that, Grimond having given the party *intellectual* credibility, his task was to give it *political* credibility. More cynically, it might be suggested that the Thorpe era was dominated by tactics rather than ideas.

In the late 1960s, the party seemed unsure how to present itself. Its projected image ranged from that of the radical alternative to two essentially conservative parties – 'which twin is the Tory?' asked one effective piece of Liberal propaganda – to that of a moderate force between two ideological extremes. In the public mind it was the latter image that predominated. Liberals were seen as pleasant, middle-of-the-road and reasonable, but without the radical cutting edge for which Grimond had striven. One opinion poll in 1968 suggested that as many as 52 per cent of the population might vote Liberal if they believed that the party had a genuine prospect of success. Such statistics fostered a simplistic belief that only a modest hurdle of electoral credibility lay between the party and the prospect of government. In practice, Liberalism had become a temporary port of call for the increasing numbers of those who wished to register a protest vote against the governmental failures of Conservatives and Labour alike.

The early years of Thorpe's leadership were dominated by financial crisis. Once the high tide of the Grimond revival had passed, the party found itself dangerously overstretched. It was a problem to which Thorpe, who had established his reputation partly though his success as Party Treasurer, responded with energy and imagination. A number of fund-raising schemes were mounted, of which the most famous was the 'Liberal Million Fund' campaign launched in 1967. A number of economy measures were also necessary, however, and in 1968 party headquarters were transferred from Smith Square in Westminster to a cheaper but less convenient location off the Strand, with a 50 per cent saving in rent. Even so, Liberal finances were still in a parlous state on the eve of the 1970 General Election. One consequence was a decline in the number of constituencies able to afford a full-time agent;

there were just 17 in April 1969. Yet, in seats that the Liberals held, their organization and the size of their local party membership stood comparison with the best of those of their opponents. The Liberals had, of necessity, learnt the importance of nursing their constituencies

Public opinion polls suggested that the level of Liberal support remained reasonably steady at between 7 per cent and 11 per cent, but the electoral history of these years offered little cause for optimism. The local government revival of the early 1960s was not sustained, and the Conservatives were the major beneficiaries of an unpopular Labour government. But one particularly worrying feature during this period was the growth of Welsh, and particularly Scottish, nationalism. The long-standing Liberal policy of Welsh and Scottish assemblies was in danger of being outflanked by the more strident demands of Plaid Cymru and the Scottish National Party (SNP). At the 1967 Liberal assembly, Ludovic Kennedy and Michael Starforth pressed the case for an electoral pact with the Scottish Nationalists. However, other leading Scottish Liberals, including Russell Johnston, MP for Inverness, were opposed, and in any case informal approaches to the SNP by the remaining MPs with Scottish seats – namely, Grimond, Steel, James Davidson and Alasdair Mackenzie – proved unsuccessful. Liberal deposits were lost in 12 of the 28 by-elections contested during the 1966 Parliament. Only the surprise victory of Councillor Wallace Lawler in June 1969 in Birmingham, Ladywood bucked the trend. In some ways this was an astonishing victory. The swing from Labour to Liberal was a staggering 32 per cent. There was, after all, no real Liberal tradition in the city. Even in the Liberal landslide of 1906, Birmingham had remained solidly Conservative/Unionist. Lawler's victory in this small and much depopulated constituency was the product of grass-roots politics, with local activists led by Lawler himself patiently building up a well-cultivated local base. At one level, the result suggested that no area was closed to the party, provided its workers were prepared to roll up their sleeves and engage with the local community. At the same time, the new MP was recognized as being unique, a Lawlerite rather than a Liberal, and the views attributed to him on some issues, including immigration, threatened to embarrass his colleagues at Westminster. Arguably, the capture of the Ladywood seat had little to do with the fortunes of the national party.

Thorpe, who never enjoyed the sort of wholehearted commitment offered to Grimond by the party hierarchy, survived a serious effort to remove him from the leadership in June 1968, launched while he was absent on his honeymoon. Only months after he became leader, a series of articles in *New Outlook* criticized his failure to confront those issues that would win support for the Liberals at the next election. Thorpe was overwhelmingly re-endorsed by a meeting of the party executive but, as a sop to his critics, he accepted a call for an element of 'collective leadership' to shape decisions. A commission was established to convert the party's principles into a coherent programme for the next election. But the timing of that election was inevitably a function of the fortunes of the Labour government. After three years of carefully and often painfully rebuilding the national economy following the devaluation of 1967, Labour finally saw the opinion polls moving in its favour and Wilson sought to capitalize on this recovery by going to the country in June 1970.

The Liberals seemed to have little new to offer. Their policies on immigration, police powers and government secrecy were distinctive, but not necessarily vote winners on any significant scale. The traditional appeal for Welsh and Scottish self-government was now being articulated with greater vigour by the Nationalists. Similarly, both Labour and the Conservatives had become converted to the virtues of British membership of the European Community. The election was focused on the state of the economy, where the choice seemed to lie between a continuation of Chancellor Roy Jenkins' Keynesian-style stewardship and the apparent return of the Conservatives, particularly following a celebrated meeting of the shadow cabinet at Selsdon Park in January 1970, to a more market-orientated alternative. For the first time for several elections, the Liberals looked less 'relevant' and, as a consequence, the party attracted less notice from either its opponents or the media. As even the chief whip later conceded, 'we had no very clear message, except the assumption of innate virtue and superiority in a host of Liberal policies'.[41]

Finance remained a serious problem. By mid-May only 286 prospective candidates were in place. Only when Thorpe announced a sudden windfall of donations to party funds, later attributed by *The Times* largely to the beneficence of the multi-millionaire businessman Jack Hayward, did this rise to 332. Within this total, about three dozen seats were designated as 'winnable' and benefited from extra injections of cash and effort. The majority of candidates, however, lacked the funds needed to conduct a comprehensive canvass of their constituencies or to hold large indoor meetings.

Thorpe himself emerged as an accomplished electioneer. With television playing a greater role in the campaign than ever before, his flair for showmanship and ability to take advantage of any available 'photo opportunity' won much praise. He was able to criticize both the main parties for the way in which they had ruined the British economy and, like so many of his predecessors, insisted that a Liberal revival was just over the horizon. In reality, the party entertained few serious hopes of an improvement in its electoral fortunes. Even so, the result was worse than expected. Seven of the 13 Liberal seats were lost, including Lawler's recent gain in Ladywood. A few hundred votes saved the seats of three further MPs, including Thorpe himself. Only Grimond in Orkney and Shetland, and Hooson in Montgomery, mid-Wales, enjoyed anything approaching comfortable majorities. For the first time in the party's history there was no Liberal representation outside Scotland, Wales and the West Country. The party's share of the total vote declined from 8.5 per cent in 1966 to 7.5 per cent, and the average constituency vote fell from 16.1 per cent to 13.5 per cent. In Scotland and Wales it was clear that the Nationalists had been particularly successful in attracting former Liberal voters. As many as 182 deposits were lost. The one redeeming feature was the way the national trend had been bucked in a handful of seats such as Rochdale, Southport and Liverpool, Wavertree, where a well-regarded, incumbent Liberal councillor had secured an increased Liberal vote, testimony it seemed to the electorate's readiness to repay patient hard work carried out at a municipal level. Otherwise, there were eerie parallels to be drawn between the 1970 result and those of the early 1950s. It was as if the progress made under Grimond had been entirely in vain.

Community Politics, Young Liberals and Direct Action

This disappointing outcome inevitably stirred active Liberals at all levels into an agonizing reappraisal of the party's strategy and organization. Fleetingly, some again questioned whether any purpose remained in trying to sustain an independent Liberal identity. It was in such an atmosphere of gloomy introspection that, at the autumn assembly, the party accepted a resolution put forward by the Young Liberals that it should now focus its campaigning at the community level. The party became committed 'to help organize people in their communities to take and use power... to build a Liberal power-base in the major cities of the country... to capture people's imagination as a credible political movement, with local roots and local successes'. This proved to be an important moment in the evolution of modern Liberalism, and both the new strategy and its proposers merit closer attention.

At one level, the adoption of the community politics resolution was the logical culmination of a strategy initiated during the Grimond era. Back in 1960, the Local Government Department had been set up, under the direction of Richard Wainwright, with the purpose, after a generation of neglect, of encouraging Liberals to participate in local government elections. The reasoning was simple enough. As Mark Bonham Carter put it, 'it is easier to change voting habits at local elections than at by-elections and at by-elections than at general elections'.[42] Significant gains at the parliamentary level would be more likely to occur once the party had established a solid foundation in local politics. Thus, suggested Grimond, though he personally had remained largely aloof from the strategy, 'every time a local Liberal councillor gets a bus stop moved to a better place he strikes a blow for the Liberal party'.[43] It was, in other words, a simple technique to strengthen the party's power base, and the following decade afforded some evidence of its success. Figures such as Lawler in Birmingham, and Cyril Carr and Trevor Jones in Liverpool, had begun the process of cutting into rock-solid Labour heartlands by associating the Liberal Party with a practical concern for the everyday needs and interests of the working-class voter. For the most part these advances seemed to be at odds with the party's scattered successes in by-elections and general elections over the same period, where it was in comfortable suburbia and at the Conservatives' expense that victories such as that in Orpington had been achieved. But Lawler's 1969 triumph in Ladywood, though not repeated in the General Election a year later, appeared to open new doors. Party workers in Ladywood were struck by the way that voters pledged their support to the Liberal candidate on the basis of services he had already rendered as their local councillor. Within a few years the new approach achieved its most spectacular success in Liverpool – like Birmingham, a city with no significant Liberal tradition over the previous half century. As late as May 1968, with the anti-Labour tide at its height, the Liberals held just one council seat as against 34 Labour and 79 Conservatives. Yet by 1973 the Liberals had become the largest single party on the Liverpool City Council.

The community politics strategy was not without its problems. While it offered genuine and active representation to the benefit of the local community, its links with Liberalism as a national political force were often tenuous. Recognizing that a Liberal councillor could be helpful in solving domestic problems did not necessarily convince a voter that the national party was an equally appropriate body for resolving an altogether different set of problems. While the planned scenario was clear enough – that a strong cohort of local councillors would form the basis for a later advance at a General Election – the danger existed of electors developing the habit of differential voting, supporting Liberals for the local council, but reverting to traditional Labour or Conservative loyalties when it was a question of choosing a government for the country. To an extent, this clearly happened. In Liverpool, for example, the Liberal Party never achieved a breakthrough in parliamentary seats comparable to its strength in the city's municipal politics, even when, as in 1979, local and national elections were held on the same day. Furthermore, the peculiarities of local situations inevitably encouraged Liberals to adjust their politics to suit the requirements of a given area, a trend which enabled critics to claim that, while the party might have a 'policy for every street corner', it lacked a consistent attitude to the great issues of national politics.

Most seriously, by 1970, the concept of community politics was no longer the preserve of the mainstream party but had been appropriated, some might have said hijacked, by the party's youth movement, the National League of Young Liberals, and the Union of Liberal Students. Indeed, the term 'community politics' appears to have been coined by two prominent Young Liberals, Gordon Lishman and Lawrie Freedman, at a strategy meeting early in 1969. The entry of enthusiastic and committed students and other young people into the Liberal ranks, first noted by Clement Davies in the early 1950s, had been an important factor in the party's subsequent revival. So-called 'commando raids', in which Liberal students undertook intensive campaigning to try to resurrect organization and enthusiasm in moribund constituencies, became a feature of the party's strategy from the late 1950s onwards. Many had been attracted by Jo Grimond's campaigning style and patent integrity. But wider forces were at work. For others, in the context of the rapid social changes of the 1960s, the Liberals offered the most appropriate political vehicle for the expression and achievement of their aims, whether or not these coincided with official party policy. The Young Liberals became particularly prominent when disillusionment set in over the failure of Wilson's Labour government to satisfy those radical and idealistic aspirations that many had entrusted to it. They became closely associated with a series of international issues, of which opposition to the Vietnam War and condemnation of the apartheid regime in South Africa enjoyed the highest public profile.

The concept of 'direct action' was advanced to compensate for the failures of conventional politics. Though the levels of disorder in Britain never reached the scale seen in the university campuses of continental Europe and the United States, the Young Liberals were widely regarded, particularly in sections of the press, as part of a wider youth movement challenging the existing assumptions of British society. As such, they posed rather more problems to the Liberal leadership than they offered advantages, for while the label 'radical' was one that, whatever their understanding of it, most prominent Liberals were happy to wear, 'revolutionary' was a different matter. At the 1966 Brighton assembly, the Youth Movement's so-called 'Red Guards' did little to enhance the party's broader appeal. They pressed the case for the withdrawal of American troops from Vietnam, for British withdrawal from NATO, for non-alignment in the Cold War and for active support to be given to the anti-apartheid movement. In 1969–70 the activities of Young Liberals, led by Peter Hain, in trying to stop a tour by the all-white South African cricket team were unlikely to enthuse the sort of 'respectable' ex-Conservative voter whom the party had been particularly successful in attracting to its cause. Not surprisingly, much effort was expended in the late 1960s in trying to curb the excesses of the Young Liberals, a process that culminated in January 1970 in a formal request to them by the party's National Executive to dismiss their chairman, Louis Eaks. In such hands, the concept of community politics became much more than a means of winning local elections, or even a longer-term political strategy to increase the Liberal party's representation at Westminster. It was seen as a form of participatory politics which, freed from the stultifying embrace of centralized bureaucracies, could begin a process of social transformation at the grass roots of British political life. In these differing conceptions – electoral strategy, or theory of political and social transformation – an important conflict entered Liberal politics: 'Jeremy Thorpe always equated [community politics] with being a good constituency MP,' recalled one activist, 'rather than with a radical platform for change.'[44]

The Heath Government and Possible Coalition

That, however, was for the future. In the shorter term, Thorpe's Liberal Party had to cope with the obvious setback occasioned by the 1970 General Election. For the first two years of the new Parliament, the Liberals performed indifferently in by-elections, most local elections and in national opinion polls. In the background lay disturbing rumours about the party leader's private life, though an internal enquiry chaired by Lord Byers in 1971 dismissed as being without foundation the accusations made by the stablehand and male model, Norman Scott, of a homosexual affair in the early 1960s. Yet, as before, events over which the Liberals had little control conspired to work in their favour. The 1970 election, against the expectations and predictions of most commentators and opinion polls, saw the return of a Conservative government and, as recent history had confirmed, the Liberals were more likely to benefit from protest votes registered against an unpopular Tory administration than would be the case with an equally unpopular Labour one. With clear evidence that Labour in opposition was moving distinctly leftwards, the propensity of disgruntled Conservatives to switch to the Liberals rather than the main opposition party was likely to be particularly marked.

The government's unpopularity was not long in coming. Considerable controversy has developed over the extent to which Edward Heath's Conservative Party set out consciously to break away from the post-war consensus. Certainly, Heath entered Downing Street pledged to 'change the course of history of this nation, nothing less' and, in its rhetoric at least, the

new government seemed determined to give the country policies that were fundamentally different from any seen since 1945.
Whatever the intention, however, the outcome was disappointing.
Notwithstanding apparently careful preparation during the years
of opposition, most of Heath's policies went badly wrong. All the
key economic indicators continued to move in an unfavourable
direction. Despite the attempt to introduce a new legal framework
through the Industrial Relations Act of 1971, industrial relations
had never been worse in the whole post-war era and the government suffered a humiliating defeat at the hands of the miners in
1972. Heath was particularly shaken when unemployment reached
the politically sensitive total of one million early that year. By that
stage, a massive U-turn was already under way, a process that led
to the nationalization of ailing industries such as Rolls-Royce and
Upper Clyde Shipbuilders, the passing of a highly interventionist Industry Bill and the adoption, in direct contravention of the
party's 1970 manifesto, of a formal incomes policy.

It was not long before the Liberal Party felt the benefits of
the government's travails. By good fortune, in October 1972 a
by-election arose in the Lancashire town of Rochdale, one of the
few seats where Liberals stood as the main challenger to Labour.
Benefiting from a popular local candidate in Cyril Smith, and
squeezing the third-placed Conservative vote, the Liberals secured
a striking victory with a majority of more than 5,000. Six weeks
later, the solid Conservative seat of Sutton and Cheam in Surrey
fell to the Liberals on a turnover of votes greater even than that
at Orpington a decade before. The victor, Graham Tope, had
entered Liberal politics inspired by the radicalism of the Young
Liberals and as an advocate of community politics. The campaign
was dominated by local issues such as concessionary travel for the
elderly and plans for comprehensive schooling, and for much of
the time it was the Liverpudlian Trevor Jones, bringing with him
his celebrated *Focus* newsletter, rather than national party headquarters, who made the running. Strikingly, a later opinion poll
showed that the majority of defecting Tories opposed the successful Liberal candidate on issues such as Europe and immigration.
None the less, the fact that the Liberal Party lost its deposit in the
not dissimilar and neighbouring constituency of Uxbridge in a by-
election held the same day forced even the most reluctant of traditional Liberals to take the new style of campaigning seriously.

The party's national rating now began to rise and, by August of the following year, had reached 20 per cent. In the meantime there were spectacular advances in the 1973 local elections, where Liberals won over 900 seats, easily their best performance since before the Second World War. Victories in parliamentary by-elections in the Isle of Ely, Cambridgeshire, and Ripon in North Yorkshire that July seemed to place a question mark over the safety of every Conservative seat in the land. Dick Taverne's resignation as Labour MP for Lincoln, after a lengthy dispute with his constituency party, and his subsequent victory as a Democratic Labour candidate at a by-election in March 1973 at which Liberals offered unofficial support, seemed to confirm that the electorate was anxious to vote for a new party of the moderate centre ground. Elsewhere the Liberals presented themselves successfully in this guise. In all the by-elections held during 1973, the Liberals won a larger total number of votes than either Labour or the Conservatives. This upsurge in the party's fortunes far outstripped those that had surrounded Torrington or Orpington. It was in fact the best Liberal performance since the Lloyd George-inspired revival of the late 1920s.

By now, and despite ongoing financial worries, the party was becoming a more professional campaigning force than ever before. Its ability to mobilize its resources in by-elections offered the most convincing evidence of the transformation. But it was also a wiser party, less inclined to be carried away by its own successes than in the heady days of the earlier false dawns of the Grimond era. As a result, many believed that the tide of Liberal advance would follow a now-established pattern and ebb once again with the approach of the next General Election. Indeed, though the party recaptured Beveridge's old seat of Berwick-upon-Tweed in November 1973, the swing against the government was less marked than of late, while the Liberals' national poll ratings were again drifting downwards. On the other hand, other factors suggested that the improvement in the party's fortunes might prove more durable. The most important long-term trend in the electoral history of the 1960s and 1970s was a clear process of dealignment. At the 1951 General Election, as many as 96.8 per cent of all votes cast had gone to the Conservative and Labour parties. By 1964 this figure had gone down to 87.5 per cent, and at the General Election of October 1974 it was to fall again to just 75.1 per cent. Put another way, back in 1951 just one voter in 30 had supported the minor parties, but by October 1974 it was as many as one in four.[45] This movement was partly the result of the beginnings of a breakdown in the pattern of class voting that had dominated British politics since the First World War. In a more fluid social structure, working-class voters were becoming less reliable adherents of the Labour Party, while the support of their middle-class counterparts could no longer be counted upon by the Conservatives. By the mid-1970s, moreover, the mood of post-war optimism was at an end. As Britain's economic and social problems mounted, and solutions to them appeared ever more illusory, it was even said that Britain was becoming ungovernable. The faith of the electorate in party politics in general inevitably waned and the Liberals, as the least party-like of the three main parties and the only one without a sullied record in government to explain or defend, were an inevitable beneficiary. Ironically, the most optimistic of political creeds picked up support in a mood of mounting pessimism. While the Liberals continued to attract votes despite, as much as because of, what they stood for, issues of constitutional reform and a new British identity inside Europe did strike a chord among those who saw the only salvation for a declining Britain lying in radical departures in public policy.

In the event, the General Election came earlier than expected. Confronted by a second major strike in the coalmines and tempted into an appeal around the theme of 'Who Governs Britain?', Heath went to the country in February 1974. With as many as 517 candidates in the field, the Liberals posed a serious national challenge for the first time in half a century. The key features in the party manifesto, *Change the Face of Britain*, were decentralization and devolution, industrial partnership, a guaranteed minimum income and a fairer distribution of national wealth. The manifesto stressed that the immediate crisis over the miners' strike was only the culmination of a long process of decline in Britain's ability to manage its affairs 'efficiently and with tolerable sanity'. It was now time to set aside sterile class conflict and question any new initiative on the basis of whether it would narrow the gulf between classes and reduce conflict. Overall, image was more important than detailed policy. Though it conflicted with ongoing aspirations to 'radicalism', Thorpe successfully presented the party as one of the moderate centre, a ground that had been deserted by the increasingly extremist Labour and Conservatives. The adversarial circumstances of the election might, in an earlier era, have sent voters scurrying back to traditional patterns of class loyalty, but with increasing numbers of voters reaching the conclusion that both the main parties had now been tried and found wanting, support for the Liberal stance of sweet reasonableness grew as the campaign progressed. One poll suggested that 40 per cent of voters would back the Liberals if the party had a chance of holding the balance of power, and a massive 48 per cent if it was believed to be capable of forming the next government.

Thorpe himself ran an effective campaign even though, aware of his fragile 1970 majority, he hardly moved out of his own constituency. There was a freshness about him in contrast to the rather shop-soiled image of both Heath and Wilson, upon which he capitalized as he sought photographic attention – leaping over fences and so on in tours of his constituency. A television link between Thorpe's Barnstaple headquarters and the National Liberal Club in London enabled him to conduct the party's daily press conference. Because of the number of candidates fielded, the party enjoyed a greater television exposure than ever before. In contrast to what had happened in both 1966 and 1970, the level of Liberal support held up remarkably well, at least until the final days of the campaign. On 25 February, Thorpe declared that the party's primary intention was to form a government. If this proved impossible, he was ready to work with 'any person of moderate and progressive views to get this country back on the rails'. At last, Liberals seemed to have buried the bogey that a vote for them was a wasted vote and, with apparent justification, the closing stages of the campaign saw the adoption of the slogan 'If you want a Liberal Government you can have one'. More soberly, Liberal headquarters were confidently thinking in terms of winning 50 seats.

The election results showed that the expected breakthrough had still not been secured. With a poll in excess of 6 million, and with more than 19 per cent of the total votes cast, the party had only 14 MPs elected. Territorially, no new ground had been taken, apart from a gain in the Isle of Wight, largely attributable to local circumstances. Liberal strategists had underestimated the extent to which the first-past-the-post electoral system worked against them. With no Liberal heartlands comparable to those enjoyed by its rivals, the party needed to poll well over 30 per cent nationally before seeing a significant difference in the number of seats won. If any Liberals had not previously understood the merits of proportional representation, the case was made for them vividly in February 1974. It had taken 432,000 votes to elect each Liberal MP, but just 40,000 and 39,000, respectively, for each Conservative and Labour counterpart.

On the credit side, the party had polled respectably throughout the country. In England only four deposits were lost. Though the party appeared to have taken votes from both its opponents, the Liberal challenge was slanted overwhelmingly against the Conservatives. Of the 100 losing Liberals with the highest percentage of votes, only two had been defeated by a Labour opponent. But there were disappointing features too. The failure to win target seats in places such as Liverpool, where the party had been building up its council base, raised question marks over the appropriateness of community politics as a strategy for a national political party. And the nationalist challenge had not been contained. The SNP was now the third party in Scotland, while Plaid Cymru's total of two seats matched that of the Welsh Liberals.

But if the overall result offered both comfort and disappointment to the Liberal Party, neither Labour nor the Conservatives had real cause for celebration. With 200,000 more votes than Labour, the Conservatives had four fewer MPs; and with only 301 MPs, Labour was 17 short of an overall majority. In this situation, Heath did not immediately tender his resignation but, arguing that over Europe and the key question of an incomes policy Conservatives and Liberals were in fundamental agreement, sought talks with Thorpe to see whether any basis existed for a deal. Despite an outcry from within the Liberal ranks, Thorpe's readiness at least to explore the situation was reasonable enough. As a minority of the parliamentary party pointed out, it made no sense for a party that espoused the cause of proportional representation not to be willing, in principle, to work with others. Moreover, Thorpe had already declared that, in the event of the Liberals holding the balance, he would be ready to co-operate with the forces of moderation in other parties. On the other hand, Thorpe's willingness to respond to Heath's overture was bound to excite a hostile reaction. Over the weekend following the election, complaints poured into party headquarters from activists throughout the country. The former chairman of the Young Liberals, Peter Hain, warned of mass resignations in the event of any deal with the Conservatives.

The Liberals did not in fact hold the balance in the new Parliament and it would have needed an additional agreement with another minority group such as the Ulster Unionists to provide Heath with a Commons majority. More important, most Liberal activists interpreted their party's huge vote as one directed primarily against the failure of the Heath government to cope with the country's deteriorating economic and industrial condition, and were not now keen to be seen propping up Heath's efforts to stay in office. Thorpe aggravated the situation by accepting the Prime Minister's invitation to talk without first seeking the views of his senior colleagues. As David Steel recalled, 'Neither I as Chief Whip, number two in the parliamentary hierarchy, or anyone else had been consulted. I was confused and irritated.'[46]

It seems that Heath was willing to offer Thorpe a cabinet seat together with junior office for some of his colleagues, but the issue of proportional representation proved to be the sticking point. Though Thorpe was clearly interested in Heath's suggestions, and hopeful that he could secure the Home Office for himself, electoral reform was understandably a *sine qua non*, especially in the light of the recent electoral outcome. Heath was ready to concede a Speaker's Conference on the subject, but remained personally uncommitted and would not pledge the government to abide by the outcome of such an investigation. In this way the negotiations were brought to a speedy end and Harold Wilson took office at the head of a minority Labour administration.

With hindsight, it is clear that Thorpe's career as Liberal leader had now peaked. The impression that he had been keen on a deal with the Conservatives undermined his position and opened up a rift with the majority of party activists. It was inevitable that another election would be held before long, with Wilson, as in 1966, seizing the first opportunity to try to secure a working parliamentary majority. The Liberals spent the intervening months arguing about whether their aim should be to boost their parliamentary representation and then strive for electoral reform within a coalition government, or to stick to the long haul of working towards a Liberal government. Thorpe himself stressed that the Liberals needed to project themselves as a national party if they were to secure a national following. His campaign received a boost when the Labour MP and former minister, Christopher Mayhew, defected to the party in July. Against accusations of treachery from Young Liberals, Thorpe succeeded in persuading the party assembly in September that the option of Liberal participation in a coalition, after proper consultation with the party, should not be closed off.

The anticipated election duly came in October 1974, and the party made great efforts to put 619 candidates into the field. Every seat in England and Wales, except Lincoln, was contested, as were all but a handful north of the border. In policy terms the Liberals offered much the same as they had put forward in February, but the emphasis now was on transforming the nature of the party political conflict by increasing the number of Liberal MPs. A strong Liberal representation would 'break up the confrontation of the two class parties and create the conditions for a broad based radical alliance led by Liberals'. By adopting the phrase 'one more heave', the party tried to encourage the belief that its ambitions were eminently realizable. In practice, however, the task of retaining the fickle support that had been attracted in February, while at the same time persuading another substantial tranche of voters to desert their traditional preferences, was enormous. Even an extra 5 per cent of the total vote, evenly distributed across the country, would only have produced six extra MPs. As it was, something of Thorpe's electoral magic seemed to have disappeared. He had always straddled an uncomfortable divide between being the accomplished professional politician and the amiable clown. Now he appeared to get the balance wrong. A hovercraft tour of the West Country was noted more for its attendant mishaps than for any political message the leader conveyed. A second tour by helicopter of Conservative marginals again smacked of gimmickry. Liberals were unable to make further inroads, despite ample evidence of continuing dissatisfaction with both the major parties. Opinion polls suggested that about half the electorate judged Labour's performance in government to be poor, while less than a third were sure that the Conservatives could do better. The election was, as the Nuffield historians described it, something of an 'unpopularity contest'.[47]

The result made only a marginal difference to the national political scene. Labour secured its overall parliamentary majority, but it was a majority of just three seats. The Liberals made one gain in Truro, Cornwall, but both Hazel Grove in Greater Manchester and Bodmin fell to the Conservatives. Since February, the total

Liberal vote had fallen from over 6 million (19.3 per cent) to 5.3 million (18.3 per cent). In fact, the decline was more marked than these figures implied. With 102 more candidates in the field than in February, the average vote per candidate had dropped quite sharply. In those seats fought on both occasions, the total Liberal vote fell by more than a million. The results in Scotland, where the SNP captured 11 seats, were particularly disappointing, despite the fact that the Liberals had promised a Scottish parliament elected by proportional representation that would have enjoyed control over 50 per cent of the revenue derived from North Sea oil. With Labour holding on to office with just 39.2 per cent of the vote on a low turnout of 72.8 per cent, the Liberals could not be other than disheartened. The party still lacked a political identity, apart from simply being neither Labour nor Conservative. Surveys showed that the party's policies were the least known or understood, and that the proportion of Liberal voters feeling a commitment to the party was much lower than in the other parties.[48]

After seven years in post, these failures were in part an indictment of the leader, Jeremy Thorpe. His enemies tended to blame the party's relatively poor performance on discussions before the election of the possibility of a coalition. More seriously, Thorpe had subordinated the creation of a clear sense of direction to the chimera of short-term political advantage. Strikingly, polling evidence suggested that Liberal voters were fairly evenly divided as to whether the Labour or Conservative Party would be their second choice in the event that no Liberal candidate was available to them. The party spent the following year campaigning for devolution and electoral reform, a natural reaction to the enormous disparity between the Liberals' popular vote in 1974 and their meagre return of MPs. Despite murmurings among Young Liberals and other activists, Thorpe secured the unanimous backing of his parliamentary colleagues at the 1975 assembly. He appeared confident that he could ride out this storm as he had others in the past. Criticism of his handling of the 1970 campaign had been stifled amid the welter of sympathy that surrounded him following his first wife's death in a road accident. Over the following 18 months he had been involved in an increasingly acrimonious and sometimes public wrangle with the Liberal Treasurer, Sir Frank Medlicott, when the latter had the temerity to question his autocratic and sometimes bizarre handling of party funds. In 1973, more general doubts emerged about Thorpe's financial judgement as a result of his involvement as a non-executive director of the ill-fated London and County Securities.

At the back of everything, however, lay the ticking time bomb of Norman Scott, whom Thorpe had befriended in the early 1960s and to whom Peter Bessell, Liberal MP for Bodmin from 1964 to 1970, had made a number of payments since 1966. By the mid-1970s it was becoming increasingly difficult to keep the lid on Scott's claims and it was later alleged that, in 1975, people close to Thorpe went so far as to stage a bungled attempt to kill the leader's troublesome tormentor. Appearing in court in January 1976, charged with defrauding the DHSS, Scott used the privilege of the courtroom to publicize his accusations against Thorpe. The following month, Richard Wainwright, MP for Colne Valley, learnt from Bessell the story of the latter's involvement in the Scott affair and began a discreet campaign for Thorpe's resignation. In a desperate attempt to pre-empt any sensational disclosures by Bessell, Thorpe allowed his letters to Scott to be published in the *Sunday Times*. Though these contained no conclusive confirmation of a homosexual affair, they did open Thorpe up to ridicule, and their publication ended any last hope he might have had of clinging on to the leadership. On 9 May 1976 he resigned. Despite widespread regret that Thorpe's career should end in such an ignominious fashion, most Liberals breathed a sigh of relief. By-elections in March and local government elections in May suggested a significant fall in the party's support. It was time for a fresh beginning.

David Steel and the Lib–Lab Pact

At a moment of evident crisis, Liberals turned, understandably enough, to the reassuring figure of Jo Grimond, who agreed to resume the leadership on a temporary basis. Such was his standing across the party spectrum that he could almost certainly have taken charge over the longer term had he so wished. He was, after all, only 63 years old. But a second sustained period with Grimond at the helm might have taken the party in an altogether different direction from that explored in the early 1960s. As he watched the economic mismanagement of the Labour government, Grimond had come to question his earlier confidence in the beneficial effects of state intervention and to toy once more with classical economic liberalism at just the time that this doctrine was making inroads into the Conservative Party of Margaret Thatcher and Keith Joseph. As it was, Grimond stayed in charge long enough to restore the party's self-confidence and hand over to David Steel, a comfortable victor over John Pardoe in the first leadership contest of the Liberals, or for that matter any major British party, determined by the wishes of the wider party membership.

Though aged only 38 at his assumption of the leadership, Steel had been an MP for 11 years, and that period had been critical in shaping his vision of the Liberal Party's future. An unequivocal disciple at least of the earlier Grimond, he believed, like his mentor, that the way forward lay in a realignment of the left in British politics. By now, moreover, the internal tensions within the Labour Party, particularly following Wilson's decision to hold a referendum on Britain's continuing membership of the European Community, had become far more acute than when Grimond had waited in vain for Labour to fragment. 'Many of the self-styled social democrats,' Steel wrote towards the end of 1975, 'would be in happier company in combination with Liberals than Socialists.' If the opportunity for realignment arose, it was important that the Liberals should be ready to join with others for the more effective promotion of liberalism and not behave 'like a more rigid sect of the exclusive brethren'.[49] Strikingly, he once confessed that, if Gaitskell had succeeded in shaping the Labour Party entirely in his own image, the need for and relevance of a separate Liberal Party would largely have disappeared.[50] This near equation of Gaitskellite social democracy with his own conception of Liberalism deserved to be more closely noted than it was.

Steel's experience in Parliament had shown that positive achievements were not the preserve of action on strictly party lines. He had risen to national prominence in sponsoring a reform of the law on abortion and, in guiding his private member's bill towards the statute book in 1967, had relied heavily on the support of like-minded members in other parties, not least Labour's Home Secretary, Roy Jenkins. Similarly, over Kenyan Asian immigration, opposition to apartheid, campaigning for the homeless and, most recently, arguing for a 'yes' vote in the European referendum, Steel had operated 'more as a Liberal working with others outside the Liberal Party than within it to advance Liberal causes'.[51] In 1968, he and a group of like-minded Liberals had formed the Radical Action Movement, designed to bring together the progressive forces in British public life, whether they were individually members of the Liberal Party or not. Though short-lived, it was indicative of his thinking at the time. The electoral setback of 1970 had convinced Steel of the pitfalls – indeed, the futility – of the long-haul approach to Liberal revival. It was impossible for the party to 'plod on as before, spending the next ten years building back up to a dozen MPs only to face near annihilation again on a sudden swing of the pendulum'.[52] He regarded the 1974 hung Parliament as a missed opportunity, and while he did not believe that a Conservative–Liberal coalition could or should have been formed that February, the ferocity of the party's reaction to the mere exploration of a possible agreement with Heath convinced him that the issue of coalition government should be addressed head-on: by 'simply pretending to be an alternative government in exile we would continue to fail'.[53] While Thorpe negotiated with Heath, Steel made tentative contacts with Roy Jenkins to see whether there might be any possibility of a Lib–Lab agreement.

In seeking the Liberal leadership in 1976, Steel made no effort to conceal his thoughts as to the direction in which, if elected, he intended to take the party. Announcing his candidacy in an address in Hampstead on 18 May, he declared:

> The role of the Liberal Party is not that of a shadow third government with a detailed policy on every single issue of the day, ready and waiting in the wings for a shift in electoral opinion to sweep us into power…We must concentrate less on giving day-to-day commentary on the policies of others, and far more on setting out our own programme. And we should combine our long-term programme with a readiness to work with others wherever we see what Jo Grimond has called the break in the clouds – the chance to implement any of [our] Liberal policies.[54]

In a *Guardian* interview within weeks of becoming leader, Steel confirmed that the Liberals had to 'start by getting a toe-hold on power which *must* mean some form of coalition'. Then, at the end of a long speech to the September assembly in Llandudno, he sought the backing of the wider party:

> I want the Liberal Party to be the fulcrum and centre of the next election argument – not something peripheral to it. If that is to

happen we must not give the impression of being afraid to soil our hands with the responsibilities of sharing power. We must be bold enough to deploy the coalition case positively.[55]

The protests of a number of Young Liberals, concerned at the possible loss of their ideological purity, were drowned out in the rapturous reception Steel received at the end of his speech, convincing him that he had captured the minds as well as the hearts of Liberal activists, and that he had a mandate to pursue his chosen course should the opportunity arise.

That opportunity was not long in coming. By the end of 1976, the Labour government, now headed by James Callaghan, was enveloped in Britain's most serious economic crisis for decades. Forced into the humiliating position of having to seek the aid of the International Monetary Fund (IMF), it had also lost its parliamentary majority as a result of by-election defeats and defections. By the following spring it faced the prospect of defeat in the Commons as the Conservative Party announced its intention of tabling a motion of no confidence. After soundings by intermediaries, Steel accepted an invitation to talks with the Prime Minister. On the basis of a modest set of demands from the Liberal leader, a pact was concluded and the government's parliamentary defeat averted. Steel wanted an ongoing consultative committee to scrutinize government business; an immediate meeting between Chancellor Denis Healey and the Liberal economics spokesman, John Pardoe, to confirm that a basis did exist for agreement on economic policy; a government bill to allow for direct elections to the European Parliament; a fresh attempt to bring devolution to Scotland and Wales; a halt to further nationalization; and an agreement to drop the government's proposed Local Government Direct Labour Bill. The pact was very much Steel's personal creation. There was no discussion with the parliamentary party about the precise terms, and no vote on those terms. Still less was there consultation with the wider party in the country. The parliamentary party accepted what Steel had negotiated with varying degrees of enthusiasm and in some cases a complete absence of it. Interestingly, the Mark II Jo Grimond was the most critical, doubting whether Callaghan's government intrinsically merited Liberal support. For the time being, at least, most Liberals were prepared to acquiesce in what Steel had done, not least because the General

Election that would otherwise have resulted would probably have produced an overwhelming victory for Thatcherite Conservatism.

It could not be claimed that Steel had driven a hard bargain. The bill for direct elections to the European Parliament, for example, would not necessarily involve proportional representation, although the government agreed to 'take account' of the Liberals' wish for this to be the system adopted. Critics argued that this revealed Steel's weakness as a negotiator, and that he had fallen an easy victim to Callaghan's greater experience and avuncular charm. In fact, Steel was more concerned with the concept of a pact and the idea of consultation – the toehold on power of which he had spoken earlier – than with specific policy commitments. It would, he hoped, be the first step in a process that, by getting the Liberal Party locked into the governmental machine, would one day lead it, via formal coalition and proportional representation, to real power.

The Lib–Lab pact lasted 18 months. Its achievements were limited and its impact upon the Liberal Party of questionable value. It certainly enabled the government to continue in office without the ever-present threat of parliamentary defeat, and during this time progress was made in stabilizing the economy and bringing down, at least temporarily, the rate of inflation. Relations between Healey and Pardoe were often strained: 'More than once Joel Barnett [Healey's deputy] had to pick up the pieces after we had sent the crockery flying.'[56] But it is difficult to sustain Steel's contention that the pact had the effect of blocking further left-wing legislation. A Labour government headed by Callaghan and Healey, and constrained by the watchful eye of the IMF, was never likely to lurch too far in the direction of socialism. The onward march of Labour's left had, in fact, been arrested at the time of the European referendum and in the very fact of IMF intervention. Furthermore, as Grimond noted, it was difficult to point to anything conspicuously 'Liberal' that could be attributed to the pact, apart from some limited profit-sharing measures in the 1978 Finance Bill. Perhaps it was wrong to expect much more. After all, the Liberal bargaining position was never strong in numerical terms – 13 MPs against Labour's 310.

More seriously, the Liberal Party associated itself in the public mind, and even more in the criticisms of the Conservative opposition, with what remained an unpopular government. Tories argued that the pact was a cynical device to save Liberal MPs from electoral defeat. There seemed to be substance in the claim. In the May local elections, held just two months after the pact was concluded, the party lost three-quarters of its county councillors. In ten by-elections held before the announcement in May 1978 of the pact's termination, the Liberal share of the poll dropped on average by 9.5 per cent. Even Steel conceded: 'We were lambasted for simply keeping in office a government which had outstayed its welcome.'[57] Steel resisted calls at the Brighton assembly in September 1977 for the renegotiation of the pact, declaring that he had 'never thought that there could be a secure or expandable future for the Liberal party as a kind of convenient temporary wastepaper basket for the ballot papers of discontented Tories'.[58] But when, in December 1977, Labour MPs declined to back proportional representation for the European elections, many Liberals, who had regarded this as the one tangible prize within their grasp, felt bitterly let down. There was now no prospect of continuing the pact into a third session of Parliament in the autumn of 1978.

Against most expectations, Callaghan did not go to the country that autumn, but soldiered on through the so-called Winter of Discontent of widespread industrial unrest to the following spring. A by-election victory in March 1979 in the Edge Hill division of Liverpool provided the Liberals with a welcome boost, but when the General Election finally came in May the party was inevitably on the defensive, easily castigated for the country's problems because of its earlier role in the Lib–Lab pact. Steel, however, fought an effective campaign, focusing his attention on existing Liberal seats and Tory-held marginals, and had the pleasure of seeing his party's poll rating climb steadily during the course of the hustings. His message dropped the charade of so many earlier elections, that a Liberal government was a realistic goal. Instead, he spoke of the need for a 'powerful wedge' of Liberal MPs in the next Parliament as the best means of ending the politics of two-party confrontation. Realignment still underlay his thinking: 'There are good people and good ideas in both [of] the other parties,' Steel insisted, 'but the party system prevents them ever co-operating. And the good people and good ideas have to give way to the extremists on both sides.'[59] The issue of Jeremy Thorpe was an unwanted distraction, as it had been at the party's autumn assembly in Southport. Most of the former leader's parliamentary colleagues had urged him not to contest his North Devon seat, but Thorpe, with strong backing from his local constituency party, put himself forward once again. As by this stage he was awaiting trial on charges of incitement and conspiracy to murder Norman Scott, his chances of electoral success were slim.

In the event, the party did less badly than might have been expected and than many had feared. The Liberals held on to 11 of their 14 seats, many with increased majorities, though Thorpe lost his seat to the Conservative candidate. While the party's share of the vote dropped from 18.3 per cent to 13.8 per cent, it tended to perform better in those seats where it was already a strong contender. On the debit side, the fact that the party performed markedly better in the local elections that were held on the same day underlined what was noted earlier, that a voter might value a Liberal councillor while still seeing national politics as a choice between Labour and the Conservatives: 'It would seem that something in the order of a million people may have voted Liberal locally whilst on the same day choosing between a Callaghan and a Thatcher government.'[60] Above all, for the first time since 1970, a government, in this case Margaret Thatcher's Conservatives, had been returned with a comfortable parliamentary majority. The Liberal party seemed as far away from 'power', however defined, as it had ever been.

The Revival: An Assessment

Almost a quarter of a century had elapsed since Jo Grimond took over the leadership of a party that was then near to extinction. At first sight it is difficult to make much sense of the bewildering series of ups and downs that characterized the fortunes of British Liberalism in the succeeding years. But some sense of pattern does exist. In the first place, the seemingly remorseless process of electoral decline had been arrested and reversed. In a remarkable comeback, the party had, against the odds, confirmed its permanent position on the British political landscape. Furthermore, though the peaks of revival had been followed by troughs of setback and disappointment, each low point had tended to be at a higher level than its predecessor, leaving the long-term trend pointing firmly upwards. Typically, the Liberals did best during periods of Conservative government, which often coincided with internal dissension within the Labour Party, though there was a tendency for disillusioned voters to return to their traditional loyalties with the approach of a General Election. Over the period as a whole, the party benefited from a gradual weakening of the class associations of the major parties, but at the same time the 'classlessness' of the Liberals worked to their disadvantage, to the extent that it prevented the development of solid Liberal heartlands and thus accentuated the disadvantages inherent in the existing electoral system.

But the most worrying feature of the Liberal revival was the nature of its vote. While a party capable of attracting the support of more than 6 million electors was clearly a major player on the political scene, too much of that vote was an essentially negative response to one or both of the two leading parties, a retrospective judgement on the governmental failings of Labour and the Conservatives. Psephologists identified a relatively small 'core' Liberal vote, espousing traditional Liberal values and ideas, and a far larger 'sympathy' vote, with a much weaker commitment to the merits of the Liberal Party. While this second group was crucial to the Liberals' further advance, its loyalty was never reliable. It has been shown that, in the General Elections from 1959 to 1979, on average less than 50 per cent of those who voted Liberal at one election did so at the next. This may be set against a figure of around 75 per cent in the case of the Labour and Conservative parties.[61] Staggeringly, just 2 per cent of the electorate offered consistent support to the Liberal Party in each of the four elections of the 1970s.

It is, then, at least arguable that the Liberal revival owed little to the efforts of the party leadership, except to the extent that Grimond, Thorpe and Steel all succeeded in conveying the image of a positive and dynamic alternative to the Labour–Conservative duopoly. All three were on the left of the Liberal Party, anxious to assert their 'radical' credentials. Grimond and Steel championed the goal of realignment, which in practice meant partnership with at least a part of the Labour Party. Though Conservative defectors would be welcomed, neither called for a realignment of the 'centre right'. Yet each proved most successful in attracting erstwhile Conservative supporters to the Liberal cause.

The volatility of the Liberal vote was matched by a continuing difficulty in identifying Liberal policies and values. Protest voters frequently turned to the party in spite, rather than because, of its views. Nowhere was this more the case than in relation to Europe: 'A disproportionate number of those voting against British membership [in the 1975 referendum] appeared from electoral and opinion-survey evidence to be drawn from Liberal ranks, suggesting that Liberal leaders and activists were out of line with over 50 per cent of the party's voters.'[62] Rather than sharing Liberal values, many transient Liberal voters attempted to project on to the party their own concerns and preoccupations as part of their dissatisfaction with the performance of the other two parties. Whatever recovery Liberalism had made, these problems remained unresolved as British politics entered the most decisive period of transformation experienced since the Second World War.

5 A Cracked Mould and a New Beginning, 1979–2001

The Changing Political Landscape

For most of the period after 1945, one of the most difficult problems facing the Liberal Party had been that of identity. Committed Liberal activists believed they knew where they stood – though often disagreeing on this issue among themselves – but the voting public was altogether less certain. In part, this reflected the way in which the post-war Conservative and Labour parties, dominated by their left and right wings, respectively, had competed for the centre ground of British politics. That convergence was often disputed and denied. The two parties had a vested interest in maintaining the outward appearance of confrontation, stressing the extremism of their opponents – that Labour threatened full-blown socialism, and the Conservatives would unleash the unbridled forces of the free market. The Liberals also saw considerable advantage in projecting their opponents as being at the extremes of the political spectrum. In 1980, David Steel suggested that post-war British politics had seen relatively small changes in public opinion result in alternating periods of Conservative and Labour government, accompanied by 'violent switches in public policy'. Thus 'each swing of the political pendulum threatens to take the country on yet more violently diverse directions to left and right'.[1] But with regard to the key areas of policy, the first post-war decades witnessed far more consistency and continuity than the rhetoric of political debate implied. In practical terms, this left very little space within the congested centre ground of British politics for the Liberals to occupy. Of course, Liberals themselves could claim that their own politics did not fit into a simple left–right linear pattern. Liberal 'radicalism' placed the party on a different plane, uncontested by its larger rivals. Average voters, however, were never comfortable with this proposition and,

218

in so far as they had any clear view of the Liberal stance, tended to locate it in the comfortable centre, an area where one or other of the major parties had generally succeeded in satisfying the majority of the electorate.

By 1979, this situation was clearly changing. The General Election that year brought to power a government, and more particularly a Prime Minister, who made something of a virtue of their determination to break the post-war consensus. To an audience in Cardiff in April 1979, Mrs Thatcher declared: 'I am a conviction politician. The Old Testament prophets did not say "Brothers, I want a consensus". They said "this is my faith. This is what I passionately believe. If you believe it too, then come with me".'[2]

The destruction of the consensus would, she hoped, become one of the lasting achievements for which she would be remembered. In her belief, consensus could be equated with the appeasement of socialism and the progressive advance of collectivism since 1945. Once in government, Mrs Thatcher began the process of dismantling many of the key aspects of the post-war settlement, upon which the Labour and Conservative parties had hitherto been in broad agreement, building instead a very different socio-economic structure, dominated by ideas about initiative and enterprise. At the same time, the emergence of a New Right within the Conservative Party was matched by the renaissance of the Left in Labour's ranks. So traumatic was the experience of the last months of Callaghan's government that the Left found it relatively easy to argue that socialism and the class struggle had been betrayed, while a Labour government sought to prop up the failing edifice of capitalism. Freed from the constraints of office, the party moved rapidly to the left, with the annual conference and the National Executive Committee achieving unprecedented power over the direction of policy. In January 1980, an opinion poll found that 60 per cent of the population believed that Labour had moved too far to the left, while 46 per cent agreed that the Conservatives had moved too far to the right. This perception of party polarization – and for the first time since 1945 there was significant evidence that it was also the reality – clearly opened up promising possibilities for the third force in British politics and, as it turned out, also for a fourth force: 'The political seas had parted as if by magic, leaving the centre ground of British politics free for the first time in recent history.'[3]

The Origins and Birth of the SDP

The history of the Social Democratic Party is quite distinct from that of the Liberal Party, but its origins must be outlined if its future troubled relationship with the Liberals is to be understood. Throughout its history, the Labour Party had existed as a somewhat uneasy coalition of ideas and beliefs which, but for the accident of its birth, might easily have developed into separate political movements. Generally speaking, the forces of non-doctrinaire moderation had managed to retain the reins of power, despite the party's theoretical commitment to the creation of a socialist state, as embodied in its 1918 constitution. Modern social democracy can be traced back to the very beginnings of the Labour movement. It flourished in the context of the Progressive Alliance and owed much to the infusion of social liberalism during and after the First World War. But its more recent manifestations are dated most usefully to the development of the Keynesian–Beveridgite welfare state and the reformulation of Labour thinking carried out in the mid-1950s by such figures as Anthony Crosland, Hugh Gaitskell and Douglas Jay. Gaitskell's leadership of the party opened up the possibility of the complete triumph of social democratic revisionism but, at the time of his death in 1963, Labour had proved strikingly resistant to some of Gaitskell's efforts at modernization. Harold Wilson's priorities as leader were focused on holding the party's competing factions together and, while the social democratic right remained dominant within his cabinets, the clear sense of vision and direction offered by Gaitskell was largely lost.

During the later years of Wilson's leadership, particularly after 1970, there was unmistakable evidence of a significant advance by Labour's left, especially within the extra-parliamentary party. The issue of British membership of the European community emerged as the acid test among the increasingly warring factions of the Labour Party, and in 1971 the votes of the parliamentary right provided crucial support to the Heath government's efforts to pilot British membership through the Commons. A few months later, Harold Lever, George Thomson and Roy Jenkins resigned from Labour's shadow cabinet rather than accept their party's decision to commit a future Labour government to submit British membership to another General Election or referendum. Thus began a process by which Jenkins, a former Labour Home Secretary,

Chancellor and Deputy Leader, started to drift away from a party in whose interest he had first been elected to Parliament in 1948. Despite serving once again as Home Secretary in Wilson's 1974 government, he failed to secure the succession to the party leadership – as had at one time seemed probable – and left the cabinet in 1976 to take up the post of President of the European Commission. From his voluntary exile in Brussels, he watched the fortunes of the Callaghan government with some dismay, while quietly allowing his Labour Party membership to lapse.

By 1979, with the end of his presidency coming into view, Jenkins began giving thought to his own future and to the future shape of British politics. Invited to give the annual Dimbleby Lecture that November, Jenkins chose the theme of 'Home Thoughts from Abroad'. Condemning the paralysing rigidity of the existing party system, he called for the creation of a new political force and spoke of the need to strengthen 'the radical centre', a somewhat confusing phrase included at the prompting of the academic and former Labour MP, David Marquand. Jenkins criticized Britain's excessive changes of policy direction, which, he claimed, were an inevitable consequence of the existing electoral system and called for the introduction of proportional representation. The address was generally well received and invited intense speculation that Jenkins intended, on returning to Britain, to launch a new political party.

How such a party would relate to the existing Liberal Party, and whether there was room in the British political spectrum for a fourth force was, of course, a matter of acute interest, not least to the Liberals themselves. Jenkins later described his thinking in characteristically relaxed terms:

> If I came quietly back from Brussels to a not very political semi-retirement, I thought that I would become a nominal Liberal, for that party was now much closer to my outlook than was either the Labour Party or the Conservatives. But if a combination of circumstances and my strength of purpose made it possible for me to mount a major political initiative then I was convinced that it ought to start separate from but in partnership with the Liberals.[4]

Perhaps more important were the views of David Steel, who was convinced that his duty as Liberal leader was 'to assess how most speedily we can reach [the] objective' of forming a government.[5]

Steel, who had exchanged thoughts with Jenkins over a period of time, made it clear that the best way to break the two-party stranglehold was to challenge it with strong, but separate, Liberal and Social Democratic parties. The experience of Christopher Mayhew, who had lost his seat at the October 1974 General Election, offered little support for encouraging a handful of further defections from Labour to the Liberals. By January 1980, Jenkins recorded that Steel

> perfectly understands that there is no question of me or anybody else joining the Liberal Party. He equally is anxious to work very closely, and possibly, if things went well, to consider an amalgamation after a general election. He would like the closeness at the time of the election itself to take the form not merely of a non-aggression pact, but of working together on policy and indeed sharing broadcasts etc.[6]

At this time, those leading social democrats still within the Labour Party, who would eventually be associated with Jenkins in the so-called 'Gang of Four', were thinking in rather different terms, though the possibility of their being forced to leave the Labour movement had no doubt crossed their minds. Unlike Jenkins, who had enjoyed the luxury of a gradual separation from his Labour roots over a number of years, David Owen, Shirley Williams and Bill Rodgers had all fought the 1979 election in support of Labour's manifesto and remained committed to it. Owen and Rodgers were still members of Labour's shadow cabinet, and Williams of the National Executive Committee, expressions of the hope of all three that their cause was not lost and that the social democratic tradition could yet be saved from inside the Labour movement. Owen, in particular, believed that the centre party envisaged in Jenkins's lecture had little in common with the sorts of ideals in which he believed. It would be 'rootless, brought together out of frustration', 'would soon split apart when faced with the real choices and could easily reflect the attitudes of a London-based liberalism that had neither a base in the provinces nor a bedrock of principles'.[7] 'For the three of us,' he recalled, 'rightly or wrongly, the Liberal Party was low on our agenda. There were other priorities.'[8]

Over the course of 1980, however, the 'gang of three' were obliged to reconsider their positions. In June, Labour's own

Commission of Inquiry endorsed the idea of the mandatory rese-
lection of MPs, together with the setting up of an electoral college
to choose the party leader. Social Democrats interpreted these
moves, fairly enough, as an attempt to place Labour MPs at the
mercy of left-wing constituency and union activists. The election
later that year (still under the old rules) of the veteran left-winger,
Michael Foot, to succeed Callaghan as party leader was a sign of
how far the balance of power had shifted, even within the parliamentary party. 'I cannot pretend that I was other than elated,'
noted Jenkins, 'as it clearly opened up a much greater prospect of
political realignment.'[9] At the annual conference, commitments
were made to an 'alternative economic strategy', including more
public ownership, a massive reflation of the economy, selective
import controls and a 35-hour working week with no reduction
in pay. Then, in January 1981, a special party conference agreed
to the creation of an electoral college for subsequent leadership
elections, in which the largest vote would be given to the trade
unions (40 per cent), with the parliamentary party and the constituency parties receiving 30 per cent each. By the end of 1980, the
Gang of Three, now in close contact with Jenkins, were, with varying degrees of conviction, agreed that the game was up as far as
their continued membership of the Labour Party was concerned.
The outcome of the special conference provided an appropriate
backdrop against which to issue the Limehouse Declaration on 25
January 1981 and launch the Council for Social Democracy. This,
as everyone now realized, would soon be transformed into a new
party, and the SDP came formally into existence on 26 March.

The Alliance

The new party found itself running before it had even attempted
to walk. It immediately secured the support of 14 sitting MPs, taking it above the Liberal total of 11, while opinion polls between
the end of January and the end of March projected support in the
country at between 23 per cent and 31 per cent. Significantly, those
same polls revealed that this figure would rise to between 38 per
cent and 48 per cent for a Liberal–Social-Democratic alliance. For
many years, the polls had suggested a marked differential between
the support actually offered to the Liberal Party and what might
be offered if electors believed that the Liberals had a chance of

winning. In a survey taken at the end of 1980, this difference was
between 13 per cent and 42 per cent. In this respect, the new party
offered clear opportunities. In combination, the Liberals and the
SDP enjoyed the image of an alternative government which the
former, standing alone, did not. The renamed Gang of Four had
all held cabinet office and presented the electorate with the gravitas which even the most able of contemporary Liberals appeared
to lack. Shirley Williams, in particular, enjoyed a standing with
the general public that might hold enormous electoral potential.
In addition, as the SDP was essentially a breakaway from Labour –
only one Conservative MP ever joined its ranks – the hope existed
that the new party could appeal to former Labour voters in a way
that the Liberals, even at the peak of their recent revivals, had never
succeeded in doing. David Owen was very clear on this point:

> If we are to realign British politics, it is vital that the Social Democrats
> cut into the Labour vote, and particularly cut into the Labour vote
> in the northern part of the country so that, in combination with
> disillusioned Tories and Liberals in seats that have hitherto been
> considered 'safe Labour', a Social Democrat can be returned.[10]

In tandem, therefore, could Liberals and Social Democrats achieve
that elusive realignment of the centre-left of British politics for
which Liberals since Jo Grimond had striven so earnestly, but as
yet so unsuccessfully?

The question of whether Liberalism and Social Democracy
were in effect the same thing exercised many minds. Traditionally,
Liberalism gave priority to the rights of individuals and minori-
ties in society, whereas social democracy seemed to be guided by
a Benthamite attachment to the search for the greatest happiness
of the greatest number. For a Liberal, the pursuit of liberty was
more important than striving for equality. In the post-war era,
moreover, social democrats had become enveloped in a cocoon of
bureaucratic centralism that was anathema to Liberal traditions
of devolution and decentralization. That said, there was a pattern of co-operation between the two traditions going back to the
Progressive Alliance of the Edwardian age and, in practice, relations between the Liberal and Social Democratic parties would be
determined more by the gut reactions of individuals on the ground
than by any perceived philosophical affinities or differences. What

did complicate these relations, however, was a lack of clarity, only half-concealed in the euphoria surrounding the new party's creation and early success, about what the SDP really represented. Many had difficulties with Jenkins' concept of a radical centre, not least in the context of a political environment in which the Bennite left and the Thatcherite right also offered their versions of 'radicalism'. More generally, a fundamental division existed between those who saw the SDP as an entirely new political force, and those for whom it was essentially a Mark II Labour Party, seeking to rebuild the Butskellite consensus from which the other parties had now departed. Did it offer the British electorate an exciting and novel future or, in Ralf Dahrendorf's telling words, and as some of the phraseology of the Limehouse Declaration implied, 'no more than a better yesterday'? Labour defectors such as Owen saw in the SDP an opportunity for creative political innovation: 'I wanted to take the ethic of redistribution into our new Party, but to lose all the trappings of state socialism; to break the institutional links with but not the respect for the trade unions.'[11] For other former Labour MPs, however, it was little more than a port of refuge from an increasingly predatory left-wing constituency party.

David Steel who, in consultation with Roy Jenkins, had already worked out a clear picture of how to proceed, welcomed the Limehouse Declaration with enthusiasm. Other Liberals were altogether less certain, however. Jo Grimond, far from seeing an SDP–Liberal alliance as the missing link in his vision of realignment, was concerned by the inherent conservatism of the new party, its nascent Butskellism and firm location in the safe centre of consensual politics. Cyril Smith, the flamboyant MP for Rochdale, famously declared that the new creation should be strangled at birth. More soberly, he had already suggested that, if Jenkins wished to join the Liberal Party, 'I for one would welcome him, but I think any electoral arrangement with Mr Jenkins and any new party that he envisages would be wholly undesirable and I would have thought that history proves that point.'[12] Similarly, the social democratic embrace held few attractions for those Liberals committed to the notion of community politics. Their strategy was 'a direct reaction to the corporatism and ineffectiveness of the old-style social democracy. Was the nature of this new beast any different?'[13] As Michael Meadowcroft, writing in 1982, explained, 'For better or worse, wittingly or unwittingly, the vast expanse of soulless council estates, the confusion of mobility with roads, and above all the wanton destruction of urban neighbourliness, are the products of the social democratic consensus of the post-war years.'[14]

Nor were the Social Democrats of one mind about their relationship with the Liberals. In personal terms, Bill Rodgers and Shirley Williams were far closer to Jenkins than was David Owen. But both were more tied to their Labour roots than was Jenkins. Furthermore, Rodgers, Williams and Owen still spoke the language of democratic 'socialism', something Jenkins had for some time excluded from his vocabulary. The first edition, at least, of Owen's *Face the Future*, published early in 1981, suggested that there was 'a yearning for a fresh and valid socialist alternative' and argued for a 'socialist philosophy'. Neither Rodgers nor Williams excluded a possible eventual merger with the Liberals but, unlike Jenkins, they did not yet see this as the desired outcome of their present actions. Owen, by contrast, was clear that the Social Democratic Party should be a permanent feature of his and the nation's political landscape, an end in itself rather than the means to an end. He rapidly developed a commitment to the new party and its values, as he understood them, unmatched by the other members of the Gang of Four. These differences, particularly between Jenkins and Owen and their respective followers, were never fully confronted, still less resolved, and translated into very different attitudes towards the Liberal Party. These in turn lay at the root of the troubled history of the Liberal–SDP Alliance.

When they came to write their respective memoirs, Jenkins and Owen sought to parody each other's position, while each capturing an element of the truth. According to Jenkins, Owen 'essentially regarded the Liberal Party as a disorderly group of bearded vegetarian pacifists, and his treatment of them as such not unnaturally brought out such of these tendencies as existed. I treated them as the statesmanlike heirs of Gladstone and Asquith.'[15] By contrast, Owen judged that,

> having sniffed the two parties as if they were bottles of claret, his nose, he kept telling us, was unable to detect a Liberal from a Social Democrat. This Olympian assessment owed too much to dining with Mark Bonham Carter and the type of old Asquithian Liberal who had little in common with the new community politicians and pavement politics.[16]

In reality, Jenkins, the biographer of Asquith and later of Gladstone, was himself an instinctive Liberal, never fully at home in Labour's working-class fraternity and always more interested in the achievement of specific political goals than in playing the party political game for its own sake. He had enjoyed working on a cross-party basis during the European referendum campaign – 'it made some of the divisions in politics seem a little artificial'[17] – and now felt perfectly at ease with the Liberal Party of David Steel, while appreciating the tactical advantages of maintaining a degree of separate identity for the time being. By contrast, Owen had been unimpressed by the Liberals' performance in the Lib–Lab Pact and was much influenced by his personal experience as a West Country MP, where the legacy of Jeremy Thorpe and Peter Bessell had left a lasting impression. He doubted whether the Liberals as a whole were tough enough to confront the problems facing British society in the 1980s: 'They constantly showed their lack of moorings in their indiscipline'; and 'when the going gets rough on a political issue they back off.' As a result, he was convinced that 'joining a Centre party based on the Liberals would be jumping out of the frying pan into the cotton wool'.[18]

For a time, relations between the two parties developed informally. In April 1981, Steel, Rodgers and Williams had the opportunity to consult at the annual meeting of the Anglo–German Society at Königswinter. Agreement was reached on the need for a minimum degree of policy co-ordination and a share-out of by-election and parliamentary seats between the two parties. The SDP was not ready to fight the May local elections, but the Liberals alone secured 250 net gains, profiting from Labour's continuing disarray and the unpopular economic policies of the Conservative government. This was followed by a joint statement of principles on 16 June, entitled *A Fresh Start for Britain*. The words 'socialist' and 'socialism' were conspicuous by their absence, and the emphasis on issues such as devolution, industrial partnership and above all proportional representation (notably missing from the Limehouse Declaration) indicated a strong Liberal input. Owen remained wary, 'increasingly worried about the way we are merging into an amorphous amalgam with the Liberal Party. I cannot put my finger on how to stop it.'[19] His instinct told him 'that it could only harm our new party if we were too identified with the Liberals'.[20] No one, however, could ignore the new party's performance at its first by-election test in Warrington, in Cheshire, in July. After some hesitation on the part of Shirley Williams, Roy Jenkins decided to throw his hat into the ring. The seat was not, on paper, promising territory for the SDP. Solidly Labour, it had no tradition of residual Liberal strength. But taking more easily to a North of England constituency campaign than might have been expected, Jenkins, with generous Liberal support, came within 1,700 votes of a dramatic victory.

A BBC computer projection extrapolated from the Warrington result suggested that, at a General Election, an SDP–Liberal alliance could win 501 Commons seats, leaving Labour with 113 and the Conservatives just one. This was, of course, exaggerated nonsense, but there seemed to be reasonable grounds for believing that, for the first time in half a century, the mould of British politics shaped around the Labour–Conservative duopoly was about to be broken. Liberal or SDP candidates were successful in almost half the local government by-elections held between the Warrington by-election and the end of 1981. Recognizing that what had been achieved at Warrington could not have been done by the Liberals acting alone, Steel renewed efforts to confirm the alliance of the two parties. After Warrington, the Liberal leader took advantage of every media opportunity to stress the benefits of a close and formalized working relationship. At the Liberals' Llandudno assembly in September, the proposal for an alliance was endorsed overwhelmingly, while Steel planted in the minds of delegates the prospect, that had eluded them for so long, of genuine political power:

> Now at last we have the reality in our grasp. We must have the nerve and courage not to let it slip. I have the good fortune to be the first Liberal leader for over half a century who is able to say to you at the end of our annual assembly: go back to your constituencies and prepare for government.[21]

Contenders for Power?

For the time being, the Alliance bandwagon continued to roll. A new wave of defections from Labour brought the SDP's tally of MPs to over 20. In October, the Liberals, fielding a relatively undistinguished candidate, captured Croydon North-West from

the Conservatives. The following month, Williams scaled a seemingly impregnable 18,000 Conservative majority to take the seat
of Crosby on Merseyside by more than 5,000 votes. Scarcely a
constituency in the land seemed invulnerable to the Alliance's
advance, as a Gallup poll in December put the two parties' combined support at 50 per cent. But the balloon was bound to burst,
or at the very least deflate. Alliance performances in such differing constituencies as Warrington and Crosby might suggest to
optimists that the SDP had succeeded in broadening the existing
third party's appeal into areas hitherto outside the Liberals' grasp.
In reality, it revealed that Alliance support was as transient and
rootless as had been the Liberals' at earlier peaks of revival. The
SDP had succeeded, even more effectively than earlier Liberals, in
mobilizing the protest vote at a time of unprecedented unpopularity for the two major parties. Many had been enthused by the
new party to get involved in political activity for the first time,
but what attracted the typical Alliance voter was the reassuring
familiarity of its message. In place of the disturbing doctrines of
socialism and monetarism were comfortable reaffirmations of the
advantages of the mixed economy. The SDP had 'sold itself at its
launch as a party of common sense, moderation and good men
and true who were against sin and in favour of virtue', making
it 'easy for many voters to regard the Social Democrats as their
sort of people'.[22] In an unguarded but revealing comment, Shirley
Williams herself admitted that the new party had attracted 'broad
and frothy support at Crosby, without much organisation or intellectual underpinning'.[23]

The downturn in the Alliance's fortunes became apparent in
the new year. Though Roy Jenkins was returned to Westminster
following victory at a by-election at Glasgow, Hillhead, the swing
to the Alliance was less dramatic than at Croydon or Crosby. Then
Conservative fortunes started to recover, with the first signs that
their unorthodox economic strategy might be beginning to bear
fruit, a process that was accelerated rapidly by the outbreak and successful conclusion of the Falklands War. By July 1982, Conservative
poll support was running at 46 per cent; but that of the Alliance had
gone down to a respectable, but not earth-shattering, 24 per cent.
Votes in the May local elections were nowhere near to being translated into a comparable proportion of seats won – clear evidence
that the Alliance would need to poll at a significantly higher level if

it was to make a real breakthrough at the expense of Labour and the Conservatives. It was also striking that the Liberals managed to win five times as many seats as the SDP. Owen was inclined to blame the loss of support on the Alliance itself. Earlier levels of public backing had been 'dissipated by constantly talking about an Alliance and giving the impression that the SDP and Liberals are in the process of merging'.[24] But it seems unlikely that voters were deserting the Alliance because of a loss of identity on the part of the SDP.

That said, clear damage was done by the public exposure of strains within and between the two parties making up the Alliance. Much had been made of a style of politics in which individuals could work constructively with others whose views were not identical to their own. But, as an earlier generation of Liberals had quickly discovered, the doctrine of agreeing to differ had strict limitations. Roy Jenkins attributed the worsening of personal relations to the decline in the Alliance's standing in the polls: 'With the change of mood there came ... a shrinkage of generosity between the two parties.'[25] But the reverse was also true, as electors recoiled from the spectacle of Alliance politicians squabbling with a relish equal to that of Labour and the Conservatives. Attentive observers may have noticed that Owen dropped references to 'socialism' from the second edition of his book, *Face the Future*, published in the autumn of 1981. But this owed more to the beginnings of the political odyssey that would eventually take him to a distinctive position on the centre-right of British politics than to any warming of feelings towards the Liberal Party. Indeed, in an interview in the *Alliance* magazine the following year, Owen spelt out publicly what would be his consistent and defining attitude towards the relationship between the two parties throughout the lifetime of the SDP and beyond:

> I'm in business to fashion a new Social Democratic party, a totally new force in British politics. If we blur our identities too much and the Liberals and the Social Democrats look as if they are 'an Alliance party', nothing would please the Conservatives and Labour party more: they would narrow us to what they would brand as a centralist band of opinion.[26]

But the issue that brought the strains within the Alliance fully into the public domain was the attempt to negotiate a deal on the division of seats at the next General Election. Deciding who should stand where in the handful of by-elections held since the launch of the SDP had been no easy matter, as the experience of Croydon had shown. Reaching a decision on the 600 or so seats on the British mainland was a task of monumental proportions. At the start of the negotiations, both sides believed they were in a strong position. The SDP felt it was they who had transformed the prospects of third-party politics in a way that the Liberals alone could not have done. Furthermore, the leading figures of the SDP enjoyed a higher public profile than, with the exception of David Steel, did their Liberal counterparts. For Owen, indeed, and those SDP MPs who thought like him, the negotiation of any electoral pact ought to involve a trial of strength with the Liberals to demonstrate that the new party could not be treated as a junior partner. On the other hand, the Liberals were far more firmly entrenched on the ground than were their new allies. In many cases they had been nursing constituencies for a number of years, watching their strength grow to the point where electoral victory was apparently within their grasp. In such situations they were understandably loath to step down in favour of a 'Johnny come lately' put forward by the SDP. So while the principle of an approximate 50–50 overall split was easy enough to agree, deciding precisely which seats would be entrusted to each party in a way that offered any chance of an equality of successful electoral outcomes was an entirely different matter. In particular, the SDP demand that the Liberals should stand aside in many of their most promising seats inevitably caused enormous resentment.

As the negotiations proceeded in the autumn of 1981, the Owenite MP, Mike Thomas, warned that 'the likely outcome of the next election is that the Liberals will win more seats (possibly twice as many as us), even though we stand at 30 per cent in the opinion polls and they stand at 8 per cent'.[27] Only if the Alliance were to win well in excess of 200 seats, an increasingly remote prospect, was the division between Liberal and SDP successes likely to come more into balance. Thomas, who often spoke for Owen, tried to convince Jenkins of the seriousness of the situation from an SDP point of view:

> What I want to communicate to you is that you are not here dealing with a little political awkwardness that has to be circumvented or

overcome, you are approaching a fundamental sticking point...for many in our Party. I don't want an Alliance party. I don't want to be a part of parachuting a few people into the upper echelons of what is essentially the Liberal Party. I want a true partnership between two distinct forces – each of which brings the Alliance its own strengths and convictions. That is why, for me, the outcome of the negotiations with the Liberals is actually about preserving the capacity of our own party to survive and develop, and thus contribute to a genuine alliance.[28]

What brought these internal disputes to public attention was the decision, during the 1981 Christmas recess, of Bill Rodgers, leading the SDP team, to announce the suspension of the negotiations, claiming that the Liberals were being too greedy in their demands. The quarrel was eventually patched up on the basis of the Liberals retaining their 50 most winnable seats, in return for the SDP standing in two-thirds of the next 100 most promising constituencies, but many believed that lasting damage had been done to the Alliance's public image. When a final deal, still very much to the Liberals' advantage, was put in place in time for the Liberal Party's annual assembly in 1982, Owen recorded his belief that a decisive moment had been reached:

When eventually the history of the SDP is written historians may have to decide at what point it became inevitable that it merged into the Liberal Party and of all the thresholds and of all the turning points it may be that they will conclude that it was this week that the final determination was made.[29]

By the beginning of 1983, minds were turning to the prospect of a General Election, with Mrs Thatcher, whose government was presiding over record levels of unemployment, being under some pressure to go to the polls before the electoral effects of the 'Falklands factor' finally disappeared. In January, a Joint Policy Resolution Group was set up, headed by Richard Wainwright for the Liberals and John Horam for the SDP, to iron out points of policy difference between the two parties. The resulting manifesto was inevitably a compromise, and as such lacked the cutting edge that the concept of the 'radical centre' had once seemed to promise. It was, judged one critic, 'little more than a rehash of that cosy, corporatist, social democracy which nearly sank this country in the 1960s and 1970s'.[30] The manifesto contained a clear commitment to constitutional reform and a thorough overhaul of the welfare state, but in economic policy – one of the key dividing lines between Labour and the Conservatives – it seemed to hark back to the Butskellite consensus of earlier years. Those who read it, suggested the *Financial Times*, were likely to 'suffer something very like nostalgia'. Owen bemoaned the dominant influence of Jenkins' views, 'rooted in the 1960s', and regretted that he had failed to attract Jenkins to the concept of a social market economy.[31] The manifesto carried the subtitle *Programme for Government,* however unlikely that outcome now appeared. A more realistic possibility was that the Liberals and SDP might together hold the balance of power in the new Parliament. In such a situation, electors would wish, reasonably enough, to know to which side Alliance support would be given to form a government. But the decision was taken to show no leaning either to the left or the right.

Thus the Alliance went into the election campaign in May as two parties united under a single manifesto, and with two leaders – Steel in charge of the campaign and Jenkins projected as Prime Minister designate in the event of an Alliance victory. The latter decision made sense in terms of Jenkins' standing and experience, and in any case, Steel, as the much younger man, could reasonably calculate that the leadership of any joint party would fall to him some time in the future. But opinion polls revealed that, both among Alliance supporters and the electorate at large, Steel enjoyed a far higher approval rating than Jenkins, who had never recovered his earlier parliamentary ascendancy since returning to Westminster. On 29 May, over an informal lunch meeting of Alliance leaders at Steel's home in the Borders, the Liberal leader attempted unsuccessfully to dethrone a startled Jenkins from his position, arguing that the Alliance would benefit if Jenkins played a less prominent role. In general, the two parties campaigned together effectively, though there was some tension in Liverpool, Leeds and the West Country, with a few Liberal candidates refusing to stand on the Alliance ticket.

As had been the Liberals' experience at several polls since the 1950s, the 1983 General Election combined both achievement and disappointment for the Alliance. In securing 25.4 per cent of the popular vote, the Alliance did better than any third party since 1923. With 7.75 million votes, it was only 0.75 million behind Labour. Under a strict system of proportional representation, this level of public endorsement would have translated into about 160 seats, almost certainly enough to force entry into a coalition government. As it was, the Alliance secured just 23 seats in the new Parliament against Labour's 209, introducing, as the *Sunday Times* put it, 'a new order of unfairness'. In terms of the strategic goal of replacing the Labour Party, little had been achieved. It was true that the left-of-centre vote had been split, but the practical effect of this was to hand Mrs Thatcher a massive 144-seat majority over all other parties combined on just 42.4 per cent of the poll. Just one seat, Leeds West, had been captured by the Liberals from the Labour Party. The Alliance had apparently reached a plateau of support, but this was not enough to make real inroads into the seats of its opponents. Meanwhile, Labour, though suffering its worst defeat since 1931, continued to pile up votes in its electoral heartlands sufficient to maintain a sizeable parliamentary presence. A further worrying feature was the shallowness of Alliance support. Polls showed that only slightly over half of its voters identified firmly with it: 'The centre vote in 1983, like the Liberal vote in 1974, was a protest vote; it did not represent a fundamental shift in voters' loyalties.'[32] The Liberals could draw one small crumb of comfort from a clear shift in the balance of power within the Alliance. The respective Liberal and SDP tallies of MPs had changed from 13 and 29 at the dissolution to 17 and just 6 in the new Parliament.

The Two Davids

This change of relative strength was qualified by post-election developments in the leadership of the two parties. Steel was taken aback by the critical tone displayed at a meeting of Liberal MPs on 15 June, which called for the election by the parliamentary party of a deputy leader and of the chief whip, clear attempts to curtail his own authority. Tired out by the recent campaign and disappointed at the failure to secure an electoral breakthrough, Steel wrote a letter of resignation as Liberal leader a fortnight later. Though eventually dissuaded from this course, Steel insisted on taking a three-month sabbatical break during which time the acting leadership passed to the chief whip, Alan Beith. Steel's authority had been badly bruised and his temporary withdrawal enabled the initiative within the Alliance to pass to the SDP. Here, Roy Jenkins rapidly gave up the party leadership, to be replaced, without a great deal of discussion, by David Owen. Within the depleted ranks of the SDP's parliamentary party, with both Shirley Williams and Bill Rodgers numbered among the electoral casualties, there was no serious alternative to his appointment. During his time within the party, Owen had greatly enhanced his public standing. After a 'good' Falklands War, he had emerged as a reasoned but trenchant critic of the Conservative government and as a formidable parliamentary and television performer whose views carried considerable authority beyond the confines of his own party.

But Owen's elevation to the leadership was a significant moment in the Alliance's history. Until the 1983 General Election, Alliance politics had been as much a partnership between David Steel and Roy Jenkins as between two parties. The two men understood and liked one another, shared a common vision of where they were going and had succeeded in carrying – and occasionally dragging – their followers along with them, while papering over the divisions and contradictions inherent since the SDP's birth. Owen, as his memoirs reveal, had travelled reluctantly along this path, while nurturing a clear and coherent alternative view of what the new party was all about. Known for his somewhat abrasive style, Owen never succeeded in establishing a relationship of warmth and trust with Steel comparable to that developed by Jenkins. 'I never underestimated David Steel's manipulative skills,' Owen once conceded. 'If they had been matched by an interest in the policies best suited to our country, he would have been a formidable politician.'[33] But, even as leader of a diminished parliamentary band, Owen now had far more scope than hitherto to influence the Alliance's future shape.

Thus, while Steel continued to believe that fusion was the logical destiny of the Alliance parties, Owen drew and promulgated a very different conclusion from the outcome of the recent election. Though in public he did not exclude the possibility of an eventual merger, Owen remained determined to preserve the SDP's independence. Its goal was the achievement, in co-operation with the Liberals, of proportional representation, after which it could look forward to a separate existence within the very different political structure that electoral reform would create. For Owen, moreover, the 1983 results showed the limited attractions of an appeal to moderation and the comfortable middle ground. 'If we could simultaneously break right on the market and left on social policy,' he later explained, 'I believed we could find an electorally attractive political mix' – an approach that perhaps explains his later sympathy for John Major's recipe of 'Thatcherism with a human face'.[34] Influenced by the American political philosopher, John Rawls, Owen differentiated between a belief in the equality of a citizen's rights and liberties and the sort of social and economic equality still espoused by the political left. He wanted to couple a high degree of social concern and responsibility with an emphasis on the primacy of the market and the importance of competition and free enterprise. Under Owen's influence, the SDP endorsed the concept of the 'social market' at its 1984 Buxton conference, though it was one about which most Liberals remained sceptical. This approach meant a readiness to apply market forces to the public services – the SDP spoke of an internal market within the National Health Service (NHS) before the Conservatives did – in a way that finally distanced Owen from his Labour past, while encouraging the belief among many Liberals that his agenda was sub-Thatcherite. Such thinking was intellectually defensible, but did little to clarify for the electorate precisely where the Alliance stood within the political spectrum. Equally seriously, it did not suggest that relations within the Alliance would run as smoothly as in the years 1981–83.

The electoral history of the 1983 Parliament revealed little that was not already known. The Alliance's average opinion-poll rating stood at 26.9 per cent. In March 1987, a Marplan survey put the level of support at 31 per cent, while Gallup suggested 31.5 per cent, two points ahead of Labour. The now-established pattern of spectacular by-election gains (and several near misses), largely at the expense of an unpopular Conservative government, was maintained. In a June 1984 by-election, held on the same day that elections to the European Parliament failed to produce a single Alliance victory, the SDP snatched Portsmouth South from the Conservatives. The constituency of Brecon and Radnor in mid-Wales was captured by the Liberals a year later, while the apparently safe Conservative seat of Ryedale in North Yorkshire fell to the Liberals with a 5,000 majority in May 1986. Only at Greenwich, South London, in February 1987 was this pattern challenged, with Rosie Barnes for the SDP taking the seat from Labour. Even here, however, it was the collapse of the Conservative vote, as electors polled tactically to defeat a left-wing Labour candidate, that largely determined the outcome. Each of these victories contributed usefully to the Alliance's parliamentary strength, while adding to the oxygen of publicity, so often denied to a third party. At the same time, they suggested that the declared goal of replacing Labour as the main non-Conservative force was an unrealizable aspiration. Indeed, as Labour began, under Michael Foot's successor, Neil Kinnock, to tread the long path back to the political centre ground, a clear blow was struck in favour of the traditional two-party mould of British politics. As Owen looked back, he saw Kinnock's attack on the Militant Tendency at Labour's 1985 party conference as a clear turning-point. As far as local politics were concerned, it was possible to discern a pattern of steady progress on the part of the Alliance. By the time of the 1987 council elections, the Liberal Party had made gains for nine consecutive years and the SDP for four. But even the 400 net Alliance gains in 1987 still left it controlling only 15 district and borough councils, and the flagship Liverpool council was lost to Labour.

Owen proved far less reluctant than Jenkins to confront the SDP's policy differences with the Liberals. He was also keen to redress the imbalance of parliamentary strength between the parties. As negotiations began to allocate seats for the next General Election, Owen expressed the hope that these would 'take as their objective to restore a balance to equality of seats with a view to not only having parity of numbers of seats fought but also some attempt to redress the imbalance of votes cast between Liberals and SDP'.[35] But the Liberals had been quick off the mark and 'most of the very best Liberal seats readopted their previous P[rospective] P[arliamentary] C[andidate]s soon after the 1983 General Election and we didn't get a look in'.[36] What particularly worried Owen was that SDP candidates, seeking selection by joint local constituency committees, would find it expedient to compromise their views on precisely those issues – 'a continuation of a British nuclear deterrent after Polaris... promising more expenditure [on social services] and generally ducking out of some of the hard edges of SDP policy' – where key differences with the Liberal Party existed. Consequently, 'we would have an Alliance policy that would look very like the Liberal policies over the years which have never been able to win sufficient support to break through'.[37] In the event, the SDP managed to secure rough parity in the allocation of seats, including those deemed most winnable.

Owen's reference to the issue of Britain's nuclear deterrent reflected the priority he gave to defence policy, an area in which he had developed a deep and detailed expertise. It had become, moreover, the issue on which he felt most profoundly separated from the now unilateralist Labour Party, the issue in fact that, he believed, disqualified Labour from fitness to govern. The issue had also always had the potential to create discord within the Alliance. The Liberals had a strong unilateralist tradition, while several leading figures in the SDP, in particular Owen and Bill Rodgers, were strong supporters of an independent British deterrent. A serious split had been averted prior to the 1983 General Election, and in the summer of 1984 a Joint Commission on Defence and Disarmament was set up to prepare proposals for an agreed defence policy. The key question was what would happen when the existing Polaris nuclear submarines, dating from the 1960s, reached the end of their useful life. Both parties opposed the Trident missile option adopted by the Conservative government – the Liberals on principle and the SDP on grounds of cost – but the latter admitted that by the time an Alliance government came to power the costs of cancellation might outweigh those of continuing with the project, and that, in such circumstances, it would be foolish to abandon what was already or almost in place. By the spring of 1986 it was becoming known that the Commission was likely to suggest that the decision on what happened after Polaris could be deferred, since Polaris itself might well remain in service until the mid- or late 1990s.

For Owen, this was precisely the sort of fudge he regarded as constitutionally characteristic of the Liberal Party, but for the time being he kept his counsel on the matter. The crisis that now arose could easily have been avoided, but reflected the lack of mutual confidence and trust existing at the highest levels of the Alliance. In mid-May, Steel briefed the *Scotsman*'s lobby correspondent, confirming that the Commission's report would not commit Liberals to replace the Polaris system. By the time this accurate, if unwise, admission reached the pages of the newspaper, it had been translated into the headline 'Alliance report rejects UK deterrent: Owen's nuclear hopes dashed'. Owen, convinced that Steel had been party to a deliberate and humiliating snub, made no attempt to resolve the matter through private investigation and discussion, but instead used his speech on 17 May to the meeting of the Council for Social Democracy in Southport, Lancashire, to reaffirm his conviction that Britain should remain a nuclear power and to state that, if the Alliance intended to campaign for the cancellation of Trident, it must be ready to find a replacement. To confirm his position, he then told a meeting of the Anglo-German society in Bonn that Britain's contribution to NATO must include, at least for the time being, a minimum nuclear deterrent.

Owen's démarche sent shock waves through the Alliance and through the SDP itself. Referring later to Owen's speech of 17 May, Roy Jenkins suggested 'that the alliance began to die on that wet Southport Saturday morning'.[38] For Shirley Williams, the maintenance of the Alliance seemed more important than the detail of policy:

> I hope … that you might welcome what [the Commission] has achieved, while making clear that your own position remains unchanged. That would strengthen cooperation between our two parties. I do hope you will not repudiate the Commission's conclusions, for the alliance between the SDP and Liberal parties offers the country the one sane alternative to the policies of the old parties, and demands all our efforts to sustain and strengthen it.[39]

Owen, his position endorsed by the SDP's parliamentary party, felt let down by Rodgers, a member of the Joint Commission, whose position had changed 'from being one of the foremost supporters … of a British nuclear deterrent to now, I gather, being "agnostic" … Your position is both unexpected and makes me in personal terms very sad.'[40] Rodgers, in turn, 'had every reason at Southport to be angry that you were undermining the Commission's report in advance of publication'. Owen had been understandably provoked by the leak in the *Scotsman*, but 'after five years' experience, we all know how difficult Liberals can often be'.[41]

Once the Commission's report was published on 11 June, Owen and Steel set about trying to repair the damage caused by their respective actions. They came to the conclusion that there was some mileage in Owen's idea of Anglo-French co-operation over nuclear weapons, and agreed to explore this possibility in a series of meetings with European and NATO leaders. But these efforts at reconciliation were undermined by events at the Liberals' annual assembly at Eastbourne in September. With the party leadership misjudging the mood of the meeting, and after passionate contributions to the debate from Simon Hughes and Michael Meadowcroft, MPs for Bermondsey in South-East London, and Leeds West, respectively, a motion opposing a nuclear element in any European defence co-operation was carried by the narrow margin of 652 votes to 625. Many of those in the majority, believing that Steel had been outmanoeuvred consistently in his partnership with the SDP leader up to that point, felt they were strengthening Steel's hand in his negotiations with Owen; others, without any serious expectation of winning the vote, felt that they were delivering a rebuke to the SDP leader. Steel criticized his party in his closing speech to the assembly, and he and Owen then redoubled their efforts to find an acceptable compromise. When it came, it represented a substantial triumph for Owen. By mid-December, a new defence statement was ready, which committed an Alliance government to maintaining, with whatever necessary modernization, a minimum British nuclear deterrent until it could be safely negotiated away as part of a global agreement involving substantial concessions on the part of the Soviet Union.

In this way, the Alliance's nominal unity was maintained, but at a significant long-term cost. The damage was immediately apparent in the opinion polls. Alliance support, as high as 35 per cent in January, was back down to 23.5 per cent in December, having been even lower immediately after Eastbourne. More profoundly, questions had been posed about the viability of the Alliance itself. Paddy Ashdown, a Liberal representative on the Joint Commission, vented his feelings:

> I will not be party to an attempt to railroad the Alliance into a position where its freedom of action after the next election is pre-empted now; or participate in a conspiracy to extract one-sided concessions which are not reciprocated; or proselytise for political partnership unless we can show rather more of it between ourselves; or make more sacrifices, or call for them from others, without some evidence that this is a two-way street.[42]

More generally, Liberal doubts about David Owen were confirmed. By now, many would have concurred with Roy Jenkins' later assessment that it was 'the especial misfortune of the Alliance to be a political grouping which stood for consensus but which contained one of the two most abrasive figures in British politics'.[43] For some, the difficulties of working with Owen stemmed from his own abandonment of the progressive left in British politics. Others believed that he had not wanted agreement over defence policy, as the continuation of separate SDP and Liberal approaches would strengthen his resolve to resist a future merger of the two parties.

It was against this background that the Alliance prepared for the General Election of June 1987. A successful rally at the Barbican Centre in January, victory in the Greenwich by-election and the comfortable retention of the seat of Truro in Cornwall, made vacant by the tragic death of David Penhaligon in a car crash, boosted morale. But underlying tensions remained. This time no attempt was made to nominate a Prime Minister designate. Despite their recent differences, Owen and Steel put themselves forward as separate party leaders and as examples of the sort of inter-party co-operation they sought to substitute for the confrontational politics which, they believed, alienated an increasing percentage of the electorate. Negotiated by teams from the two parties, the joint manifesto, *Britain United: The Time has Come*, was inevitably something of a compromise. In a jointly signed foreword, Owen and Steel insisted that Britain could only be drawn together by 'political, economic and social reform on a scale not contemplated in our country for over forty years'. Yet, in its detail, apart from constitutional issues, it was a less radical document than these words implied. As Owen later explained:

> We could not openly endorse the social market for Liberals felt that positioned us too close to the Conservatives; we could not wholeheartedly support the British nuclear deterrent for the Liberals were still deeply divided on the issue. Nor could we present Labour as totally unfit to govern because that meant closing the option of being able to form a coalition with them.[44]

The manifesto was described as a 'programme for government' but, as everyone recognized, the most to which the Alliance could realistically aspire was to hold the balance of power in the new Parliament. Inevitably, this raised the question of which way the balance would be tipped in the event that the Alliance got hold of it. It was a question Steel and Owen were reluctant to answer, recognizing that a clearly stated preference either way would inevitably chase away the votes of some potential supporters. In a joint letter to Alliance candidates some months earlier, the two leaders put forward the agreed line: 'We shall not allow ourselves, nor should you, to express a preference between working with Labour or Tory MPs.' Only in a general sense, however, was this position maintained. It was fairly obvious to the attentive observer that Steel's Liberal Party was more of an anti-Conservative force than an anti-Labour one. Equally, Owen's SDP seemed more sympathetic to the Conservative Party, especially if that party was no longer led by Mrs Thatcher. Once again, the issue of defence divided the two parties. As Owen later explained, 'for me [Labour's defence policy] was the disqualifying factor for being the government, for David [Steel] it was one very good issue to measure Labour by, no more and no less'.[45] Yet it was Owen himself who did the most to open the rift to public inspection when, in the course of a joint television interview with the two leaders by Robin Day, he declared:

> In the last analysis, the one issue on which I will always judge anyone –
> and that is somebody who would put at jeopardy the defences
> and security of this country – unless the Labour Party changes
> its defence policy, in my judgement they are not fit to govern the
> country.[46]

Despite these divisions, the Alliance waged a reasonably effective campaign. Both leaders came over well and impressed the electorate as being committed and serious politicians. Some argued, particularly once the electoral outcome was known, that the joint leadership was a disadvantage, confusing the electorate and contrasting unfavourably with the way in which both Labour and the Conservatives presented their respective leaders in quasi-presidential terms. But later detailed studies failed to produce hard evidence that large numbers of voters had been alienated by the fact that the Alliance consisted of two parties with two leaders. In practice, the Alliance's fortunes were largely determined, as had so often been the case for the Liberals in the past, by the performance of the two leading parties. It was widely agreed that Labour had waged a highly competent campaign. But the electorate remained unconvinced that Neil Kinnock had yet gone far enough to pull Labour back from socialist extremism, and it had profound doubts about his personal fitness for the premiership. In contrast, the Conservatives were rewarded for low inflation, falling unemployment and widespread prosperity. Mrs Thatcher, if not always liked, was admired for her leadership qualities. This was not a situation in which the Alliance was likely to improve on its 1983 performance. In the event, the Alliance secured 22 seats, one fewer than four years before, on 22.7 per cent of the vote. Three seats were gained, all by the Liberals, but these were more than offset by losses, which included that of Roy Jenkins at Glasgow, Hillhead. Overall, a net loss of five seats was recorded from the Alliance's standing at the dissolution.

The mould, then, had not been broken. It had perhaps been cracked to the extent that, in tandem with the SDP, the Liberals had performed better in two successive General Elections than at any time since the 1920s. But the goal of replacing Labour as the main non-Conservative party in British politics, which had seemed not beyond the bounds of possibility in 1981–83, was now fading from view. Indeed, throughout its history, the Alliance was more of a threat in Conservative seats than in those held by Labour, especially in the heartlands of industrial Britain. In the 1987 election, only six of the 20 seats in which Alliance candidates came closest to victory were Labour-held. Labour had proved remarkably resilient for precisely the same reasons that the Alliance had failed to break through. The concentration of Labour's vote, class-based if on a diminishing foundation, meant that, however badly it performed, it was never likely in the existing electoral system to secure fewer than 150 Commons seats. By contrast, the even spread of the Alliance vote meant that even an impressive share of the popular vote of up to 30 per cent was unlikely to be matched by a comparable representation in Parliament. Only in the event of a freak result, with a relatively small number of Alliance MPs holding the balance between equally matched Labour and Conservative parties, would the Liberals and SDP have had the chance – but by no means the certainty – of forcing through the introduction of proportional representation and thereby transforming the pattern of British politics. Ironically, therefore, the Alliance needed Labour to perform better and not worse than it did in the 1980s.

Thus the Alliance failed to remedy the weaknesses from which the Liberal Party, standing alone, had long suffered. The Alliance, like the Liberals, enjoyed no solid ideological or geographical base, its vote coming 'from everywhere in general and nowhere in particular'.[47] As a result, and again in common with the Liberals, the Alliance enjoyed its greatest success – and sometimes that success was quite spectacular – as a repository for protest votes in individual by-elections, rather than as a serious aspirant for power in national contests. By 1987, moreover, the scope for attracting disillusioned Tory and Labour supporters was narrowing. Many of the Conservatives' reforms and innovations now seemed less radical than when Mrs Thatcher had first advocated them, while Labour was beginning to move back to the middle ground, its new programme being, in the words of *The Times*, 'Gaitskellism from the left of centre'. On policy and image too, the Alliance showed little advance over the performance of the Liberals. Individual policies appear to have played only a small part in generating Alliance support. Polls showed that the electorate had only a hazy notion of what the Alliance stood for. It was little more than 'a safe and decent alternative to the two established parties ... a moderate force in an increasingly immoderate age'.[48] Ironically, as Labour under Kinnock became reconciled to staying in Europe, the policy issue that had been most important for the Gang of Four in their original decision to jump ship, and on which the Liberals had a long and consistent record, it appeared that the majority of Alliance voters actually supported Britain's withdrawal.

Merger Most Foul

With the Conservative government comfortably re-elected, the period immediately after the 1987 General Election was, from an Alliance point of view, an appropriate one for reflection and re-evaluation. It was not to be, however. The question of merging the two parties was bound to come on to the agenda. Steel had taken the opportunity in July 1986, on the tenth anniversary of his assumption of the Liberal leadership, to make clear his own belief that a formal union of the two parties was, in the long term, inevitable. That summer, Jenkins told a meeting of the Tawney Society that the Alliance was, in ideological terms, 'about as cohesive as any decent democratic grouping ought ever to be'. Even Owen had suggested, at the fifth anniversary of the founding of the SDP, that a merger might one day be the natural destiny of the two parties.

On the ground, local Liberal and SDP activists often acted as if they were now part of a united party and, in constituencies such as Cambridge and Saffron Waldon in Essex, fusion had already taken place.

But merger was by no means an inevitable outcome. Whatever he had said in public, it was not what Owen wanted, and the majority of the diminished SDP parliamentary party agreed with him. Indeed, as his own views had evolved, he had begun to feel, if anything, less comfortable in Liberal company and more distant from his erstwhile colleagues in the Gang of Four. The party's Owenite trustees no doubt spoke for their leader:

> From the beginning the SDP was seen by some members of the Gang of Four as simply a device to get people out of the Labour Party. They thought, therefore, that as soon as possible it should be merged with the Liberal Party. This view, which was no doubt a careful political decision at the beginning, has become an article of faith, if not an obsession.[49]

With Owen included, the strains within a united party would not have gone away. Indeed, they would have become more acute in the event of that party ever entering government. Differences over defence and the market economy had already surfaced and would one day have been joined by the issue of a federal Europe, which Owen had always opposed. It was perhaps his understanding of this position that persuaded David Steel that nothing would be gained by delay or waiting for a process of organic merger to occur of its own accord. Over the weekend following the General Election, Steel called for a 'democratic fusion' of the two parties. Owen responded by declaring his opposition and calling for a ballot of SDP members. That ballot was cleverly worded to maximize the numbers of those opposing total fusion, because the conciliatory alternative was to negotiate for a closer constitutional framework for the existing Alliance that still preserved the SDP's separate existence. In the event, the proposal to begin merger negotiations was carried by 25,897 votes (57.4 per cent) to 19,228 (42.6 per cent). This result prompted Owen's resignation as party leader and a clear indication that he intended to work for the creation of a new fourth party in British politics based on those who had voted to retain an independent SDP. His decision, though consistent with the views he had held since the party's foundation, seemed to defy the democratic decision of the membership and earned Owen the lasting animosity of the majority of Liberals and of many members of the SDP. Meanwhile, on the Liberal side, the path to union seemed at this stage altogether smoother. At Harrogate in September the party's annual assembly voted over-whelmingly to begin merger negotiations, and preliminary talks between the two sides began on 29 September.

The prospective loss of David Owen, the most high-profile fig-ure within the Alliance, was a considerable blow, but this was as nothing compared with the way negotiations towards union now proceeded. It was not just that many obstacles remained to be over-come before the two parties could be combined. In the words of the historians of the SDP, the negotiations themselves 'resembled a cross between the Twilight of the Gods and a Feydeau farce, with the farcical element increasingly to the fore as time went on'.[50] The chances of agreement were not improved by the inclusion within the Liberal negotiating team of figures such as Tony Greaves, head of Liberal publications, Michael Meadowcroft, the former MP for Leeds West, and Rachael Pitchford, Chair of the Young Liberals, who were most suspicious of the SDP, its policies, its structure and its decision-making processes. Such figures represented a strong strand of opinion that the Liberals had conceded too much in earlier negotiations between the two parties. When a draft con-stitution for a new joint party was published on 18 December, it was clear either that Steel, in the wake of Harrogate, was taking the Liberals too much for granted or else that Robert Maclennan, the new, often diffident and sometimes patently nervous, leader of the Social Democrats, was proving a more formidable negotia-tor than had been anticipated. The new party was to have a fed-eral structure and, as in the SDP, responsibility for policy would be divided between the annual conference and a special policy committee. The inclusion in the preamble to the constitution of a commitment that Britain should play a full and constructive role in NATO was curious. This was something that Liberals were more inclined to accept as an item of current policy rather than as part of a declaration of abiding principles. Nomenclature also proved controversial. 'Liberal and Social Democrats' might have been fair to both sides, but produced an unfortunate acronym. In the event, the proposed name of the new party – 'The New Liberal and Social Democratic Party' – was cumbersome; the proposed shorthand – 'the Alliance' – insensitive to those who wanted to build something new rather than be reminded of past tensions.

Despite clear warnings from the meeting of the Liberal Party Council in December, Steel compounded his difficulties by pressing ahead, apparently regardless of mounting unease among party activists. Matters came to a head with the conclusion of the merger negotiations in the early hours of 13 January 1988. By the end of the night, four Liberal negotiators had resigned, either over the question of the new party's name or the commitment to NATO. A joint policy document, *Voices and Choices for All*, supposedly the work of the two leaders but in practice largely the creation of Maclennan, proved even more contentious. For Maclennan, this was a key element in the merger negotiations, necessary in order to pin down the Liberals' 'softness' on policy issues, of which Owen had so often complained, and to have any chance of attracting Owenites, if not Owen himself, to the new party. When the details of the Steel–Maclennan package emerged, it appeared that the Liberal leader had put his name to an astonishing list of unpopular and potentially damaging policies. These included the extension of VAT to food, children's clothing, newspapers, financial services and domestic fuel; the phasing out of tax relief on mortgage interest payments; the ending of universal child benefit; and a commitment to retain the Trident missile system. Steel had failed to foresee that this package would be completely unacceptable to his colleagues. For a man with an impressive record of political dexterity and surefootedness, combining for more than a decade understated persuasiveness with resolute determination, it was an untypical aberration and one that probably ended any chance that he would lead the new party. But Steel had always enjoyed a closer rapport with the electorate than with his own party. Before the day was out, the Liberal Party *en masse* seemed ready to disown him and, to the embarrassment of all concerned, a press conference, intended to proclaim agreement on the new party, had to be postponed. Borrowing a phrase from the well-known Monty Python sketch, Des Wilson soon dubbed the Steel–Maclennan document a 'dead parrot'.

For a time it seemed that the entire merger process might unravel. But enough goodwill existed on both sides to save the situation. A new six-man team was set up to draft a replacement policy document, which took as its basis the 1987 Alliance manifesto. The earlier controversial proposals were dropped and the new document quickly gained the leaders' acceptance: 'It was a third of the length of the dead parrot; it was hardly uplifting, but it was unexciting and anodyne; it was largely uncontroversial within the parties; it served its purpose and was soon forgotten by most.'[51] Only Maclennan's dramatic but unsuccessful attempt, at the eleventh hour and in a blaze of publicity, to secure David Owen's adherence to the agreement provided one final twist to an unedifying tale. Special Liberal and SDP conferences at the end of January then endorsed the deal. That of the Liberals at Blackpool, carefully controlled by the leadership, produced an overwhelming victory for the advocates of merger – by 2,099 votes to 385, with 23 abstentions. In this way the historical Liberal Party formally came to an end. Liberal opponents of fusion, seeing themselves as the heirs of a north of England radical tradition in danger of being watered down in any new party, eventually organized themselves under the leadership of Michael Meadowcroft into the Continuing Liberal Party. This body put up 73 candidates in the 1992 General Election, and polled 100,000 votes in the 1994 European elections, before fading into insignificance. Divisions within the SDP were more serious and more damaging to the new party's prospects. Though a motion for merger was passed overwhelmingly, Owen's supporters tried to show their strength by taking no part in the proceedings. A subsequent ballot of SDP members revealed 65 per cent support for merger, but the size of the minority and the low overall poll were sufficient to encourage Owen to announce that a rump SDP would fight on. Thus, against a background of division and recrimination, the new Social and Liberal Democratic Party (the Democrats for short), formally came into existence in March 1988.

The New Party's Uncertain Beginnings

Founded more on the ruins of its predecessors than as the beneficiary of their respective political traditions, the new party got off to a bad start. The public divisions and disputes since the 1987 General Election had had an inevitable impact on its standing in the opinion polls, shattering the image of co-operation and consensus that had been the most potent appeal of the old Alliance at its height. Now, the continuation of the Owenite SDP threatened to split the centre vote, to the electoral detriment of both parties. Grass-roots morale had been badly shaken and, by the summer of 1988, resignations were reaching party headquarters at an alarming rate. The local elections in May offered meagre comfort. The Social and Liberal Democratic Party (SLD) suffered a net loss of over 60 seats, but its vote held up better than opinion polls had predicted. The SDP, by contrast, was all but wiped out. With Steel declining to stand for the leadership of the new party, the membership was offered a straight choice between two former Liberals – Alan Beith and Paddy Ashdown. The former committed himself to protecting the values of the old Liberal Party within its successor, but few genuine policy differences emerged. In the event, the party opted by a decisive margin for Ashdown's more exciting personality and style, but, with only five years' parliamentary experience under his belt, an element of risk attached to this choice.

The new leader faced, by any criteria, a daunting challenge. When Ashdown took over, the SLD was 'confused, demoralised, starved of money and in the grip of a deep identity crisis'.[52] By the autumn of 1988 the party was, with debts of more than £500,000, technically bankrupt, and drastic economies had to be effected. The position improved only gradually, though for a time it seemed that, for each dragon slain, a fresh one was waiting in the wings to take its place. A by-election in Kensington, Greater London, in July offered no evidence of a revival. In December, the Conservatives held on in Epping Forest, Greater London, even though the SLD and SDP candidates combined secured 38 per cent of the vote, which was more than the victorious Tories. Two months later, in the North Yorkshire constituency of Richmond, the Owenites forced the SLD into third place, prompting Ashdown to make a final but unsuccessful gesture of reconciliation to Owen: 'otherwise I can see only protracted trench warfare which will destroy both our parties and give Labour the chance it needs'.[53] In the 1989 council elections the SLD suffered a further net loss of more than 100 seats, though its vote again held up reasonably well. North of the border, the Scottish Nationalists were racing ahead of the Democrats in the opinion polls. Worse, however, was to come. In the third set of direct elections to the European Parliament in June 1989, the party was pushed into a humiliating fourth place on just 6.4 per cent of the popular vote, behind a sudden, unexpected and spectacular advance by the Green Party. This was a particular blow in view of the efforts the Liberals had made since the 1970s to focus on environmental issues. The upsurge of the Greens, reflective of mounting concerns about global warming and the depletion of the ozone layer, would fade as quickly as it had arrived. Yet this was precisely the voice of passing protest that the Liberals and the Alliance had been so adept at attracting. Now, as one leading Democrat quipped, 'we are no longer the cop-out vote'.[54] Even the party's name proved to be contentious and divisive, and was changed to the 'Liberal Democrats' following a postal ballot of members in October 1989. That membership had by then fallen to around 75,000. Ashdown confessed to being haunted by the nightmare that the party that had started with Gladstone would end with himself: 'A very, very black week,' he recorded at the end of June, 'which may well mark the end of the Party altogether. It's down to me and a few others to try and keep the thing together.'[55] As late as September 1990, the party's Gallup rating stood at just 9.3 per cent. Changes of name appeared only to have exacerbated long-standing problems over image and identity. Nearly three-quarters of those questioned could not give the party's proper name, while 80 per cent were unable to say with any accuracy what the Liberal Democrats stood for. Inevitably, questions were asked as to whether the price of the merger had been too high.

Salvation arrived in a familiar fashion. By the end of 1988, the Conservatives were trailing Labour in the polls. The government's reputation for economic competence was badly dented as the boom engineered by Chancellor Nigel Lawson turned sour and inflation began to rise once more. In introducing the community charge (or poll tax), Mrs Thatcher appeared to have lost her acute and instinctive sensitivity to the public mood, a key feature in her earlier ascendancy. With the government shaken by a succession of ministerial resignations and the Conservative Party increasingly divided by the Prime Minister's strident opposition to further European integration, the Liberal Democrats had their chance to profit once again at the expense of an unpopular Tory government. At a by-election in October 1990 in Eastbourne, Sussex, solidly Conservative throughout the century, the Liberal Democrat candidate, David Bellotti, captured the seat on an anti-Conservative swing of more than 20 per cent. By this time too, the threat from the Greens and the Owenite SDP had passed.

Owen abandoned any pretensions to be leading a national party following the 1989 local elections, and his group was effectively wound up after its candidate at the May 1990 Bootle, Merseyside, by-election secured fewer votes than Screaming Lord Sutch of the Monster Raving Loony Party – the one consequence of any political importance during the latter body's overlong and undistinguished political lifetime. Further by-election successes followed at Ribble Valley, Lancashire (March 1991) and Kincardine and Deeside in Scotland (November 1991) on swings of 25 per cent and 11.4 per cent, respectively. But it was the 1991 local elections that gave most cause for celebration. Despite defending a high base-line secured by the Alliance in 1987, the Liberal Democrats registered a further 520 net gains through effective targeting, winning control of 19 councils.

With the party enjoying a stronger base in the country, Ashdown had more opportunity to mould the Liberal Democrats in his own image. He personally had emerged as a politician of stature – though there were always those who found him sanctimonious. His particularly forthright views on foreign policy issues, including Yugoslavia and the Gulf, which aroused resentment among some of his parliamentary followers, ensured him a high public profile and an approval rating that always ran ahead of his party's. As chairman of the Liberal Democrats' Policy Committee, Ashdown used the force of his personality to remove the last vestiges of what he once called 'soggy corporatism' – the old-style Liberal commitment to the managed economy of incomes policies and governmental control. In their place he encouraged a wholehearted espousal of the free market, competition and enterprise. With both Labour and the Conservatives showing renewed signs of convergence, Ashdown also sought to broaden the agenda of political debate, with a new emphasis on constitutional reform, the rights of women and the family, environmental issues and improved public services. Overall, he succeeded in making Britain's third party appear to be a more serious political force than at any time in the previous 60 years. It was at this time that the party finally shook off the 'beards and sandals' image that had dogged its predecessor for so long. As Ashdown later explained:

the thing which drove me through my leadership of the Liberal Democrats was getting the Party into power. I have never been at all attracted by the notion that it was sufficient for us to be the unpaid think tank for new ideas in British politics; or the repository for community politics without a purpose.[56]

It was, then, a very different and rejuvenated party that faced the 1992 General Election from the one that had emerged from the botched merger process of four years before. The political landscape too was showing a distinct change from the pattern of the 1980s. After the General Election of 1987, its third successive defeat, Labour had begun its first major policy review since the 1950s. Seven policy groups were set up to rethink its approach to domestic and international affairs, with the clear aim of throwing out the policies that had made Labour unelectable. In practice, this meant coming 'to terms with the irreversibility of many Thatcherite reforms by recognizing that the market economy should be regarded as innocent until found guilty, rather than vice versa'.[57] The results were startling. Any residual commitments to extend public ownership soon disappeared. The 1989 policy statement, *Meet the Challenge, Make the Change*, bound a future Labour government to work through a successful market economy. It was perhaps the least socialist policy statement in the party's history to date. State intervention would now be limited to specific areas such as industrial training, where the market was perceived to be failing. In 1990, Labour's *Looking to the Future* declared that only the water industry among those enterprises privatized by the Conservatives since 1979 was to be returned to the public sector. Two years later, even this commitment was dropped, with the party settling now merely for 'public control'. Similarly, in the area of industrial relations, Labour had by 1990 moved towards accepting much of the legal framework constructed by the Conservatives. The party also swung back to support for British membership of the European Community, its path eased by the perception that, under the Commission presidency of Jacques Delors, that body was more sympathetic to Labour's aspirations than had once been the case. Perhaps most striking of all, in view of Neil Kinnock's well-known personal views, the 1989 Labour conference abandoned the party's policy of unilateral nuclear disarmament.

These dramatic changes opened up both opportunities and dangers for the Liberal Democrats. At the time of his campaign for the party leadership in 1988, Ashdown had declared that his strategic aim remained that of the Alliance throughout its history – to replace Labour as the main opposition to the Conservatives. Yet if the 1987 General Election had already shown that this ambition was unlikely to be achieved, by the early 1990s it had become totally unrealistic. Most commentators agreed that Labour looked electable for the first time in a decade, and opinion polls indicated that this perception was shared by the wider electorate. Ashdown was not blind to this evolving situation, and began to think in terms of a political realignment not unlike the one that had attracted Jo Grimond a generation earlier. Though he was unimpressed by Kinnock, and in his own mind ruled out any formal relationship with Labour before the next election, he believed that a fourth Conservative electoral victory would place realignment firmly on the political agenda. Such a possibility became more likely following Margaret Thatcher's replacement by John Major in November 1990. The new Prime Minister's easy-going, moderate image registered an immediate appeal with the electorate. On the other hand, it was also possible that the next General Election would leave the Liberal Democrats holding the balance of power in the Commons and able to negotiate their way into a coalition government.

Major delayed holding an election until April 1992, and most observers predicted a close outcome. The Liberal Democrats' manifesto, *Changing Britain for Good*, pledged a counter-inflation strategy centred on an independent Bank of England able to set interest rates free from political interference, wide-ranging constitutional reform and a more constructive role for Britain within the European Community. It stressed the need to invest in the public services and, defying conventional wisdom that electors will not support higher taxation, promised to raise income tax by a penny in the pound to fund investment in education. In addition, the Liberal Democrats would repeal some of the Conservative government's recent innovations in health and education, in particular GP fund-holding schemes, hospital trusts and City Technology Colleges. In its editorial, the *Guardian* enthused that the Liberal Democrats, unlike the Liberals of old, were a 'proper party', which had produced a 'proper manifesto' – one that 'far out-distances its competitors with a fizz of ideas and an absence of fudge'. It was an appropriate tribute to the party's recovery under Ashdown's leadership, and to the importance of its inheritance from the SDP of an efficient party structure and an effective policy-making process.

Ashdown himself waged an impressive campaign, and his personal standing was unharmed, perhaps even enhanced, by recent newspaper disclosures of an earlier affair with his secretary. Though a hung Parliament seemed an increasing possibility, he resolutely refused to express a preference as between supporting a minority Labour or a minority Conservative administration. In practice, this was an unrealistic stance. On several key issues, including devolution for Scotland and investment in education, Labour was clearly closer to the Liberal Democrat position. In the course of the campaign, moreover, Major ruled out the possibility of proportional representation – which would have been the Liberal Democrats' bottom line in any coalition negotiations – while Labour was at least prepared to examine the pros and cons of electoral reform. But Ashdown was wary about making any statement that might alienate potential supporters and believed that, by at least holding out the possibility of a Liberal Democrat–Conservative coalition, he would make Labour more inclined to concede proportional representation for Westminster. In fact, Ashdown had, characteristically, worked out a clear negotiating position for the eventuality of a hung Parliament.

The outcome was among the more intriguing of post-war election results. The Conservatives finished 8 percentage points ahead of Labour in the popular vote, but their overall parliamentary majority was cut to just 21 seats. After many years, the electoral system had begun to work against them. The Liberal Democrats' performance was in many ways disappointing – just 20 seats on 18.3 per cent of the vote, with a million fewer supporters than had rallied to the Alliance in 1987. Nor did the party's challenge appear to be growing, as the number of second place results dropped from 261 to 154. In many promising constituencies, Labour's partial recovery thwarted Liberal Democrat hopes. There was some comfort to be had when comparisons were made with the 6 per cent rating the party had enjoyed when Ashdown assumed its leadership, and even with the 15 per cent recorded at the start of the campaign. But most activists found it hard to sustain the inveterate optimism that had seen the party and its predecessor through so many past setbacks. In particular, the tantalizing prospect of a hung Parliament, predicted even in the BBC's supposedly reliable exit polls, quickly faded from view as the results came in. Yet, beyond these disappointments lay some interesting features.

The first was evidence of an increasingly sophisticated electorate. The Liberal Democrats had hoped to boost their parliamentary representation as a result of anti-Conservative tactical voting. In most seats in which the Alliance had come second in 1987 – and these were overwhelmingly Conservative seats – the party sought to emphasize the opportunities for tactical voting, attempting to squeeze Labour support by stressing the impossibility of a local Labour victory. This strategy enjoyed only limited success. Tactical voting clearly had occurred, reducing Major's prospective majority by about half, but Labour rather than the Liberal Democrats had been the main beneficiary. Even so, two and possibly three of the four seats gained by the Liberal Democrats could be attributed to tactical voting. The hope had to be that, if this apparent desire to remove the Conservatives from office were to grow, increasing numbers of voters would see the need to support the Liberal Democrats where their party was the main challenger. In the second place, the party's vote was less evenly, and therefore more effectively, distributed across the country than at any election since the Liberals resumed standing on a fully national basis. The South-West in particular was beginning to look like a Liberal Democrat stronghold where further success might be anticipated.

Ashdown Ends 'Equidistance'

At least Ashdown seemed well satisfied with the outcome:

> There is a real opportunity now for us to drive a wedge in Labour on PR. Despite the disappointment, this is the result I always said I wanted, with the Tories ahead and Labour going down to a fourth defeat and into an internal battle. We must make use of this opportunity to realign the left.[58]

It was his belief that if, after 13 years in power and with the country at the bottom of a recession, the Conservatives could secure a fourth successive victory, Labour would realize they could no longer win a General Election on their own. Forthcoming boundary changes were likely to entrench the Conservative position still further before the next General Election was held. If nothing was done to change this pattern, Britain faced the very real prospect of one-party government. As the twentieth century neared its close,

Ashdown increasingly viewed the current situation within the historical context of the century as a whole. The breakdown of the Progressive Alliance in the 1910s had, he believed, opened the way to a long era of Conservative domination sustained on a minority of the popular vote. The restored unity of the forces of progressivism became his mission. Events would show that Ashdown's calculations were, in key respects, wide of the mark. But they formed the starting point of the strategy that would guide and inform his leadership of the party, sometimes obsessively so, from then on.

Ashdown moved quickly to prepare his party for a major strategic review. The speech he delivered to a tiny audience of his constituents in Chard, Somerset, on 9 May 1992 was probably the most important of his whole career. Ashdown declared that his purpose was to initiate a wide-ranging discussion about the Liberal Democrats' strategic options in the wake of the recent election. But he left few doubts about the direction in which he personally hoped the party would travel. Its purpose, he insisted, should be to 'create the force powerful enough to remove the Tories; to assemble policies capable of sustaining a different government; and to draw together the forces in Britain which will bring change and reform'. Labour had become a 'drag factor' on those others who wished to fight the Conservatives and had lost its historic role as the only left-of-centre party capable of holding power: 'The Tory–Labour duopoly is finished.' It was time for Liberal Democrats to seize the initiative, but they could not do so on their own. They must 'reach out beyond the limits of [their] own party' and 'be the catalyst, the gathering point for a broader movement dedicated to winning the battle of ideas which will give Britain an electable alternative to Conservative government'. That alternative would have a reformed voting system at its heart. The notion of equidistance, tenuously sustained during the election campaign, was not mentioned, but the implication of Ashdown's words was clear. Like Grimond and Steel before him, he saw the Liberal Democrats' future lying primarily in partnership with the non-socialist wing of the Labour Party.[59]

Also like his predecessors, however, and for all his brave words about the end of the Tory–Labour duopoly, Ashdown would find that the Liberal Democrats' fortunes were largely determined by events inside the two main parties. The Conservative government's honeymoon was short-lived. The events of 'Black Wednesday',

16 September 1992, when Britain was forced ignominiously to withdraw from the European Exchange Rate Mechanism (ERM), hitherto trumpeted as a vital component of the government's anti-inflation strategy, destroyed for years to come the Conservatives' reputation for economic competence. A Gallup poll revealed a halving in public satisfaction with John Major and his government's record, and in optimism about the British economy. It was a slump from which the government never recovered. Despite a steady improvement in economic indicators achieved *outside* the ERM, ministers waited in vain for the much-vaunted 'feel-good' factor to translate into signs of electoral approval. Major's difficulties were exacerbated by increasingly open divisions within the party and inside the cabinet itself on the question of Europe, particularly during and after the passage through Parliament of the Maastricht Treaty, paving the way for a further tranche of measures of European integration. The government also became associated in the public mind with the idea of 'sleaze', as a succession of ministers and MPs became embroiled in personal and financial scandals. With Major seemingly lacking the strength of purpose to hold his party together, all these misfortunes were skilfully manipulated by their opponents, especially by a rejuvenated Labour Party.

Liberal Democrats prospered as they and their predecessors had been doing for over 30 years whenever there was an unpopular Tory administration, and the party enjoyed four by-election gains during the course of the Parliament. That at Christchurch, Hampshire, in July 1993, where a 23,000 Conservative majority was overturned, witnessed an astonishing 35 per cent swing. With a couple of defections included, Liberal Democrat strength in the Commons at the 1997 dissolution stood at 26, and the picture in local government was even more gratifying. Building on the unexpected successes of 1991, the party made a further 308 net gains in 1992, 341 in 1993, and 388 in 1994. Following the 1996 council elections, the Liberal Democrats held approximately 5,100 council seats against the Conservatives' 4,700. To emerge as the second party in local government was no small achievement for a party whose standing in some opinion polls at the time of Ashdown's accession to power had been 'within the statistical margin of error of zero'.[60]

But the fortunes of the Labour Party were probably of greater long-term significance from a Liberal Democrat point of view than were those of an unprecedentedly unpopular Conservative government. Contrary to Ashdown's expectations, Labour responded in a disciplined and businesslike manner to the renewed tasks of opposition. It was a sign of the times that, in the contest between John Smith and Bryan Gould to succeed Neil Kinnock as party leader, Gould – who, in another era, might have been described as an unrepentant Keynesian – was seen as the candidate of the Left. But it was also a sign of the times that Smith emerged the comfortable victor. A cautious Scottish lawyer, Smith's leadership did not witness any significant change of direction from that already mapped out by his predecessor. But he won the respect and support of a united party, less disheartened than it might have been by the 1992 result. In general terms, the decline of Labour's Left continued, with Smith's close allies, Gordon Brown and Tony Blair, securing election to the National Executive Committee. Smith was not interested in formal co-operation with the Liberal Democrats at Westminster, but an encouraging development was the way in which he placed constitutional reform firmly on Labour's agenda and the two parties worked well together on the Scottish Constitutional Convention that had first met in 1989. Labour and the Liberal Democrats agreed on a joint programme centred on the creation of a Scottish parliament. Ashdown, however, was disappointed by what he regarded as Labour's opportunistic opposition to the Maastricht Treaty, an issue for him of principle and not of party politics. European integration was, after all, an issue on which the Liberal Party, unlike its opponents, could point to a long, honourable and consistent record of support. Liberal votes in the Commons helped the government to survive the opposition of its own Eurosceptic backbenchers. Smith was committed to a patient, long-term strategy to return Labour to government, but he died suddenly in May 1994. It was his successor, Tony Blair, who transformed the prospects not only of the Labour Party but also of the Liberal Democrats.

The Project

Blair soon made it clear that he intended to take Labour even further towards the centre ground of British politics. One of his first major initiatives as party leader was to propose to the 1994 Labour conference the replacement of the much-venerated Clause

IV of the party's constitution, one of the last remaining symbols of its commitment to traditional socialism. He got his way with surprising ease. A special conference in April 1995 approved his proposed change with just over two-thirds of the total vote. Labour was now pledged 'to work for a dynamic economy, serving the public interest, in which the enterprise of the market and the rigour of competition are joined with the forces of partnership and cooperation ... with a thriving public sector and high quality public services'.[61] Before long, Labour was explicitly endorsing the market economy and proclaiming a 'Third Way' in which a stake-holding society would develop policies of social inclusion for all its citizens. So dramatic was the transformation since Labour had offered itself to the electorate under Michael Foot's leadership little over a decade earlier that the assumption of a changed name, albeit an unofficial one – New Labour – seemed entirely appropriate. Liberal Democrats could not ignore these developments. On the one hand, it could now be asked whether any space remained within the political spectrum for the Liberal Democrats to occupy. David Marquand, whose shifting political allegiance left him well-placed to judge, concluded that New Labour and the Liberal Democrats 'belong to the same broad-based progressive tradition that goes back, by way of Beveridge, Keynes and the Attlee government, to the ethical socialists and the New Liberals of the early century'.[62] On the other hand, New Labour reopened the genuine possibility of that realignment of the left, of which Liberal leaders had dreamed for almost four decades, or at the very least presented itself as a viable partner for Liberal Democrats in coalition government.

Paddy Ashdown's published diaries describe in voluminous, agonized, and sometimes repetitive, detail the way in which he wrestled with this dilemma. Though as yet largely uncorroborated, they provide the historian of this period with his most important primary source. While Smith remained at Labour's helm, Ashdown continued to think in terms of Labour's fragmentation. The Liberal Democrats' covert aim was to promote debate within the Labour Party between its modernizers and its traditionalists in order to drive a wedge between the two groups. By April 1994, shortly before Smith's death, Ashdown had decided privately to abandon the policy of equidistance, to declare publicly that the Liberal Democrats could not support a Conservative government after the next election, and then to set tough conditions for a relationship with Labour. But Blair's arrival – 'the deepest and most desperate point of depression in my whole leadership of the party'[63] – forced a rethink:

> I have been building the Party to fill a certain gap in politics, which I know is there and which would give us real electoral appeal. But then along comes Blair with all the power of Labour behind him, and fills exactly the space I have been aiming at for the last seven years![64]

Ashdown started meeting Blair some months before the latter succeeded Smith. He found him congenial and, unlike Smith, ready to consider co-operation between the two parties, and he quickly realized that Blair's political vision was very like his own: 'There is very little difference between his thinking and mine. We have come to the same analysis from different directions.'[65] For Blair, there was the added advantage that an arrangement with the Liberal Democrats would serve to dilute the power of the 'old left' and the trade unions within the Labour movement.

Blair's leadership forced the abandonment of any lingering belief that the Liberal Democrats could replace Labour as the major left-of-centre force in British politics. Instead, Ashdown came to the conclusion that the best option was to forge a new relationship between the two parties, based on a common progressive agenda in which the introduction of proportional representation would form an indispensable element. In a series of usually clandestine meetings with Blair over the next three years, concealed from the majority of the Liberal Democrat parliamentary party, Ashdown explored this 'Project'. A small group of trusted advisers – the 'Jo Group' – offered advice as to the parameters within which the negotiations should proceed. Ashdown's preferred option was the so-called 'Big Thing' – that the two parties should go into the next election as separate entities but offering the electorate a joint heads of agreement document. The two men began with the assumption that Labour would not be able to win the election on its own but, as the Conservative government's fortunes failed to show any significant signs of recovery despite an improving economic climate, the possibility of a majority Labour government had to be admitted. In such a situation the question was whether

Labour–Liberal Democrat co-operation would prove to be more than a matter of electoral convenience. Ashdown recorded a conversation with Blair in October 1994:

Ashdown: If you got a majority, do you still see us working together in government?
Blair: Yes.
Ashdown: In which case I think we have the opportunity to do something really historic in politics.[66]

On this basis, the policy of equidistance was formally renounced in May 1995 and the Liberal Democrats became an overtly anti-Conservative party.

It was a high-risk strategy and at times Ashdown seemed to lose confidence in it, not least because of his failure to extract from Blair a formal promise to reform the Westminster electoral system. The Labour leader repeatedly declared himself unconvinced by the arguments, making it clear that he faced strong opposition to the 'Project' in the upper echelons of his party. The popularity of New Labour, as registered in the opinion polls, was part of the problem. 'I am becoming really worried,' Ashdown wrote in June 1995:

I can't see a role for us. If the Tories collapse completely I suppose we could become HM Opposition. But then what? Our policies are too close to Labour's for us to be a genuine Opposition and the Tories would simply recover again. Meanwhile, Labour has stolen our ground comprehensively.[67]

But Ashdown received repeated assurances, not least from Roy Jenkins (by then leader of the Liberal Democrat peers but also a confidant and adviser of Blair, and hopeful that New Labour offered the prospect of resurrecting his failed mission to break the mould of British politics), that Blair would prefer to head a government which contained Liberal Democrats than one made up entirely from the ranks of the Labour Party, irrespective of whether Labour won an overall majority. Increasingly, indeed, he believed that, despite the disparity in resources and parliamentary strength between the two parties, it was essentially a Liberal agenda around which realignment could take place. 'If, as it appears, I have more in common with Blair than he has with his left wing,' reasoned Ashdown, 'surely the logical thing is for us to create a new, powerful alternative force which would be unified around a broadly liberal agenda.'[68] Even Gordon Brown, Labour's shadow chancellor, assured Ashdown that he was in practice adopting a classical Liberal programme, based on competition, enterprise and equality of opportunity. Blair and Ashdown repeatedly reflected on the historical context of their plans. 'The real shame,' noted Blair, 'was that our two parties weren't able to stay together in the early part of the century... Lloyd George was incomparably the most radical figure in the second and third decades of the twentieth century, but he wasn't in a party that could deliver. We have to bring these two streams back together again.'[69] In 1996, the two leaders asked two of their senior parliamentary colleagues, Robert Maclennan and Robin Cook, to lay the groundwork for a stable relationship by exploring the possibilities of co-operation on questions of constitutional reform. The outcome was the Cook–Maclennan agreement of March 1997, outlining the areas in which Labour and the Liberal Democrats could work together in the next Parliament.

It was, then, with a more realistic prospect of being in government than at any time since the 1920s, that the Liberal Democrats went into the General Election of April 1997, delayed by John Major for almost as long as the constitution permitted in the ultimately forlorn hope of a Conservative revival. They had hardly put a foot wrong throughout the Parliament, and only at the 1994 annual assembly, at a time when Ashdown was trying to convince Blair that the Liberal Democrats were a responsible party that could be trusted with power, had they come near to scoring an own goal. Then, an exasperated Ashdown had walked off the platform after a badly organized debate on the possible legalization of soft drugs. Otherwise, both the party and its leader had developed a gravitas that had previously been lacking. Most observers believed that the Liberal Democrats were better prepared for an election than a third party had ever been. The party called for constitutional reform, entry into the Single European Currency and investment in the public services paid for by income tax rises. Even the demand for electoral reform seemed to be gaining ground as Ashdown, with scant recognition of what many regarded as a finely balanced argument, repeatedly and insistently equated proportional representation with 'fair votes'. With a modernizing agenda, the party also called for a written constitution, a bill of rights and sweeping changes to the institution of Parliament.

Both Blair and Ashdown understood the importance of tactical voting. A secret agreement was reached not to invest resources in a number of seats where one or other party had no realistic chance of victory over the Tories. The Labour-supporting *Daily Mirror* was given, and subsequently published, a list of seats where Liberal Democrats could beat the Conservatives if Labour supporters voted tactically. Targeting was therefore central to the Liberal Democrats' campaign, and Ashdown covered more than 17,000 miles in visiting 75 seats where, he believed, his party had a realistic prospect of victory. Once again, the party campaigned on its unashamed readiness to increase taxes to invest in public services. Despite the now well-established links with Labour, Liberal Democrats sought to claim the high moral ground, dismissing the 'Punch and Judy' spats of the two larger parties. None the less, voters were left in no doubt that support for the Liberal Democrats would primarily help to secure the defeat and removal of an unpopular Conservative government.

The outcome revealed both how much progress the Liberal Democrats had made, and why Ashdown had been right to view Blair's arrival on the scene as a mixed blessing. The Liberal Democrats secured 46 seats, by far the best third-party performance for almost 70 years and twice as many as won by the Alliance in 1983. But they did so on just 17 per cent of the popular vote, the party's second-worst performance since it had resumed contesting General Elections on a truly national basis. The election was a huge triumph for New Labour (with 419 seats), taking votes and seats from the Conservatives, including protest votes that might normally have been expected to benefit the Liberal Democrats. The latter's success in terms of seats reflected the fact that anti-Conservative tactical voting had been more prevalent than ever before. Had the movement of votes been consistent across the country, the Liberal Democrats would have won just 28 seats. As it was, they prospered in constituencies where they were already well-placed; with tactical support from Labour voters to unseat a Conservative incumbent; and in areas where their credibility had been enhanced by their record in local government. These also tended to be constituencies that the Liberal Democrats had been targeting for at least the previous four years. Such seats were over-whelmingly in the South and South-West.

Where did this result leave the Project? Ashdown's first reaction was that the scale of Labour's victory made co-operation between the parties more difficult. It would, he thought, be 'somehow unseemly' to join forces and deprive the country of an effective opposition: 'I am plagued by the idea that it would be seen as an undemocratic, self-serving act.'[70] When, however, he met the new Prime Minister on 2 May, Blair discussed the prospect of Liberal Democrat representation on two cabinet committees. More sig-nificantly, he stressed that the 'end position' remained Liberal Democrat participation in the government, and even held out the possibility of an eventual merger between the two parties 'some way down the track'.[71] But Ashdown was struck by a change in Blair's demeanour. In what must strike the outsider as a curiously naïve passage, he later reflected:

> Was Blair 'got at' by some of the 'anti-project' people on the night of 1 May? I am unable to say, but there was certainly a curious change in tone between the telephone call I took from him … on the morning of 1 May and our conversation the following morning.[72]

What had definitely changed was that the electorate had under-mined the assumption with which the Project had begun, that Labour could not, on its own, unseat the Conservatives. Though the opinion polls had long predicted a Labour landslide, even the most sanguine tenant of Millbank Tower nurtured a sneak-ing suspicion that, on the day, the gap between Labour and the Conservatives would be much narrower, with many voters conceal-ing their Conservative inclinations until entering the privacy of the polling booth, as was believed to have happened in 1992. In the event, Labour secured an overall majority of 177 seats. To proceed now with the Project would mean depriving a number of expect-ant Labour politicians of office, depriving a considerable number of Labour MPs of their seats at the next General Election and, with the introduction of proportional representation, depriving the Labour Party itself of any realistic prospect of forming a major-ity government in the future. All this would probably be accompa-nied by a major split in the Labour movement. The Deputy Prime Minister, John Prescott, was reported to have warned that 'the day that man [Ashdown] walks through the door is the day that I walk out of it', while the new Chancellor, Gordon Brown, was also hostile.[73] If Blair now hesitated, his caution was entirely understandable. Had the result of the election been a hung Parliament or even a narrow Labour victory, his room for manoeuvre would have been altogether greater.

Being outside the government, at least for the moment, yet broadly sympathetic to much of its programme, created a difficult situation for the Liberal Democrats. Ashdown feared that the inevitable pressures of Britain's confrontational political structure could easily destroy his hopes of long-term realignment if his party remained on the opposition benches for too long. He therefore determined to adopt a stance of 'constructive opposition', which involved criticizing the government where the two parties differed but working with it where agreement existed, especially on the programme of constitutional reform worked out by Cook and Maclennan. Over the following months, the public saw clear manifestations of a new style of politics emerging. Five Liberal Democrats took seats on the cabinet committee on constitutional change; a Liberal Democrat MP became chairman of the Commons Social Security Select Committee; and two Labour junior ministers spoke to fringe meetings at the Liberal Democrats' conference in Eastbourne. In the meantime, Blair continued to suggest that he would bring Liberal Democrats inside his government 'within a matter of months'.[74] But not everyone in the party was comfortable with these new arrangements. Bill Rodgers argued that the presence of Liberal Democrats on the new consultative committee could create a situation of responsibility without power, 'inhibiting the Liberal Democrats with nothing in exchange except the symbol of closeness'.[75] Peter Mandelson, one of the principal architects of New Labour and a committed supporter of the Project, seemed to confirm this point when he warned Ashdown publicly that the evolving relationship between their parties required him to ensure that the Liberal Democrats behaved responsibly and did not revert to a stance of 'oppositionitis', 'making invalid criticisms and promising pointless profligacy'.[76] But there was much in the government's conduct that the party felt obliged to criticize, not least Gordon Brown's determination not to raise direct taxation and to stick for two years to the public-spending plans of the outgoing Conservative government. Such policies, argued the

Liberal Democrats' Treasury spokesman, Malcolm Bruce, would delay much-needed investment in education and the health service. Concern was also expressed at Labour's failure to give a clear commitment to take Britain into the Single European Currency.

In the meantime, Ashdown could not convince Blair of the centrality of proportional representation to any further progress on realignment. He argued that electoral reform would guarantee Blair a two-term government, with no possibility of the Conservatives regaining power, and thus the opportunity to transform and modernize the country. But the Prime Minister, worried about the long-term implications, remained sceptical, and suggested that the formal merger of the two parties might be a necessary consequence of a change to the electoral system: 'Look, I must tell you that if I give you guys PR, without getting from you a guarantee of merger, or at least some bottom-line assurance that you won't break away later, my party will think I have lost my marbles.'[77]

Blair needed to be sure that, once a change in the voting system had been made, Liberal Democrats would not abandon the Project, leaving Labour stranded in a permanent minority position:

> I think the basic question is: Are our two parties in fact both modern social democratic parties? The answer is, substantially, yes. At the moment I am being asked to sacrifice a large part of my party and accept permanent coalition politics with no guarantee that our coalition partner remains constant.[78]

Ashdown's response was to accept that there was a broad identity between New Labour and the Liberal Democrats, but also to remind Blair that much of the Labour Party, particularly in local government, had still to be converted to the new variant. Merger might well come at some time in the future, but was 'not an option in the short term' and certainly not something to which Ashdown could commit his party.[79]

On this basis, the dialogue continued throughout 1998, though the prospect of a formal coalition was postponed repeatedly and ultimately abandoned. Blair continued to make encouraging noises, telling the post-election Labour Party conference that he numbered Keynes, Beveridge and Lloyd George, as well as Bevin, Bevan and Attlee, among his heroes. From a Liberal Democrat point of view there were some positive achievements, of which the introduction of proportional representation for elections to the European Parliament and to the newly created Scottish Parliament and Welsh Assembly were the most notable. For a time it seemed that even 'the citadel of Westminster [was] surrounded by PR forests – creeping like Birnam Wood, in the last act of Macbeth, ever closer to the walls'.[80] In September 1998, Blair proposed strengthening existing links by broadening the joint cabinet committee to include issues beyond merely constitutional ones. But there were also disappointments. Ashdown reached the reluctant conclusion that constitutional reform was not 'the iron in Blair's soul' that he had hoped.[81] New Labour seemed keener on the theory of devolution than on its practical consequences and, in key respects, showed itself as much inclined to centralization as its Conservative predecessor had been. Government proposals for a Freedom of Information Act were quietly watered down and their leading champion dropped from the cabinet. The first stage in the reform of the House of Lords, which allowed for the temporary survival of 92 hereditary peers, resulted from a backstairs pact between the government and the Conservative leader in the upper chamber, for which the latter was summarily dismissed: 'The deal was done without reference to the Liberal Democrats and a thoroughly unsatisfactory dog's breakfast of a deal it turned out to be.'[82] Ashdown found the pace of change disappointingly slow and had to try to reassure his increasingly sceptical party. But his diaries reveal mounting exasperation with Blair's failure to deliver:

> It's always us who put the propositions to you. Then you and I agree how to go forward. Then, at the last moment, it's discovered you can't. Then we – never you – go off and find a different way to keep the project on track and the whole depressing cycle starts over again. Frankly, I don't know how long we can keep doing this. [83]

But the decisive moment probably came in October 1998 with the publication of the report of a commission headed by Lord Jenkins into the reform of the Westminster electoral system. Jenkins proposed replacing the existing first-past-the-post system with a scheme that was called 'AV plus'. It involved the majority of MPs being elected by single-member constituencies using the system of the Alternative Vote. This would retain the widely valued link between the voter and his/her local MP. But the remaining 100 or so MPs would be elected by a list system within wide geographical areas to create a broadly proportional overall outcome. These proposals, as might be expected from a commission headed by Jenkins, were welcomed warmly by Liberal Democrats but met with a lukewarm response in the Commons from the Home Secretary, Jack Straw, apparently endorsed by the Prime Minister. No serious attempt was made to take the matter further.

On the ground, the Liberal Democrats experienced some difficulty in differentiating themselves from the Labour government, especially when that government was putting in place many key Liberal Democrat policies. It might now have been appropriate to project the party's appeal somewhat to the left of Labour. On public expenditure, in particular, its approach seemed closer to that espoused by an earlier incarnation of the Labour movement. 'My concern,' wrote William Rodgers, who became Liberal Democrat Leader in the Lords in 1998, 'is that the Blair government is not facing up to the question of inequality which, for me, is central to any party of the centre-left.'[84] Ashdown, however, was wary of any overt move to the left, especially as the party's most promising prospects of further electoral advance remained in Conservative-held constituencies. In the circumstances, the party's electoral record during the 1997 Parliament was surprisingly impressive. In line with the experience of earlier periods of Labour government, there were some signs of a Conservative recovery at the Liberal Democrats' expense at a local level. The 1998 council elections witnessed substantial Tory gains in places such as Tunbridge Wells in Kent, Richmond upon Thames in Surrey, and the Isle of Wight. Two years later, the Conservatives made striking gains in Torbay, Devon and Eastbourne, Sussex at the Liberal Democrats' expense. The latter's record against Labour was more impressive. The Liberal Democrats recaptured Liverpool in 1998 and took control of Sheffield (which had supported Labour since 1929) in 1999. On the other hand, the country showed no enthusiasm for the return of a Conservative government, and the Liberal Democrats took the usually safe Tory seat of Romsey, Hampshire, in a by-election in May 2000. A proportional system of voting helped the party to take ten seats in the 1999 European elections, though the national turnout was only 24 per cent. In elections that year to the Scottish Parliament and Welsh Assembly, the same reform allowed for some recovery of the Conservative position, leaving the Liberal Democrats in fourth place in terms of seats in both countries. As, however, proportional representation deprived any one party of an outright majority, the Liberal Democrats joined Labour in a coalition administration in Scotland, and eventually also in Wales.

In August 1999, Ashdown stood down from the party leadership after 11 years in the post. Arguably, he had been the most significant leader since Grimond: 'He created, out of the wreckage of the Liberal–SDP Alliance, a professional, modernized and effective Liberal Party. He took the party... to a new respectability, stunning local election and by-election victories and – finally overcoming the barriers of the first-past-the-post electoral system – a higher number of Commons seats than at any time since 1929.'[85] The party he handed over had 46 MPs, 10 MEPs, 17 members of the Scottish parliament, six of the Welsh Assembly and around 4,800 local councillors. Ashdown always had a plan and a clear set of objectives. But his last two years at the helm witnessed increasing disagreement over the party's future direction. Judgements on the Project must remain tentative. Blair's memoirs added little on this matter to the account already set down by Ashdown. As the latter always recognized, one interpretation of what happened is likely to be that Ashdown, the dupe, was led by the nose by the charlatan Blair. More charitably, it remains questionable whether even a fully committed Blair could have taken his party with him. Bill Rodgers heard from one senior minister that, apart from the Prime Minister and Peter Mandelson, there was no real support for the Project inside the cabinet.[86] Events after Ashdown's departure – continuing Labour reticence over Lords reform and the euro, and the disappearance of proportional representation from the Westminster agenda – did not suggest that the path to realignment would have been an easy one. The problem perhaps lay in what Ashdown once described as 'the compromises of power', something with which Liberals had not had to grapple for 80 years. Even selling the abandonment of a specifically Liberal identity to the Liberal Democrat Party would have been a task of Herculean proportions. The announcement of the extension of the remit of the Joint Cabinet Committee in late 1998 caused consternation to the parliamentary party which had not been consulted about this important development. 'Liberal Democrats loved their leader,' commented Tony Greaves, 'but, insofar as they sensed his strategy, most wanted none of it.'[87] Despite an abiding sense of history and a belief that the twentieth century might end as it had begun with a Progressive Alliance of the centre-left, Ashdown seemed curiously blinkered about the historical fate of the junior partners of peacetime coalitions. As earlier groups of Liberals had discovered, it was the lot of such as the Liberal Unionists and the Liberal Nationals to be absorbed within the embrace of their more powerful ally and to disappear without trace from the political stage. Though New Labour had unashamedly appropriated many of the policies first espoused by the Liberals, there was always something fanciful, granted the disparity of strength between the two parties, about Ashdown's perception that realignment might take place around a *Liberal* agenda, 'a sort of reverse takeover process'.[88]

In the contest to determine Ashdown's successor, the party opted for Charles Kennedy over Simon Hughes. The choice of the former Social Democratic MP for Ross, Cromarty and Skye was evidence that the scars left from the process of merger had finally faded from view. In terms of his relaxed style and personality, the new leader was very different from his predecessor, but the party's strategy in the period before the 2001 General Election remained largely unchanged. Liberal Democrats were still ready to criticize New Labour's shortcomings in the fields of social and educational reform, but they also left no doubt about their overwhelming preference for Labour over the Conservative Party of William Hague. Moreover, the party went into the General Election with the advantage that the main opposition party was showing few signs of recovery from its 1997 nadir. Once again, the Liberal Democrats presented themselves as the only party ready to increase taxes to invest in the underfunded public services. They were now fully established as a national party. They could point to their achievements in government in Scotland, where their effective opposition to tuition fees in Scottish universities demonstrated the practical consequences of devolution; they could draw attention to a positive record in local government. But they had also learnt the advantages of ruthlessly targeting their resources on their most promising seats. Broadly speaking, this meant trying to attract tactical Labour votes in the South of England and Conservative ones in the North. The party and its leader waged an effective campaign. Mounting confidence led in the final week to the claim that the Liberal Democrats were the most likely party to provide an effective opposition to a re-elected Labour government. It was a striking (albeit somewhat exaggerated) commentary on reversing party fortunes that the Liberal Democrats could now turn on its head the old Conservative slogan of earlier campaigns and warn the electorate not to waste its votes on the Tories. Yet there was something of a contradiction in the suggestion that the Liberal Democrats could replace the Conservatives as the main party of opposition when, on issues such as taxation, public expenditure, crime and asylum, the party seemed to be positioning itself somewhere to the left of Labour. There was always likely to remain a strong right-of-centre constituency among the British electorate. Paddy Ashdown's scepticism was well-founded: 'Some believe that we can somehow replace the Tories. I have never shared this view ... We will not be able to hold perpetually on to the bulk of this "borrowed" vote, because we are not a centre right party, we are a centre left party.'[89] Furthermore, there remained a question mark over how firmly Liberal Democrat support was entrenched. Only 55 per cent of those who voted for the Alliance in 1987, and who voted again in 1992, supported the Liberal Democrats in the latter year, and between 1992 and 1997 the Liberal Democrats held on to just 59 per cent of their support.[90] Such statistics suggested that the new party, like the Liberals of earlier elections, was overly dependent on the 'protest' vote and unable to rely on the backing of a sufficient number of voters committed to its own cause on its intrinsic merits.

That said, there remained good cause to be pleased with the 2001 outcome. The party polled 4.8 million votes – 18.3 per cent of the total – and captured 52 seats, its best parliamentary tally since 1929, and the first time that the party had increased its vote after a full-term Labour government. The decline in the share of the vote, apparent since the Alliance's high point in 1983, had finally been arrested. As in 1997, the party was a clear beneficiary of tactical voting, with the electorate displaying a continuing determination to resist the return of a Conservative government. This was fostered by a secret understanding between the Labour and Liberal Democrat parties to inflict the maximum possible electoral damage on the Tories. By most standards of judgement it was a heartening performance, though critics suggested that, in the context of a deeply unpopular opposition and a government for which, judging by the turnout of just 59.4 per cent, the electorate lacked real enthusiasm, it should have been even better. Large numbers seemed to prefer to stay at home rather than register a protest vote in favour of the Liberal Democrats.

6 Right into Government, 2001–11

The Drift Away from New Labour

If, as is inevitably the case, a political party's success is measured primarily by its performance in General Elections, then the first decade of the twenty-first century was a period of only modest progress for the Liberal Democrats. In the election of 2001, the party secured 52 seats from 18.3 per cent of the popular vote, while, in 2010, the corresponding figures were 57 seats and 23 per cent of the vote. Yet such statistics conceal a fundamental transformation in the party's position, taking it from informal and essentially powerless co-operation with a centre-left Labour Party to full partnership in a coalition government led by a centre-right Conservative Party. It was a development that few could have envisaged as the new century opened.

Despite the Liberal Democrats' showing in the 2001 election, Kennedy's relationship with his parliamentary party was never easy and he could not rely on the unqualified support of a significant number of leading MPs. It was said that Ashdown himself was persuaded to excise some critical references to his successor from the draft manuscript of his diaries before they were published. After the initial relief at the change from Ashdown's energetic, controversial and sometimes divisive approach, it became clear that Kennedy's critics in the party wanted something more from their leader than the agreeable and easy-going bonhomie that seemed to satisfy a substantial proportion of the wider electorate. The charge that Kennedy was an intellectual lightweight was perhaps exaggerated, but he certainly saw his party's future in broad-brush terms rather than at the level of detailed policy and ideological development. Even his sympathetic biographer concedes that Kennedy's book *The Future of Politics*, published in 2000, revealed 'a startling lack of original thinking on policy or a strain of political thought that was identifiably his own'.[1] Yet Kennedy did have a vision for the Liberal Democrats. He sought to end the strategy, embraced in their different ways by Grimond, Steel and Ashdown, of a realignment of the political left, seeking instead an independent role for his party which might lead to an eventual coalition, but not fusion, structured around electoral reform. With hindsight, this may have been a crucial first step on the path that ultimately led to coalition government with the Conservatives in 2010, even though Kennedy himself was in no doubt that his own sympathies tilted to the left rather than the right. His ambitions for his party were no doubt encouraged by the failure of the Conservatives to make any significant advances in 2001 from their catastrophic defeat of four years earlier, and the increasing perception that they were drifting towards right-wing irrelevance under their new leader, Iain Duncan Smith. Against this background, Kennedy told the party conference in Brighton in 2002 that the party should seek to overtake the Tories and become the principal alternative to Labour. The stance of 'effective opposition' to the Blair government made increasing sense as 'New Labour' evolved away from the promise of its early years, which Ashdown and others had found so seductive. After a cautious first term, in which Blair's over-riding concern seemed to be to ensure re-election for a second term, even at the expense of progress in the fields of social and educational reform, the Labour government, partly in response to the mounting threats of international terrorism, became increasingly authoritarian and illiberal.

For a time, the trappings of Labour–Liberal Democrat co-operation were maintained. But Kennedy was unhappy about continuing the Joint Consultative Committee and it was allowed to lapse in the autumn of 2001. At a meeting the preceding March, Blair assured the Liberal Democrat leader that he would carry out a review of the voting system and reassess the Jenkins Report in the light of devolved elections in Scotland and Wales in 2003. The promise was never kept. The existing Liberal Democrat propensity to vote with Labour in parliamentary divisions fell back sharply, particularly once the libertarian David Davis became the Conservatives' shadow Home Secretary in 2003. The party increasingly found itself in the same lobby as the Tories in defence of civil liberties. By the end of the 2001 Parliament, Liberal Democrats were already opposing Labour in 75 per cent of whipped votes.[2]

The turning point in Labour–Liberal Democrat relations came with the terrorist attack on New York's Twin Towers on 11 September 2001 ('9/11'). The seemingly unquestioning support for the Blair–Bush 'war on terror' offered by the Conservatives opened up a clear opportunity for the Liberal Democrats to carve out a distinctive position. That position became increasingly relevant as Britain moved towards collaboration in an American invasion of Iraq. After Iraq, recalled Blair, 'our relations soured completely'.[3] Kennedy's appearance at a mass anti-war rally in London in February 2003 was the sort of gesture for which the radical wing of the Liberal Democrats had long waited. In the absence of a second United Nations resolution, without which the legality of Anglo-American action was at least questionable, Liberal Democrat MPs took a principled and united stance in the crucial Commons vote on 18 March. The entire parliamentary party joined with 139 rebel Labour MPs and 15 dissenting Conservatives in voting against the government. The ensuing war, suggested Menzies Campbell, gave Kennedy a platform, and the party 'definition and distinctiveness'.[4] Though Liberal Democrat support in the polls initially fell as British troops went into battle, the embarrassing failure to find those Iraqi 'weapons of mass destruction', which Blair had used to justify the war, led to a surge in the party's standing. A net gain of 174 seats was secured in the local elections in May on a record-breaking overall poll of around 30 per cent.

This story of electoral success continued with a spectacular by-election victory in East Brent, a seat with a substantial Muslim population but little Liberal Democrat infrastructure in terms of council representation, in September 2003. On a low turnout, the youthful Sarah Teather took the seat on a massive 29 per cent swing from Labour. Significantly, this was the first seat won from Labour in a by-election since Simon Hughes took Bermondsey in 1983.[5] An opinion poll in the *Guardian* suggested that the Liberal Democrats now stood at 28 per cent, just behind the Conservatives on 30 per cent and Labour on 35 per cent. The result in East Brent strengthened Kennedy's hand and he performed well at the party's annual conference shortly afterwards, following this up with a wide-ranging reshuffle of his front-bench team. In what many interpreted as a move to the right, Vince Cable, supported by David Laws, took over responsibility for economic policy, while Mark Oaten shadowed the Home Office.

All this activity took some, but not all, of the pressure off the leadership. Problems, however, remained. Despite his experience as a student debater, Kennedy did not always perform well at Prime Minister's Questions (PMQs), and the approachability implied to the general public by his successful appearances on television light entertainment shows was not matched by his relationship with his own party, where he increasingly withdrew behind the protective shield of his private office. As was becoming widely known, although not formally acknowledged, Kennedy was waging a personal battle with alcohol throughout his period as leader. The matter was raised – and denied – in a television interview in July 2002, and a year later Kennedy was on the verge of calling a press conference to announce that he would stand down temporarily as leader to seek professional help. At the last moment, however, he changed his mind and, on television in March 2004, again denied that he had a problem. But the reality was difficult to disguise. Kennedy had been absent from the Commons in June 2002 when Chancellor Gordon Brown made his crucial statement on the euro, effectively kicking into the long grass British membership of the Single European Currency, an issue that had once seemed to unite New Labour and the Liberal Democrats. Similarly, Kennedy was unfit to respond to the 2004 Budget Statement, delegating the task at short notice to Vince Cable, while Menzies Campbell, now deputy leader, stood in at Prime Minister's Questions. A few days later the leader did speak at the party's spring conference in Southport, but he was sweating profusely and visibly shaking. The impact of the resulting television pictures was damaging.

Yet the contrast between a leader now seen as a liability within the upper reaches of his party and one who remained an asset as far as the voters were concerned persisted. As the journalist, Jackie Ashley, put it, the party needed Kennedy's popular appeal; but it also needed him fit and well.[6] The local elections in June 2004 saw the Liberal Democrats make more than 130 gains, winning control of Newcastle. Better still, the BBC's calculation of the national vote suggested that they had pushed Labour into third place. Then, in July, a swing of more than 21 per cent saw the party take the parliamentary seat of Leicester South from Labour and only narrowly fail on the same day in Birmingham, Hodge Hill, where the swing, at 27 per cent, was even greater. Both were ethnically mixed constituencies in which the party's stance on the Iraq War worked strongly in its favour. Only the European elections in June were disappointing. The party's proclaimed enthusiasm for European integration did not resonate with an increasingly Eurosceptic public, and it suffered the indignity of being relegated to fourth place behind the United Kingdom Independence Party (UKIP). Even so, the Liberal Democrats' share of the vote rose by more than 2 per cent and they increased by two their tally of MEPs.

Electoral success could not disguise a certain intellectual confusion in the party's position on the political spectrum. The stated aim remained to replace the Tories, yet the latter were inevitably showing some signs of revival themselves in the context of an increasingly unpopular Labour government. Under Michael Howard, chosen to replace Duncan Smith in November 2003, the Conservatives looked more unified and professional than previously, though the extent of the new leader's appeal to the wider electorate remained unclear. Furthermore, on a range of issues, the Liberal Democrats now seemed to project themselves to the left of Labour and the evidence of local elections was that they were making progress at Labour's expense in the towns and cities of Northern England, but might struggle to contain a Conservative revival in the more prosperous south. Against this background, a group of largely younger Liberal Democrats produced a volume of essays, *The Orange Book*, designed to show the relevance and applicability of liberal principles and solutions to the challenges of the twenty-first century. David Laws, a joint editor of the collection, later wrote that it had been designed to remedy 'the lack of a clear narrative distinguishing the Liberal role and expectation of the state from that of an historically more statist Labour party'.[7] In practice, this meant reclaiming the doctrine of economic liberalism from the Conservative Party, which had appropriated and, in many Liberal eyes, discredited it from the late 1970s onwards. Yet, as Jo Grimond had written as long ago as 1980, 'Much of what Mrs Thatcher and Sir Keith Joseph say and do is in the mainstream of liberal philosophy'.[8]

Liberal Democrats are understandably keen to play down any fundamental split between social and economic liberalism, and Laws himself has insisted that *The Orange Book* 'sought to explain how "social liberal" ends could be delivered by "economically liberal" means'.[9] Yet, at the very least, such a tension had existed within the party's ranks throughout the twentieth century, often translating – especially once the Liberals had fallen into third-party status – into a preference between Conservatives and Labour as a partner in coalition or a more informal arrangement. 'Technically as well as ideologically,' argued Conrad Russell, the blend between the two Liberal traditions is 'extremely difficult to mix in the right proportions.'[10] At all events, the appearance of *The Orange Book* caused a considerable stir at the party's 2004 autumn conference.

Among the more important contributions, Laws argued that, between the 1930s and the 1980s, Liberal commitment to the principles of the free market had slowly been watered down, while the party was progressively seduced by 'forms of soggy socialism and corporatism' which were mistakenly seen as the necessary vehicles for social liberal ambitions.[11] Elsewhere, Vince Cable called for a reduction in the size of the 'regulatory state' and the provision of greater choice in the public services, while Nick Clegg argued that enthusiasm for the European ideal was not incompatible with opposing the unnecessary accretion of further powers by the EU or with the case for repatriating powers from the EU that were exercised more appropriately at a local level. Perhaps most controversially, Laws claimed that the NHS was failing to meet the expectations of its users and proposed a continental-style insurance scheme in which a range of providers would compete to offer the necessary services. The fact that Kennedy was persuaded to provide a seal of endorsement by writing a foreword to *The Orange Book* enraged the party's left, while its brevity confirmed the suspicion of others that the leader lacked the intellectual capacity to engage in such debates. At all events, its publication inevitably 'increased speculation about the scope for co-operation between the Liberal Democrat and Conservative parties'.[12]

Notwithstanding these internal problems, the Liberal Democrats went into the General Election of May 2005 with considerable grounds for optimism. Their campaign was well financed (albeit partly by a benefactor whose foreign domicile would later cause the party embarrassment) and the polls suggested support running at around 20 per cent nationally. It was hoped that Kennedy's engaging personality would attract additional backing during the campaign at the expense of a Prime Minister (Blair) who had now lost much of the country's trust and a Leader of the Opposition (Howard) who had never really enjoyed it. Unexpected support came via the defection of the retiring left-wing Labour MP, Brian

Sedgemore, who accused Blair of 'stomach-turning lies'. But the campaign got off to a disastrous start when, at the launch of the manifesto, Kennedy proved incapable of explaining the detailed implications of the party's plans to replace the Council Tax with a local income tax. The explanation that the leader was the victim of sleepless nights following the birth of his first child was not wholly convincing. The party's manifesto was entitled *The Real Alternative* – an attempt to emphasize that the Liberal Democrats had opposed Labour across a range of policies, often with greater clarity and effectiveness than the Tories. No one could question that, over the previous Parliament, Labour had injected substantial additional resources into the public services, though the benefits of such investment were less evident. So it now made sense for the Liberal Democrats to drop their commitment to increase the basic rate of income tax, leaving the emphasis on a fairer overall system of taxation. In the light of what had happened since 2001, party headquarters decided to target around three dozen Labour-held seats; but it was also hoped to unseat a number of leading Conservatives, such as Oliver Letwin and David Davis, as part of a so-called 'decapitation' strategy.

At one level the result was very pleasing – a tally of 62 seats was the best Liberal performance since 1923, and the share of the vote at over 22 per cent was the highest since the Alliance in 1983. Eleven seats had been taken from Labour, including the unexpected bonus of Manchester, Withington. Student and ethnic votes appeared to have been crucial. But nothing could disguise a sense of disappointment and a belief that the party could and should have done much better. 'Would we ever again have a governing party so riven by its rightward drift and war and a Conservative opposition so unattractive', reflected Menzies Campbell.[13] There had been no electoral breakthrough. The decapitation strategy had failed almost completely. Indeed, the Liberal Democrats suffered a net loss of two seats to the Tories and lost ground in the majority of their target seats.

The election thus failed to give Kennedy's personal position within the party the boost for which he must have hoped. He quickly announced a wide-ranging policy review, but the public statement by Simon Hughes – whom Kennedy had only just asked to shadow the Deputy Prime Minister, John Prescott – about the disappointing outcome of the election brought internal discontent into public view and did little to soothe relations at the top of the party. A decidedly lacklustre performance by the leader at the first meeting of the parliamentary party after the election was followed at the end of June by one at which Kennedy implicitly accused a minority of his parliamentary colleagues of spreading rumours about him. Perhaps only victory in the Cheadle by-election in July following the death of the sitting Liberal Democrat MP, Patsy Calton, postponed a crisis. With mounting tension between the social and economic wings of the party in greater evidence than before at the 2005 annual conference, Kennedy sought to restore unity by insisting that there was no inherent contradiction between the two approaches, and that economic rectitude was perfectly compatible with social justice. At the same time, he insisted that the British people did not want and did not deserve another Conservative Party. What the Liberal Democrat Party needed, however, was a clear strategic direction for the future and this Kennedy seemed either reluctant or unable to provide. Matters were not helped when his former speech-writer, Richard Grayson, suggested that Kennedy's style was more that of a chairman than a leader – this at a time when the party wanted desperately to be led rather than chaired. Where previous Liberal and Liberal Democrat leaders had proudly displayed the scars of conference defeats inflicted by the party rank and file, it was Kennedy's usual practice to avoid committing himself in such internal battles.

The election in December of the youthful and progressive David Cameron to replace Michael Howard as Conservative leader 'brought a new ingredient to the political landscape' and only increased the pressure on Kennedy.[14] Later that month, Kennedy demanded the loyalty of his front-bench team, but Campbell privately urged him to step down while publicly declaring that Kennedy would have his full support 'for as long as he remained leader' – a less than wholehearted endorsement. Meanwhile, in the run-up to Christmas, Vince Cable drafted, but did not send, a letter calling for the leader's resignation. It attracted eleven signatures from the party's front bench, including those of Norman Baker, Ed Davey, Chris Huhne, David Laws and Sarah Teather. Matters came to a head early in the New Year. On 5 January, Kennedy issued a personal statement, finally admitting to his drink problem and announcing a leadership contest in which he challenged any of his colleagues who thought they could do a better job to stand against him. This, however, merely prompted an ultimatum from the parliamentary party with two dozen party spokespersons threatening to give up their portfolios if Kennedy did not resign. He thus had no option but to stand down, which he did on 7 January. The resulting contest for the succession nearly descended into farce. Mark Oaten, a potential candidate, quickly resigned his position as home affairs spokesman following newspaper revelations of his use of male prostitutes, while Simon Hughes, who did stand, was also obliged to admit that he was bisexual. The party clearly needed a leader whose private life was beyond reproach. A by-election in the seemingly rock-solid Labour seat of Dunfermline and West Fife seemed an unwanted distraction. In the event, the Liberal Democrats scored an unexpected victory with a swing of 16.2 per cent. The significance of the result was underlined by the fact that the constituency bordered that of Gordon Brown, the Chancellor of the Exchequer and, almost certainly, the next Prime Minister. In the leadership contest, Campbell's victory over Huhne by 29,697 votes to 21,628 was surprisingly narrow. Huhne had only been an MP since 2005, but he polled well among party activists attracted by his proposals to take those earning the minimum wage out of income tax, and to introduce environmental taxes.

Campbell's Interregnum

In choosing Campbell, the Liberal Democrats seemed to confirm the widely held belief that parties have an ingrained predisposition to select a leader as unlike his or her predecessor as possible. But what might have been seen as assets at the disposal of the new leader led inexorably to his downfall. Campbell was reliable, dignified, intellectually capable and, in every sense of the word, sober. But he was also – at least in the context of a televisual age dominated by the political soundbite – unequivocally dull. He had established his reputation as the party's thoughtful and convincing spokesman on foreign affairs (and, for a time, defence) since 1997. He had won respect for his polite, reasoned and often incisive critique of Labour's foreign policy, especially at the time of the Iraq War. He was listened to and was well-regarded. But these qualities did not translate easily into the effective leadership of a political party, and his performance in Parliament, especially at PMQs, proved unimpressive. In a perceptive assessment, Vince Cable later argued that 'after twenty years of being listened to with deference and respect, he was not psychologically equipped to deal with the noisy hostility and mockery of the Commons'. Furthermore, rather than rushing out eye-catching policy proposals, Campbell was always 'concerned not to stray too far from the responsible, nuanced position he would have taken as a minister'.[15] Perhaps most important, Campbell was already 64 years of age and looked somewhat older. However unfairly, he was mercilessly portrayed in the media as an old man, not up to the task at hand. Campbell was inevitably seen as a stopgap leader, most unlikely to fight more than one General Election. This left younger aspirants for the top job inclined to tread water and calculate their own future prospects. It says much for the contrast between the demands of the party and those of the wider electorate that the average three-month figure of 19 per cent support for the Liberal Democrats in the opinion polls, achieved in the final period of Kennedy's leadership, was not equalled again until the spring of 2010. The polls also suggested that more than half of Liberal Democrat voters believed that Kennedy should have remained leader.

Campbell's leadership began reasonably enough. The *Guardian* suggested that a 'low-key opening spell' had 'put a smile back on the face of the party's MPs' after the traumatic experience of Kennedy's last weeks in office.[16] The local elections in May were at first sight encouraging. The Liberal Democrats secured 27 per cent of the vote and pushed Labour into third place. But they made few overall gains and the most striking feature of the contest and – from a Liberal Democrat perspective – the most disquieting was the performance of the Conservatives, who had their best results since 1992. Not for the last time, Simon Hughes showed his capacity to damn with faint praise when he used a television interview to stress that Campbell's expertise was in foreign affairs, implying that the leader's abilities were less apparent in the domestic arena. Yet the Liberal Democrats could still focus their resources successfully on a parliamentary by-election campaign and they came near to capturing the archetypal Tory seat of Bromley and Chislehurst in June. At the party conference in September, the proposed 50p top rate of income tax was dropped. It was, Campbell believed, 'against aspiration', it 'discouraged ambition' and it 'didn't produce large sums of money'.[17] But the party's underlying intentions remained redistributive. There were proposals, spelt out in detail the following July, for a substantial cut in the basic rate of tax, to be financed by ending exemptions for higher-rate taxpayers and bringing in environmental taxes. Indeed, the publication in September 2007 of *Re-inventing the State*, a collection of essays edited by Duncan Brack, Richard Grayson and David Howarth, suggested that the economic liberal prescriptions proposed in *The Orange Book* did not enjoy a monopoly within the party's thinking.

Campbell's position remained insecure, partly because of the party's disappointing showing in the polls. Though figures fluctuated more markedly from month to month than was usually the case, the *Guardian* showed support for the Liberal Democrats standing at just 18 per cent at the end of 2006. Albeit for different reasons, Campbell found himself subjected to the same sort of murmurings of discontent among the party's MPs and peers as had undermined Kennedy. Local elections in 2007 offered little comfort – except that they were less dreadful than had been predicted. The Liberal Democrats suffered net losses of around 250 seats, though they did take control of Hull in East Yorkshire, Rochdale in Lancashire and Eastbourne in Sussex. Elections held on the same day for the Scottish Parliament and the Welsh Assembly left them in fourth place in both contests. Gordon Brown finally succeeded Tony Blair as Prime Minister on 27 June 2007 and enjoyed a brief political honeymoon with the British electorate. His efforts to create a government 'of all the talents' were less wide-ranging than his rhetoric suggested and his rather clumsy offer of a cabinet post to Paddy Ashdown had little chance of being accepted. But Campbell's problems continued. Even a respectable performance in by-elections in Ealing Southall in West London and Sedgefield in the North-East of England on 19 July, when the Conservatives were pushed into third place, failed to silence the leader's critics, and Campbell soon found himself being urged to resign by some of the party's elders. Yet it was the Labour Prime Minister rather than Liberal Democrat malcontents who finally prompted his decision to step down.

With Brown winning praise for his handling of a number of crises, ranging from an outbreak of foot and mouth disease to the collapse of the Northern Rock bank, and with Labour once more comfortably ahead of the Tories in the polls, speculation was rife that the Prime Minister would call a snap General Election to secure the personal endorsement from the British electorate that he craved. Some observers even pencilled in the date of 8 November for the poll. At the last minute, however, Brown pulled back, fearful that his premiership might turn out to be the shortest of the last 100 years. Labour was wrong-footed when the Conservative shadow chancellor announced plans to reduce the burden of inheritance tax on middle-income estates. Its lead in the polls rapidly diminished and Brown's inner circle concluded that the result of any contest would be too close to call. Brown now announced that there would be no election in 2007, denying – unconvincingly – that his decision had been influenced by the movement in the polls. Many commentators later concluded that Brown had destroyed his premiership by his indecision. Almost certainly, Campbell's leadership of the Liberal Democrats was one of the Prime Minister's collateral casualties. The apparent imminence of a General Election had offered Campbell some security. The knowledge that it was now unlikely to be held until at least 2009 reopened the floodgates of criticism. Campbell's wife posed the key question: 'Can you take it for another two years?'[18] Quietly, and with dignity, he announced his resignation on 15 October. He had been at the helm for only 19 months, but his leadership was not without its modest achievements. While in terms of policy he had largely followed an agenda tentatively begun under his predecessor, Campbell had restored a degree of professionalism to the party's operations and of stability to its internal organization, which had been in danger of collapse under Kennedy.

Yet prospects for the future were far from encouraging. As Vince Cable, who assumed temporary leadership pending the election of Campbell's successor, noted: 'Party morale was low; membership and income were falling; MPs were torn between a sense of relief and foreboding that the downward spiral would continue.'[19] As the party's most prominent and respected figure, Cable might have been well-placed to seek the leadership on a permanent basis, but he was himself 64 years old and, after the unremitting focus on Campbell's age, it was probably inevitable that the party would now look to a younger generation. In the event, the contest was between Nick Clegg (aged 40) and Chris Huhne (aged 53), both first elected to Westminster in 2005, though both had previously served in the European Parliament. As in his contest against Campbell, Huhne sought to position himself somewhat to the left of his opponent, but in reality there was little in terms of policy to separate the two men beyond Huhne's call for the scrapping of Trident in favour of a minimal nuclear deterrent. When the result was announced, Clegg emerged the winner by the narrowest of margins, with just 511 votes separating the candidates on a total poll of nearly 62,000 – a margin of victory that took on added significance when it became known that a number of late votes had not been counted.

Clegg as Leader: The World Economic Crisis and a Hung Parliament

It would be wrong to suggest that Clegg's election began a process that led inexorably towards coalition with the Conservatives two and a half years later. None the less, the generational change was important. At its top the party now had a group of individuals including Clegg, Huhne, Laws and Danny Alexander who were both more pragmatic and more market-orientated than their predecessors. This was a generation that had come into politics after the Thatcher years, a period which, somewhat illogically, granted the espousal of the market and an economically liberal approach by the Conservative New Right, had convinced many Liberal Democrats that partnership with Labour was the only conceivable option in the event of a hung Parliament. 'Most of us,' Paddy Ashdown later confessed, 'had been bred to be anti-Tory during the Thatcher years.'[20] Neither should the disillusionment of this new generation with Labour be discounted. Ashdown, Kennedy and Campbell had all held out the hope that New Labour might live up to its name and concede some form of electoral reform. Instead, a decade of increasingly centralizing Labour government had produced a long list of disappointments, ranging from a war in Iraq of questionable legality to a tentative programme of constitutional reform via limited action on the environment. At the same time, the Conservative Party had changed – though by how much remained a matter of debate. David Cameron and those around him fully recognized that the possibility of a future Conservative government depended on the party's ability to appeal far beyond its core vote, and that this in turn depended on 'detoxifying its brand'. Under Hague, Duncan Smith and Howard, the Tories had been seen to be extremely right-wing, an image assiduously encouraged by their opponents, though even a Conservative frontbencher had conceded that they were viewed as the 'nasty' party. Cameron, by contrast, presented himself as a 'liberal' Conservative, a move no doubt designed in the first instance to seduce wavering Liberal Democrat voters, but one that could also be significant in the event of a hung Parliament. At all events, under Clegg's leadership the assumption that the Liberal Democrats 'could only do a "deal" with Labour was no longer valid'.[21]

In his first important speech as leader, Clegg was at pains to avoid the impression that he belonged to any particular faction within the party. His task was to marry the traditions of economic and social liberalism and to refuse 'to accept that one comes at the cost of the other'. Yet Clegg's policy agenda, in which he supported the establishment of 'free schools', released from local authority control, and a requirement for the NHS to pay for treatment by a private provider once a maximum waiting time was exceeded, suggested a clear inclination towards an economic liberal stance.[22] Furthermore, it was difficult to dispute the fact that the new leader's shadow cabinet was located to the right of the parliamentary party as a whole. Party divisions were apparent when Parliament debated the ratification of the Lisbon Treaty in March 2008. A sizeable number of Liberal Democrat MPs rebelled against a three-line whip to abstain on a motion for a referendum on the treaty, and three front-bench spokesmen resigned. Evidence was mounting of a Eurosceptic tendency within the party's ranks.

For the time being, Vince Cable, whose gut instincts – if not necessarily his policies – made him more sympathetic to Labour than to the Tories, remained the star of the Liberal Democrat team. His brief spell as acting leader had been an unqualified success. A Commons joke at the expense of the Prime Minister, that the hapless Brown had seamlessly transmogrified from Stalin to Mr Bean, immediately entered the lexicon of one-line put-downs. In terms of economic policy, Cable always seemed to be ahead of both the government and the Conservative opposition. In February 2008, the government was finally obliged to nationalize the troubled Northern Rock bank, a course of action Cable had been advocating for some time. Then, in the face of the mounting worldwide economic crisis, Cable found himself elevated from 'the humble status of Liberal Democrat spokesman to Global Financial Wizard'.[23] Cable had long enjoyed good personal relations with the Prime Minister and former Chancellor. But this did not prevent him from pointing out that Brown, while proclaiming that he had put an end to the post-war pattern of 'boom and bust', had in fact presided over the toxic mix of an inflated housing market and huge personal debt, a dangerous combination of which Cable had long warned. As one of the very few British politicians who could now legitimately cry 'I told you so', Cable's standing in popular esteem steadily rose.

Local elections in May saw the Liberal Democrats secure a small gain in seats, while narrowly pushing Labour into third place in the popular vote. The party took control of Burnley in Lancashire, Hull (taken first in 2007, but subsequently lost again through defections), St Albans in Hertfordshire, and Sheffield. Yet it was also clear that the Conservatives were the real beneficiaries of Labour's precipitous decline. The Conservative candidate, Boris Johnson, won the contest to be London's mayor, leaving the Liberal Democrats' Brian Paddick in a poor third place. A Tory victory in the parliamentary by-election in Crewe and Nantwich in Cheshire suggested levels of voter approval last seen in the heyday of Margaret Thatcher. Once again, the Liberal Democrats came third. Perhaps most strikingly, a concerted Liberal Democrat effort in a subsequent by-election at Henley in Oxfordshire, the sort of concentrated assault that had so often reaped benefits in the past, failed to wrest the seat from Tory control. It was perhaps appropriate that Chris Rennard, the party's chief executive since 2003 and the mastermind behind its by-election strategy since the late 1980s, left his post in 2009. In many ways, Rennard had been brilliantly successful, as a series of stunning by-election victories testified. He had brought to a fine art the notion of using targeted local campaigning to secure national political success, boosting party morale and encouraging further effort. But it had also meant adopting a stance to suit local circumstances, an 'intellectual fuzziness' at the expense of a clear national image of what the Liberal Democrats were about.[24] The party was now led by a group of men hungry for power, for whom periodic by-election triumphs, often reversed at a subsequent General Election, were not enough.

Clegg hoped that the party's 2008 conference would give it a clear identity and a new sense of direction. An ambitious plan was revealed to identify £20 billion in savings in the government's budget to finance a 4p reduction in the basic rate of income tax. By the beginning of 2009, however, it was becoming clear that cuts in government spending would be needed, not to reduce tax, but to deal with the country's mounting burden of debt. In an episode whose significance would not become fully apparent until after the formation of the 2010 coalition, the party's Federal Policy Committee met in January 2009 to debate whether to drop its commitment to abolish university tuition fees. By a vote of 18 to five, it was decided to keep the policy unchanged, but Clegg was among the minority. The following month the leader called for government cuts of £20 billion, which would mean ending tax credits for middle-income families, the closure of Labour's child trust fund and a moratorium on the road-building programme. The government's unpopularity ensured another strong Liberal Democrat performance in the local elections in June, though the Tories were again the main beneficiaries. The realities of the pre-vailing electoral map suggested that, at the next General Election, the Liberal Democrats should focus their attack on vulnerable Labour seats, while protecting their existing position where the Conservatives were the main opposition. Yet the mood of the electorate remained volatile and other polls were less encouraging from a Liberal Democrat point of view. The party came fourth behind UKIP in the European elections and performed badly in a parliamentary by-election in Norwich North in July. Its performance in Glasgow North-East in November was even worse. With fewer than 500 votes and in sixth place, this was one of the worst results since the formation of the merged party in 1988. All parties were tainted from the early summer onwards by the scandal over MPs' expenses, but at least the most newsworthy cases – ranging from the infinitely flexible designation of second homes to the provision of an ornamental duckhouse – seemed to relate to Labour and the Tories. Clegg won praise for his support of Gurkha veterans in their campaign for settlement rights in Britain and for taking a leading role – somewhat against parliamentary convention and protocol – in calling for the resignation of the Commons Speaker, Michael Martin, for his apparent acquiescence in the expenses scandal.

For all that, 2009 closed with no sign of an imminent break-through. The party's average rating in the opinion polls was still below that routinely secured during Kennedy's leadership. The annual conference in Bournemouth in September revealed some uneasiness at the direction in which the leadership was heading.

In a *Guardian* interview, Clegg called for 'bold and even savage cuts' in public spending, but however realistic, his blunt words caused disquiet on the party's left wing. The Liberal Democrats' decision-making process had often been criticized for being overly bureaucratic, but its value was shown when Cable announced a surprise, and poorly thought-out, proposal for a so-called 'mansion tax'. Likely to hit many potential Liberal Democrat voters in the South-East, the plan was soon modified. Yet if there were few signs of a major Liberal Democrat advance, the polls were showing another significant development. Cameron's path to Downing Street looked less certain than for the previous two years. Indeed, a partial Labour recovery meant that, by the turn of the year, most polls were pointing to a hung Parliament resulting from the election that would have to be held by the spring of 2010.

The Liberal Democrats appear to have given the possibility of a hung Parliament greater consideration than either of their rivals. Towards the end of 2009, Clegg appointed a group of four MPs – Danny Alexander, Chris Huhne, David Laws and Andrew Stunell – to make preparations for and be the party's negotiators in a situation where the electors decided not to give any one party an overall majority in the House of Commons. This group met several times in advance of the General Election to consider possible outcomes and negotiating strategies. Its composition would prove to be crucial. In Alexander and Laws, Clegg had two of his closest ideological soulmates; Huhne, despite his appeal to the party's left wing, had now reached the intellectual conclusion that partnership with the Conservatives was a realistic possibility; and Stunell would both reassure the party's grass-roots and bring a wealth of experience of the sorts of negotiations that might ensue. Just as important as who was in it was the exclusion of any figure such as Vince Cable, whose natural inclination might be towards a deal with Labour. Meanwhile, Clegg declared on television in November 2009 that the party receiving the strongest mandate from the British people should have the first right to try to form a government, though it was not immediately apparent whether this mandate would be judged in terms of votes, seats or both. The negotiating team concluded that a formal coalition was the preferred option; that, if numbers permitted, this would be more likely to occur as the outcome of an arrangement with Labour; but that the Tories were likely to emerge as the largest single party and that the most probable deal that could be struck with them was a 'confidence and supply' agreement, falling short of a full coalition, unless the Conservatives made significant concessions on key Liberal Democrat priorities, including progress on electoral reform. This would mean the Liberal Democrats staying on the opposition benches, but offering a minority Conservative government support on economic matters and votes of confidence. It also carried with it the danger of a second election, perhaps as early as the autumn, something the Liberal Democrats were keen to avoid. Significantly, the stipulation about electoral reform did not involve a commitment to full proportional representation, as had been the case when Campbell and senior colleagues had considered the possibility of a post-election coalition back in the autumn of 2006.

Gordon Brown finally called an election for 6 May 2010. That the personality of Nick Clegg would become a key element in the campaign was not immediately obvious. Indeed, the party's campaign bus entered the fray bearing pictures of both Clegg and Cable, in the clear hope that the latter's public standing would boost the party's fortunes. A list of the 50 most influential Liberal Democrats published in the *Daily Telegraph* in 2009 had had Cable rather than Clegg at its head. The party's manifesto was based around the theme of fairness, a more equitable distribution of power in all its manifestations. In addition to political and constitutional reform, there were promises to increase the income tax threshold, break up the banks, invest in a low-carbon infrastructure and introduce a 'pupil premium' to benefit children from poorer backgrounds. But the traditional niceties of party manifestos, set-piece speeches and daily press conferences were soon overtaken by the decision, for the first time in British electoral history, to hold three televised debates between the competing would-be Prime Ministers. Such gladiatorial contests had always been blocked in the past by one or other of the larger parties. Now Cameron was convinced that he could out-perform a Prime Minister renowned for his somewhat wooden persona; and Brown was sure he could catch the more charismatic Conservative leader out when it came to a detailed scrutiny of economic policy. What neither seemed fully to appreciate was the potential a televised debate offered to the leader of the third party, never previously accorded this sort of equal billing.

The first debate was watched by an audience of almost 10 million. All three leaders had prepared carefully – perhaps too carefully – for the occasion, with well-rehearsed anecdotes and soundbites they were determined to introduce at, they hoped, a propitious moment. But at least Clegg's set-pieces appeared more spontaneous and natural than those of his rivals. He also dealt better with the camera, made a point of noting and using the first names of his questioners in the studio audience and cashed in on the feeling that the Labour and Conservative leaders were the representatives of an old-style politics that had produced both the debt crisis and the scandal over MPs' expenses – 'two old parties who have been playing pass the parcel with your government for 65 years'.[25] It was soon clear, not least from almost instant polls, that Clegg had 'won' the first round. The effect was dramatic. As 'Cleggmania' entered the political lexicon, 'the man who began the campaign as the also-ran in the shadow of his deputy was transformed overnight into the star who had stolen the show'.[26] Liberal Democrat support surged by about 10 points; some polls actually put the party in the lead. Clegg achieved a level of popular approval for a political leader usually associated only with the wartime Winston Churchill. Large numbers of small donations poured into the party's coffers, while a 100,000-strong Facebook group emerged committed to supporting the Liberal Democrats' campaign. At one level it was all a sad commentary on the state of British democracy that a single television programme, which had more to do with emotional engagement than rational debate, should have had such an impact. Yet that impact could not be denied, not least in terms of a greater readiness on the part of the Tories to turn their fire on the Liberal Democrats and, in the event that this assault failed, in private to consider more seriously the possibilities of a Conservative–Liberal Democrat arrangement.

The rest of the campaign went less well for the Liberal Democrats. Though the *Observer* and *Guardian* came out in support, Clegg was vilified in the Tory tabloids. More seriously, the party seemed to lose its way and had neither the strategy nor the resources to build on its surge in the polls. Clegg performed less well in the remaining television debates, particularly the third. By this stage his tone was becoming too sanctimonious as he strained to distance himself from the 'old politics', a fault seen earlier in Paddy Ashdown. Meanwhile, the Conservatives tried to play on the fear that a hung Parliament would be damaging to the country at a time when the economic crisis demanded 'strong' (that is, single-party) government. By contrast, Brown sought belatedly to woo the Liberal Democrats. The Conservatives, he insisted, were opposed to the 'new politics', whereas Labour and the Liberal Democrats shared some 'common ground' on constitutional matters.[27] Labour had already committed itself to a referendum on the Alternative Vote, but Clegg, in a phrase that would be thrown back at him over the months to come, declared that he was 'not going to settle for a miserable little compromise thrashed out by the Labour Party'.[28] By the eve of the vote, Liberal Democrat support had declined from its post-debate peak. But the polls still suggested that the party was heading for its best result since the early 1920s, and that Labour might yet be pushed into third place in terms of the popular vote.

In these circumstances, the actual result of the election – a result that would take the party into government in a matter of days – came as a bitter disappointment, as Clegg himself was quick to concede. On election night, the BBC's television audience heard Ashdown dismiss its exit poll – which turned out to be remarkably accurate – as 'rubbish'. After the heady euphoria surrounding the first television debate, it was difficult to believe that the party was actually losing seats. While the Liberal Democrats' share of the vote had gone up by 1 per cent compared with 2005, they suffered a net loss of five seats. 'Cleggmania' had encouraged the party to spread its limited resources more widely than was wise, thus diluting the impact of the targeting strategy that had served it so well over the previous two decades. Moreover, the party's vote fell significantly in Liberal Democrat seats being contested by new candidates, suggesting that the link developed between the electorate and an established MP remained important. Only four seats had been gained from Labour, a particular disappointment granted the outgoing government's patent unpopularity. Indeed, there were some indications that Labour was fighting back against the Liberal Democrat challenge. In local elections, held the same day but inevitably overshadowed by the national contest, Labour regained control of Liverpool. What had gone wrong? Detailed analysis of the party's surge following the televised debate revealed that it was never as substantial as the crude figures implied. Its increased support base derived largely from the young and others who were the least likely sections of the electorate actually to cast their votes.

Despite an inevitable feeling of anti-climax, the Liberal Democrats were still left holding the balance of power in the new Parliament – the position for which the leadership had long yearned. But it was one that needed to be handled with exceptional skill. All Clegg's possible choices were accompanied by distinct dangers. Whatever the ultimate outcome, it was important not only to maintain party unity but also to convince as many Liberal Democrats as possible that the course chosen was the only viable option. The Conservatives now had 307 seats, 19 short of the number required for an overall majority in the Commons. Labour had 258 seats, but its share of the vote was its third-lowest since before the First World War. While this book has argued that the changes that had taken place over the previous decade had made possible the formation of a Conservative–Liberal Democrat coalition government, there was nothing inevitable about such an outcome. Only the events that took place over the five days immediately following the General Election in May 2010 determined this result. The detailed negotiations of 7–11 May have been chronicled authoritatively by a Liberal Democrat who took part in them, and by a well-informed Conservative observer.[29] The discussion here will be restricted to the most significant elements of these dramatic days.

The initial assumption was that David Cameron would seize on the fact that the Tories were comfortably the largest single party to form a minority government. Such an eventuality carried with it the probability of an early – and, from a Liberal Democrat point of view, unwanted – second election, following Harold Wilson's precedent of 1974. Yet, on the day after the election, the Conservative leader announced that, in the national interest, he wanted to make 'a big, open and comprehensive offer to the Liberal Democrats' to work with him. Such a statement implied, though it did not guarantee, a full coalition. Granted Clegg's earlier statements that the largest party in a hung Parliament should have the first option, he had to respond positively. Many rank-and-file Liberal Democrats were unenthusiastic, but the logic of the parliamentary arithmetic was compelling. As Ashdown put it, the electorate had managed to produce 'an instrument of excruciating torture for the Liberal Democrats, where our hearts and emotions went one way but the mathematics the other'.[30]

In a glare of publicity, negotiations now opened between teams from the Liberal Democrat and Conservative parties and, soon afterwards but at first clandestinely, between the Liberal Democrats and Labour. The latter were necessary, both to convince the wider party that its preferred option had at least been explored, and with a view to using them as a bargaining counter further down the line in talks with the Tories. Formal negotiations were accompanied by meetings and telephone calls between the party leaders and contacts, authorized and unauthorized, between leading figures in the three parties. In all cases, personal factors were of fundamental importance: 'Were one to have replaced any one of the three party leaders with a rival from the same party,' writes the former Conservative Foreign Secretary, Malcolm Rifkind, 'one would almost certainly have seen a different outcome.'[31] The significance of the Liberal Democrat negotiating team has already been noted. But the composition of the corresponding Conservative group – George Osborne, William Hague, Oliver Letwin and Ed Llewellyn – was also important. David Laws has been lavish in his praise of Hague, whom he did not know previously. Laws found him 'friendly, warm, pragmatic, helpful and relaxed', and his conduct in the negotiations 'straightforward, respectful and businesslike'. Letwin, whose shortcomings as a front-line politician had been cruelly exposed during the election campaign of 2001, turned out to be 'warm, cheerful, honest, trustworthy and pretty liberal-minded'.[32] He was also extremely well-informed about the detailed policy priorities of the two parties, with a keen eye for the potential for compromise and co-operation.

Against this background, the Conservative–Liberal Democrat negotiations soon made substantial progress. Operating in what were, in British terms, largely uncharted waters, both sides seemed intent on bringing matters to a speedy conclusion and avoiding the sort of protracted haggling that often characterized comparable proceedings on the Continent. All were convinced that the markets might react unfavourably to any suggestion of political deadlock. Overall, the mood was very positive. As Laws recalled: 'We were negotiating with a moderate and reasonable group of Conservatives, who were willing to make real concessions to reach agreement, and who behaved in an honest and constructive way, rapidly building trust.'[33] Even so, the Liberal Democrat team was surprised by the apparent readiness of the Tories to drop some of their flagship policies, such as the raising of the inheritance tax threshold. At the same time, the Liberal Democrats had to give ground on some of their declared policy positions. Perhaps the most striking instance came over the question of public expenditure cuts. During the election, the party had agreed with Labour that total government spending should not be reduced in 2010 because of the danger that this might stifle economic activity before the country's economic recovery had had a chance to take root. The Conservatives, by contrast, had called for cuts of £6 billion in 2010–11 and this had developed into one of the key dividing lines of the election campaign. In practice, this relatively modest figure was unlikely to become a deal-breaker. More important, the Liberal Democrat leadership's view appears to have evolved over the course of the campaign in the light of the mounting crisis in Greece, which threatened to spread to other countries carrying a large deficit. 'Bluntly,' Laws concludes, 'we thought that the signalling value of these limited cuts was important and we were prepared to take the political pain in order to do the right thing for the country.'[34] Such was the change of heart in fact, that the Liberal Democrats declined the offer, suggested by their Tory counterparts, of independent briefings on this matter from Treasury and Bank of England officials. What had appeared on the surface to be a major obstacle to agreement was soon surmounted.

Despite the widespread – and fully justified – perception that Labour had 'lost' the election, Gordon Brown responded energetically once he sensed that there was some chance of remaining in office. Though a Labour–Liberal Democrat coalition could not command an overall parliamentary majority, there was some talk of a 'rainbow' alliance involving the Welsh and Scottish Nationalists and the solitary Green MP. Guiding Brown was an innate belief that Labour and the Liberal Democrats were both on the 'progressive' side of politics and formed an altogether more natural combination than did the Liberal Democrats and the Tories. Yet this was a somewhat curious conviction on the part of one who had been unsympathetic to the Blair–Ashdown 'project', and was seen by many as something of a deathbed conversion. Contacts made with Labour over the weekend of 8–9 May by such senior Liberal Democrats as Cable and Ashdown may have served to exaggerate the realistic prospects of a deal, but it was always in Clegg's interests to keep the Labour option in play for as long as possible.

For all that, formal discussions with Labour proved extremely difficult. Most of the 'positives' that characterized the talks with the Tories were markedly absent when negotiations opened with a hastily assembled Labour team. The personal chemistry between the two groups was poor, especially at the beginning, when the Liberal Democrat negotiators did not feel they were being treated as equals. The Labour team appeared ill-prepared, lacking a coherent strategy and divided among themselves. The commitment to reach an agreement shown by the Conservatives was missing. While Peter Mandelson and Andrew Adonis seemed positive in their approach, Ed Balls and Ed Miliband were altogether less enthusiastic. The lack of a credible plan to deal with the country's deficit posed a particular problem, with Balls even rejecting the plans of the outgoing Labour Chancellor, Alistair Darling. Labour was also unwilling to make a commitment on two of the Liberal Democrats' most important policies – a £10,000 income tax allowance and the pupil premium. 'It was difficult,' recalled Laws, 'to regard the negotiations as entirely serious while this remained the case.'[35] On Monday, 10 May, it became clear that even over electoral reform, where Labour had seemed to be offering more than the Tories, their commitment was lukewarm. Balls explained that Labour's promise of a referendum on AV was in doubt: 'Many of our colleagues are opposed to it. It cannot be guaranteed.' This was, judged Laws, 'a deadly intervention and, I felt, a calculated wrecking device'. The same witness concludes of this 'historic meeting': 'instead of ushering in the long anticipated Lib–Lab partnership, it had buried thirty years of Lib–Lab dreams'.[36]

Underlying the difficulties thrown up by these negotiations was the position of the Prime Minister himself: 'If his own Cabinet cannot work with him,' reasoned Laws, 'what chance do four or five Lib Dem ministers have?'[37] Relations between Clegg and Brown were already poor. The Liberal Democrat leader found his Labour counterpart patronizing and overbearing. Brown's attempts over the weekend to convince Clegg of the logical inevitability of a 'progressive' coalition were probably counter-productive, and obliged Clegg to point out that more than policy issues were involved. If the election had revealed nothing else, it had shown that the country did not want Gordon Brown as Prime Minister. Indeed, subsequent opinion polls suggested that the premier's personal unpopularity may have cost Labour anything between 20 and 40 seats. On 10 May, Brown finally announced his readiness to step down in the wider national interest, though even then the timetable for his departure remained obscure. Only at this point could talks with Labour offer any real prospect of success. But Brown's delay in reaching his decision meant that Labour had much ground to make up if it were to overtake the Tories in the quest for an agreement.

Brown's move inevitably placed increased pressure on the Conservatives and led to one of the most important and controversial moments in the formation of the new government. Clegg and Cameron spoke by telephone on the afternoon of 10 May. Later that day, Cameron addressed Tory MPs and persuaded them to accept a referendum on the Alternative Vote (AV) as the only way of trumping, or at least competing with, Labour's offer of legislation to introduce AV without a referendum. The connection, if any, between these two events remains unclear. Labour had made no such offer. It is possible that Cameron had genuinely misunderstood what Clegg had told him. Alternatively, Clegg may have deliberately exaggerated Labour's position to try to coax the Conservatives into greater concessions. Or Cameron may have misled his party into making the sort of offer on electoral reform without which the Conservative–Liberal Democrat talks could have collapsed. At any event, the Conservative move on AV proved crucial. AV is not, of course, proportional representation (PR). Indeed, it is capable of producing even greater distortions than the first-past-the-post voting system. But it was believed that it would usually increase Liberal Democrat representation and thus make future hung Parliaments, from which a genuinely proportional system might be extracted, more likely. A meeting of senior Liberal Democrat leaders concluded that evening that the party should join a full coalition with the Conservatives, and immediately afterwards, a meeting of the parliamentary party moved, with a surprising lack of dissent, towards the same conclusion. Negotiations with Labour continued into Tuesday, 11 May, but by this stage Brown was losing patience and, conscious that his continuing position as Prime Minister was becoming increasingly anomalous, anxious to tender his resignation to the Queen. Clegg still hoped to keep Labour in play a little longer, if only to extract further concessions from the Tories. For perhaps the first time in the negotiating process, however, he lost control of the agenda when Brown insisted on going to the Palace. Cameron was thus invited to form a government before the final details of the coalition agreement with the Liberal Democrats had been concluded.

The formation of a Conservative–Liberal Democrat government still took some observers by surprise. After all the talk little over a decade earlier of making the twenty-first century, in contrast to its predecessor, a 'progressive' century, coalition with Britain's right-of-centre party seemed an odd way to proceed. But was it such an unnatural outcome? Parliamentary arithmetic, of course, always pointed in this direction. Yet the case against a Labour–Liberal Democrat alignment was only partly based on numbers. Though a coalition between the two parties could not, on its own, have commanded a Commons majority, it could probably have formed the basis of a viable government. Granted the permanent absence of the Sinn Fein representatives from Westminster and the known predilections of the Welsh and Scottish Nationalists, it seems unlikely that the Conservatives could ever have mustered the numbers to bring such a government down. More important, however, a Labour–Liberal Democrat combination, especially under Gordon Brown, would have been seen, whatever the ambiguities of the election result, as propping up a defeated government, 'chaining ourselves to a decaying corpse', as David Laws put it.[38] A coalition under a new Labour leader would have created the probably unacceptable situation of a second successive Prime Minister not chosen by the British people, despite the increasingly presidential nature of modern General Elections. By the end of the negotiating process, moreover, senior Labour figures such as David Blunkett, John Reid and Jack Straw, their thirst for power perhaps quenched by years in office, were lining up to denounce the idea of a coalition with the Liberal Democrats.

But partnership with the Conservatives was not just a reluctant response to the rejection of the Labour alternative. The political landscape that had determined the thinking of the Steel–Ashdown–Campbell generation of Liberal Democrats had changed significantly. Writing in 1999, Conrad Russell had argued that it would be impossible for the Liberal Democrats to remain 'permanently equidistant between two moving points ... In 40 years' time our positioning of 1999 may seem as antiquated as our position of 1955 seems now.'[39] In practice, this change took considerably less than 40 years. By 2010, the Liberal Democrats, whose own centre of gravity had changed significantly, were already sharing power with the Tories in 14 councils, including Birmingham and Leeds. David Cameron had brought about sufficient change to the Tory party to suggest a re-drawing of the central dividing line in British politics. In this, progressive/conservative antagonism was replaced by a

> view in which the fundamental divide was between a 'statist' Labour Party, whose answer to problems was invariably more government intervention, and 'liberal' Conservative and Liberal Democrat Parties, in which both sought to encourage 'social responsibility' at an individual and community level and to buttress individual liberties against the encroachment of the state.[40]

On this basis, Britain's third party entered government for the first time since the end of the war against Adolf Hitler.

Coalition Government

Matters began well enough. The party accepted the leadership's choice with a surprising display of near unanimity. Under the so-called 'triple lock' mechanism, established in 1998 as a reaction to Ashdown's apparent readiness to bounce the party into an arrangement with New Labour, any such initiative now needed 75 per cent support from both the parliamentary party and the Federal Executive. If this was not forthcoming, two-thirds support would be needed at a special conference, failing which a simple majority in a full ballot of the party membership. A joint meeting of the parliamentary party and the Federal Executive on 11 May offered an overwhelming endorsement of the coalition – 50 to 0 on the part of the MPs and 27 to 1 (David Rendel) among the Executive. Though technically now unnecessary, the party went into the second stage of the triple lock process on 16 May, when a special conference also pledged overwhelming support. This outcome was a tribute to the way in which Clegg and his colleagues had handled the post-election negotiations, and indicated that the party as a whole had fully committed itself to the coalition. At least on this point of principle there would be little room for later recriminations.

Five cabinet posts out of 22 in the new government went to the Liberal Democrats. Clegg himself became Deputy Prime Minister, with special responsibility for constitutional reform. Cable took office at the Department for Business, Innovation and

Skills, Huhne became Secretary for Energy and Climate Change, Alexander was made Scottish Secretary, and Laws became Chief Secretary to the Treasury. On 29 May, however, Laws, a key architect of the coalition, resigned after disclosures about his parliamentary expenses and private life. Alexander then moved into his place, while Michael Moore became Scottish Secretary. Liberal Democrat junior ministers were placed in most other government departments. Overall, the party's representation was in line with, or slightly greater than, its representation in the Commons.

The Prime Minister and Deputy Prime Minister appeared at a joint press conference in the Downing Street rose garden on Wednesday, 12 May. The personal chemistry between the two men of similar age, background and education was obvious – too obvious for some Liberal Democrats, who nurtured fears of the eventual loss of their party's identity. When Cable stepped down from the deputy leadership to concentrate on his ministerial responsibilities, he was replaced by Simon Hughes who, like the party president, Tim Farron, clearly saw himself as a guardian of the party's conscience. The introduction to the full coalition programme, published on 20 May, put forward a bold claim: 'We have found that a combination of our parties' best ideas and attitudes has produced a programme for government that is more radical and comprehensive than our individual manifestos.' Some potential points of friction were skilfully circumvented. The key date in the decision-making process on the replacement of the Trident nuclear weapon system was deferred until 2016, beyond the date of the next General Election. Accepting that Britain would not adopt the euro over the course of the Parliament was less controversial than it might have been in happier economic times, and the Liberal Democrats moved with the mood of the country in agreeing that there would be no further transfers of power to Brussels in the same period. At the same time, the party could take satisfaction from the inclusion of a surprising number of its key policies in the government's plans. These included the £10,000 income tax threshold, the pupil premium, reform of the banking system, the abandonment of identity cards, fixed-term five-year Parliaments, and the restoration of the earnings link for state pensions. One academic study suggested that 75 per cent of the Liberal Democrat manifesto had been included in the coalition programme compared with just 60 per cent of the Tories' proposals. Such mathematical exactitude must be treated with caution, but there were certainly right-wing Conservatives who believed that Cameron, like Baldwin in the 1930s, welcomed the excuse afforded by the coalition to ditch some of his party's more controversial policies and anchor it firmly in the political centre-ground. It was certainly to the Prime Minister's advantage that some of the government's most difficult policy decisions fell within the remit of Liberal Democrat ministers, including university tuition fees (Cable, at Business, Innovation and Skills) and nuclear power (Huhne, at Energy), not to mention detailed spending cuts (Alexander as Chief Secretary).

When the Chancellor, George Osborne, presented his emergency budget on 22 June, four Liberal Democrat MPs tabled an amendment to the proposed rise in VAT, while two actually voted against the government. The following month, Simon Hughes and Menzies Campbell sought to steady Liberal Democrat nerves by insisting that there would be no coalition at the next election. But August saw rumours, quickly denied, that Charles Kennedy was so upset by his party's involvement in spending cuts that he was having confidential talks with Labour. Then, on the eve of the party's annual conference in Liverpool in September, Cable declared that the government's cap on immigration was in danger of damaging the economy. For the most part, however, the coalition's first months saw the Liberal Democrats rallying loyally, if without great enthusiasm, behind the government's programme of spending cuts. Osborne's comprehensive spending review, unveiled in October, envisaged the most severe restraint on public spending since the end of the Second World War. The Liberal Democrats' first major problem arose over the issue of tuition fees. The party had gone into the 2010 election committed to scrapping them, and all its MPs had signed a very public pledge to vote against any proposed increase. Several leading party figures, including Clegg and Laws, believed this had been a mistake in the context of the grave economic situation, but it was not one that was easy to undo, especially as the Liberal Democrats had polled well among students, not least in Clegg's own Sheffield constituency. The coalition agreement on this issue was based on the on-going Browne enquiry, set up by the Labour government, whose report was due in the autumn. In the expectation that this would recommend raising fees, the Liberal Democrats were given the right to abstain on any resulting government proposals. The matter was further complicated by the fact that it fell within Cable's area of responsibility, and at one point it was even suggested that the minister might himself abstain on a proposal which he would have to take through the House of Commons. Cable failed to persuade his critics that a scheme that would not involve any student payments until after graduation was in fact fairer than the one it replaced. In the event, in a division on 9 December, 28 Liberal Democrat MPs voted to increase fees to a maximum of £9,000 per annum, 21 (including the former leaders Kennedy and Campbell) defied the coalition agreement and voted against, while a further eight, including two who were necessarily absent abroad, abstained.

It would, of course, have been unrealistic for the Liberal Democrats to expect that the whole of the government's programme would meet with their approval. Compromise and concession are the very essence of coalition, especially from the point of view of the junior partner in government. But the effect on the party's popular standing of abandoning the position held at the time of the election was dramatic. Liberal Democrat support had already dropped to 14 per cent by the end of July 2010, and by December it was down to 11 per cent, while Clegg's personal approval rating fell even more sharply. A YouGov poll in January 2011 suggested that 41 per cent of those who had voted Liberal Democrat at the General Election would now back Labour. Clegg, declared *The Spectator*, had become the most hated politician in Britain: 'It is as if someone has thrown compost accelerator over him, speeding up the process of degeneration from hope to has-been from ten years to ten months.'[41] Actual polls were, if anything, even worse. The party came sixth in a by-election in Barnsley Central, behind UKIP, the British National Party (BNP) and an independent candidate. Out of such disappointments, which might, it was hoped, prove only temporary, the Liberal Democrats needed to rescue the jewel of electoral reform. AV was not the same as PR, and the party had some difficulty in extricating itself from Clegg's earlier jibe about a 'miserable little compromise'. But AV was likely to increase Liberal Democrat representation and had the merit, Liberal Democrats believed, of reducing the number of 'safe' parliamentary seats. Under it, MPs would have to secure 50 per cent of the vote, even if that plurality was to be achieved with second preferences.

The AV referendum held in May 2011 was the most significant event in the history of the coalition to date. Its result (a 68 per cent 'no' vote) came as a heavy blow to the Liberal Democrats. It suggested that the whole issue of electoral reform might now be off the political agenda for a generation. Yet, for many, electoral reform had been the party's deal-breaker at the time of the coalition negotiations, and the Tory concession of a referendum the bottom line of the Clegg–Cameron agreement. Just as important, the referendum campaign itself soured relations between the coalition parties. In reality, the 'yes' campaign had not been effective. AV came across as unduly complex and its supporters failed to come up with a slogan to match the earlier simple (if contentious) equation of PR with 'fair' votes. The Liberal Democrats were annoyed that Cameron, having agreed to play a low-key role, figured prominently in the campaign, and by what they claimed was a concerted Conservative attempt to smear Clegg. The Deputy Prime Minister himself suggested that the 'no' campaign was led by a 'nasty right-wing clique'.[42] Free from the constraints of office, Lord Ashdown criticized the Prime Minister for failing to dissociate himself from a 'regiment of lies', and predicted that for the coalition it would never again be glad confident morning.[43] But when Chris Huhne appeared to liken the Conservative Co-Chairman, Sayeeda Warsi, to the Nazi propaganda minister, Joseph Goebbels, and to note that the Tories, in opposing AV, found themselves in the same camp as the BNP, without also pointing out that a referendum on full PR would have found that party on the same side as the Liberal Democrats, it was clear that the Conservatives had no monopoly of the Black Arts. If the disappointment of the referendum was not enough, English local elections held the same day were equally depressing, not least because the Conservatives made unexpected gains. The electorate chose to punish the Liberal Democrat side of the coalition. The party lost around 700 seats, some 40 per cent of the total being defended. Nine councils fell, including Hull, Stockport, Bristol and Sheffield. Meanwhile, in elections in Scotland, Liberal Democrats lost 12 of their 17 Members of the Scottish Parliament (MSPs). In Wales, the picture was marginally better. Just one Assembly seat was lost, but the party's share of the vote fell to 10.6 per cent.

More generally, the first months of 2011 saw a greater readiness on the part of leading Liberal Democrats to criticize publicly and distance themselves from their Conservative colleagues. When, in March, Clegg inadvertently left his microphone on, he was heard joking with Cameron that the two of them were in danger of having nothing on which to disagree in the television debates that would accompany the next General Election. In spite of, or perhaps because of, this, the Liberal Democrat leadership became more outspoken, partly to give voice to genuine disagreements, but more importantly to reassure the wider party that there was no danger of its distinct identity being swamped by participation in the coalition. At its crudest, this tended to degenerate into the claim that caring Liberal Democrats were saving the country from the rampant Thatcherism of their coalition partners. Cable had already told two *Telegraph* journalists, posing as Liberal Democrat supporters, that the Conservatives were too intent on change and that, if he were pressed too hard, he might use the 'nuclear option' of resigning and bringing down the government. In April he criticized a 'very unwise' speech by the Prime Minister on immigration, claiming that it risked inflaming extremism. Even Clegg clashed with Cameron over the ethics of internships. In the House of Lords in May, rebel Liberal Democrat peers helped to defeat a government proposal for elected police commissioners. But perhaps the most divisive issue on the government's agenda was the proposal for a radical reform of the NHS put forward by Health Secretary, Andrew Lansley. The party's spring conference saw a major revolt led by Baroness Williams of Crosby – the former Shirley Williams. The leadership decided to accept a critical resolution, calling for extensive changes to Lansley's plans, even though Clegg had signed up to them as Deputy Prime Minister. In his speech to the conference, Clegg defended participation in the coalition and insisted that the Liberal Democrats had in no sense lost their soul. But it was clear that the rank and file were uncomfortable about the situation and expected the leader to fight harder for Liberal Democrat values. Pressure was maintained over the following weeks. Norman Lamb announced that he might have to resign as Clegg's chief political adviser if the NHS reforms went through in their present form, and Warren Bradley, Liberal Democrat leader on the Liverpool City Council told Clegg bluntly to pull out of the coalition. Such signs of independence and differentiation were only likely to increase.

Conclusion

Continuity and Change

A survey of more than 100 years of the history of the Liberal Party and its successor, the Liberal Democrat Party, demands that some tentative conclusions be drawn. The most intriguing question concerns the relationship between the party as it stood in 1900 and that existing in the second decade of the twenty-first century. The name on the bottle has certainly changed, but are its contents essentially the same? At the most fundamental level, a clear institutional continuity is apparent. The party may have come near to going out of business in the decade after the end of the Second World War, but it never actually did so, and it has been handed on by successive generations of leaders, activists and followers without interruption. It has been the victim of many defections, most notably in 1931–32, and, more recently, has benefited from the arrival of new recruits, especially following the merger with the majority of the Social Democratic Party in 1988. But enough of the core has always been retained to guarantee a legitimate pattern of descent from Campbell-Bannerman to Clegg. This institutional continuity is confirmed by the party's extra-parliamentary structure. The organizational history of the modern party may be traced back to the setting up of the National Liberal Federation (NLF) in May 1877, a body designed to create a channel of communication between the leadership and the wider party, and to aid the 'participation of all members of the party in the formation and direction of its policy'.[1] This initiated a tradition of activist independence from the party at the centre, often but not invariably of a creative nature, which persists to this day. Indeed, in its role as the party's chief policy-making body, the Council of the NLF may be seen as the forerunner of the modern party conference. The structure created in 1877 lasted essentially unchanged until the replacement of the NLF by the Liberal Party Organisation in 1936, following the report of the Meston Committee into party organization. At that point, the newly created Liberal Assembly took over responsibility for policy-making from the annual Liberal Council. This arrangement was modified in 1946, when the report, *Coats off for the Future*, while leaving the assembly's central role essentially unchanged, proposed a permanent party committee, whose membership would be largely a matter for the leader, to act in the manner of a shadow cabinet and issue policy statements on pressing issues. The fused party of 1988 took over many detailed ideas from the SDP, but the decentralized Liberal tradition was maintained and the party's twice-yearly conference enjoys to this day the basic policy-making role created for the extra-parliamentary party in the late nineteenth century.

The realm of ideology, policy and ideas offers a more complex picture. All parties must develop and adapt if they are to survive. Detailed policies are often appropriate only for a specific time. But parties also need to ensure that their core beliefs and values are retained. The balance of importance between political and economic Liberalism has inevitably varied greatly over the period under review but, arguably, a continuity of Liberal principles has been upheld. Liberalism remains committed to the rights of the individual and to personal liberty. The twenty-first-century party is at the forefront of the defence of civil liberties, even though the challenges and threats to those liberties are in many respects very different from those that existed in the era of Campbell-Bannerman and Asquith. The party retains its faith in the market and the need to restrict the intrusions of government. It continues to proclaim the need for social justice and a fairer society. Within the coalition government it has championed the idea of redistribution through the tax system, in a way that has echoes of Lloyd George's famous budget of 1909. It insists on the need for a moral component in the conduct of British foreign policy, and the reader will be struck by parallels between the opposition of radical Liberals to the conduct of the Boer War and that of the entire parliamentary party to a possibly illegal invasion of Iraq just over 100 years later. In neither case did Liberals believe that a valid *casus belli* really existed. More generally, Liberalism upholds the ideal of internationalism above that of the nation state. And it has given a new lease of life to the quest for political

Liberalism by championing such issues as devolution and freedom of information.

Though the party has not often been in government during the period under review, much has been achieved. Indeed, the history of the twentieth century is not just about the survival of the Liberal Party; it is also in part the story of the triumph of liberalism. Britain has become a more 'liberal' society, one more permeated with 'liberal' values than it was 100 years ago. Yet herein lies one of the party's most formidable problems. The Liberal Party has survived within an increasingly 'liberal' democratic polity. Liberals have looked on while their rivals have appropriated many of their most characteristic aims and policies. To this extent, such aims and policies have ceased to be distinctively 'Liberal' even if they remain essentially 'liberal'. Since the late 1970s first the Conservatives and then New Labour have discovered the virtues of the liberal market economy. At the same time, Labour became, not always convincingly, the champion of constitutional reform, including devolution. Thus, as during much of the period covered by this book, the contemporary Liberal Democrat Party still struggles to lay claim to a distinctive identity. Ironically, the one policy area over which the Liberal Democrats may assert their greatest claim to a unique ownership is the party's consistent espousal of the ideal of a united Europe, including acceptance of a federal dimension. This separates them from both Labour and the Conservatives, which have both changed course and significantly divided on this issue. And it also probably separates the Liberal Democrats from the majority of the British electorate, which remains at best unenthusiastic about this goal. Indeed, the present crisis within the Eurozone compels speculation as to whether the Liberal Democrats will in future need to modify their Euro-enthusiasm to take into account the widespread perception that Britain's non-membership of the single currency has been one of the country's few significant advantages in combating the effects of the present global economic crisis.

Uncertainty over Liberal identity and the appropriation of its policies and ideas by its rivals would matter less to the Liberal Party if it had ever succeeded in regaining the position – which it had lost by the end of the second decade of the twentieth century – as one of the two contenders for power operating within an electoral system that disadvantages the prospects of any third force. The Liberal Democrats may at present be part of a coalition government, but they enjoy this status still very much as the third party in the state. Indeed, it needs to be remembered that, until the General Election of 2001, the party's vote had been on a consistently downward trajectory since the high-point achieved by the Alliance in 1983. The steady improvement in the party's *parliamentary* strength has resulted from more effective electioneering rather than a surge in popular support. Even the result that brought Liberal Democrats into government with 57 seats in 2010 was weaker in percentage terms than that of the Alliance in 1983, which resulted in just 23 MPs. The party remains more disadvantaged by the recently confirmed first-past-the-post electoral system than either the Conservatives or Labour. In terms of the total national vote, it took considerably more than three times the number of electors to secure one Liberal Democrat MP in the 2010 General Election as it did a representative of either of the two main parties. Liberal Democrat popular support will need to exceed 30 per cent by a good margin for this situation to change. Such an achievement may still be far away. Most commentators confidently predict that the party's vote will fall, perhaps significantly, at the next General Election.

But at least the Liberal Democrats can now claim realistically that, as at the beginning of the twentieth century, their party is a significant national force throughout Great Britain. The often-repeated line that Liberal Democrats are the main challengers to the Conservatives in the south of England, and to Labour in the north, may exaggerate the party's inherent strength, but it at least indicates that it has a viable institutional presence throughout the land. For much of the twentieth century, this was simply not the case. The geographical pattern of Liberal Democrat strength offers some interesting comparisons with the picture from 100 years ago. In some cases, the party has managed to re-establish itself in former strongholds such as rural Scotland and the South-West of England. But Liberal Democracy is also prominent in towns and cities where there is no long-standing Liberal tradition – for example, Birmingham and Liverpool. Yet it remains difficult to speak of Liberal Democrat 'strongholds'. If around 15 parliamentary seats might now be regarded as reasonably 'safe', a comparable number can be classified as 'marginal' and vulnerable to a relatively modest upsurge on the part of Labour or the Conservatives.

The diversity of Liberal Democrat parliamentary seats – two of the party's longest-serving MPs represent such different constituencies as Ross, Skye and Lochaber in the Scottish Highlands, and Bermondsey in inner London – makes it difficult to generalize about the socio-economic basis of Liberal Democrat popular support. At the start of the twentieth century, the Liberal Party, notwithstanding the beginnings of the Labour movement, had strong claims to be the chief representative of the British working class. Liberals enjoyed substantial support among the business community, and the correlation between voting Liberal and belonging to the nonconformist churches was also marked. A century later, the concept of class-based voting is self-evidently much weaker. Where it does persist, it is Labour that can still count on the support of the least prosperous sections of the population. All parties now claim to be 'business-friendly', but it is the Conservatives who are most associated with notions of enterprise and wealth creation. At the same time, voting patterns based on religious affiliation have now all but disappeared, at least outside the province of Northern Ireland. The modern Liberal Democrat Party polls reasonably well across the social spectrum, but not strongly enough to be able to claim any particular socio-economic group as its own. In 2010, the party seemed to have done well among female voters, particularly younger ones. It also improved its performance from 2005 among members of the lower middle class, but lost ground among the unskilled and unemployed. Such, however, has been the volatility and inconsistency of the party's vote that it would be dangerous to delineate with certainty any long-term trends.

The Future

If, by definition, the historian's obvious role is to look into the past, he may find it difficult, when history is traced to the present day, not to indulge in a few speculative observations about the future. Back in 2009, two seasoned Liberal Democrat activists (and party historians) debated the pros and cons, from their party's point of view, of a hung Parliament. Roy Douglas could not 'conceive of a more certain cause of disaster' than leaving the party to choose whether Labour or the Conservatives took office. Duncan Brack, by contrast, saw a 'much more desirable outcome: Liberal Democrats taking part in government, having a say in legislation and actions, implementing at least some Liberal Democrat policies and demolishing the image of the party as one doomed to permanent opposition'.[2] It is, as yet, too soon to endorse with any certainty either of these contrasting views. History certainly offers its warnings. Previous associations with the Tories have led to fragmentation and the eventual absorption of both the Liberal Unionists and the National Liberals into the Conservative fold. At one level, some damage is almost inevitable. As long ago as 1926, J. M. Keynes pointed out that Liberals, forced to make the choice, would divide into those who would vote Conservative and those who would back Labour.[3] Not all Liberal Democrat voters approved of the coalition with the Tories, and the support of some of them was lost, at least temporarily. Yet others would have reacted similarly in the event of a Labour–Liberal Democrat arrangement. Seemingly permanent opposition had granted the party the luxury of leaning one way and then the other – and occasionally both at the same time. The realities of power and government demanded a clear choice to be made. Perhaps the Liberal Democrats have at least given a definitive answer to the question with which they and their predecessors have long had to grapple, usually in a theoretical context, of whether their best advantage lies in preserving a fully independent identity or whether, despite the ultimate fate of earlier schismatics, the best course is to co-operate with one or other of the two leading parties.

The year 2010 was never going to be the easiest moment for a party to return to government after a lapse of 65 years. The Governor of the Bank of England has been reported as saying that the decisions that would have to be taken would prove so unpopular as to render the parties involved unelectable for a generation. Even in happier times, it would not be easy for the junior partner to a coalition to claim credit for a government's successes; and it is only too easy to be tarred by its failures. The circumstances in which the coalition ends – the party's 'exit strategy' – may prove all-important. If it lasts until the next election, the Liberal Democrats may have insufficient time to re-establish a distinct identity in the mind of the electorate. Following the disastrous 2011 local election results, there was much talk of Liberal Democrat ministers resigning in advance of the General Election and merely sustaining a minority Conservative government in office until 2015.

Many believe that, however it ends, the coalition has fundamentally redrawn the dividing lines of British politics. In explaining why he could not formally support the coalition deal (he abstained in the vote of Liberal Democrat MPs), Charles Kennedy argued that it would 'drive a strategic coach and horses through the long-nurtured "realignment of the centre-left" to which leaders in the Liberal tradition, this one included, have all subscribed since the Jo Grimond era'.[4] Yet even this conclusion is open to question. As Conrad Russell pointed out in 1999, at a time when coalition with Labour seemed a much stronger possibility, 'the year of greatest closeness to [the Conservatives] in my memory' was 1955. 'The next year, we had Suez, and the closeness vanished in a puff of smoke. What will be the next puff of smoke?'[5] At all events, future General Elections are likely to produce further opportunities for the Liberal Democrats. Even under the existing electoral system there is a strong likelihood of more hung Parliaments to come. A clear pattern has emerged since the 1950s of the two major parties winning an ever-smaller share of the popular vote. Securing a majority Conservative or a majority Labour government becomes in this context an increasingly difficult proposition.

The Liberal and Liberal Democrat revival that has run in parallel with this trend has not been smooth or consistent. But its general upward direction is clear and should not be measured solely in terms of representation in the House of Commons. The growing strength of its power base in local government is also striking. For most of the lifetime of the Liberal Democrat Party it has had more than 4,000 councillors. Additionally, Liberal Democrats have shared power in coalitions in Scotland and Wales, and maintained a presence in the European Parliament. The party has grown up. As one writer has put it, the Liberal Democrats are now some way down a path transforming them from being 'a movement of protest and centre-left posturing into a centrist party of government'.[6] The first-past-the-post electoral system continues to work against the party at Westminster, but its effects have been somewhat mitigated by a successful policy of targeting effort on winnable seats. The party is also associated more clearly in the public mind than was the case in the early stages of its revival, with specific policies on, for example, taxation, the environment, and defence and foreign affairs. This makes its electoral support less dependent on the protest vote, a negative endorsement based on voter disillusionment with periods of Labour and Conservative government. Even so, Liberals and Liberal Democrats have not always made it easy to attract consistent voter allegiance, which perhaps explains why, to this day, the party's vote is less reliable and less loyal than that of either of its main rivals. For around a quarter of a century, beginning with Jo Grimond, Liberal leaders positioned their party as a radical, non-socialist alternative to Labour, while nurturing hopes of a realignment of the centre-left. At the height of Labour's internal disputes of the 1980s, Liberals (and the Alliance) spoke optimistically of replacing Labour as Britain's main non-Conservative force, but by the 1990s they moved again towards a realignment strategy as the only means of removing the Tories from power. Ironically, some would say inexplicably, throughout this period the party was seen by the electorate as being closer to the Conservatives than to Labour. In the first years of the twenty-first century, Charles Kennedy talked of replacing the Conservatives, but succeeded at the same time in positioning his party to the left of Labour on a number of issues. Only then did the voters see the Liberal Democrats as leaning towards Labour, yet the decade ended in the formation of a Conservative–Liberal Democrat government.[7] Even if, as academic investigation has shown, the party draws its strength disproportionately from the educated professional and managerial classes and attracts a high percentage of university graduates, its chequered course has sometimes challenged comprehension and has not been best designed to consolidate voter loyalty.

The prospects for the coalition itself remain uncertain. 'Leading the Liberal Democrats,' maintains Vince Cable, 'is like leading a biblical tribe of nomadic pastoralists across a semi-arid landscape, constantly looking for the water of favourable publicity. There are frequent droughts for which the leader is held responsible. What sustains us is a sense that there is a promised land.'[8] If the promised land remains beyond the horizon, Liberal Democrats must hope that participation in government has finally broken the two-party stranglehold that has dominated British politics since the 1920s. But many of them fear that Clegg will only succeed in consigning his party to opposition for decades to come. The next few years should reveal which of these two scenarios is nearer to the truth.

Chronology of Main Events

1899	Sir Henry Campbell-Bannerman becomes Liberal leader.
1900	Unionists win General Election held during Boer War.
1902	End of Boer War and Unionist Education Act help heal Liberal divisions.
1903	Joseph Chamberlain launches tariff reform campaign. MacDonald–Gladstone Pact concluded.
1905	Balfour resigns. Campbell-Bannerman forms minority Liberal administration.
1906	Landslide Liberal victory in General Election. Trades Disputes Act.
1908	H. H. Asquith succeeds Campbell-Bannerman as Prime Minister. Lloyd George moves to Exchequer.
1909	People's Budget rejected by House of Lords. Constitutional Crisis begins.
1910	Two General Elections leave Liberals in office, but dependent on Irish Nationalists and Labour for parliamentary majority.
1911	Parliament Act removes Lords' veto. National Insurance Act introduces benefits for sickness and unemployment.
1913	Lloyd George launches Land Campaign.
1914	Deadlock over Irish Home Rule circumvented by outbreak of First World War. Two cabinet ministers resign. Defence of the Realm Act.
1915	Formation of first wartime coalition.
1916	Conscription introduced. Lloyd George replaces Asquith. Coalition now dominated by Tories.
1918	Franchise greatly extended by Representation of the People Act. Maurice Debate and Coupon Election harden Liberal divisions. Independent Liberal Party reduced to a parliamentary rump.
1921	First Liberal Summer School.

1922	Labour replaces the still divided Liberals as the Official Opposition.
1923	Liberals reunite uneasily in defence of free trade. Partial Liberal recovery in General Election.
1924	Disastrous Liberal performance in General Election after sustaining first Labour government.
1926	General Strike. Lloyd George replaces Asquith as party leader.
1928	The 'Yellow Book' suggests revival of Liberalism as intellectual force.
1929	Liberals secure nearly a quarter of the popular vote, but only 59 seats in General Election.
1931	Further Liberal splits over policy towards second Labour government. Formation of National Government with Liberal representation. Herbert Samuel replaces Lloyd George as leader.
1932	Split between Liberals and Liberal Nationals confirmed. Former leave government.
1935	General Election sees Liberal strength reduced to 21 MPs. Archibald Sinclair replaces Samuel.
1939	Outbreak of Second World War. Liberals decline to serve in government under Neville Chamberlain.
1940	Liberals join Churchill Coalition. Sinclair at Air Ministry.
1942	Beveridge Report published.
1945	Coalition dissolved. Liberals reduced to 12 MPs at General Election. Clement Davies chosen as leader.
1947	Woolton–Teviot Agreement allows for amalgamation of Liberal Nationals and Conservatives at constituency level.
1950	Disastrous Liberal performance at General Election. Only nine MPs elected.
1951	General Election sees further reduction to six MPs, but Clement Davies preserves party's independence by declining Churchill's offer of cabinet post.
1955	Liberals retain six seats at General Election. First faint suggestion of revival, or at least stabilization.
1956	Suez Crisis dispels notion of Conservative–Liberal affinity. Davies replaced by Jo Grimond.
1958	Mark Bonham Carter wins Torrington by-election. First by-election gain since 1929.

1959	General Election sees significant increase in Liberal vote. Possibility of realignment of political left after third successive Labour defeat.
1962	Eric Lubbock wins famous Orpington by-election.
1964	Labour narrowly wins power. Liberal representation increases to nine MPs.
1966	Liberals win 12 seats at General Election, but large Labour majority takes realignment off the political agenda.
1967	Grimond replaced by Jeremy Thorpe.
1970	Liberals fall back to six seats at General Election. Party Assembly votes in favour of 'Community Politics'.
1972–3	Five Liberal by-election gains at expense of unpopular Conservative government.
1974	Liberals secure six million votes but only 14 seats at General Election. Talks on possible Conservative–Liberal Coalition break down over Proportional Representation. Second election in October sees Liberal strength decline slightly to 13 seats.
1975	EEC referendum sees Liberals campaign alongside pro-European Tories and Labour ministers.
1976	Thorpe resigns amid allegations about his private life. Succeeded by David Steel.
1977	Lib–Lab Pact sustains minority Callaghan government in power.
1978	Lib–Lab Pact ends.
1979	Conservatives return to power under Margaret Thatcher. Liberals fall to 11 MPs.
1981	Social Democratic Party founded by so-called 'Gang of Four' Labour defectors. In partnership with the Liberals the 'Alliance' achieves stunning initial success.
1983	Alliance wins 25.4 per cent of the vote at General Election, but only 23 seats.
1986	Tensions within Alliance revealed, especially over defence policy.
1987	Alliance secures 22.6 per cent of the vote and 22 MPs at General Election. Immediate calls for merger of two parties opposed by SDP leader, David Owen.

1988	Fused party, initially called 'Social and Liberal Democrats' under leadership of Paddy Ashdown, gets off to uncertain start.
1989	SLD pushed into fourth place by Greens in European elections. Name changed to Liberal Democrats.
1990	Victory in Eastbourne by-election signals restoration of party's fortunes.
1992	Liberal Democrats win 20 seats in General Election on 17.8 per cent of vote. Chard speech by Ashdown signals end of policy of 'equidistance'.
1994	Arrival of Tony Blair and 'New Labour' presents both opportunities and dangers for Liberal Democrats.
1997	Liberal Democrat vote falls but 46 seats captured in General Election as a result of successful targeting and tactical voting. Labour landslide removes need for Labour–Lib Dem coalition.
1998	Labour government fails to endorse Jenkins Report on electoral reform.
1999	Ashdown resigns and is replaced by Charles Kennedy. Liberal Democrats enter coalition in Scottish parliament.
2000	Liberal Democrats enter coalition in Welsh Assembly.
2001	Party wins 52 seats in General Election.
2003	Opposition to war in Iraq gives Liberal Democrats distinctive policy stance.
2004	Party pushes Labour into third place in local elections. Publication of *The Orange Book* indicates revival of economic liberalism.
2005	Liberal Democrats secure 62 seats in General Election.
2006	Kennedy forced to resign after belatedly admitting drinking problem. Sir Menzies Campbell chosen to replace him.
2007	Indifferent poll ratings force Campbell's resignation. Vince Cable performs well as acting leader, but Nick Clegg chosen as Campbell's successor.
2009	Scandal over MPs' expenses sees mounting disillusionment with political class.
2010	General Election campaign transformed by Clegg's performance in first televised debate between party leaders. Liberal Democrats hold balance in hung parliament.

After five days of intense negotiations Conservative–Liberal Democrat Coalition is formed with five Lib Dem cabinet ministers.

2011   Decisive 'No' vote in AV referendum. Liberal vote falls sharply in local, Scottish and Welsh elections.

Appendix 1: Liberal Performance at General Elections since 1900

Year	A	B	C	D
1900	670	406	184	44.6
1906	670	539	400	49.0
1910 (Jan.)	670	516	275	43.2
1910 (Dec.)	670	467	272	43.9
1918[a]	707	411	161	25.6
1922[a]	615	490	116	29.1
1923	615	453	159	29.6
1924	615	340	40	17.6
1929	615	513	59	23.4
1931[b]	615	119	37	7.0
1935[b]	615	161	21	6.4
1945	640	306	12	9.0
1950	625	475	9	9.1
1951	625	109	6	2.6
1955	630	110	6	2.7
1959	630	216	6	5.9
1964	630	365	9	11.2
1966	630	311	12	8.5
1970	630	332	6	7.5
1974 (Feb.)	635	517	14	19.3
1974 (Oct.)	635	619	13	18.3
1979	635	577	11	13.8
1983[c]	650	633	23	25.4
1987[c]	650	633	22	22.6
1992[d]	651	632	20	17.8
1997[d]	659	639	46	16.8
2001[d]	659	639	52	18.3
2005[d]	646	626	62	22.0
2010[d]	650	631	57	23.0

Key:

A Number of seats in the House of Commons
B Number of Liberal candidates
C Number of Liberal MPs elected
D Liberal percentage of the total vote

Notes:

[a] Figures for supporters of Lloyd George and Asquith are combined.

[b] Excludes Liberal Nationals but includes followers of Lloyd George.

[c] Includes figures for Social Democrat wing of the Alliance.

[d] The Liberal Democrats.

Appendix 2: Leaders of the Liberal (and Liberal Democrat) Party since 1900

Party Leader

1899	Sir Henry Campbell-Bannerman
1908	Herbert Henry Asquith (from 1925, Earl of Oxford and Asquith)
1926	David Lloyd George
1931	Sir Herbert Samuel
1935	Sir Archibald Sinclair
1945	Clement Davies[a]
1956	Jo Grimond
1967	Jeremy Thorpe
1976	David Steel
1988	Paddy Ashdown
1999	Charles Kennedy
2006	Sir Menzies Campbell
2007	Nick Clegg

Leader in the House of Lords

1900	Earl of Kimberley
1902	Earl Spencer
1905	Marquess of Ripon
1908	Marquess of Crewe
1923	Viscount Grey
1924	Earl Beauchamp
1931	Marquess of Reading
1936	Marquess of Crewe

---

[a] Technically, Davies was only Leader of the Parliamentary Party

1944	Viscount Samuel
1955	Lord Rea
1967	Lord Byers
1984	Lady Seear
1988	Lord Jenkins
1997	Lord Rodgers
2001	Lady Williams
2004	Lord McNally
2010	Lord Shutt

Notes

Introduction

1. M. Bentley, *The Climax of Liberal Politics: British Liberalism in Theory and Practice 1868–1918* (London, 1987), p. 123.
2. M. Pottle (ed.), *Daring to Hope: The Diaries and Letters of Violet Bonham Carter* (London, 2000), p. 178.
3. R. Muir, *The Liberal Way* (London, 1934), p. 169.
4. Cited in M. Pugh, *The Making of Modern British Politics 1867–1939* (Oxford, 1982), p. 22.
5. S. Koss, *Asquith* (London, 1976), p. 30.
6. A. Sykes, *The Rise and Fall of British Liberalism 1776–1988* (London, 1997), p. 269.
7. H. C. G. Matthew (ed.), *The Gladstone Diaries*, Vol. XI (Oxford, 1990), p. 341.
8. Bentley, *Climax*, p. 106.
9. J. Spender, *Sir Robert Hudson: A Memoir* (London, 1930), p. 53.
10. Cited in D. Tanner, *Political Change and the Labour Party 1900–1918* (Cambridge, 1990), p. 60.
11. John Rylands Library, University of Manchester, MacDonald MSS, RMD/1/1/10, MacDonald to W. Allard, Secretary Home Counties Division, National Liberal Federation, 9 December 1893.
12. Ibid., RMD/1/1/27, J. Randolph to E. Pease 10 May 1894.
13. University of Liverpool Library, Bruce Glasier MSS, GP/1/1/569, Glasier to K. Hardie, 21 October 1902.
14. L. T. Hobhouse, *Democracy and Reaction* (London, 1904), pp. 209–10.
15. M. Rathbone, 'The Rainbow Circle and the New Liberalism', *Journal of Liberal History*, 38 (2003), p. 26.
16. R. Barker, 'Socialism and Progressivism in the Political Thought of Ramsay MacDonald', in A. J. A. Morris (ed.), *Edwardian Radicalism 1900–1914* (London, 1974), p. 116.
17. Koss, *Asquith*, p. 77.
18. P. Clarke, *Liberals and Social Democrats* (Cambridge, 1978), p. 63.

1 Strange Death or Edwardian Summer, 1902–16?

1. L. S. Amery, *My Political Life*, Vol. 1 (London, 1953), p. 235.
2. H. W. McCready, 'The Revolt of the Unionist Free Traders', *Parliamentary Affairs*, 16 (1963), p. 188.

3. A. K. Russell, *Liberal Landslide: The General Election of 1906* (Newton Abbot, 1973), p. 145.
4. Bodleian Library, Oxford, Selborne MSS 2/118, St John Brodrick to Selborne, 24 November 1905; W. A. S. Hewins, *The Apologia of an Imperialist*, Vol. 1 (London, 1929), p. 155.
5. P. F. Clarke, *Lancashire and the New Liberalism* (Cambridge, 1971), p. 375.
6. *Northern Daily Telegraph*, 22 December 1905, cited in Clarke, *Lancashire*, pp. 355–6.
7. Russell, *Liberal Landslide*, p. 71.
8. Clarke, *Lancashire*, p. 234.
9. A. Sykes, *The Rise and Fall of British Liberalism 1776–1988* (London, 1997), p. 270.
10. Clarke, *Lancashire*, p. 398.
11. Crewe to Campbell-Bannerman, 14 November 1905, cited in Russell, *Liberal Landslide*, p. 33.
12. Campbell-Bannerman to Asquith, 17 January 1906, cited in Russell, *Liberal Landslide*, p. 210.
13. J. F. Harris and C. Hazlehurst, 'Campbell-Bannerman as Prime Minister', *History*, 55 (1970), p. 376.
14. Ibid., pp. 382–3.
15. University of Liverpool Library, Bruce Glasier MSS, GP/1/1/812, Glasier to Elizabeth Glasier-Foster, 5 July 1907.
16. C. Hazlehurst, 'Asquith as Prime Minister, 1908–1916', *English Historical Review*, 85 (1970), p. 514.
17. J. M. McEwen (ed.), *The Riddell Diaries: A Selection* (London, 1986), p. 39.
18. Ibid., p. 43.
19. E. David (ed.), *Inside Asquith's Cabinet: From the Diaries of Charles Hobhouse* (London, 1977), p. 74.
20. B. K. Murray, 'The Politics of the "People's Budget"', *The Historical Journal*, 16 (1973), pp. 555–70; J. Grigg, *Lloyd George: The People's Champion 1902–1911* (London, 1978), p. 180.
21. S. Koss, *Asquith* (London, 1976), p. 103.
22. N. Blewett, *The Peers, the Parties and the People: The General Elections of 1910* (London, 1972), p. 407.
23. N. and J. MacKenzie (eds), *The Diary of Beatrice Webb*, Vol. 3 (London, 1984), p. 149.
24. Ibid., p. 134.
25. McEwen (ed.), *Riddell Diaries*, p. 46.
26. B. K. Murray, *The People's Budget: Lloyd George and Liberal Politics* (Oxford, 1980), p. 54.
27. G. Dangerfield, *The Damnable Question* (London, 1979), p. 53.
28. David (ed.), *Inside Asquith's Cabinet*, p. 171.
29. W. S. Churchill, *The World Crisis*, Vol. 1 (paperback edn, 1968), p. 114.
30. McEwen (ed.), *Riddell Diaries*, p. 64.
31. T. Morgan, *Churchill: Young Man in a Hurry 1874–1915* (New York, 1982), p. 315.
32. McEwen (ed.), *Riddell Diaries*, p. 76.

33. T. Wilson (ed.), *The Political Diaries of C. P. Scott 1911–1928* (London, 1970), p. 70.
34. I. Packer, *Lloyd George, Liberalism and the Land: The Land Issue and Party Politics in England, 1906–1914* (Woodbridge, 2001), p. 194.
35. House of Lords Record Office, Bonar Law MSS 39/4/40, Steel-Maitland to Law, 23 June 1914.
36. B. K. Murray, ' "Battered and Shattered": Lloyd George and the 1914 Budget Fiasco', *Albion*, 23(3) (1991), p. 503.
37. Carrington diary, 8 July 1914, cited ibid., p. 505.
38. M. and E. Brock (eds), *H. H. Asquith: Letters to Venetia Stanley* (paperback edn, Oxford, 1985), p. 89.
39. B. B. Gilbert, 'David Lloyd George: The Reform of British Land-Holding and the Budget of 1914', *The Historical Journal*, 21(1) (1978), p. 141.
40. I. Packer, 'The Liberal Cave and the 1914 Budget', *English Historical Review* 442 (1996), pp. 621, 628.
41. Liverpool Record Office, Holt-Durning MSS, Holt diary, 19 July 1914.
42. David (ed.), *Inside Asquith's Cabinet*, p. 125.
43. P. Stansky, cited in C. W. White, ' "The Strange Death of Liberal England" in its Time', *Albion*, 17 (1985), p. 446.
44. T. Wilson, *The Downfall of the Liberal Party 1914–1935* (London, 1966), p. 17.
45. G. Dangerfield, *The Strange Death of Liberal England* (London, 1936), p. 10.
46. The 'franchise factor' is discussed below; see pp. 71–3.
47. H. Pelling, 'Labour and the Downfall of Liberalism', in H. Pelling, *Popular Politics and Society in Late Victorian Britain* (London, 1968), p. 120.
48. Ibid., p. 118.
49. R. McKibbin, *The Evolution of the Labour Party 1910–1924* (paperback edn, Oxford, 1983), pp. xiv, 244.
50. Wilson, *Downfall*; Clarke, *Lancashire*.
51. Clarke, *Lancashire*, p. 406.
52. Ibid., p. 6.
53. Samuel Storey, Chairman of the Northern Liberal Federation, cited in G. R. Searle, *The Liberal Party: Triumph and Disintegration, 1886–1929* (Basingstoke, 1992), p. 72.
54. Memorandum by J. Herbert for H. Gladstone, 6 March 1903, cited in F. Bealey, 'Negotiations between the Liberal Party and the Labour Representation Committee before the General Election of 1906', *Bulletin of the Institute of Historical Research*, 29 (1956), p. 266.
55. Gladstone memorandum, 6 March 1903, cited in Clarke, *Lancashire*, p. 314.
56. Gladstone memorandum, 13 March 1903, cited in D. Powell, 'The New Liberalism and the Rise of Labour, 1886–1906', *The Historical Journal*, 29 (1986), p. 383.

57. F. Bealey and H. Pelling, *Labour and Politics 1900–1906* (London, 1958), p. 155.

58. Bryce to Goldwin Smith, 16 June 1906, cited in M. Petter, 'The Progressive Alliance', *History*, 58 (1973), p. 45.

59. Clarke, *Lancashire*, p. 376; J. A. Spender, *Sir Robert Hudson: A Memoir* (London, 1930), p. 198.

60. J. Herbert to H. Gladstone, 6 February 1906, cited in Bealey, 'Negotiations', p. 273.

61. Powell, 'New Liberalism', p. 383.

62. C. Hazlehurst and C. Woodland (eds), *A Liberal Chronicle: Journals and Papers of J. A. Pease, 1908 to 1910* (London, 1994), p. 141.

63. Petter, 'Progressive Alliance', p. 48.

64. Cited A. Hetherington, *The Guardian Years* (London, 1981), p. 326.

65. R. Douglas, 'Labour in Decline 1910–14', in K. D. Brown (ed.), *Essays in Anti-Labour History* (London, 1974), p. 125.

66. *The Nation*, 31 January 1914, cited in Petter, 'Progressive Alliance', p. 49.

67. Douglas, 'Labour in Decline', p. 124.

68. McKibbin, *Evolution*, p. 71.

69. Petter, 'Progressive Alliance', p. 60; G. L. Bernstein, 'Liberalism and the Progressive Alliance in the Constituencies, 1900–1914: Three Case Studies', *The Historical Journal*, 26 (1983), p. 637.

70. K. Laybourn and J. Reynolds, *Liberalism and the Rise of Labour 1890–1918* (London, 1984), p. 154.

71. A. W. Purdue, 'The Liberal and Labour Parties in North-East Politics, 1900–14: The Struggle for Supremacy', *International Review of Social History*, 26 (1981), p. 15.

72. P. Thompson, *Socialists, Liberals and Labour: The Struggle for London 1885–1914* (London, 1967), pp. 295–6. It should be noted that both Peter Clarke and Neal Blewett have questioned Thompson's conclusions and believe that his findings are compatible with growing working-class support for the Liberal Party.

73. C. Cook, 'Labour and the Downfall of the Liberal Party, 1906–14', in A. Sked and C. Cook (eds), *Crisis and Controversy: Essays in Honour of A. J. P. Taylor* (London, 1976), pp. 55, 58, 62.

74. D. Tanner, *Political Change and the Labour Party 1900–1918* (Cambridge, 1990), p. 317.

75. Ibid., p. 332.

76. Ibid., p. 337.

77. B. B. Gilbert, *David Lloyd George: The Architect of Change 1863–1912* (London, 1987), p. 290.

78. McEwen, *Riddell Diaries*, p. 44.

79. Tanner, *Political Change*, p. 44.

80. Searle, *The Liberal Party*, p. 85.

81. M. Bentley, *The Climax of Liberal Politics: British Liberalism in Theory and Practice 1868–1918* (London, 1987), p. 144.

82. Powell, 'New Liberalism', p. 383.

83. G. L. Bernstein, *Liberalism and Liberal Politics in Edwardian England* (London, 1986), p. 200.

84. Hazlehurst and Woodland (eds), *Liberal Chronicle*, p. 74.
85. Wilson (ed.), *Political Diaries of C. P. Scott*, pp. 100–1.
86. Bernstein, 'Three Case Studies', pp. 617–40.
87. Laybourn and Reynolds, *Liberalism and Rise of Labour*, pp. 168, 173.
88. M. D. Pugh, 'Yorkshire and the New Liberalism', *Journal of Modern History*, 50(3) (1978), p. D1155.
89. Purdue, 'Liberal and Labour Parties', pp. 1–24; K. O. Morgan, 'The New Liberalism and the Challenge of Labour: The Welsh Experience, 1885–1929', in Brown (ed.), *Essays in Anti-Labour History*, pp. 163–4.
90. K. Laybourn, *The Rise of Labour: The British Labour Party 1890–1979* (London, 1988), p. 26.
91. Glasier MSS, GP/1/1/944, Glasier to Hardie, 17 December 1908.
92. C. Wrigley, 'Labour and the Trade Unions', in K. D. Brown (ed.), *The First Labour Party 1906–1914* (London, 1985), p. 151.
93. Bentley, *Climax*, p. 124.
94. Searle, *The Liberal Party*, p. 122.
95. K. O. Morgan, *The Age of Lloyd George: The Liberal Party and British Politics, 1890–1929* (London, 1978), p. 58.
96. Wilson, *Downfall*, p. 18.
97. R. Douglas, *The History of the Liberal Party 1895–1970* (London, 1971), p. 91.
98. C. Addison, *Politics from Within*, Vol. 1 (London, 1924), p. 38.
99. Holt diary, 2 August 1914.
100. Ibid., 9 August 1914.
101. John Rylands Library, University of Manchester, MacDonald MSS, RMD/1/3/1, Trevelyan to MacDonald, 7 August 1914 and MacDonald's later annotation.
102. I. Packer (ed.), *The Letters of Arnold Stephen Rowntree to May Katherine Rowntree, 1910–1918* (London, 2002), pp. 159–60.
103. R. E. Dowse, 'The Entry of the Liberals into the Labour Party, 1910–1920', *Yorkshire Bulletin of Economic and Social Research*, 13 (1961), p. 86.
104. MacDonald MSS, Trevelyan to MacDonald, 6 January 1924.
105. William Llewelyn Williams, MP for Carmarthen District, 5 July 1915, cited in E. David, 'The Liberal Party Divided 1916–1918', *The Historical Journal*, 13 (1970), p. 511.
106. MacDonald MSS, RMD/1/3/41, Trevelyan to Simon, 22 August 1915.
107. McEwen (ed.), *Riddell Diaries*, p. 95.
108. McKibbin, *Evolution*, p. 238.
109. G. Bernstein, 'Yorkshire Liberalism during the First World War', *The Historical Journal*, 32 (1989), pp. 107–29.
110. M. D. Pugh, 'Asquith, Bonar Law and the First Coalition', *The Historical Journal*, 17 (1974), p. 813.
111. V. Bonham Carter, *Winston Churchill as I Knew Him* (London, 1965), p. 404.
112. Holt diary, 30 May 1915.

113. Newcastle University, Runciman MSS 136, Hobhouse to Runciman, 28 May 1915.
114. C. Hazlehurst, *Politicians at War July 1914 to May 1915: A Prologue to the Triumph of Lloyd George* (London, 1971), pp. 286–7.
115. Holt diary, 20 June 1915.
116. *The Nation*, 22 May 1915, cited in Wilson, *Downfall*, p. 80.
117. R. Jenkins, *Asquith* (London, 1964), p. 371.
118. Bodleian Library, Oxford, Simon MSS, SP52, fols 26–7, Asquith to Simon, McKenna and Runciman, 28 December 1915.
119. *The Nation*, 1 January 1916, cited in Wilson, *Downfall*, p. 82.
120. McEwen (ed.), *Riddell Diaries*, p. 138.
121. P. F. Clarke, *Liberals and Social Democrats* (Cambridge, 1978), p. 181.
122. Packer (ed.), *Letters of Arnold Stephen Rowntree*, p. 198.
123. Hazlehurst, 'Asquith as Prime Minister', p. 530.
124. Wilson (ed.), *Political Diaries of C. P. Scott*, p. 216.
125. Jenkins, *Asquith*, p. 410.
126. D. Lloyd George, *War Memoirs*, Vol. 2 (London, 1933), p. 997.
127. Clarke, *Lancashire*, p. 394.
128. Wilson (ed.), *Political Diaries of C. P. Scott*, p. 242.

2   The Liberal Civil War, 1916–35

1. Liverpool Record Office, Richard Holt MSS, diary, 10 December 1916.
2. A. J. P Taylor, 'Politics in the First World War', in A. J. P. Taylor (ed.), *Politics in Wartime* (London, 1964), p. 32; E. David, 'The Liberal Party Divided, 1916–1918', *The Historical Journal*, 13 (1970), pp. 527, 529, 531.
3. B. McGill, 'Asquith's Predicament, 1914–1918', *Journal of Modern History*, 39 (1967), p. 297.
4. T. Wilson, *The Downfall of the Liberal Party 1914–1935* (London, 1966), p. 123.
5. Ibid., p. 125.
6. D. Tanner, *Political Change and the Labour Party 1900–1918* (Cambridge, 1990), p. 382.
7. House of Lords Record Office, Lloyd George MSS F/21/2/30, Guest to Lloyd George, 3 August 1918.
8. Holt diary, 18 December 1917.
9. R. Douglas, 'The Background to the "Coupon" Election Arrangements', *English Historical Review*, 86 (1971), p. 322.
10. D. Dutton (ed.), *Paris 1918: The War Diary of the British Ambassador, the 17th Earl of Derby* (Liverpool, 2001), p. 316.
11. Douglas, 'Background', p. 329.
12. Asquith to Spender, 6 October 1926, cited in S. Ball, 'Asquith's Decline and the General Election of 1918', *Scottish Historical Review*, LXI(171) (1982), p. 61.
13. Memorandum by Gladstone, 18 November 1924, cited in M. Hart, 'The Decline of the Liberal Party in Parliament and in the Constituencies', Oxford D. Phil. thesis (1982), p. 145.

14. Crewe to Grey, 12 June 1928, cited Hart, 'The Decline', p. 93.
15. Manchester Central Library, E. D. Simon MSS, M11/11/5 addtl, diary, 16 November 1918.
16. P. Harris, *Forty Years In and Out of Parliament* (London, n.d.), p. 76.
17. G. Bernstein, 'Yorkshire Liberalism during the First World War', *The Historical Journal*, 32 (1989), p. 129.
18. E. D. Simon MSS, M11/11/5 addtl, diary, 27 April and 15 December 1918.
19. Ibid., 15 December 1918.
20. M. Pugh, *The Making of Modern British Politics* (Oxford, 1982), p. 201.
21. H. C. G. Matthew, R. I. McKibbin and J. A. Kay, 'The Franchise Factor in the Rise of the Labour Party', *English Historical Review*, 91 (1976), pp. 723–52.
22. Ibid., p. 740.
23. D. Tanner, 'The Parliamentary Electoral System, the "Fourth" Reform Act and the Rise of Labour in England and Wales', *Bulletin of the Institute of Historical Research*, 56 (1983), pp. 205–19.
24. M. Childs, 'Labour Grows Up: The Electoral System, Political Generations, and British Politics 1890–1929', *Twentieth Century British History*, 6(2) (1995), p. 142.
25. Holt diary, 15 and 23 December 1918.
26. E. D. Simon MSS, M 11/11/5 addtl, diary, 15 December 1918.
27. Viscount Simon, *Retrospect* (London, 1952), p. 121.
28 Lloyd George MSS F/40/2/24, Montagu to Lloyd George, 16 November 1918.
29. University of Liverpool Library, Veitch MSS D40/15, Muir to G. Veitch, 25 October 1928.
30. R. Jenkins, *Asquith* (London, 1986), p. 517.
31. A. C. Murray's diary, 12 May 1920, cited in Wilson, *Downfall*, p. 212.
32. M. Bentley, *The Liberal Mind 1914–1929* (Cambridge, 1977), p. 66.
33. St Deiniol's Library, Hawarden, Glynne-Gladstone MSS 965, Henry Gladstone to Herbert Gladstone, 10 March 1921.
34. Newcastle University, Runciman MSS 177, McKenna to Runciman, 4 January 1919.
35. Cecil to Runciman, 24 January 1920, cited in M. Bentley, 'Liberal Politics and the Grey Conspiracy of 1921', *The Historical Journal*, 20 (1977), p. 465.
36. Herbert Gladstone to Henry Gladstone, 27 February 1921, cited ibid., p. 467.
37. E. D. Simon MSS, M/11/11/5 addtl, diary 7 February 1920.
38. R. Muir, *An Autobiography and Some Essays* (London, 1943), p. 181.
39. Wilson, *Downfall*, p. 216.
40. Glynne-Gladstone MSS 964, Henry Gladstone to Herbert Gladstone, 3 April 1919.
41. M. Bentley, 'The Liberal Response to Socialism 1918–29', in K. D. Brown (ed.), *Essays in Anti-Labour History: Responses to the Rise of Labour in Britain* (London, 1974), p. 47.
42. Glynne-Gladstone MSS 964–5, Henry Gladstone to Herbert Gladstone, 30 August 1919 and 26 February 1922.

43. P. F. Clarke in V. Bogdanor (ed.), *Liberal Party Politics* (Oxford, 1983), p. 36.
44. E. D. Simon MSS, M/11/11/5 addtl, diary, 2 June 1920.
45. Ibid., diary, 2 October 1921.
46. D. Cregier, *Chiefs without Indians* (Washington, 1982), pp. 149–63.
47. Glynne-Gladstone MSS 965, Henry Gladstone to Herbert Gladstone, 18 November 1921.
48. Lord Riddell, *Intimate Diary of the Peace Conference and After 1918–1923* (London, 1933), p. 139.
49. K. Morgan, 'Lloyd George's Stage Army: The Coalition Liberals 1918–22', in A. J. P. Taylor (ed.), *Lloyd George: Twelve Essays* (London, 1971), p. 246.
50. J. Ramsden (ed.), *Real Old Tory Politics* (London, 1984), p. 131.
51. *The Nation*, 11 November 1922, cited in M. Kinnear, *The Fall of Lloyd George: The Political Crisis of 1922* (London, 1973), p. 135.
52. T. Wilson (ed.), *The Political Diaries of C. P. Scott 1911–1928* (London, 1970), p. 434.
53. S. Koss, *Asquith* (London, 1976), p. 255.
54. M. Pottle (ed.), *Champion Redoubtable: The Diaries and Letters of Violet Bonham Carter 1914–1945* (London, 1998), p. 137.
55. Bodleian Library, Oxford, J. Simon MSS, SP 5, diary 18 November 1922.
56. Wilson (ed.), *Political Diaries of C. P. Scott*, p. 433.
57. J. Campbell, *Lloyd George: The Goat in the Wilderness 1922–1931* (London, 1977), p. 58.
58. Hart, 'Decline of the Liberal Party', p. 205.
59. C. Cook, *The Age of Alignment: Electoral Politics in Britain 1922–1929* (London, 1975), p. 92.
60. Jenkins, *Asquith*, p. 498.
61. E. D. Simon MSS, M 11/11, diary, 21 January 1924.
62. *The Times*, 19 December 1923.
63. E. D. Simon MSS, M 11/11, diary, 21 January 1924.
64. Ibid., note by Simon, 22 February 1924.
65. Ibid., note by Simon, March 1925.
66. MacDonald to G. Murray 10 October 1924, cited in Bentley, 'Liberal Response', p. 57.
67. Speech at Llanfairfechan, 22 April 1924, cited in Campbell, *Goat*, pp. 94–5.
68. Wilson (ed.), *Political Diaries of C. P. Scott*, p. 462.
69. Harris, *Forty Years*, p. 97.
70. E. D. Simon MSS, M/11/11, parliamentary diary for 1924, March 1925.
71. House of Lords Record Office, Stansgate MSS, ST/66, diary, 20 February 1924.
72. Glynne-Gladstone MSS 966, Henry Gladstone to Herbert Gladstone, 14 January 1924.
73. House of Commons Debates, 5th Series, vol. 169, col. 601.
74. University of Birmingham, Chamberlain MSS, AC 35/4/19, Chamberlain to S. Hoare, 28 January 1924.
75. Amery to Baldwin 21 December 1923, cited Campbell, *Goat*, p. 87.

76. Stansgate MSS, ST/66, diary, 8 October 1924.
77. Hudson to Herbert Gladstone, 4 July 1924, cited in S. Koss, 'Asquith versus Lloyd George: The Last Phase and Beyond', in A. Sked and C. Cook (eds), *Crisis and Controversy: Essays in Honour of A. J. P. Taylor* (London, 1976), p. 80.
78. J. A. Spender, *Sir Robert Hudson: A Memoir* (London, 1930), p. 199.
79. V. Phillipps, *My Days and Ways* (Edinburgh, *c.*1943), p. 113.
80. Lloyd George to Viscount Inchcape, 5 November 1924, cited in R. Douglas, *History of the Liberal Party 1895–1970* (London, 1971), p. 184.
81. M. Cole (ed.), *Beatrice Webb's Diaries, 1924–1932* (London, 1956), p. 48.
82. G. Searle, *The Liberal Party: Triumph and Disintegration, 1886–1929* (Basingstoke, 1992), p. 154.
83. C. Cook, 'Liberals, Labour and Local Elections' in G. Peele and C. Cook (eds), *The Politics of Reappraisal 1918–1939* (London, 1975), pp. 166–88.
84. Stansgate MSS, ST/66, diary, 10 November 1924.
85. Glynne-Gladstone MSS 966, Henry Gladstone to Herbert Gladstone, 30 October 1924.
86. British Library Add. MS 46477, Gladstone MSS, Runciman to Herbert Gladstone, 21 November 1924.
87. J. M. Keynes, *Essays in Persuasion* (London, 1931), p. 343.
88. E. D. Simon, *The Inheritance of Riches* (London, 1925), p. 12.
89. Gladstone to Samuel, 30 April 1927, cited in Campbell, *Goat*, p. 159.
90. E. D. Simon MSS, M/11/11/5, diary, 27 February 1925.
91. *Daily Chronicle*, 1 November 1924, cited in Campbell, *Goat*, p. 108.
92. A. J. P. Taylor (ed.), *Lloyd George: A Diary by Frances Stevenson* (London, 1971), p. 246.
93. Wilson (ed.), *Political Diaries of C. P. Scott*, p. 472.
94. Lady Kennet's diary, January 1925, cited in Koss, 'Asquith versus Lloyd George', p. 82.
95. A. J. P. Taylor (ed.), *My Darling Pussy: The Letters of Lloyd George and Frances Stevenson 1913–41* (London, 1975), p. 101.
96. Hart, 'Decline of the Liberal Party', p. 225.
97. J. Simon MSS, SP 60, Simon and others to Asquith, 31 May 1926.
98. Ibid., memorandum by J. Rowland Evans, 20 June 1926.
99. Holt diary, 24 October 1926.
100. *Manchester Guardian*, 19 October 1926.
101. Pottle (ed.), *Champion Redoubtable*, p. 171.
102. Holt diary, 25 November 1926.
103. Pottle (ed.), *Champion Redoubtable*, p. 171.
104. J. Wallace, 'The Political Career of Walter Runciman, First Viscount Runciman of Doxford', Ph.D. thesis, Newcastle University, 1995, p. 291.
105. E. D. Simon MSS, M/11/11/5, diary, 1929–35.
106. Taylor (ed.), *Darling Pussy*, p. 108.
107. Ibid., p. 121.

108. Glynne-Gladstone MSS 968–9, Henry Gladstone to Herbert Gladstone, 15 October 1928 and 19 April 1929.
109. Holt diary, 29 March 1929.
110. Campbell, *Goat*, p. 230; *Manchester Guardian*, 16 May 1929.
111. British Library, Simon MSS Eur F77/5/56, Simon to Irwin, 6 June 1929.
112. Runciman MSS 221, note by D. Maclean, 14 June 1929.
113. E. D. Simon MSS, M/11/11/5, diary, 18 June 1929.
114. Ibid., diary, 27 July 1929.
115. Ibid., Simon to R. Hutchison, July 1930 (not sent).
116. O. Mosley, *My Life* (London, 1968), p. 249.
117. J. Simon MSS 249, Simon to Lloyd George, 25 October 1930.
118. E. D. Simon MSS, M/11/11/5, Simon to R. Hutchison, July 1930 (not sent).
119. F. Trentmann, *Free Trade Nation* (London, 2008), passim; J. Campbell, 'The Renewal of Liberalism: Liberalism without Liberals', in Peele and Cook (eds), *Politics of Reappraisal*, p. 94.
120. *Sunday News*, 1 March 1931.
121. E. D. Simon MSS, M/11/11/5, diary, 27 November 1930.
122. J. Simon MSS, SP 249, diary, 27 November 1930.
123. Churchill College, Cambridge, Thurso MSS I/17/4, Sinclair to V. Finney, 19 March 1931.
124. Lloyd George to Lansbury, 16 February 1931, cited in Campbell, *Goat*, p. 283.
125. J. Simon MSS, SP68, Simon to Sinclair, 26 June 1931.
126. T. Clarke, *My Lloyd George Diary* (London, 1939), p. 121; Beatrice Webb unpublished diary, 15 March 1931.
127. B. Wasserstein, *Herbert Samuel: A Political Life* (Oxford, 1992), p. 326.
128. Glynne-Gladstone MSS 945, report by Maclean, 19 September 1931.
129. Wasserstein, *Samuel*, p. 327.
130. K. Morgan, *The Age of Lloyd George: The Liberal Party and British Politics, 1890–1929* (London, 1978), p. 104.
131. Lloyd George to R. Muir, 13 April 1932, cited in T. Stannage, *Baldwin Thwarts the Opposition* (London, 1980), p. 88.
132. Flintshire Record Office, Henry Morris Jones MSS 12, diary, 2 October 1931.
133. Taylor (ed.), *Darling Pussy*, p. 192.
134. Morris Jones MSS 12, diary, 2 November 1931.
135. Glynne-Gladstone MSS 945, Maclean to Herbert Gladstone, 29 January 1932.
136. National Library of Wales, Clement Davies MSS C1/16, Davies to S. Clement-Davies, 3 November 1943.
137. J. Simon MSS, SP71, Simon to I. Macpherson, 5 February 1932.
138. *The Times*, 27 May 1932.
139. House of Lords Record Office, Samuel MSS A/89/26, MacDonald to Samuel, 10 September 1932.
140. University of Birmingham, Chamberlain MSS, NC 7/11/25/35, Runciman to N. Chamberlain, 21 September 1932.

141. Runciman MSS 254, Shakespeare to Simon, 23 September 1932.
142. Cambridge University Library, Baldwin MSS 46, Simon to Baldwin, 28 September 1932.
143. Wasserstein, *Samuel*, pp. 360–1.
144. Simon MSS, SP73, Baldwin to Simon, 26 October 1932.
145. E. Granville, 'The Liberal Resignations', *Contemporary Review*, November 1932, p. 539.
146. Thurso MSS, III/1/3, Sinclair to Samuel, 14 October 1933.
147. Ibid., II/1934/37, Samuel to Sinclair, 30 October 1933.
148. Morris Jones MSS, diary, 28 November 1932.
149. M. Baines, 'The Survival of the British Liberal Party 1932–1959', University of Oxford, D.Phil. thesis, 1991, p. 30.
150. D. Rees, 'The Disintegration of the Liberal Party 1931–33', MA thesis, University of Wales, 1980, p. 191.
151. Lloyd George MSS G/19/7/6, notes on the political situation, 26 November 1933.
152. A. Sinclair, 'Crossing the Floor', *Contemporary Review*, December 1933, p. 9.
153. G. De Groot, *Liberal Crusader: The Life of Sir Archibald Sinclair* (London, 1993), p. 98.
154. Memorandum by Lord Lothian, 16 November 1932, cited in M. Baines, 'The Samuelites and the National Government: A Study in Liberal Survival, August 1931–November 1933', MA thesis, University of Lancaster, 1983, p. 73.
155. West Briton, 26 March 1931, cited in G. Tregidga, *The Liberal Party in South-West Britain since 1918: Political Decline, Dormancy and Rebirth* (Exeter, 2000), p. 58.
156. De Groot, *Liberal Crusader*, p. 84.
157. R. Muir, *The Liberal Way* (London, 1934), p. 120.
158. Muir to Lothian, 29 October 1934, cited in De Groot, *Crusader*, p. 105.
159. Sinclair to Samuel, 21 January 1935, cited in De Groot, *Crusader*, p. 105.
160. Cook, 'Liberals, Labour and Local Elections', pp. 178–9.
161. Wilson, *Downfall*, p. 377.
162. Glynne-Gladstone MSS 945, Johnstone to Herbert Gladstone, n.d. (but 1932).
163. Tregidga, *Liberal Party in South-West Britain*, p. 83.
164. Johnstone to Lothian, 19 November 1934, cited in Stannage, *Baldwin Thwarts Opposition*, p. 104.
165. Stannage, *Baldwin Thwarts Opposition*, p. 207.

3 So Few and So Futile, 1935–55

1. C. Cook, *A Short History of the Liberal Party 1900–1976* (London, 1976), p. 124.
2. M. Steed, 'The Liberal Party', in H. M. Drucker (ed.), *Multi-Party Britain* (London, 1979), p. 76.

3. Churchill College, Cambridge, Thurso MSS II, 71/2, Sinclair to Scott, 19 November 1935.

4. T. Wilson, *The Downfall of the Liberal Party 1914–1935* (London, 1966), pp. 377–8.

5. House of Lords Record Office, Lloyd George MSS G/141/28/28, Lothian to Lloyd George, 25 November 1935.

6. Flintshire Record Office, Henry Morris Jones MSS 13, diary, 10 November 1932.

7. Sinclair to General Secretary, Scottish Liberal Federation, 4 February 1937, cited in M. Baines, 'The Survival of the British Liberal Party 1932–1959', University of Oxford D.Phil. thesis, 1991, p. 29.

8. Hammond to Crewe, 13 January 1939, cited in M. Hart, 'The Decline of the Liberal Party in Parliament and in the Constituencies', D.Phil. thesis, Oxford University, 1982, p. 91.

9. Baines, 'Survival of the British Liberal Party', p. 138.

10. D. Johnson, *Bars and Barricades* (London, 1952), pp. 73–4.

11. R. Grayson, *Liberals, International Relations and Appeasement: The Liberal Party, 1919–1939* (London, 2001), p. 75.

12. G. De Groot, *Liberal Crusader: The Life of Sir Archibald Sinclair* (London, 1993), p. 114.

13. Horabin to G. White, 7 June 1939, cited in Baines, 'Survival of the British Liberal Party', p. 46. For a more positive assessment of Liberal–Labour co-operation within a Popular Front, see M. Pugh, 'The Liberal Party and the Popular Front', *English Historical Review*, cxxi, p. 494.

14. *Oxford Guardian*, 21 February 1939, cited in G. Sell, 'Liberal Revival: Jo Grimond and the Politics of British Liberalism 1956–1967', University of London, Ph.D. thesis, 1996, p. 16.

15. Baines, 'Survival of the British Liberal Party', p. 40.

16. P. Harris, *Forty Years In and Out of Parliament* (London, n.d.), p. 127.

17. M. Pottle (ed.), *Champion Redoubtable: The Diaries and Letters of Violet Bonham Carter 1914–1945* (London, 1998), p. 308.

18. W. Beveridge, *Power and Influence* (London, 1953), p. 350.

19. Baines, 'Survival of the British Liberal Party', pp. 51, 62.

20. Ibid., p. 51; A. Watkins, *The Liberal Dilemma* (London, 1966), p. 42.

21. De Groot, *Liberal Crusader*, p. 206.

22. Morris Jones MSS 24, diary, 13 and 28 July 1943.

23. *The Times*, 19 July 1943.

24. National Library of Wales, Megan Lloyd George MSS, 20475, C3173, Foot to M. Lloyd George, 7 August 1943.

25. National Library of Wales, Clement Davies MSS C/1/16, C. Davies to S. Clement-Davies, 3 November 1943.

26. Harris, *Forty Years*, p. 184. See also A. Thorpe, *Parties at War: Political Organisation in Second World War Britain* (Oxford, 2009).

27. Pottle (ed.), *Champion Redoubtable*, p. 312.

28. De Groot, *Liberal Crusader*, p. 215.

29. R. McCallum and A. Readman, *The British General Election of 1945* (Oxford, 1947), p. 61.

30. M. Baines, 'The Liberal Party and the 1945 General Election', *Contemporary Record*, 9(1) (1995), p. 54.
31. McCallum and Readman, *General Election of 1945*, p. 166.
32. De Groot, *Liberal Crusader*, p. 224.
33. Baines, 'Liberal Party and 1945', p. 59.
34. J. Rasmussen, *The Liberal Party: A Study of Retrenchment and Revival* (London, 1965), p. 12.
35. *Liberal Magazine*, August 1945.
36. Baines, 'Liberal Party and 1945', p. 60.
37. J. G. Jones, 'Churchill, Clement Davies and the Ministry of Education', *Journal of Liberal Democrat History*, 27 (2000), p. 7.
38. *Liberal Magazine*, August 1946, cited ibid., p. 8.
39. *Montgomeryshire Express*, 11 October 1947, cited ibid., p. 8.
40. J. Grimond, *Memoirs* (London, 1979), p. 148.
41. J. Stevenson, *Third Party Politics since 1945: Liberals, Alliance and Liberal Democrats* (Oxford, 1993), p. 33.
42. Davies MSS J/3/26i, Davies to G. Murray, 11 May 1950.
43. John Rylands Library, University of Manchester, Leonard Behrens MSS 4, V. Bonham Carter to Behrens, 4 April 1949.
44. D. Roberts, 'The Strange Death of Liberal Wales', in J. Osmond (ed.), *The National Question Again: Welsh Political Identity in the 1980s* (Llandysul, 1985), p. 80.
45. J. G. Jones, 'The Clement Davies Papers: A Review', *The National Library of Wales Journal*, xxiii(4) (1984), p. 413.
46. M. Young, *The Chipped White Cups of Dover* (London, 1960), p. 2.
47. Grimond, *Memoirs*, p. 148.
48. R. Garner and R. Kelly, *British Political Parties Today* (Manchester, 1993), p. 204.
49. Johnson, *Bars and Barricades*, p. 285.
50. McCallum and Readman, *General Election of 1945*, pp. 141, 185.
51. R. Douglas, *The History of the Liberal Party, 1895–1970* (London, 1971), p. 253.
52. *The Times*, 18 November 1946.
53. Douglas, *Liberal Party*, p. 253.
54. H. Macmillan, *Tides of Fortune* (London, 1969), p. 288.
55. A. Horne, *Macmillan 1894–1956* (London, 1988), p. 298.
56. I. Hunter, 'The Final Quest for Liberal Reunion 1943–46', *Journal of Liberal Democrat History*, 32 (2001), pp. 14–16.
57. Macmillan, *Tides of Fortune*, p. 310.
58. *The Times*, 27 November 1947.
59. M. Pottle (ed.), *Daring to Hope: The Diaries and Letters of Violet Bonham Carter 1946–1969* (London, 2000), p. 36.
60. Megan Lloyd George MSS 20475, C3168, V. Bonham Carter to M. Lloyd George, 17 November 1947.
61. N. Nicolson (ed.), *Harold Nicolson: Diaries and Letters 1945–62* (London, 1968), pp. 111–12.
62. Pottle (ed.), *Daring to Hope*, p. 28.
63. *Western Morning News*, 12 January 1949.

64. Megan Lloyd George MSS 20475, C3174, Foot to Lloyd George, 15 August 1949.
65. Davies MSS J/3/4 and 6, V. Bonham Carter to Davies, 2 and 9 May 1949.
66. The Liberal Nationals were renamed National Liberals in 1948.
67. H. G. Nicholas, *The British General Election of 1950* (London, 1951), pp. 83–4.
68. Watkins, *Liberal Dilemma*, p. 50.
69. Nicholas, *General Election of 1950*, pp. 83–4.
70. Davies MSS J/3/12, Davies to Sinclair, 17 January 1950.
71. Ibid., J/3/10, Davies to Sinclair, 6 January 1950.
72. Pottle (ed.), *Daring to Hope*, p. 75.
73. Lord Kilmuir, *Political Adventure* (London, 1964), p. 170.
74. Davies MSS J/3/25i, G. Murray to Davies, 10 May 1950.
75. Nicholas, *General Election of 1950*, p. 299.
76. J. Thorpe, *In My Own Time: Reminiscences of a Liberal Leader* (London, 1999), p. 94.
77. Pottle (ed.), *Daring to Hope*, p. 84.
78. Nicolson (ed.), *Harold Nicolson: Diaries and Letters*, p. 188.
79. S. Ball (ed.), *Parliament and Politics in the Age of Churchill and Attlee: The Headlam Diaries 1935–1951* (London, 1999), p. 615.
80. M. Gilbert, *Winston S. Churchill*, Vol. 8 (London, 1988), p. 529.
81. House of Commons Debates, 5th Series, vol. 472, col. 592.
82. *The Times*, 1 and 3 May 1950.
83. Ibid., 17 April 1950.
84. Davies MSS J/3/23, Sinclair to Davies, 3 May 1950.
85. Pottle (ed.), *Daring to Hope*, p. 83.
86. Macmillan, *Tides of Fortune*, p. 318.
87. N. Fisher, *Harold Macmillan* (London, 1982), p. 132.
88. A. Howard, *RAB: The Life of R. A. Butler* (London, 1987), p. 170.
89. Ibid., pp. 168–71.
90. Davies MSS C/1/54, 'Liberal position as put by me to Mr Winston Churchill and Lord Woolton', n.d.
91. Ibid., J/3/45, Davies to V. Bonham Carter, 15 November 1950.
92. Ibid., J/4/17, Davies to Churchill, 4 May 1950.
93. Ibid., J/3/43, V. Bonham Carter to Davies, 27 October 1950.
94. D. Butler, *The British General Election of 1951* (London, 1952), pp. 94–5.
95. Ibid., pp. 146–7.
96. M. McManus, *Jo Grimond: Towards the Sound of Gunfire* (Edinburgh, 2001), p. 92.
97. Davies MSS J/3/58, Teviot to Davies, 4 October 1951.
98. Gilbert, *Churchill*, Vol. 8, p. 646.
99. *The Times*, 27 October 1951.
100. *Manchester Guardian*, 27 October 1951.
101. Butler, *General Election of 1951*, pp. 242, 266–7.
102. Macmillan, *Tides of Fortune*, pp. 360–1.
103. Jones, 'Churchill, Davies and Education', pp. 6–14.

104. *News Chronicle*, 29 October 1951.

105. *The Times*, 19 May 1952.

106. Davies MSS J/3/67i, Davies to G. Murray, 15 November 1951.

107. Ibid., J/3/65, Davies to Murray, 9 November 1951.

108. House of Lords Record Office, Samuel MSS, A/155(xiii)161, M. Lloyd George to Samuel, 9 November 1951.

109. R. Cockett (ed.), *My Dear Max: The Letters of Brendan Bracken to Lord Beaverbrook 1925–1958* (London, 1990), p. 128.

110. Davies MSS C/1/76.

111. J. Bowle, *Viscount Samuel* (London, 1957), p. 357.

112. Davies MSS J/3/66, Murray to Davies, 12 November 1951.

113. D. Wilson, *Gilbert Murray OM 1866–1957* (Oxford, 1987), p. 391.

114. Sell, 'Liberal Revival', p. 51.

115. R.S. Milne and H. C. Mackenzie, *Marginal Seat, 1955: A Study of Voting Behaviour in the Constituency of Bristol North East at the General Election of 1955* (London, 1958), p. 19.

116. Ibid., p. 50.

117. Rasmussen, *Liberal Party*, p. 24.

118. Stevenson, *Third Party Politics*, p. 41.

119. M. Egan, *Coming into Focus: The Transformation of the Liberal Party 1945–64* (Saarbrucken, 2009), p. 23.

120. Ibid., p. 108.

121. Behrens MSS 4, Behrens to President, Liberal Party Organisation, 4 September 1973.

4   Two Steps Forward and One Back, 1955–79

1. M. Pottle (ed.), *Daring to Hope: The Diaries and Letters of Violet Bonham Carter 1946–1969* (London, 2000), pp. 148–51.

2. *The Times*, 10 July 1956.

3. B. Pimlott (ed.), *The Political Diary of Hugh Dalton 1918–40, 1945–60* (London, 1986), p. 671.

4. A. Watkins, *The Liberal Dilemma* (London, 1966), p. 82.

5. G. Sell, '"A Sad Business": The Resignation of Clement Davies', *Journal of Liberal Democrat History*, 24 (1999), p. 16.

6. K. Morgan, *The People's Peace* (Oxford, paperback edn, 1992), p. 155.

7. Pottle (ed.), *Daring to Hope*, p. 170.

8. See, for example, John Rylands Library, University of Manchester, Leonard Behrens MSS 4, J. MacCullum Scott to Editor, *Liberal News*, 9 November 1956.

9. *The Spectator*, 29 November 1957, cited in G. Sell, 'Liberal Revival: Jo Grimond and the Politics of British Liberalism 1956–1967', University of London Ph.D. thesis (1996), p. 180.

10. Elliot Dodds, 'Liberty and Welfare' in G. Watson (ed.), *The Unservile State* (London, 1957), p. 25.

11. L. Behrens, 'Why Do We Do It?', *The Liberal Forward*, 266 (September 1956).

12. M. McManus, *Jo Grimond: Towards the Sound of Gunfire* (Edinburgh, 2001), pp. 107, 119.
13. A. Cyr, *Liberal Party Politics in Britain* (London, 1977), p. 101.
14. *News Chronicle*, 29 March 1958, cited in McManus, *Grimond*, p. 129.
15. Sell, 'Liberal Revival', p. 95.
16. Cyr, *Liberal Party Politics*, p. 179.
17. J. G. Jones, 'The Liberal Party and Wales, 1945–79', *Welsh History Review*, 16(3) (1993), p. 354.
18. D. Butler and R. Rose, *The British General Election of 1959* (London, 1960), p. 51.
19. R. Douglas, *History of the Liberal Party 1895–1970* (London, 1971), pp. 271–2.
20. *The Times*, 17 March 1962.
21. W. Rodgers, *Fourth Among Equals* (London, 2000), p. 40.
22. Jones, 'Liberal Party and Wales', p. 342.
23. Behrens MSS 4, Patrick Lort-Phillips to Harold Granville, 6 April 1960.
24. Ibid., memorandum by Grimond, 13 April 1961.
25. Pottle (ed.), *Daring to Hope*, p. 242. See also M. Cole, *Richard Wainwright, the Liberals and Liberal Democrats* (Manchester, 2011), p. 141.
26. H. Macmillan, *At the End of the Day* (London, 1973), p. 58.
27. C. Cook and J. Ramsden (eds), *By-Elections in British Politics* (London, 1973), p. 213.
28. Douglas, *Liberal Party*, p. 278.
29. Behrens MSS 4, memorandum by Grimond, 13 April 1961.
30. D. Butler and A. King, *The British General Election of 1966* (London, 1966), pp. 74–5.
31. H. Cowie, *Why Liberal?* (Harmondsworth, 1964), p. 40.
32. Butler and King, *Election of 1966*, p. 36.
33. Jones, 'Liberal Party and Wales', p. 345.
34. J. Grimond, *Memoirs* (London, 1979), p. 212.
35. Jones, 'Liberal Party and Wales', pp. 346–7.
36. Grimond, *Memoirs*, p. 254.
37. Butler and King, *Election of 1966*, p. 269.
38. Sell, 'Liberal Revival', p. 247.
39. *The Times*, 30 December 1968.
40. D. Steel, *Against Goliath: David Steel's Story* (London, 1989), p. 109.
41. D. Steel, *A House Divided: The Lib–Lab Pact and the Future of British Politics* (London, 1980), p. 10.
42. Watkins, *Liberal Dilemma*, p. 109.
43. Ibid., p. 108.
44. J. Tankard, 'The Sutton and Cheam By-election', *Liberal Democrat History Group Newsletter*, 14 (March 1997), p. 13.
45. C. Cook, 'The Challengers to the Two-Party System', in C. Cook and J. Ramsden (eds), *Trends in British Politics since 1945* (London, 1978), p. 132.
46. Steel, *Against Goliath*, p. 79.

47. D. Butler and D. Kavanagh, *The British General Election of October 1974* (London, 1975), p. 272.
48. Ibid., p. 285.
49. Steel, *Against Goliath*, pp. 87–8.
50. Steel, *House Divided*, p. 2.
51. Steel, *Against Goliath*, p. 65.
52. *Liberal News,* July 1970, quoted ibid., p. 70.
53. Steel, *House Divided*, p. 16.
54. Ibid., p. 22.
55. Ibid., p. 25.
56. D. Healey, *The Time of My Life* (paperback edn, London, 1990), p. 403.
57. Steel, *House Divided*, p. 153.
58. P. Bartram, *David Steel: His Life and Politics* (London, 1981), p. 161.
59. Ibid., p. 177.
60. M. Steed, 'The Liberal Party', in H. M. Drucker (ed.), *Multi-Party Britain* (London, 1979), p. 106.
61. J. Curtice in V. Bogdanor (ed.), *Liberal Party Politics* (Oxford, 1983), p. 102.
62. A. Butt Philip, ibid., p. 224.

5   A Cracked Mould and a New Beginning

1. D. Steel, *A House Divided: The Lib–Lab Pact and the Future of British Politics* (London, 1980), p. 160.
2. R. Rose, *Do Parties Make a Difference?* (London, 1980), p. 4.
3. P. Zentner, *Social Democracy in Britain: Must Labour Lose?* (London, 1982), p. 8.
4. R. Jenkins, *A Life at the Centre* (London, 1991), p. 514.
5. Speech at Llandudno assembly, September 1976.
6. R. Jenkins, *European Diary 1977–1981* (London, 1989), p. 553.
7. D. Owen, *Time to Declare* (London, 1991), p. 428.
8. Ibid., p. 448.
9. Jenkins, *European Diary*, p. 645.
10. Owen, *Time to Declare*, p. 489.
11. Ibid., p. 500.
12. H. Stephenson, *Claret and Chips: The Rise of the SDP* (London, 1982), p. 26.
13. D. Thomson, *The Shocktroops of Pavement Politics? An Assessment of the Influence of Community Politics in the Liberal Party* (Hebden Bridge, 1985), p. 22.
14. J. Josephs, *Inside the Alliance: An Inside Account of the Development and Prospects of the Liberal–SDP Alliance* (London, 1983), p. 86.
15. Jenkins, *Life at the Centre*, p. 587.
16. Owen, *Time to Declare*, p. 653.
17. I. Bradley, *Breaking the Mould? The Birth and Prospects of the Social Democratic Party* (Oxford, 1981), p. 35.
18. Owen, *Time to Declare*, pp. 441, 614, 446.

19. Ibid., p. 522.
20. Ibid., p. 485.
21. Stephenson, *Claret and Chips*, p. 84.
22. Bradley, *Breaking the Mould?* p. 149.
23. Josephs, *Inside the Alliance*, p. 73.
24. University of Liverpool Library, Owen MSS, D709 3/11/1/1, Owen to Geoff White, 23 September 1982.
25. Jenkins, *Life at the Centre*, p. 569.
26. I. Crewe and A. King, *SDP: The Birth, Life and Death of the Social Democratic Party* (Oxford, 1995), p. 160.
27. Owen MSS, D709 3/11/1/1, Thomas to Owen, 19 October 1981.
28. Ibid., D709 3/11/1/1, Thomas to Jenkins, 7 September 1982.
29. Owen, *Time to Declare*, p. 559.
30. I. Bradley, *The Strange Rebirth of Liberal Britain* (London, 1985), p. 4.
31. Owen, *Time to Declare*, pp. 496–7. Critics have argued that Owen's idea of a 'social market economy' was little more than a slogan, designed to differentiate himself from his opponents, whoever they were at any particular time. See D. Brack, *The Myth of the Social Market: David Owen's Economic Policy* (London, 1989).
32. Crewe and King, *SDP*, p. 289.
33. Owen, *Time to Declare*, p. 507.
34. Ibid., p. 599.
35. Owen MSS, D709 3/11/1/1, Owen to M. Thomas, 5 March 1984.
36. Ibid., D709 3/11/1/1, W. Rodgers to Owen, 31 October 1985.
37. Ibid., D709 3/11/1/1, Owen to G. Saltmarsh, 30 October 1984.
38. Jenkins, *Life at the Centre*, p. 590.
39. Owen MSS, D709 3/11/2/8, Williams to Owen, 9 June 1986.
40. Ibid., D709 3/11/2/8, Owen to Rodgers, 9 June 1986.
41. Ibid., D709 3/11/2/8, Rodgers to Owen, 12 June 1986.
42. Ibid., D709 3/11/2/8, Ashdown to Constituency Party Chairman, copied to Owen, 25 June 1986.
43. Jenkins, *Life at the Centre*, p. 603.
44. Owen, *Time to Declare*, p. 682.
45. Ibid., p. 694.
46. D. Steel, *Against Goliath: David Steel's Story* (London, 1989), p. 279.
47. Crewe and King, *SDP*, p. 292.
48. Ibid., p. 298.
49. Owen, *Time to Declare*, p. 724.
50. Crewe and King, *SDP*, p. 416.
51. R. Pitchford and T. Greaves, *Merger: The Inside Story* (London, 1989), p. 134.
52. *Independent*, 7 September 1991, cited in S. Ingle, 'Britain's Third Party', in L. Robins, H. Blackmore and R. Pyper (eds), *Britain's Changing Party System* (London, 1994), p. 104.
53. P. Ashdown, *The Ashdown Diaries 1988–1997* (London, 2000), p. 30; P. Ashdown, *A Fortunate Life* (London, 2009), p. 247.
54. D. Butler and D. Kavanagh, *The British General Election of 1992* (Basingstoke, 1992), p. 69.

55. Ashdown, *Diaries 1988–1997*, p. 56.
56. P. Ashdown, *The Ashdown Diaries 1997–1999* (London, 2001), p. 493.
57. K. Jefferys, *The Labour Party since 1945* (London, 1993), p. 122.
58. Ashdown, *Diaries 1988–1997*, p. 159.
59. D. Brack and T. Little (eds), *Great Liberal Speeches* (London, 2001), pp. 423–8; Ashdown, *Fortunate Life*, p. 268.
60. Brack and Little (eds), *Speeches*, p. 421.
61. E. Shaw, *The Labour Party since 1945* (Oxford, 1996), p. 199.
62. P. Joyce, *Towards the Sound of Gunfire: A History of the Liberal Democrats* (Dorchester, 1994), p. 62.
63. A. Rawnsley, D. Brack and H. Smith, 'Ashdown as Leader', *Journal of Liberal Democrat History*, 30 (2001), p. 7.
64. Ashdown, *Diaries 1988–1997*, p. 273; Ashdown, *Fortunate Life*, p. 276.
65. Ashdown, *Diaries 1988–1997*, p. 244.
66. Ibid., p. 287.
67. Ibid., p. 324.
68. Ibid., p. 419; T. Blair, *A Journey* (London, 2010), p. 118.
69. Ashdown, *Diaries 1988–1997*, p. 456.
70. Ibid., pp. 557–8.
71. Ibid., p. 560.
72. Ashdown, *Diaries 1997–1999*, p. 498.
73. A. Rawnsley, *Servants of the People: The Inside Story of New Labour* (London, 2000), p. 199.
74. Ashdown, *Diaries 1997–1999*, p. 3.
75. W. Rodgers, *Fourth Among Equals* (London, 2000), p. 287.
76. P. Joyce, *Realignment of the Left? A History of the Relationship between the Liberal Democrat and Labour Parties* (Basingstoke, 1999), p. 297.
77. Ashdown, *Diaries 1997–1999*, p. 30.
78. Ibid., p. 36.
79. Ibid., p. 15.
80. *The Times*, 25 July 1997.
81. Rawnsley, Brack and Smith, 'Ashdown as Leader', p. 9.
82. Rodgers, *Fourth Among Equals*, p. 288.
83. Ashdown, *Diaries 1997–1999*, p. 319.
84. Rodgers, *Fourth Among Equals*, p. 293.
85. Brack and Little (eds), *Great Liberal Speeches*, p. 421.
86. Rodgers, *Fourth Among Equals*, p. 289; P. Mandelson, *The Third Man* (London, 2010), p. 564.
87. Brack and Little (eds), *Great Liberal Speeches*, p. 421.
88. Ashdown, *Diaries 1997–1999*, p. 153.
89. Ibid., p. 504.
90. Joyce, *Realignment of the Left?*, p. 286.

6 Right into Government, 2001–11

1. G. Hurst, *Charles Kennedy: A Tragic Flaw* (London, 2006), p. 119.
2. S. Lee and M. Beech (eds), *The Cameron–Clegg Government: Coalition Politics in an Age of Austerity* (Basingstoke, 2011), p. 42; P. Cowley and

M. Stuart, 'From Labour Love-In to Bona Fide Party of Opposition', *Journal of Liberal History*, 43 (2004), p. 18.

3. T. Blair, *A Journey* (London, 2010), p. 122.
4. D. Brack, 'Campbell as Leader', *Journal of Liberal History*, 60 (2008), p. 42.
5. The SDP had won Greenwich in 1987.
6. M. Campbell, *My Autobiography* (London, 2008), p. 209.
7. D. Laws, in J. Margo (ed.), *Beyond Liberty: Is the Future of Liberalism Progressive?* (London, 2007), p. 146.
8. P. Marshall and D. Laws (eds), *The Orange Book: Reclaiming Liberalism* (London, 2004), p. 29.
9. D. Laws, *22 Days in May: The Birth of the Lib Dem–Conservative Coalition* (London, 2010), p. 139.
10. C. Russell, 'Liberalism and Liberty from Gladstone to Ashdown', *Journal of Liberal Democrat History*, 20 (1998), p. 10.
11. Marshall and Laws (eds), *Orange Book*, pp. 28–9.
12. Laws, *22 Days*, p. 64.
13. Campbell, *Autobiography*, p. 222.
14. Ibid., p. 228.
15. V. Cable, *Free Radical* (London, 2009), pp. 287–8.
16. Campbell, *Autobiography*, p. 256.
17. Brack, 'Campbell as Leader', p. 43.
18. Ibid.
19. Cable, *Free Radical*, p. 289.
20. A. Rawnsley, *The End of the Party: The Rise and Fall of New Labour* (paperback edn, London, 2010), p. 746.
21. Laws, *22 Days*, p. 270.
22. R. Ingham and D. Brack (eds), *Peace, Reform and Liberation: A History of Liberal Politics in Britain 1679–2011* (London, 2011), p. 348.
23. D. Kavanagh and P. Cowley, *The British General Election of 2010* (Basingstoke, 2010), p. 105.
24. J. Gerard, *The Clegg Coup* (London, 2011), p. 242.
25. Kavanagh and Cowley, *General Election 2010*, p. 164.
26. Rawnsley, *End of Party*, p. 723.
27. *Independent*, 21 April 2010.
28. Ibid., 24 April 2010.
29. Laws, *22 Days*; R. Wilson, *5 Days to Power: The Journey to Coalition Britain* (London, 2010).
30. Wilson, *5 Days*, p. 100.
31. Lee and Beech (eds), *Cameron–Clegg Government*, p. vii.
32. Laws, *22 Days*, pp. 63–4, 66.
33. Ibid., p. 269.
34. Ibid., p. 111.
35. Ibid., p. 173.
36. Ibid., pp. 153, 156.
37. Ibid., p. 22.
38. Ibid., p. 156.
39. C. Russell, *An Intelligent Person's Guide to Liberalism* (London, 1999), p. 16.

40. Wilson, *5 Days,* p. 47.
41. *The Spectator,* 13 January 2011.
42. *Independent on Sunday,* 24 April 2011.
43. *Guardian,* 5 May 2011.

Conclusion

1. R. Ingham and D. Brack (eds), *Peace, Reform and Liberation: A History of Liberal Politics in Britain 1679–2011* (London, 2011), p. 374. My brief discussion of party organisation draws heavily on the excellent appendix to this book: S. Whitehead and D. Brack, 'Party Organisation from 1859'.
2. D. Brack and R. Douglas, 'Holding the Balance', *Journal of Liberal History,* 64 (2009), pp. 28, 30.
3. S. Lee and M. Beech (eds), *The Cameron–Clegg Government: Coalition Politics in an Age of Austerity* (Basingstoke, 2011), p. 5.
4. *Observer,* 16 May 2010.
5. C. Russell, *An Intelligent Person's Guide to Liberalism* (London, 1999), p. 122.
6. J. Gerard, *The Clegg Coup* (London, 2011), p. 273.
7. Ingham and Brack (eds), *Peace, Reform and Liberation,* pp. 340–1.
8. V. Cable, *Free Radical* (London, 2009), p. 300.

Guide to Further Reading

The history of the Liberal Party since the early twentieth century has been covered by a vast array of books and articles, and no attempt has been made below to list more than just some of the most important works. Readers wishing to keep up to date with an ongoing historiography are urged to consult the *Journal of Liberal History*, published by the Liberal Democrat History Group. The same body has also produced four valuable works of reference: Duncan Brack (ed.), *Dictionary of Liberal Biography* (1998); Duncan Brack and Robert Ingham (eds), *Dictionary of Liberal Quotations* (1999); Duncan Brack and Tony Little (eds), *Great Liberal Speeches* (2001); and Duncan Brack and Ed Randall (eds), *Dictionary of Liberal Thought* (2007). It maintains a website at www.liberalhistory.org. uk.

Each work is listed only under the heading where it has been found most useful. Many, however, are relevant to more than one chapter of this book. The place of publication is London unless otherwise indicated.

General Topics and Introduction

Chris Cook, *A Short History of the Liberal Party* was first published in 1976 but successive editions have now taken the story up to 2010. It provides a readable introductory narrative, particularly useful for the party's electoral history. Roy Douglas, *Liberals: The History of the Liberal and Liberal Democrat Parties* (2005) contains much of value, but is clearly written from a position of commitment. Alan Sykes, *The Rise and Fall of British Liberalism 1776–1988* (1997) has the advantage of a wide chronological framework, but has now been superseded by Robert Ingham and Duncan Brack (eds), *Peace, Reform and Liberation: A History of Liberal Politics in Britain 1679–2011* (2011). Iain Dale (ed.), *Liberal Party General Election Manifestos, 1900–1997* (2000) provides easy access to important electoral material, while Peter Joyce, *Realignment of the Left? A History of the Relationship between the Liberal Democrat and Labour Parties* (Basingstoke, 1999) usefully considers Liberal–Labour relations over the entire twentieth century. Anthony Howe, *Free Trade and Liberal England, 1846–1946* (Oxford, 1997) expertly charts a key theme. For the origins of the party, John Vincent, *The Formation of the Liberal Party 1857–68* (1966) remains indispensable. Michael Bentley, *The Climax of Liberal Politics: British Liberalism in Theory and Practice, 1868–1918* (1987) offers much food for thought. The history of nineteenth-century Liberalism falls largely outside the scope of the present work, but readers may be directed to Jonathan Parry, *The Rise and Fall of Liberal Governments in Victorian Britain* (New Haven, CT, 1993); Eugenio Biagini, *Liberty, Retrenchment and Reform: Popular Liberalism in the Age of Gladstone, 1860–1880* (Cambridge, 1992), T. A. Jenkins, *The Liberal Ascendancy, 1830–1886* (1994); D. A. Hamer, *Liberal Politics in the Age of Gladstone and Rosebery* (Oxford, 1972); Colin Matthew, *The Liberal Imperialists* (Oxford, 1973); Stephen Koss, *Nonconformity in Modern British Politics* (1975); and Peter Stansky, *Ambitions and Strategies: The Struggle for the Leadership of the Liberal Party in the 1890s* (Oxford, 1964).

1 Strange Death or Edwardian Summer, 1902–16

George Dangerfield, *The Strange Death of Liberal England* (1935) may be enjoyed as literature, but should also be read – with caution – as history because of the huge impact it has had on later writing. The General Elections of Edwardian England have been well covered by A. K. Russell, *Liberal Landslide: The General Election of 1906* (Newton Abbot, 1973), and Neal Blewett, *The Peers, the Parties and the People: The General Elections of 1910* (1972), while Peter Rowland, *The Last Liberal Governments* (2 vols, 1968 and 1971) offers a solid narrative account of the Liberals in office. For early relations with the embryonic Labour Party, reference should still be made to two articles by Frank Bealey: 'The Electoral Arrangements between the LRC and the Liberal Party', *Journal of Modern History* (1956) and 'Negotiations between the Liberals and the LRC before the 1906 Election', *Bulletin of the Institute of Historical Research* (1956). Martin Petter, 'The Progressive Alliance', *History* (1973) offers a broader perspective. For the impact of the New Liberalism, the seminal work is Peter Clarke's *Lancashire and the New Liberalism* (Cambridge, 1971). Important additional material may be found in the same author's *Liberals and Social Democrats* (Cambridge, 1978) and in Michael Freeden, *The New Liberalism: An Ideology of Social Reform* (Oxford, 1978). George Bernstein, *Liberalism and Liberal Politics in Edwardian England* (1986); Keith Laybourn and Jack Reynolds, *Liberalism and the Rise of Labour 1890–1918* (1984); and David Powell, 'The New Liberalism and the Rise of Labour, 1886–1906', *The Historical Journal* (1986) offer much less optimistic interpretations of Liberalism's fortunes in the face of the rise of a new political party. For the most recent assessment of the key by-elections of 1911–14, see Ian Packer, 'Contested Ground: Trends in British By-elections, 1911–1914', *Contemporary British History* (2011). Though their primary focus is not the Liberal Party, Ross McKibbin, *The Evolution of the Labour Party 1910–1924* (Oxford, 1974) and Duncan Tanner, *Political Change and the Labour Party 1900–1918* (Cambridge, 1990) are key works within the historiographical debate.

Among significant monographs relating to the Edwardian era, mention should be made of Bruce Murray, *The People's Budget 1909–10* (Oxford 1980); H. V. Emy, *Liberals, Radicals and Social Politics, 1892–1914* (Cambridge, 1973); and Ian Packer, *Lloyd George, Liberalism and the Land:*

The Land Issue and Party Politics in England, 1906–1914 (Woodbridge, 2001). K. D. Brown (ed.), *Essays in Anti-Labour History* (1974); Alan O'Day (ed.), *The Edwardian Age: Conflict and Stability 1900–1914* (1979); Henry Pelling, *Popular Politics and Society in Late Victorian Britain* (1968); and Alan Sked and Chris Cook (eds), *Crisis and Controversy: Essays in Honour of A. J. P. Taylor* (1976) all contain important essays. If the reader remains confused by the diversity of interpretations of the Liberal Party's fortunes, reference may profitably be made to G. R. Searle, *The Liberal Party: Triumph and Disintegration, 1886–1929* (Basingstoke, 1992); Searle writes lucidly, carries his learning lightly and offers a balanced and persuasive account. Keith Laybourn, 'The Rise of Labour and the Decline of Liberalism: The State of the Debate', *History* (1995) is also helpful.

Among the biographies of Liberal leaders, John Wilson, *C. B. – A Life of Sir Henry Campbell-Bannerman* (1973) should be supplemented by José Harris and Cameron Hazlehurst, 'Campbell-Bannerman as Prime Minister', *History* (1970). Roy Jenkins, *Asquith* (1964) and Stephen Koss, *Asquith* (1976) paint rather different pictures from one another. See also Cameron Hazlehurst, 'Asquith as Prime Minister, 1908–1916', *English Historical Review* (1970). Lloyd George has been undergoing multi-volume biographical treatment à la Churchill. That by John Grigg (4 vols, 1973–2002) has reached 1918 but will not now be completed, unless by another hand, because of the author's untimely death. The late Bentley Gilbert's two volumes only reached 1916: *David Lloyd George: The Architect of Change 1863–1912* (1987) and *David Lloyd George: Organizer of Victory 1912–1916* (1992). Pending completion, the best, if somewhat plodding, single-volume life is probably Peter Rowland, *Lloyd George* (1975), though Ian Packer, *Lloyd George* (Basingstoke, 1998), Martin Pugh, *Lloyd George* (1988) and Chris Wrigley, *Lloyd George* (1992) all managed to say a lot within a small compass. Kenneth Morgan, *The Age of Lloyd George: The Liberal Party and British Politics, 1890–1929* (1971) also deserves to be mentioned.

Historians of this period are fortunate in the number of important diaries and collections of letters that have been published. These include: Mark Bonham Carter and Mark Pottle (eds), *Lantern Slides: The Diaries and Letters of Violet Bonham Carter 1904–1914* (1996); Michael and Eleanor Brock (eds), *H. H. Asquith: Letters to Venetia Stanley* (Oxford, 1982); Edward David (ed.), *Inside Asquith's Cabinet: From the Diaries of Charles Hobhouse* (1977); David Dutton (ed.), *Odyssey of an Edwardian Liberal: The Political Diary of Richard Durning Holt* (Gloucester, 1989); Cameron Hazlehurst and Christine Woodland (eds), *A Liberal Chronicle: Journals and Papers of J. A. Pease, 1908 to 1910* (1994); John McEwen (ed.), *The Riddell Diaries: A Selection* (1986); Kenneth Morgan (ed.), *Lloyd George: Family Letters 1885–1936* (Cardiff, 1973); and Trevor Wilson (ed.), *The Political Diaries of C. P. Scott, 1911–1928* (1970).

Trevor Wilson, *The Downfall of the Liberal Party, 1914–1935* (1966) remains the best starting point for an examination of the impact of the First World War on Liberal politics. But its argument is now somewhat dated and some of its analysis should be treated with care. Cameron Hazlehurst, *Politicians at War: July 1914 to May 1915* (1971) offers a microscopic study of Liberal high politics in the early months of the war, while Martin Pugh, 'Asquith, Bonar Law and the First Coalition', *The Historical Journal* (1974) presents a convincing explanation of the end of Britain's last Liberal government. Matthew Johnson, 'The Liberal War Committee and the Liberal Advocacy of Conscription in Britain, 1914–1916', *The Historical Journal* (2008) stresses the ideological flexibility of many wartime Liberals. Michael Fry, 'Political Change in Britain, August 1914 to December 1916: Lloyd George Replaces Asquith: The Issues Underlying the Drama', *The Historical Journal* (1988); and John McEwen, 'The Struggle for Mastery in Britain: Lloyd George Versus Asquith, December 1916', *Journal of British Studies* (1978) seek to explain Lloyd George's rise to the premiership.

2   The Liberal Civil War, 1916–35

The most useful works on the second half of the First World War are John Turner, *British Politics and the Great War: Coalition and Conflict 1915– 1918* (New Haven, CT, 1992), Edward David, 'The Liberal Party Divided 1916–1918', *The Historical Journal* (1970) and Barry McGill, 'Asquith's Predicament, 1914–1918', *Journal of Modern History* (1967). Michael Hart's unpublished Oxford D.Phil. thesis, 'The Decline of the Liberal Party in Parliament and in the Constituencies' (1982) is indispensable and carries the story beyond the end of hostilities. The controversy over the 'franchise factor' may be followed in H. C. G. Matthew, R. I. McKibbin and J. A. Kay, 'The Franchise Factor in the Rise of the Labour Party', *English Historical Review* (1976); Duncan Tanner, 'The Parliamentary Electoral System, the "Fourth" Reform Act and the Rise of Labour in England and Wales', *Bulletin of the Institute of Historical Research* (1983); and Michael Hart, 'The Liberals, the War and the Franchise', *English Historical Review* (1982). Michael Childs, 'Labour Grows Up: The Electoral System, Political Generations and British Politics 1890–1929', *Twentieth Century British History* (1995) adds usefully to the debate. Roy Douglas, 'The Background to the "Coupon" Election Arrangements', *English Historical Review* (1971) clarifies arrangements surrounding the 1918 General Election. Kenneth Morgan, *Consensus and Disunity: The Lloyd George Coalition Government 1918–1922* (Oxford, 1979) is likely to remain the standard work on the post-war coalition, but see also Chris Wrigley, *David Lloyd George and the British Labour Movement* (Hassocks, 1976) and the same author's *Lloyd George and the Challenge of Labour: The Post War Coalition 1918–1922* (Hemel Hempstead, 1990). Lloyd George's loss of office is dealt with in Michael Kinnear, *The Fall of Lloyd George: The Political Crisis of 1922* (1973).

For Liberal thought in the inter war years, see Michael Bentley, *The Liberal Mind, 1914–1929* (Cambridge, 1977) and Michael Freeden, *Liberalism Divided: A Study in British Political Thought* (Oxford, 1986). Frank Trentmann, *Free Trade Nation* (2008) compellingly traces the post-war erosion of free trade within the pantheon of Liberal ideology. Chris Cook, *The Age of Alignment: Electoral Politics in Britain 1922–1929* (1975) explores the Liberal Party's decline at the ballot box, and there is much useful material in John Campbell, *Lloyd George: The Goat in the Wilderness 1922–1931* (1977), though not all will find his argument totally convincing. Richard Toye, *Lloyd George and Churchill: Rivals for Greatness* (2007) charts a celebrated political relationship. There are important essays in A. J. P. Taylor (ed.), *Lloyd George: Twelve Essays* (1971); Gillian Peele and Chris Cook (eds), *The Politics of Reappraisal 1918–1939* (1975); and Don Cregier, *Chiefs without Indians* (Washington, DC, 1982). The Liberal role in the formation of the National Government may be traced in Philip Williamson, *National Crisis and National Government: British Politics, the Economy and Empire, 1926–1932* (Cambridge, 1992), while the General Elections of 1931 and 1935 are well covered by Andrew Thorpe, *The British General Election of 1931* (Oxford, 1991) and Tom Stannage, *Baldwin Thwarts the Opposition* (1980), respectively. David Dutton, '1932: A Neglected Date in the History of the Decline of the British Liberal Party', *Twentieth Century British History* (2003) argues for the importance of the split with the Liberal Nationals, and the same author's *Liberals in Schism: A History of the National Liberal Party* (2008) follows the fortunes of the breakaway group through to the 1960s. Revealing light is thrown on Lloyd George's continuing role in Liberal politics by A. J. P. Taylor (ed.), *Lloyd George: A Diary by Frances Stevenson* (1971) and *My Darling Pussy: The Letters of Lloyd George and Frances Stevenson 1913–41* (1975). The privately published Vivian Phillipps, *My Days and Ways* (Edinburgh, c. 1943) sees matters from a different perspective.

3 So Few and So Futile, 1935–55

The period of Liberal impotence is inevitably less well covered, but some important works have been written. Mark Egan, *Coming into Focus: The Transformation of the Liberal Party 1945–64* (Saarbrucken, 2009) provides a well-researched study of the survival and early revival of Liberalism at constituency level. Malcolm Baines, 'The Survival of the British Liberal Party 1932–1959' (1991), Oxford D.Phil. thesis unfortunately remains unpublished, but is indispensable. Baines' argument is summarized in a chapter of the same title in A. Gorst, L. Johnman and W. S. Lucas (eds), *Contemporary British History, 1931–61: Politics and the Limits of Policy* (1991). Matt Cole's important study, 'The Identity of the British Liberal Party 1945–62' (2006), University of Birmingham Ph.D. thesis also remains unpublished. Two recent works have illuminated different aspects of the 1930s: Richard Grayson, *Liberals, International Relations and Appeasement: The Liberal Party, 1919–1939* (2001) and Garry Tregidga, *The Liberal Party in South West Britain since 1918: Political Decline, Dormancy and Rebirth* (Exeter, 2000). Martin Pugh, 'The Liberal Party and the Popular Front', *English Historical Review* (2006) explores moves to co-operate with Labour. Successive Liberal leaders of this period have been well served by their biographers: Bernard Wasserstein, *Herbert Samuel: A Political Life* (Oxford, 1992); Gerard De Groot, *Liberal Crusader: The Life of Sir Archibald Sinclair* (1993); Ian Hunter (ed.), *Winston and Archie: The Collected Correspondence of Winston Churchill and Archibald Sinclair* (2005); Alun Wyburn-Powell,

Clement Davies: Liberal Leader (2003); and David Roberts, 'Clement Davies and the Liberal Party, 1929–56', University of Wales M.A. thesis (1975), supplemented by several articles by J. Graham Jones listed in the notes of this book. For relations with the Liberal Nationals, see David Dutton, *Simon: A Political Biography of Sir John Simon* (1992) and, by the same author, 'John Simon and the Post-War National Liberal Party: An Historical Postscript', *The Historical Journal* (1989). John Vincent has found interesting information about the outbreak of the Second World War: 'Chamberlain, the Liberals and the Outbreak of War, 1939', *English Historical Review* (1998). John Stevenson provides an accessible introduction to the post-war era in *Third Party Politics since 1945: Liberals, Alliance and Liberal Democrats* (Oxford, 1993), but this does not entirely replace Jorgen Rasmussen, *The Liberal Party: A Study of Retrenchment and Revival* (1965), which remains of value. David Dutton, 'On the Brink of Oblivion: The Post-War Crisis of British Liberalism', *Canadian Journal of History* (1992) analyses the threat to Liberal independence in the years after 1945. For the whole of the period since the war, the Nuffield General Election studies are invaluable. The memoirs of Percy Harris, *Forty Years in and out of Parliament* (*c.* 1947); the biography of Megan Lloyd George, Mervyn Jones, *A Radical Life* (1991); and the published diaries of Violet Bonham Carter, Mark Pottle (ed.), *Champion Redoubtable: The Diaries and Letters of Violet Bonham Carter 1914–1945* (1998) and *Daring to Hope: The Diaries and Letters of Violet Bonham Carter 1946–1969* (2000) may all be used with profit.

4   Two Steps Forward and One Back, 1955–79

Vernon Bogdanor (ed.), *Liberal Party Politics* (Oxford, 1983) contains an important collection of essays. Michael Steed, 'The Liberal Party' in H. M. Drucker (ed.), *Multi-Party Britain* (1979) is also worth reading. Two significant studies have appeared recently on the Grimond era: Michael McManus, *Jo Grimond: Towards the Sound of Gunfire* (Edinburgh, 2001), and Geoffrey Sell, 'Liberal Revival: Jo Grimond and the Politics of British Liberalism 1956–1967' (1996), University of London Ph.D. thesis, are both scholarly and perceptive. Grimond's own *Memoirs* (1979) offer only occasional insights. The leadership of Jeremy Thorpe is, as yet, less well served: Lewis Chester, Magnus Linklater and David May, *Jeremy Thorpe: A Secret Life* (1979) is journalistic, but contains some useful information. The same is true of Simon Freeman and Barrie Penrose, *Rinkagate: The Rise and Fall of Jeremy Thorpe* (1996). Thorpe's reminiscences, *In My Own Time: Reminiscences of a Liberal Leader* (1999) are largely inconsequential. David Thomson considers the rise of community politics in *The Shocktroops of Pavement Politics? An Assessment of the Influence of Community Politics in the Liberal Party* (Hebden Bridge, 1985). Alan Watkins, *The Liberal Dilemma* (1966) is now interesting largely as a period piece. Very much in that mould and therefore helpful for the evolution of Liberal thought, are Harry Cowie, *Why Liberal?* (Harmondsworth, 1964) and George Watson (ed.), *The Unservile State: Essays in Liberty and Welfare* (1957). David Steel has, to date, largely been his own historian: *Against Goliath: David Steel's Story* (1989) surveys his career as a whole, while *A House Divided: The Lib–Lab Pact and the Future of British Politics* (1980) is important for the period of co-operation with the Callaghan government. For this, see also Alistair Michie and Simon Hoggart, *The Pact: The Inside Story of the Lib–Lab Government, 1977–8* (1978). David Torrance, *David Steel: Rising Hope to Elder Statesman* (2012), appeared too recently to be considered. Matt Cole, *Richard Wainwright, the Liberals and Liberal Democrats* (Manchester, 2011) is a well-written biography of a prominent Liberal MP of this era.

5   A Cracked Mould and a New Beginning, 1979–2001

Not surprisingly, there are fewer quality monographs relating to the years since the early 1980s. A shining exception is Ivor Crewe and Anthony King, *SDP: The Birth, Life and Death of the Social Democratic Party* (Oxford, 1995), in which the authors combine scholarship with much inside information. Earlier works, such as Ian Bradley, *Breaking the Mould? The Birth and Prospects of the Social Democratic Party* (Oxford, 1981); Jeremy Josephs, *Inside the Alliance: An Inside Account of the Development and Prospects of the Liberal–SDP Alliance* (1983); and Hugh Stephenson, *Claret and Chips: The Rise of the SDP* (1982), remain valuable. The fusion of the Liberals and the SDP is chronicled from an admittedly hostile standpoint in Rachael Pitchford and Tony Greaves, *Merger: The Inside Story* (Hebden Bridge, 1989). The best work so far on the Liberal Democrats is Don MacIver (ed.), *The Liberal Democrats* (1996). But see also Peter Joyce, *Towards the Sound of Gunfire: A History of the Liberal Democrats* (Dorchester, 1994). Fortunately, while further academic analysis is awaited, the historian has at his or her disposal several important memoirs and diaries. Among these are David Owen, *Time to Declare* (1991); Roy Jenkins, *A Life at the Centre* (1991); Bill Rodgers, *Fourth Among Equals* (2000); Shirley Williams, *Climbing the Bookshelves* (2009); Roy Jenkins, *European Diary 1977–1981* (1989); and Paddy Ashdown, *A Fortunate Life* (2009) and *The Ashdown Diaries* (2 vols, 2000–1).This material is bound to grow considerably in the years to come, though the memoirs so far written by New Labour insiders add little to our understanding of the 'project'.

6   Right into Government, 2001–11 and Conclusion

Historical perspective will come later, but a surprising amount of useful material has already been published covering the decade 2001–11. Greg Hurst, *Charles Kennedy: A Tragic Flaw* (2006) offers a sympathetic and perceptive portrait, but Duncan Brack, 'Liberal Democrat Leadership: The Cases of Ashdown and Kennedy', *Political Quarterly* (2007) is much less favourable to Kennedy's performance and abilities. Menzies Campbell, with *My Autobiography* (2008) and Vince Cable, perhaps prematurely, with *Free Radical* (2009) lost no time in producing their memoirs. Nick Clegg will eventually merit something more penetrating than Chris Bowers,

Nick Clegg: The Biography (2011). Andrew Russell and Edward Fieldhouse, *Neither Left nor Right? The Liberal Democrats and the Electorate* (Manchester, 2005) and Paul Whiteley, Patrick Seyd and Antony Billinghurst, *Third Force Politics: Liberal Democrats at the Grassroots* (2006) cover, respectively, the electoral support and the membership and views of the modern party. Tudor Jones, *The Revival of British Liberalism: From Grimond to Clegg* (Basingstoke, 2011) traces the party's ideological evolution since the early 1960s. Kevin Hickson (ed.), *The Political Thought of the Liberals and Liberal Democrats since 1945* (Manchester, 2009) offers a different approach to the same subject. Much will be gained by going straight to the competing Liberal Democrat protagonists: Paul Marshall and David Laws (eds), *The Orange Book: Reclaiming Liberalism* (2004) and Duncan Brack, Richard Grayson and David Howarth (eds), *Reinventing the State: Social Liberalism for the 21st Century* (2007).

Two accounts of the negotiations leading to the formation of the 2010 coalition are unlikely to be bettered, at least in terms of the detailed accounts provided: David Laws, *22 Days in May* (2010) and Rob Wilson, *5 Days to Power* (2010). From a Labour perspective, Peter Mandelson, *The Third Man* (2010) adds little. The coalition itself will attract its historians in due course. But Simon Lee and Matt Beech (eds), *The Cameron–Clegg Government* (Basingstoke, 2011) provides a useful preliminary assessment of the government's policies.

Index